AN

A View From Moscow

In memory of
comrade Chris Hani
and all South African comrades
who were assassinated or killed in action;
and also those who, due to age or illness, never reached home.

ANC

A View From Moscow

Vladimir Shubin

Mayibuye History and Literature Series No. 88

MAYIBUYE
BOOKS-UWC

Published 1999 in South Africa by Mayibuye Books, University of the Western Cape, Private Bag X17, Bellville 7535, South Africa

Mayibuye books is the book publishing division of the Mayibuye Centre at the University of the Western Cape. The Mayibuye Centre is a pioneering project helping to recover areas of South African history that have been neglected in the past. It also provides space for cultural creativity and expression in a way that promotes the process of change and reconstruction in a democratic South Africa. The Mayibuye History and Literature Series is part of this project.

ISBN 1-86808-439-6

Cover design, layout and typesetting by jon berndt Design
PRINTED AND BOUND IN THE REPUBLIC OF SOUTH AFRICA BY THE RUSTICA PRESS,
NDABENI, WESTERN CAPE

D7131

CONTENTS

PART THREE : THE ROAD TO POWER
(1985-1991)

"The important events of history should not be shrouded in myths, even though myths are inevitably part of the spice of political life."

(Nelson Mandela, speech at the opening of the University of Cape Town Centre for Russian Studies, 17 August 1994)

INTRODUCTION

This book describes the history of the African National Congress of South Africa in the three decades following its banning. There are many myths surrounding the ANC: some harmless, the products of enthusiastic supporters; others malicious, disseminated by those in South Africa and abroad who did their best to prevent the victory of the ANC and still cannot accept that victory as a reality.

I strongly believe that the comprehensive history of the ANC should and will be written by South Africans. However, of non-South African historians, it is perhaps Soviet/Russian scholars who are best placed to undertake such a study. This is because of the multi-faceted relationship that developed between Moscow and the South African liberation movement. Inevitably, that relationship occupies a significant place in this book.

In writing the book, I have endeavoured always to use primary sources. In the main I have used the following invaluable collections: ANC and South African Communist Party documents in the Historical Papers Archive of the Mayibuye Centre at the University of the Western Cape; documents located at the Centre for Storage of Contemporary Documentation (the former Archive of the Soviet Communist Party); and documents in the Archive of the Soviet Afro-Asian Solidarity Committee in Moscow. Then there are those documents, not attributed to archives here, which I have (or had) at my disposal as a result of my personal and professional contact with the ANC. A substantial part of my personal archive was lost in August 1991. Therefore, in some cases, particularly when referring to discussions with South African friends, I have had to rely on my memory. I apologise in advance for any errors that may have resulted from this, and will welcome any amendments and corrections; generally, I am confident of the accuracy of my recollections.

This book is intended as an academic text but, because of my long involvement with the South African liberation movement, it has a

7

somewhat personal flavour as well.

However, I would be extremely concerned if readers were to imagine that I was the only Soviet contact with the South African liberation movement, or, as one South African paper put it, the "ANC man in Moscow".[1]

Many people were involved. The names of those who dealt directly with the ANC and the SACP at different times from 1960 should be mentioned. Those in the CPSU International Department were: Vitaly Korionov, Petr Manchkha, Yury Ivanov, Vladimir Shemyatenkov, Rostislav Ulyanovsky, Andrei Urnov, Vadim Dudin, Boris Belyakov, Alexei Makarov, Andrei Chuzhakin, and Alexander Pirozhenko. On the Solidarity Committee were: Dmitry Dolidze, Nikolay Bazanov, Alexander Dzassokhov, Valery Zhikharev, Tatyana Kravtsova, Eduard Samoylov, Yury Golovin, and Vyacheslav Tetyokin. Dr Andrei Urnov should be singled out as the person responsible for Soviet relations with the ANC and its allies for almost 25 years.

There were other friends of the ANC and its armed wing (whose surnames are not given here): the two Ivans, Fyodor, George, Valery, the two Michaels, and Victor. One can be named in full: Major General Nikolay Vassilyevich Kurushkin, who was a guest of honour at the celebration of the first anniversary of Namibian independence in 1991.

Not all of these comrades are still alive. I am convinced that those who remain active in political, diplomatic and academic life, or have been edged out into the business world by the recent stormy events in Moscow, all cherish the memory of the period of co-operation with the freedom fighters from South Africa.

I started writing this book a long time ago, but it would probably never have been completed had I not been given a research fellowship by the University of the Western Cape (UWC) in 1993-5. I express my sincere gratitude to the then Rector, Professor Jakes Gerwel; to Professor Robert Davies, Professor Peter Vale, and other colleagues at the UWC Centre for Southern African Studies; as well as to Professor André Odendaal and the staff of the Mayibuye Centre for History and Culture in South Africa.

I am deeply indebted to Brian Bunting and Barry Feinberg, who brought their deep knowledge of the liberation history and their superior editorial skills to the task of making my original text readable. Thanks are also due to Robin Malan and Linda Pithers who formed part of the editorial team.

PART ONE

HARD TIMES (1960-74)

1 960 has become known in history as "Africa Year". It was a year in which, one after another, African countries gained independence, while at the two extremes of the continent – Algeria in the North and the countries of Southern Africa – the struggle for liberation was intensifying and developing.

During the long fight for Algerian independence in which hundreds of lives were lost daily, the Front of National Liberation (FLN) was, slowly but steadily, tilting the balance of power in its favour. In South Africa the liberation forces were preparing themselves for decisive battles against the apartheid regime, while still hoping to avoid armed conflict and to limit the form of struggle to mass protests.

In the summer of 1960 several Soviet-made Ilyushin-14 transport planes landed at the Athens International Airport (at the time also a NATO air base). They were painted combat-grey, with the inscription *Rèpublique du Congo* on their fuselages, and they were on their way to Leopoldville (Kinshasa) to support Patrice Lumumba's government. In this way the Soviet Union announced to both friends and foes its active involvement in the anti-colonial and anti-racist struggles in Africa.

For me 1960 marked my first acquaintance with Africa, when as a young undergraduate student I experienced for the first time the inferno that is Cairo in the hot season.

It was Soviet policy during the sixties to play a more active role in support of liberation struggles; and this was seen specifically in relation to South Africa. In 1960, after a break of more than twenty years, the ruling Communist Party of the Soviet Union (CPSU) resumed ties with what were the major opposition forces in South Africa. Two streams were meeting. The first was the energetic (sometimes even unrealistic) new policy of "Khrushchev's Russia", ready to support each and every revolt against imperialist domination in the Afro-Asian world. The second was the South African liberation movement, seeking to establish international contacts and to generate assistance abroad, particularly vital after the banning on 8 April 1960 of the African National Congress (ANC) and the Pan-Africanist Congress (PAC) (which had split from the ANC a year earlier).

The bannings formed part of a wave of repression after the massacres in Sharpeville and Langa on 21 March 1960. Around two thousand leaders and activists of the ANC, the PAC, the South African Congress of Trade Unions (Sactu), the South African Indian Congress (SAIC), the Coloured People's Congress (CPC), the (white) Congress of Democrats (COD) and the (moderate) Liberal Party were detained. Under the State of Emergency declared by the Pretoria government, the South African Police, assisted by the South African Defence Force, moved to impose rigid control in the black townships.

The ANC and the Congress Alliance faced a difficult task in determining the forms and methods of struggle to be adopted under the new conditions. The outright banning of the ANC had not come as a complete surprise. The banning of the Communist Party of South Africa (CPSA) ten years earlier under the so-called Suppression of Communism Act provided an early warning of things to come, and the ANC had protested against it, along with other anti-racist organisations. The banning and restriction of ANC leaders and activists followed. Among them were Nelson Mandela and Walter Sisulu, who were forbidden to serve in the ANC leadership, although they secretly continued to do so. ANC President Albert Luthuli was banished to Groutville, his village in Natal; Deputy President Oliver Tambo was confined to the Johannesburg and Benoni areas. Also, following localised peasant revolts, in 1958 the ANC had been banned in areas of the Northern Transvaal and the Transkei.

These early signals of repression were not taken seriously enough. People believed that the ANC would remain a legal organisation, and no one prepared in any real way for having to work underground. "Congress leadership did not anticipate the speed and depth of impending crisis or of the sweeping counter-measures and the adoption of Nazi rule by the all-white government."[2]

After the bannings, "the methods of organisation that had been tested and employed by Africans over decades of political acting became obsolete."[3] The ANC leaders were somewhat confused about what to do. As one later said, they understood that a political party could go underground and still operate successfully, but they did not know how to organise the illegal activities of the mass movement. Some argued that the ANC as a mass organisation had ceased to exist at the moment of its banning, but most of the leadership thought that it should not be dissolved.

As Moses Kotane, a long-standing ANC leader and General Secretary of the SACP, commented: "It is very easy to say yes [to the question of whether the underground apparatus could have been prepared] ... So theoretically you can prepare people to be flyers where there are no airplanes."[4] Kotane was in fact speaking about the Communist Party's experience after its banning in 1950, but what he said was perhaps even more relevant for the ANC in 1960. For many ANC members, accustomed to mass rallies and regular public conferences, functioning in secrecy was not something that came easily. Nevertheless, as soon as the government announced the banning of the ANC, an Emergency Committee was formed. It declared that the ANC would continue to provide leadership and organisation for the people under its own name. Kotane chaired that Committee, while simultaneously heading the communist underground organisation.

While about 150 members of the Communist Party (its total membership was 450-500) were among the detained, Kotane himself managed to evade arrest. His appointment to chair an interim body of the ANC was clear evidence not only of his personal influence but also of the important contribution made by communists in the ANC and the Congress Alliance.

The role of communists in the South African liberation struggle remains a subject for academic research and political dispute. Whether inadvertently (owing to the lack of available sources concerning the activities of the illegal structures) or intentionally, the role of communists in the struggle has been widely distorted. At one extreme, there are those who say communist influence was profound; at the other, the communist contribution is negated. I will pay close attention to this, in order to bring some of the distortions into a sharper focus.

Before the Suppression of Communism Act was passed in 1950 the Central Committee of the Communist Party of South Africa (CPSA) decided to dissolve the Party to protect its members. To re-create it under conditions of secrecy was no easy task, and the first inaugural conference of the new South African Communist Party (SACP) took place only in 1953. Even then it was decided not to publicise the re-emergence, and it was not until July 1960 that the existence of the Party became generally known. Paradoxically, the banning of the party had a positive spin-off that was not, of course, either expected or intended by the South African government. It undoubtedly weakened the prejudice against communists that was prevalent within the anti-racist movement. Oliver Tambo, who as a leader of the Youth League in the mid 1940s had himself stood for the expulsion of communists from the ANC, said much later: "Before 1950 there was the feeling that there are two camps; some belong to one, some to the other. But after

1950 we were all together and when we discussed politics we never thought of the differences in our philosophies. We were all equals deciding what to do."[5]

How did the communists of South Africa view the situation at that time, on the threshold of the 1960s? Though the external contacts of the South African communists were very limited and were mainly channelled through the Communist Party of Great Britain, the SACP's position on international issues was largely influenced by the views then prevailing in the world communist movement. An unwarranted optimism, typical of the Soviet leadership of the early 1960s, headed by Nikita Khrushchev, was regularly expressed in the publications and documents of the SACP. Report, an internal document prepared in early 1960, spoke of "a steady strengthening of the position of the forces working for peace, of socialist and other anti-imperialist countries in relation to 'the West'."[6] The "African revolution" was regarded as a part of a world transition from capitalism to socialism.

But, more importantly, the SACP leadership was at the same time giving expression to a more sober approach to political developments in South Africa. The replacement of the National Party government "by a more progressive one, however far short of the ideal such a government might be" was regarded as a possible "step forward", which might create "conditions in which we could envisage the peaceful transition of South Africa towards a true democracy of the people."[7]

The power of the ruling party was not underestimated, and the need for an active and organised nation-wide struggle was underlined. It is very important to note that the opinion of the SACP was that leadership in this struggle was to be provided by the Congress Movement, and the Communist Party itself was to play a dynamic and constructive role in promoting such leadership. This task was to be achieved not by securing the leading positions, but by taking concrete initiatives to define policy, and by winning broad support for such initiatives and policy through persuasion and convincing argument. This approach, which had proved valuable in the 1950s, was pursued by the Party in the decades that followed, and undoubtedly helped the SACP, as distinct from many other communist parties in Africa and elsewhere, to maintain and strengthen its prestige among both leaders and participants of the mass movement.

Opposing "senseless and adventurist stunts", the SACP was at the same time in favour of "all methods of struggle which drew the *masses*

13

into *action*, which raise[d] the level of mass consciousness and organisation." This stand provided a basis for reconsidering the Party's attitude "to the often-repeated slogan of 'non-violence'."[8] The principle of non-violence was not seen as absolute, nor did the SACP exclude the possibility of adopting new forms of struggle, even before Sharpeville.

The Party regarded itself as a loyal and committed supporter of the aims of the Congress Alliance, though it was not a formal member. At that stage it believed that "the majority of the people of the various national groups" were not yet ready to support "organisational union between certain partners of the alliance", though such proposals had already been put forward.[9]

The SACP leadership discussed the need to announce publicly the re-emergence of the Party. The decision to do so had been taken a couple of years earlier, although some of the prominent Party leaders, including Moses Kotane and its Chairman Yusuf Dadoo, had initially opposed it, and so delayed its implementation.

It was intended that a draft of the Party Programme would be published in the *African Communist* magazine, which had been launched in 1959 (though not at first openly as a Party publication). Developments after Sharpeville accelerated the process of going public. After the first wave of repression under the State of Emergency, several local Party Committees were resurrected; and in June 1960 the Central Committee managed to convene a meeting of those Committee members who had not been detained, together with other activists. It was at this meeting that the decision to go public was taken. "Above all the party has decided to issue statements, addressed to the workers, in its own name."[10] It was decided to increase the number of full-time officials and to start publishing an underground monthly, Inkululeko (Freedom).

The Central Committee elected at the Party conference in 1958 consisted of fifteen members, seven of whom were Executive Committee members and three of whom were members of its Secretariat. Apart from Moses Kotane (General Secretary) and Yusuf Dadoo (Chairman), the Executive Committee included Bram Fischer, Lionel ("Rusty") Bernstein, Joe Slovo, Michael Harmel, and one other, an African, whose identity cannot be revealed.

Three people, including Kotane and Harmel, constituted the Secretariat. Other members of the Central Committee were John ("Uncle JB") Marks, Dan Tloome, Ruth First, Brian Bunting, Fred

Carneson, Ray Alexander (Simons), Raymond Mhlaba, and Mariemuthu ("MP") Naicker.[11]

Four new members were co-opted to the Central Committee during the State of Emergency.[12] In the circumstances of illegality and detention, these co-options may have been necessary, although the lack of consultation with grassroots structures was to have a negative impact. All 15 members of the Central Committee elected in 1958 continued for many years to work actively in the Party and in the liberation movement as a whole, but the experience of those co-opted in 1960 was different. Bartholomew Hlapane soon became a state witness. Robert Hepple also agreed to become one in 1963, but saved himself from the disgrace of giving evidence by managing to escape from the country. Joe Matthews, after playing a leading role for some years in the SACP and the ANC, later concentrated on his private business and finally found his political home in the Inkatha Freedom Party. The fourth is today an active and respected member of the ANC, and no longer a member of the Communist Party.

The situation which confronted the SACP and the Congress Alliance during the State of Emergency was vividly expressed by Michael Dingake in his book *My Fight against Apartheid*: "Compromise and confrontation clashed for prominence in the new unfolding scenario in the liberation struggle ... Yesterday's freedom fighters changed into dedicated revolutionaries overnight. It was not easy and the morale of the masses was ailing. Then [after the lifting of the Emergency] came ex-detainees, triumphant and confident. Public morale picked up quickly. The leaders were back. Expectations, vague and untranslatable, were in the air. Political magicians had arrived." [13]

To meet such high expectations, to play the role of "magicians", was not an easy task. The first major project for the leaders of the ANC was the preparation of the African All-in Conference to be convened in Pietermaritzburg on 25 March 1961. At that stage, both the ANC and the Congress Alliance hoped that a broad front of opposition forces would be created, and tried to encourage unity between the ANC and the PAC. The SACP shared this point of view.

But this attempt failed when PAC representatives and members of the Liberal Party withdrew from the Preparatory Committee. One of the Liberal Party leaders, Jordan Ngubane, accused the ANC of attempting to control the conference preparations, and receiving financial assistance from the SACP. He wrote of the "invisible hand of communism". Prominent American historians Thomas Karis and Gail

Gerhart noted: "There is some irony in these charges by Ngubane ... since a reliable source ... has said that money was being channelled at this time to the organisers of the All-in Conference from non-Communist sources, including African governments and members of the Liberal Party." [14]

The failure of these joint actions again sharpened the differences between the ANC and the PAC. The PAC leadership attempted to foil a stay-away on the eve of the proclamation of the Republic of South Africa on 31 May 1961. Helen Joseph later wrote: "The PAC took the shameful way of destructive opposition through leaflets issued from underground, calling upon the people to go to work and not stay at home. This political scabbing, by the very organisation which had brought about Sharpeville, aroused a new, deep and lasting resentment in the ANC." [15]

Government repression on the eve of the strike and during it increased the polarisation of South African society. Prime Minister Verwoerd declared that South Africa was resisting "the grabbing hand of communism" and seeking to preserve itself as a "pillar of Christian Western civilisation in Africa." [16] On the same day Nelson Mandela, who was elected Chairman of the National Action Council at the All-in Conference, warned the government: "As long as grievances remain, there will be protest actions of this kind or another. If peaceful protests like these are put down by the mobilisation of the army and the police, then the people might be forced to use other methods of struggle." [17]

The position of the SACP leadership was similar: "With practically every channel of legal opposition stopped by Verwoerd's dictatorship, it is inevitable that patriots and democrats will be compelled to an increasing extent to find new methods of struggle which are unconstitutional and illegal. Such methods will require courage, resourcefulness and imagination: the liberation movements of South Africa have given ample proof in the past that they possess these qualities in good measure." [18]

So, the question of a change in the form of struggle arose, imposed on the opposition forces by the actions of the government.

BEGINNINGS OF THE ARMED STRUGGLE

When the decision was taken, how it was taken and the role played by South African communists are all subjects of debate among academics, a debate fuelled by the fact that the evidence of those who participated in the events directly is somewhat contradictory.

The possibility of turning to armed struggle was discussed in Congress Alliance and communist circles immediately after Sharpeville, if not before. The belief was growing that under repressive conditions a position of non-violence was becoming more and more untenable. Some even considered it treachery.

Tom Lodge in his book *Black Politics in South Africa since 1945* claims that, at its conference in December 1960, the SACP "resolved itself in favour of a campaign of economic sabotage to precede a guerrilla war." [19] His claim echoes information provided in the book written by a police agent, Gerard Ludi, who can hardly be regarded as a reputable source for any academic work. Ludi himself did not have firsthand information but referred to the evidence of a deceased person who had never been a member of the Communist Party. [20]

May 1961 and the events around 31 May 1961 were a watershed. The *African Communist* criticised some aspects of the general strike organisation, such as "repeated eve-of-strike calls for non-violence from the people" which "were not only unnecessary but ... dampening to militancy" as it was the police and not the people who were preparing for violence. The same criticism was applied to the strictures against picketing and demonstrations. [21]

A rather contradictory picture emerges around the decision to change the form of struggle. Tom Lodge, referring to Ludi as well as to a seminar paper presented in Britain [22], writes that "there was no internal debate on the adoption of violence within the upper echelons of the Congress alliance." [23] On the same page, however, he contradicts himself by referring to Nelson Mandela's statement in court that such a move had been discussed at the ANC Executive meeting in June 1961 – in other words, in those very same "upper echelons". [24]

What is correct is that not all members of the ANC leadership participated in taking this decision. There was a delay in informing the banished ANC President-General Albert Luthuli. According to Brian

Bunting, who based his account mostly on interviews with Moses Kotane, "Luthuli was not involved in the discussions which led to the formation of Umkhonto." This was due not only to organisational difficulties and the lack of communication with Luthuli in Natal but also to a reluctance on the part of some ANC leaders "to engage in a discussion that might result in a presidential veto before it was necessary."[25]

In Kotane's view, it was only after armed operations had begun that the ANC leadership, at Luthuli's behest, sent its representatives to him to explain the decision. But Luthuli was not satisfied and demanded that Moses Kotane come to Groutville. After a lengthy talk in the bush near Luthuli's house, the ANC President-General finally stated that he would not condemn the participation of ANC members in armed actions, though he himself could not advocate violence. With some humour he said to Kotane: "When my son decides to sleep with a girl, he does not ask for my permission, but just does it. It is only afterwards, when the girl is pregnant and the parents make a case that he brings his troubles home."[26] According to Mary Benson, when Luthuli met Mandela later in August 1962, he "criticised the failure to consult him and the ANC grassroots." But in the opinion of Nelson Mandela the action of the ANC leadership had been "tactically correct" because it wanted to protect "Luthuli and the ANC from involvement in the drastic change in policy."[27]

Umkhonto we Sizwe (Spear of the Nation), or MK, was formed as a special organisation, formally separate from the ANC but in practice subordinate to its political leadership. This meant that the regime could not accuse the members of the ANC as a whole of direct involvement in the armed struggle. Ultimately, this could have made the eventual unbanning of the ANC possible.

There was, perhaps, a further rationale behind this form of organisation. Since the liberation struggle at that stage was united in the Congress Alliance, and different national groups participated in it mostly through their own organisations, the combat structure, too, needed to be a united endeavour. The creation of a military structure by only one of the organisations, even the strongest, might well have been regarded as a violation of the Alliance's professed unity of action. Also, the legal position of the Alliance members was different. Only the ANC was officially banned at that time.

The evidence that the idea of armed resistance was not imposed from above or imported from outside South Africa is contained in the memoirs of Umkhonto members. According to Andrew Masondo, who became the National Commissar of the ANC and later a Major-General in the new South African National Defence Force, "the idea of the movement moving away from its non-violence stance was discussed within youth circles even earlier than 1960. I remember that a group of us at Fort Hare actually formed a group to prepare for the eventuality of an armed struggle taking place."[28]

Steve Tshwete, Commissar of Umkhonto we Sizwe in the late 1980s and now Minister of Sport and Recreation, analysed the situation in this way: "[After the banning of the ANC] there were views that the struggle could still be prosecuted and led by the same movement under a different name. But such a conception would have presupposed a smothering of the revolutionary demands and aims of the movement. It would also mean a deep-going revision of our entire tactical approach to a struggle whose mass character could not be jettisoned for purposes of protecting legality. At the same time there was the more popular idea that some other methods of struggle other than 'legal' should be pursued for the realisation of the freedoms enshrined in the Freedom Charter," though, as Tshwete indicates, at that stage "there could ... be no precise stipulation or identification" of these methods, and that "the reality of armed struggle still remained a strange concept to the whole of the subcontinent."[29] Tshwete described the Pietermaritzburg conference as a watershed.

Another key witness-participant is Joe Modise, the Umkhonto Commander for many years and Minister of Defence from May 1994. He said that, even before Sharpeville and the ANC banning, the youth, while adhering to it, questioned the policy of non-violence. Later, but prior to the formation of Umkhonto, a group of young people including Modise tried "to stop the trains that ran between Soweto and Johannesburg" in order to strengthen the call for a strike in May 1961, and attempted to destroy telephone communications.[30]

Apart from the pressure within the membership, especially from the youth, international developments also influenced the decision to take up arms. If in the past the Indian experience of non-violent struggle had been an example for many South Africans (more so because of Mahatma Gandhi's connections with the country), they now sought inspiration from African countries, where armed struggle was already being waged or planned. India's stance had also modified with the liberation of Goa from Portuguese rule by the Indian Army in December 1961.

Events in Algeria were perhaps the greatest inspiration: by the end of 1961 it was clear that France would have to withdraw and concede victory to the Algerian liberation forces. Soon after the first actions of Umkhonto, the SACP magazine wrote: "Militarily, strategically, the South African government starts off weaker than the French in Algeria. Its armed forces are smaller; the exclusively white pool from which it can draw further recruits is minute by comparison with the French 'reserves' of population; its armaments are inferior; its industrial base is infinitely smaller; incapable of producing an internal combustion engine, a tank or an airplane. It is isolated. Not a single supporter – neither British reactionaries with fascist leanings nor millionaires with heavy investments in 'Kaffirs' – would dare raise a hand to support Verwoerd in civil war."[31]

Such optimism was to prove excessive. The South African authorities managed to draw into the SADF an adequate number of whites, as well as those of other races; the production of sophisticated military equipment was instituted; and, perhaps most importantly, reactionaries from Britain and other Western countries more than once "raised a hand" covertly or overtly to support Verwoerd and his successors.

The theory of "*foco*" advanced by Che Guevara had some influence, too, though it was not supported directly. "Experience, particularly in Cuba and Algeria," wrote Michael Harmel (A. Lerumo) in the *African Communist*, "has shown that it is an academic and mistaken approach for revolutionaries to observe events in a detached spirit, awaiting the situation where 'conditions are ripe for insurrection'. While adventurism and 'playing with revolution' are always to be avoided, the overwhelming lesson of the events in these countries is that the starting of their building of people's armed forces, however small to begin with, is in itself a tremendously important factor, helping to ripen and mature the revolutionary crisis, to create the conditions for victory, to act as the detonator of repercussions and reverberations far beyond the calculations of those who forget the revolutionary spirit of the masses, who attempt to gauge the outcome of a people's struggle against tyranny merely by counting the size and fire-power of the units which each, at the beginning, is able to put in the field."[32]

And, last but not least, the adoption of a new course of action was engendered by the experience of anti-colonial struggle within South Africa itself, the traditions of armed resistance to foreign domination, and militant action in some rural areas towards the end of the 1950s.

To what extent did South African communists influence the ANC and the other Congresses in changing the form of struggle, and to what extent did they initiate the structural re-arrangements?

The SACP Central Committee's statement "South Africa – What Next?" gave an indication that the methods of struggle were being reassessed. Before it was made public, the draft (written, I later learned, by Michael Harmel) was circulated among members in August 1960 as a confidential document for comment and criticism. Under the section titled "Violent or Non-violent", it stated: "Non-violence is not an absolute principle. It was correct in the past, and still is today, to warn the people against being provoked into desperate and useless acts of unorganised retaliation. But if the Verwoerd regime continues to butcher unarmed and defenceless people, it becomes worse than futile – even treacherous. The stage may be reached in the life of any nation when the stern and sacred duty presents itself to organise for battle. Should that day come the world will know who is the aggressor and who is responsible for the bloodshed and suffering that will result."[33]

The situation in South Africa after Sharpeville was analysed in the Political Report to the SACP Conference held at the end of 1960: "The declaration of the State of Emergency in April last should have been foreseen, expected and prepared for by us. But it must be admitted that in fact it caught us unprepared. Overnight we were faced with the arrest of a large part of our membership, the dislocation of all our leading committees and units, and simultaneously with the outlawing of the ANC, our foremost ally in struggle and the main public platform through which our views could be voiced."[34]

Nevertheless the system of contacts was soon pulled together, "not because we had planned and prepared for such a situation, but rather because the revolutionary training which we all had during the years gone by enabled us to respond rapidly, courageously and sensibly to a difficult situation." Moreover, during the months of Emergency, "in the conditions of the most extreme difficulty, our membership rose by 25%" [35], and "... the spirit and morale of our organisation is better that it had been before."[36]

The Political Report to the Conference raised the question of the role of the armed struggle in South Africa: "We do not seek to use force, but we are not pacifists who refuse under any and all circumstances to resort to force. We do not, either, play at revolution, using force where forceful actions are not properly prepared for, or attempting to substitute armed putschist bands for mass struggle .... What the government is preparing for throughout the country in the future is armed counter-revolution. We must ask ourselves seriously whether the non-violent tactics and the methods of the past are adequate to deal with even more bitter battles which are looming ahead."[37]

The report underlined that, by preparing a pamphlet with the title "South Africa – What Next?", the SACP "opened the discussion on this matter of violence and non-violence .... That discussion deals chiefly with slogans; but we must concern ourselves not only with slogans, but also with tactics and methods of struggle. We must consider whether armed counter-revolution can be effectively opposed by passive resistance."[38]

But the approach of the SACP leadership was still very cautious: "We must remind ourselves that just as the possibility of peace can disarm us in the international field if we are not vigilant, so too illusions about the inevitability of non-violence can disarm us in the local struggle."[39]

That approach was confirmed in a special resolution, "On Forms of Struggle". It spoke of the probability of "a violent people's struggle" against "the military counter-revolution" of the government. "While the people seek peaceful solutions to their problems at all times where such solutions exist, we would be betraying our duty to the people if we do not warn of the prospect of violent clash, and prepare the people for the use of force against armed counter-revolution."

It recognised that "the use of organised armed forces against the state, directed by the leading organisations of the people, is a part of the tactics of the revolutionary struggle, and is a necessary complement of the mass political agitation in such situations as that now developing [but not yet developed] in South Africa."[40] At the same time it strongly opposed dangerous "acts of violence and terror" undertaken as "individual acts of protest against society". These could bring "heavy retaliation by the authorities" and "serve to divide the people and to undermine the confidence of the masses in their political organisations and leaders."[41]

The actual circumstances surrounding the taking of the decision and the role of communists in that act are interpreted differently by various sources. As has already been mentioned, the government sources claimed that the decision on this matter was taken by the SACP in 1960. But even the sensitive documents of that period, such as "Notes on Some Aspects of the Political Situation in the Republic of South Africa", a working paper written by Moses Kotane in November 1961 during his visit to Moscow, contradict that view. Kotane stated that it was in 1961 that the leaders of the liberation movement, including communists, decided to use "some elements of violence" during future mass struggle, "such as picketing and breaking of communications".[42] It appears that when Kotane left South Africa for Moscow (arriving in mid October 1961) he did not yet know that the first actions of Umkhonto would start in two months' time. At least, no mention of it was made during a confidential discussion with his Soviet counterparts.

Valuable sources on the history of the ANC and the SACP in this period are the interviews conducted by Brian and Sonia Bunting in preparing Brian Bunting's political biography of Moses Kotane. Those interviews (now in the Mayibuye Centre Historical Papers Archive) give a valuable insight into many aspects of the liberation struggle in South Africa, including the dramatic change of form in 1961 as well as the relationship between the ANC and the SACP. Nevertheless, even this firsthand information is rather contradictory. For example, a prominent ANC Executive member M B Yengwa claimed that "MK had nothing to do with communists at all, it flowed out of the national movement."[43]

However, another participant, whom I will not name for ethical reasons, painted a different picture: "Rusty [Lionel Bernstein, member of the SACP Executive Committee] gave this report for armed struggle. It was discussed at some length and accepted, it was very unspecific but everybody knew that some steps would be taken in this direction and in fact it was a very important decision. If I remember rightly, Nelson [Mandela] was against violence, I think he had some reservations in this particular meeting. I don't say he was opposed to it, but he did have some reservation and said it would be difficult to sell this to the ANC, particularly to Luthuli."[44]

Nelson Mandela said at his trial in 1964: "It is a fact that for a long time the people had been talking of violence – of the day they would fight the white man and win back their country – and we, the leaders of the ANC, had nevertheless always prevailed upon them to avoid violence and pursue peaceful methods. When some of us discussed this in May and June 1961, it could not be denied that our policy to achieve a non-racial state by non-violence had achieved nothing and that our followers were beginning to lose confidence in this policy and were developing disturbing ideas of terrorism."[45]

He explained that the SACP rendered support to Umkhonto shortly after it was constituted.[46] Karis and Gerhart write, however: "This seems academic in the light of the intimate de facto co-operation between African nationalists like Mandela and Sisulu and white, Indian and African communists like Slovo, Ahmed Kathrada, Kotane and Marks."[47]

Important evidence of the decision-making process in 1961 is contained in the minutes of discussions that took place between the delegations of the ANC and the SACP in May 1969, immediately after the ANC Consultative Conference in Morogoro. At this highly confidential gathering Joe Slovo, having noted that this was "the first formal meeting ever to take place between two organisations which walked with hands clasp[ed] together for many years," emphasised "the simultaneous decision by both leaderships to chart the new way – the way of armed struggle. Many of our members - the cream, in fact - volunteered for MK training on the authority and with the encouragement of our party."[48]

In the Umkhonto magazine *Dawn* in 1986, on the occasion of its 25th anniversary, Joe Modise recalls that after preliminary discussions with some members of the ANC leadership, in particular Duma Nokwe (the Secretary General) and Walter Sisulu, he was invited to Stanger in Natal, "where the African National Congress, South African Communist Party, Coloured People's Congress, South African Indian Congress and Congress of Democrats met to discuss this new method of struggle. After two days of consultation it was agreed that the ANC and SACP were going to undertake this new form of struggle whilst the other movements that were still legal should continue working legally. It was then decided that MK was going to be launched." [49]

In implementing this decision the major role players were Nelson Mandela and Joe Slovo, who was at that time a member of the SACP Central Committee and a veteran of World War Two.

Joe Slovo perceived the creation of Umkhonto and the move from a policy of non-violence to one of violence as one of the "major struggles" initiated by the leadership of the SACP. [50] The South African communists were in a unique position. At that time only whites in South Africa had easy access to arms, only they were allowed to handle arms in the army, and therefore, in the practical sense, only whites could be military instructors for other members of Umkhonto inside South Africa. White communists such as Arthur Goldreich, who acquired his skills from Jewish military units in Palestine, and, especially, Jack Hodgson, who fought in World War Two, played an important role.

Govan Mbeki, ANC and SACP veteran, who was later to become Deputy President of the Senate in the South African parliament, wrote: "The South African Communist Party lost no time in setting up sabotage units while the ANC also formed its own. Towards the end of the year [1961], however, these units were merged."[51] In a confidential memorandum brought to Moscow, South African communists emphasised that "the Party is not, and under present conditions does not in the immediate future expect to be, of a mass character. Any exclusively Party fighting force, therefore, could not possibly have the mass popular character which a people's force of national liberation should rightly have."[52]

Further details were given by Joe Slovo in the issue of *Dawn* mentioned earlier: "To constitute the High Command the ANC appointed Mandela and the Party appointed me. We were instructed by both bodies to make recommendations about the balance of members of the High Command, which we did and it was endorsed. We were then given the mandate to proceed to create MK structures in all the main regions. Regional commands were established in the main urban centres."[53]

At first the High Command of Umkhonto comprised three people from each organisation: Mandela, Sisulu and Andrew Mlangeni from the ANC; and Slovo, Govan Mbeki and Raymond Mhlaba from the SACP. Joe Modise was appointed later. Ahmed Kathrada, Arthur Goldreich, Dennis Goldberg, Jack Hodgson and Elias Motsoaledi constituted the Johannesburg Regional Command and assisted the High Command.[54]

However, another leader of the SACP described the initial role of the Party in the creation of Umkhonto differently. John ("J B") Marks, at that time the SACP National Chairman, wrote in the Moscow *Pravda* in 1971 that the Party re-considered the issue of non-violence at its Congress in 1962 and that the ANC leaders agreed with their position. "The revolutionaries, communists and non-communists, decided to create their own armed force – Umkhonto we Sizwe." [55] One cannot exclude the possibility that the text of Marks's article was "improved" by the *Pravda* editors. Certainly, the reference to the SACP congress that took place at the end of 1962, a year after the commencement of Umkhonto operations, does not inspire confidence.

One would expect that after the 1990 unbanning of the ANC and SACP, when leaders and activists of these organisations were free to tell their story – not in a hostile courtroom but to a broad local and international audience – the historical account would become more accurate and comprehensive. Joe Slovo wrote in his *Unfinished Autobiography*: "The short accounts that have been published about the formation of MK have been drawn from the court speeches by Nelson Mandela and Bram Fischer in their respective trials. Understandably, the racist courtroom is not the most appropriate forum for establishing this kind of history, and some elaboration is required."[56]

However, newly emerging evidence is again contradictory. It is hard to imagine a more authoritative source than Nelson Mandela, the first MK Commander-in-Chief. Mandela's autobiography *Long Walk to Freedom*, prepared with the assistance of Richard Stengel, an American journalist, gives an account of Luthuli's attitude to the launching of the armed struggle that is different from the report given by Kotane to Bunting. According to Mandela, during the ANC Executive Committee meeting in Durban, Luthuli initially resisted Mandela's argument in favour of the use of violence. However, "we worked on him the whole night and I think that in his heart he realised we were right. He ultimately agreed that a military campaign was inevitable," but "the Chief and others suggested that we should treat this new resolution as if the ANC has not discussed it."[57]

Mandela offers this explanation of the conflicting reports about Luthuli's position: "The Chief was not well and his memory was not what it had been once. He chastised me for not consulting him about the formation of MK. I attempted to remind him of the discussions we had in Durban about taking up violence, but he did not recall them. This is in large part why the story has gained currency that Chief Luthuli was not informed about the creation of MK and was deeply opposed to the ANC taking up violence."[58]

As to the actual formation of the Umkhonto Command, Mandela writes: "Although the Executive of the ANC did not allow white members, MK was not thus constrained. I immediately recruited Joe Slovo and along with Walter Sisulu we formed the High Command with myself as chairman. Through Joe I enlisted the efforts of white Communist Party members who had resolved on a course of violence."[59]

On the other hand, Slovo in his *Unfinished Autobiography* virtually repeats the version published by him in the *Dawn* article mentioned above: "A High Command was appointed consisting, in the first place, of Mandela representing the ANC's working group in Johannesburg and me representing the Central Committee. We were asked to make recommendations on the rest of the High Command and these were considered and decided upon by the ANC and the Party leadership." [60]

The birth of the armed struggle in South Africa was the subject of a special conference organised by the Mayibuye Centre in December 1995. Some questions were answered, although many remain for future historians.

The first actions of Umkhonto we Sizwe on 15 and 16 December 1961 and those which occurred in the following months are well documented. According to Nelson Mandela, sabotage was chosen as the form of action specifically to avoid loss of life and to offer "the best hope for future race relations" in the light of "the ANC heritage of non-violence and racial harmony."[61]

Slovo addressed the other major consideration when he later wrote that "the immediate unleashing of the armed struggle" was not possible in South Africa in the early 1960s because of "a gap between the people's disenchantments with exclusively non-violent methods and their readiness and capacity to storm the citadels of the enemy."[62]

Such an approach proved to be partially correct. Many staunch supporters of non-violence were ready to agree with actions against objects but not people. A reluctance of the broad masses to risk their lives in armed struggle persisted throughout the early 1960s and beyond. Joe Slovo wrote: "The response of the regime was increased repression. It was clear to all and we had demonstrated to the movement and to the leadership elements which were in doubt that there was no way forward short of preparing for effective escalation of revolutionary violence."[63] When it became clear that "a real people's army" had to be built, the High Command and its structures devoted a great deal of energy "to sending out of the country a contingent of many hundreds of experienced political cadres at all levels who were subsequently trained in the art of guerrilla warfare and military struggle." [64]

A primary aim of Nelson Mandela's trip abroad in 1962 was to secure such training. He was greatly assisted in his mission by Oliver Tambo, who had left South Africa at the end of March 1960 to organise an international solidarity campaign. Though Mandela was well received in several African countries, he sometimes met with a lack of understanding of certain aspects of ANC activity and in particular with "uneasiness ... at the ANC's alliance with whites and Indians and at the fact that some were communists."[65]

When the ANC was banned, followed later by the Congress of

Democrats, there was a perception that the leadership of the national liberation movement would pass to the remaining Alliance members who were still legal: the South African Indian Congress, the Coloured People's Congress and the South African Congress of Trade Unions. This did not happen. While co-operation essentially continued and this was reflected in the composition of the groups sent for training abroad (though Africans were strongly in the majority), the Alliance ceased to exist as a formal structure.

The efforts of the Umkhonto High Command to build a people's army met with a popular response. Michael Dingake recalls: "The organisation was inundated with applicants for training abroad. Although not all known former members of the ANC were members of MK, the ordinary man in the street was not aware of the distinction between the political and military structures of the underground. On a number of occasions I was approached by senior citizens of Alexandra [Johannesburg township] who had known me as an office bearer of the ANC and presumed I was now a member of the underground: 'M'tanami (My child), my son is unemployed and gravitating towards delinquency. Won't you take him for training so that he can come back and fight amabunu (Boers)? Please, m'tanami. We are tired of amabunu and I don't want my boy to go and rot in gaol for stupid crimes.'"[66]

This example helps to explain some of the difficulties experienced by Umkhonto and the ANC in exile for many years: the weak discipline of some members, especially newcomers to political struggle, who would cling to certain negative conventions of township life, such as carrying a knife wherever you go. Not that unemployed youth or petty criminals formed a major component of Umkhonto recruits. According to Wilton Mkwayi, a prominent trade unionist and later head of the Umkhonto second High Command, "most of the chaps who left the country first were involved in Sactu."[67] Eric Mtshali, one of the first MK members in Natal, confirmed that he and other trade unionists were well placed to recruit "the best out of the working class" to Umkhonto. "Therefore people who went out for military training during that period of the 60s were mostly workers."[68]

The first groups of recruits were sent to independent African states. The closest to South Africa was Tanganyika, which gained independence in December 1960. While it was not possible to organise military training there at that time, Tanganyika became a major transit base on the road north. Joe Modise actively participated in the transportation of recruits abroad. When the first recruits arrived in Johannesburg from the Eastern Cape, and then from Natal and the Western Cape, they were placed in safe houses before moving illegally across the South African border into Bechuanaland (Botswana). The very first group was taken straight to Francistown, where a truck was hired to take them into Southern Rhodesia (Zimbabwe), at that time a self-governing British colony. From there they proceeded to Lusaka and then on to Dar es Salaam.

The second group (also travelling via Francistown) reached Kazangula on the banks of the Zambezi River. Here the borders of Bechuanaland, South West Africa (Namibia), Northern Rhodesia (Zambia) and Southern Rhodesia almost met, leaving a narrow passage from Bechuanaland to Northern Rhodesia for those who managed to cross the Zambezi by ferry. Travel was further complicated by the fact that the road from Francistown to Kazangula was "a little bush track, which was so faint, and at some places there was nothing at all."[69] The alternative route via Southern Rhodesia, described above, was used only once because the second group (which included Thabo Mbeki, now South Africa's Deputy President) was detained by the Southern Rhodesian authorities and deported, fortunately to Bechuanaland and not to South Africa.

For these reasons, aircraft had to be chartered to move the ANC activists from Bechuanaland. This method was used for only a short period. The costs of chartering aircraft were very high. The South African and British authorities exerted pressure on the aircraft owners. Even more critically, Pretoria introduced new rules in September 1963 which required all aircraft flying to, from or between the British protectorates to land at one of South Africa's airports, inform the South African authorities of the purpose of their flight, and provide lists of passengers.

The situation deteriorated further when, after two or three successful flights, South African agents sabotaged an aircraft that was supposed to transport a group of Umkhonto leaders. So, the road to Kazangula again became the main route. Groups of 30 to 35 would travel by truck through the bush, then cross the Zambezi, to reach Livingstone. There the local branch of Kenneth Kaunda's United National Independence Party (UNIP) would assist them, despite the fact that the British colonial authorities were still in power in the country.

In Northern Rhodesia travel was not yet safe. One group was arrested there by the British colonial authorities and deported to South

Africa, where they stood trial and were subsequently imprisoned. The inevitable leaking of information that resulted from this forced Joe Modise to leave South Africa. He and Raymond Mhlaba managed to cross the Southern Rhodesian territory with false Malawian documents, claiming that they had been deported from South Africa.[70] Only after arriving in Tanzania could the ANC and Umkhonto activists expect some (limited) help from the authorities. All the expenses on the long route had to be provided by Umkhonto and the ANC.

The first large group of Umkhonto recruits arrived in Dar es Salaam in July 1962, led by Johnstone (Johnny) Makatini, who later became a prominent member of the ANC Executive and the Head of its International Department. There the contingent was divided into two: in October eleven members went via Nairobi, Juba (Southern Sudan) and Khartoum to Morocco, and twenty members (also via Nairobi) to Addis Ababa.[71]

After short-term training in Ethiopia the group returned to Dar es Salaam to be divided again: nine men were sent home to South Africa while the others went to Algeria to continue their military studies. The route of their travels indicates the obstacles the ANC representatives abroad had to overcome. From Dar es Salaam to Nairobi they went by plane; from Nairobi to Juba by hired taxis on poor roads; from Juba to Khartoum by ship down the Nile; from Khartoum to Cairo by train; and from Cairo to Algiers again by plane.

This small group in Algeria was joined in February 1963 by another 25 and soon after by 34 more, arriving from South Africa. After they completed their training, some were sent home, and the rest were sent outside the African continent, to the USSR. There the group that had completed their basic initial training in Morocco joined them. In addition, nineteen members who arrived in Dar es Salaam in December 1962 left for Cairo the following month. After studying there, most went to the USSR and some returned to South Africa. All in all, from September 1962 to March 1963, 135 Umkhonto fighters were dispatched from Dar es Salaam to various countries.

The list of African countries used to organise training immediately after Nelson Mandela's trip is worth noting. Morocco, in the first years of independence, took an active anti-colonial position and its territory was used as a base by Algerian freedom fighters. The leaders of newly independent Algeria considered their country to be a vanguard of the liberation movement in Africa; even the ruling party's journal was called *Revolution Africaine*. While Emperor Haile Selassie of Ethiopia maintained fairly close links with Western countries (especially the United States), he claimed the role of "Patriarch" for the emerging independent African states. He facilitated the convening of the first African Summit in May 1963 in Addis Ababa, and insisted on locating the Headquarters of the Organisation of African Unity there.

Egypt played a special role in African nationalist movements. I personally witnessed the concern shown in 1960, the "Africa Year", and in subsequent years for the liberation struggles throughout Africa. This concern was shown not only by the Egyptian leadership, especially Gamal Abdel Nasser, but also by the media and, more surprisingly, by almost every educated Egyptian. Egypt gave both political and practical support, including military assistance. Soviet transport planes found their way to the Congo via Cairo, and Patrice Lumumba's family found asylum in Egypt after his assassination. In 1962 when I spent a few weeks in the Kulliat al-Harbia, the military college near Cairo International Airport, I saw many African cadets being trained by the Egyptian Army. Their training, especially in Saiqa (the Commandos), was very rigorous.[72]

MK transportation and training in Africa and elsewhere were prime targets for South African special services, working in co-operation with their Western colleagues. Many years later an Umkhonto fighter, who came to Moscow for medical treatment after serving a long sentence on Robben Island, told me that during interrogation in South Africa he had been shown a picture of himself and his friends taken in Heliopolis, a Cairo suburb.

Joe Modise recalls: "I think we sent one group to China; from then onwards we acquired most of our training from the Soviet Union."[73] There were apparently several reasons for the ANC and the SACP leadership requesting this kind of assistance from the Soviet Union. Facilities in the African countries were limited and the political situation not always helpful. In Algeria, for example, the situation was unstable because of severe differences within the ruling FLN. The Moroccan authorities demanded political references for trainees (perhaps worried about their "communist connections"), and the Ethiopians even suggested using American servicemen stationed there to train the South Africans.

There is a widespread view that the friendly relations between the USSR and the ANC, and the assistance provided to the South African liberation movement over three decades, arose from the ANC's alliance (informal as it was) with the South African Communist Party. How accurate is this perception and what led to the co-operation? What were the political structures and who were the individuals involved?

Firstly, it should be noted that a fresh start was needed in 1960 in relations between the Soviet Union and the South African liberation forces. Whatever ties existed earlier between the Communist Party of South Africa (and to an extent the ANC) and the Soviet Union had been severed after the beginning of World War Two and the subsequent dissolution of the Comintern. The Soviet Consulate in Pretoria and its branch in Cape Town naturally maintained some contact with the CPSA (until its banning in 1950) and the Congress Movement, but those contacts did not serve as a channel of communication between the South African political organisations and the ruling Communist Party of the Soviet Union.

Unfortunately a number of publications have confused the issue. I refer here not only to the propaganda of the Verwoerd-Vorster-Botha period, but also to recent "academic" writing, such as *Comrades Against Apartheid* co-authored by Stephen Ellis (former editor of *Africa Confidential*) and "Tsepo Sechaba". They quote police agent Gerard Ludi, who alleged that even the Freedom Charter was "sent to the Moscow Africa Institute for approval".[74] Excessive confidence in their intelligence sources has betrayed the authors: the decision to establish the Africa Institute was taken in June 1959, exactly four years after the Charter was adopted by the Congress of the People in Kliptown.

Equivalent sources of information have appeared recently in Moscow. When the much-praised *glasnost* deteriorated into a free-for-all, some former Soviet intelligence operatives also started talking. In an interview in the Moscow newspaper *New Bridge*, Vassily Dazhdalev (from 1952 to 1956 Head of the Soviet Mission in Cape Town and for some time Acting Consul General in Pretoria, and now a self-confessed retired KGB General) confirmed that he had been acquainted with several leading South African communists. Dazhdalev claimed that he had transmitted messages from Bram Fischer "to the Soviet leadership" and, as he recalled, one message contained "a request for material assistance," though he emphasised that he "did not pass money to Fischer or to any of his comrades."[75] He did not elaborate on the content of the messages, as, apparently, there was nothing to elaborate on. His memory may have betrayed him: the names of the South African communists he mentioned were most probably prompted by the journalist. He spoke, for example, about "Mr

Ruth First".

The CPSU archives do not contain any record of bilateral relations between the South African and Soviet Communist Parties in the 1950s. Some prominent members of the illegal SACP and the ANC did visit Moscow in that period, but declassified documents say nothing about inter-party contacts. According to the documentation, the first South African communists to visit the USSR after World War Two were Brian and Sonia Bunting. They arrived in March 1954, as the guests of the All-Soviet Society for Cultural Ties with Foreign Countries (VOKS), "to get acquainted with the life in the Soviet Union"[76], and were followed by Ruth First, who was a guest of the Anti-Fascist Committee of Soviet Women.[77] Archive documents concerning these visits do not, however, make any reference to requests by the SACP for assistance, nor do they mention the Party's existence. Neither Ruth First nor the Buntings were sent to the USSR by the SACP to establish contacts with the CPSU, nor did they have meetings with its representatives in Moscow. Both the archival documents and my discussion with Brian and Sonia Bunting confirm that those trips were not part of a resumption of inter-party relations.[78]

Sam Kahn, referred to in the Soviet documents as "a progressive figure of the Union of South Africa, who is at present in England", did mention his intention "to discuss matters concerning the work of the Communist Party" in his request to visit the USSR.[79] Kahn came to Moscow soon after the Buntings but was denied a meeting with CPSU Headquarters because he had not participated in efforts to rebuild the Party underground.

Others, including ANC leaders Walter Sisulu and Duma Nokwe, toured the USSR after participating in the World Youth and Student Festival. Many years later Sisulu recalled his trip by train from Moscow to Beijing in 1953 in the company of very friendly but very noisy Latin Americans (15 or 20 years younger than he was), as well as his visit to Azerbaijan, where the memory of British intervention and occupation in 1918 was still fresh.[80]

Two prominent black South African women – Lilian Ngoyi (President of the ANC Women's League) and Dora Tamana (National Secretary of the Federation of South African Women) – were also invited to the USSR in 1955 on the initiative of Helen Joseph. In her autobiography *Side by Side* Helen Joseph wrote with some bitterness about her experience: "I had hoped secretly and vainly that perhaps I too might have been invited to visit some other country for there

33

seemed to be many invitations floating around though almost entirely to black women. However, it did not happen. I think my disabilities were that I was white and not ideologically committed." [81] But in fact she herself insisted on the invitation of the African women. In Geneva at the session of the International Federation of Democratic Women she met Soviet delegates and wrote a letter to the Anti-Fascist Committee of Soviet Women, recommending her African friends. No question of their relationship with communists or their ideological views was raised. The Soviet women's organisation, however, underlined the fact that "representatives of the African women have not yet visited the USSR."[82] This was not strictly correct, however, because Josie Mpama, the wife of Communist leader Edwin Mofutsanyana, visited the USSR in the 1930s and participated in the Seventh Congress of the Comintern.

In 1959 Solly Sachs, a veteran of the South African trade union movement, was invited on the initiative of his old friend, prominent Soviet Africanist Professor Ivan Potekhin. In Potekhin's letter to the CPSU Central Committee, Sachs's relationship with the Communist Party (a rather complicated one) was not mentioned. [83]

The first stone was laid in building regular relations between the USSR and the SACP and the Congress Alliance when the official representatives of the South African communists came to Moscow in July 1960 and had meetings in the CPSU Headquarters. They were Yusuf Dadoo (SACP Chairman), who played an outstanding role in the Congress Alliance for many years, and Vella Pillay (the Party's representative in Europe).

Another prominent South African communist, Moses Kotane, described Dadoo much earlier, in 1954, as "the only non-African who has been accepted as their own leader and brother by the Africans."[84] Dadoo left South Africa at the beginning of April 1960 for Bechuanaland. From there, together with Oliver Tambo, he travelled on Indian documents by charter plane to Tanganyika. Unfortunately the plane had to land in Blantyre in Nyasaland, where the danger of deportation to South Africa was very real. But they managed to get permission to go on to Dar es Salaam and later to Accra, where Kwame Nkrumah provided them with Ghanaian travel documents. Soon they moved to London, which, in the words of Dadoo, was "a very suitable centre from many points of view to operate from."[85]

The request for SACP representatives to go to Moscow to discuss the "establishment of contacts and rendering of support" was passed on to the Soviet Embassy in London by the Communist Party of Great Britain. The CPSU International Department officials communicated the request to the leadership. These communications clearly show the absence of a bilateral relationship, as well as a lack of information: "In 1952 [*sic*] the Communist Party of South Africa announced its self-dissolution but according to British friends [read: British communists], it continues its activity underground. The leadership of the Party regularly conducts meetings, directing the main efforts at the work in the mass organizations. During the recent pogroms [this word was used to describe the arrests after Sharpeville] many South African Communists underwent repression and others are in difficult material conditions." [86]

Evidence of the pioneering character of this mission was a letter of recommendation sent to the CPSU Central Committee by John Gollan, the General Secretary of the CP of Great Britain (CPGB). For many years the CPGB interfaced between communist parties and anti-colonial organisations in the former British Empire and the socialist countries. It is therefore not surprising that in the CPSU in the late 1940s and early 1950s South African affairs were a part of the responsibility of the "Sub-Department of the British Empire [*sic*] of the Foreign Policy Commission". October 1955 saw the terminology modernised and the department became the "Section of Great Britain". In 1960 a special Section of African Countries was formed in the International Department of the Central Committee. The Department itself was created in 1957, when foreign contacts were separated into two spheres, one headed by Yury Andropov dealing with socialist countries, and the other, the International Department, headed by Boris Ponomarev and dealing with the rest of the world.

The spirit of the meeting in July 1960 and of subsequent discussions with the CPSU representatives was later described by Yusuf Dadoo: "We have open honest discussions as between Communists, and the Soviet comrades have never insisted on this or that line."[87] The SACP delegation presented their Soviet counterparts with documents on the "Political Situation in the Union of South Africa"[88] and on "The Situation in the South African Communist Party"[89], which described the "deep crisis" after Sharpeville and gave a self-critical analysis of the actions of the opposition forces.

The SACP documents explained that in spite of arrests the Party had continued its activity. Its work was hindered, however, by economic constraints. These were caused by declining donations after the introduction of the State of Emergency (previously, many contributions had come from the Indian community, in which Yusuf Dadoo was extremely popular and respected), and by additional expenditure on maintaining the families of detainees and assistance to the ANC Emergency Committee.[90]

Much attention was paid by the SACP delegation to the involvement of the USSR and other socialist countries in the international campaign to isolate and boycott South Africa. The SACP leadership expected speedy results in the Western countries (in reality it took many years before any substantial limitations in trade with South Africa were achieved); and there was concern that the "Eastern countries" would become South Africa's new major partners. The problem for the USSR in introducing sanctions against South Africa, as the SACP saw it, was not so much one of possible losses (bilateral trade was very limited), but that this could undermine Moscow's policy of "trade with all countries". This policy was Moscow's response to the Cold War restrictions placed on the USSR by the USA and other major Western states.

These questions, as well as "forms of fraternal assistance from the CPSU and workers' parties of the Socialist Countries"[91], were discussed at the meeting in the International Department of the Central Committee. The South African communists were also interested in the outcome of a Bucharest meeting of several Communist parties in June 1960, where Soviet-Chinese differences became apparent for the first time.

When the question of financial assistance to the anti-racist struggle in South Africa was discussed, perhaps Yusuf Dadoo recalled the words of Mahatma Gandhi at their meeting in Patna, India, in 1947. Dadoo, as the President of the Transvaal Indian Congress, had raised the matter, and Gandhi had replied: "Well, of course, you know, when you have the struggle, money will come; don't worry about funds, funds will come, you carry on with the struggle and if the struggle goes on, funds would be there."[92]

The funds did indeed materialise. The newly declassified archive material shows that by the end of 1960 the SACP was allocated $30 000 from the so-called "International Trade Union Fund for Assistance to Left Workers' Organisations, attached to the Romanian Council of Trade Unions".[93] This fund was established ten years earlier on the initiative of the Soviet Party to render material assistance to "foreign left parties, workers' and public [non-governmental] organisations, which are subjected to persecution and repression."[94]

There are many stories about "Kremlin gold", but originally only half of the contributions to this fund came from the USSR, with the remainder coming from China, Czechoslovakia, Romania, Poland, Hungary and the GDR. Bulgaria joined later, in 1958. China withdrew in 1962 after the Sino-Soviet split. The choice of Romania as a venue was not accidental as in the early 1950s the Cominform (a weak replica of the Comintern) and its newspaper were based in Bucharest. Initially the Fund's Board was comprised of representatives from the Soviet, Romanian and Polish parties, and the decision taken by the Politbureau envisaged that "material assistance will be rendered according to unanimous decisions of the Board," whose members were to be appointed annually by the agreement of the contributing parties.[95]

The international character of the Fund was maintained, at least on the surface. A CPSU Politbureau decision on the distribution of financial assistance for 1963 specifically entrusted "Com. Semichastny [KGB Chairman] to ensure that while transferring the [financial] means it should be advised that assistance is rendered from the International Trade Union Fund."[96] It should be emphasised that as a matter of mutual trust the SACP and other friendly parties have never been asked to account for these donations.

The visit in July 1960 was followed by another later in the year when the SACP delegation, headed again by Dadoo and including Michael Harmel, Joe Matthews and Vella Pillay, travelled to Moscow to participate in the International Meeting of the Communist and Workers' Parties. Joe Matthews was the first to speak at the meeting on behalf of the SACP, possibly because he was the only African in the group. He and Michael Harmel (who was the second to speak on the SACP's behalf) had arrived in Moscow directly from South Africa.

On the eve of the meeting, Dadoo had visited China. At that stage the Chinese communist leadership treated guests from the Afro-Asian world with considerable respect. Dadoo was received personally by Mao Zedung. According to Dadoo the visit to China was "extraordinary, perhaps even bizarre." In preliminary discussions Chinese representatives tried to convince the SACP delegation that the CPSU was revisionist. They "elevated into a law-governed principle of revolutionary struggle the Chinese experience of the long march and forms of armed struggle."[97] Dadoo explained to Mao Zedung that conditions in South Africa were very different from those in China and that the struggle would take different forms. Mao Zedung was very friendly and listened carefully but refrained from comment. He did suggest that they meet the Chinese delegation (headed by Deng Xiaoping) in Moscow.

There the Chinese representatives did their best to win support for their line, possibly overstepping what was appropriate. At one point Michael Harmel warned them that the SACP would seriously have to reconsider the distribution of materials from the Chinese Communist Party inside South Africa.[98] Overall, the SACP delegation was happy with the outcome of meeting: the joint documents were approved by both the Chinese and the Soviets. For several years, while Soviet-Chinese relations deteriorated and the split became public, the position of the Central Committee of the SACP was to avoid criticising Beijing, in order "not to inflame the differences."[99]

The Soviets also treated the SACP delegation with respect, though recognition was not at the highest level. The delegation twice had discussions with Nuretdin Mukhitdinov. One of the youngest in Khrushchev's team, he had previously been the Party leader in Uzbekistan and was now the Secretary of the Central Committee and Member of the Presidium (the highest Party body, later called the Politbureau). The South Africans described the situation in their country, outlined plans to convene an SACP conference underground, and once more requested that political literature be sent to South Africa.

Again the boycott of South African goods received attention. The SACP was concerned about the passive attitude of the World Federation of Trade Unions, headed by communists, particularly when compared with the active stand of the "pro-Western" International Confederation of Free Trade Unions. The delegation was also worried by reports of the sale of South African wool to the USSR, especially as these sales were given prominence in propaganda aimed at subverting the boycott movement.

Mukhitdinov immediately checked this by *"vertushka"* (the famous bug-safe intercom of Soviet high officials) with the Ministry of Foreign Trade and relayed the information that the wool, bought in London, was purported to be of Australian origin. He also assured the SACP delegation that Ministry data indicated that Soviet organisations had stopped signing contracts with South African companies in November 1960 and no longer responded to their proposals. Steps that had been taken by the Soviet Union to curtail economic ties with South Africa before the passing of the relevant UN resolution in 1962 allowed the SACP to state that the USSR "imposed a full trade embargo at the request of the South African liberation movement."[100]

In particular, the relevant Soviet state bodies were instructed to stop dealing with De Beers and to find alternative ways of selling Soviet diamonds. De Beers Chairman Harry Oppenheimer noted in the 1963 Annual Report that "on account of Russian support for the boycotting of trade with South Africa, our contract to buy Russian diamonds has not been renewed."[101] The CPSU International Department was informed that an alternative buyer had been found in London, although it later became clear (to participants in the deal it may have been clear all along) that this company, portrayed as British, was controlled by De Beers.

Other questions discussed in Moscow in 1960 included broadcasting Moscow radio programmes to South Africa. This soon began in English and some years later in Zulu. Further practical steps in the development of co-operation followed, such as the purchase and distribution of the *African Communist* magazine in the USSR.[102] Bilateral relations between the two parties were thus resumed, although for years to come all contact with the SACP was maintained through the CPGB leadership in London. This included a message of congratulations on the 40th anniversary of the SACP, which was not published in the USSR.[103]

In its first report to the Party at home, the SACP delegation stated that it had been active both at the conference and in the editing commission. "Though representing a small organisation, your delegation played a not unimportant part .... It addressed the plenary session twice, first on general questions ... and the second time on the special question of factional activities, basing itself on our own experiences." It proposed two amendments to the main document of the meeting – on the newly independent African states, and on support for the struggle against apartheid – both of which were unanimously supported.[104]

The SACP leadership was satisfied with "the development of world Communist Unity". Having acknowledged that "the leaders of the Chinese Party apparently differ in view from the majority of the Communist Parties," it nevertheless believed that "the very controversial nature of the Chinese contribution to [the debate] has served also a valuable purpose."[105]

Yusuf Dadoo visited Moscow again in October 1961, this time together with Moses Kotane, who left South Africa illegally and was now back in the USSR after a quarter of a century. Those who met Kotane in 1961 remember him as a very colourful, impressive and powerful person, who took the lead in the Moscow discussions. The very fact that he was a communist in the "Comintern mould" also contributed towards the re-establishment of full-scale relations between the two parties. It was lucky that he returned to the USSR in the days of Khrushchev, after the criticism of Stalin's "cult of personality", when old assessments of people underwent a critical review. Certain references, "inherited" by the International Department from the Comintern, associating Kotane with the "Roux-Gomas factionist group", may otherwise have influenced his Soviet associates.

A distinct feature of Kotane was his independence, as his new Moscow friends were soon to discover. Shortly after his arrival he asked to be taken from his "special flat", provided by the Central Committee, into the centre of Moscow, where he then promptly disappeared. Imagine, the General Secretary of an illegal party getting lost in Red Square! Fortunately the alarm was called off in a matter of hours: Kotane rediscovered some parts of Moscow after his 25-year absence, took a few rides on the metro and by trolley-bus, and then successfully found his way back to his "hideout".[106]

The South African communists were invited to attend the 22nd CPSU Congress, which, under the leadership of Khrushchev, adopted the new Programme of the Party, which promised to build a communist society in the lifetime of one generation.

On 21 October 1961 a discussion took place in the CPSU Headquarters between the South African delegation and Vitaly Korionov, Deputy Head of the International Department. Though of a preliminary nature, it had special significance: for the first time the South Africans touched upon the possibility of using an armed form of struggle. They said that the SACP had created a special Sub-Committee whose task it was to elaborate the practical steps (together with ANC representatives) necessary to train cadres and to prepare for sabotage. The Party leadership had already arranged military and political studies with the Chinese for the first group of trainees, who were on their way. (This group included prominent ANC members Raymond Mhlaba, Wilton Mkwayi, Joe Gqabi, Andrew Mlangeni, the SAIC member Steve Naidoo, and Patrick Mtembu, who later became a state witness.)[107]

After the CPSU Congress, at the first meeting of the newly elected Central Committee Secretariat, Boris Ponomarev was instructed to receive the South African delegation jointly with Korionov.[108] For the next 25 years Ponomarev was the main interlocutor with SACP and ANC delegations in Moscow. Many issues were discussed, from Moses Kotane's impressions of how Moscow had changed since his first visit a quarter of a century earlier ("Many things changed, one cannot recognise the streets, though the Red Square and the Bolshoy Theatre are in their place.") to the Party Rules. Two issues were of special importance: the degree of openness of the Party, and the use of various forms of struggle.

Before the meeting on 18 November the SACP delegation handed the International Department a document headed "Notes on Some Aspects of the Political Situation in the Republic of South Africa", signed by Moses Kotane. Preparatory documents of this sort became a tradition, providing a preview of items for discussion and therefore sometimes advance solutions to problems.

The approach of the Soviet side was summarised in Ponomarev's words: "You know better." It was this that led him to endorse the SACP's cautious approach to the recruitment of new members, even though in his opinion a mass Party was needed when the "social battles" began. He believed that, apart from working in the ANC and other mass organisations, communists should inform people of the SACP's existence. The SACP had already been doing this for more than a year, but perhaps Kotane and Dadoo wanted to test this against the opinion of the Soviets. The question of the public re-emergence of the Party was highly controversial and Kotane and Dadoo may have had lingering reservations about their decision.

Nor was the SACP urged to proclaim immediate socialist aims: instead, the Soviet side simply referred to the document of the International Communist meeting of 1960 which called for the creation of "states of national democracy" in Africa. A cautious position was also taken on the question of armed struggle. Ponomarev regarded this matter as important enough to be reported to the CPSU's top leadership. He endorsed the opinion of the South African communists that "under the conditions of the reign of terror by the fascist government which has at its disposal a huge military and police machinery, the peaceful way of reaching the tasks of liberation and revolutionary movements at present are excluded. The Party has decided to proceed from the necessity of the preparation for the armed forms of struggle. They ask the Central Committee of the CPSU to express its opinion whether such course is correct. At the same time the

41

comrades request ... support in training several military instructors."[109]

The report, sent to the Central Committee on 24 November, further stated: "The Marxist Leninist doctrine on the combination of all forms of struggle was elucidated to the South African comrades. At the same time they were informed that the opinion of the Central Committee would be conveyed to them later on the question of their tactics on a new stage of struggle." They were also informed that the USSR "would be able to render the SACP possible assistance using for this in particular the facilities in some friendly African countries, for example in Guinea and Ghana."

Ponomarev requested official permission from the Central Committee to convey the following to Kotane and Dadoo: "Taking into account the situation in [South Africa] we agree with the opinion expressed by comrades Kotane and Dadoo. At the same time the intention of the SACP to take a course of armed forms of struggle places on the Party great responsibility. It is necessary not to counterpoise one form of struggle to the others but to combine skilfully all these forms. The armed struggle is a struggle of the broad people's masses. It means that in the conditions of the preparation for the armed struggle the political work to win the masses acquires decisive importance. Without consistent political and organisational work among the masses victory is impossible. The winning of the masses to your side and preparation for the armed struggle are two sides of the same question. Both these tasks should be accomplished in close interconnection."

"Certain assistance" was also promised in the training of instructors.[110]

On 28 November 1961 Ponomarev's opinion was endorsed by the Central Committee Secretariat.[111] As a matter of historical record it should be noted that the position of the CPSU leadership was conveyed to Moses Kotane (who stayed in the USSR for some time) after Umkhonto we Sizwe had carried out its first actions. (A hand-written confirmation of this fact was made later, in February 1962, on a document by Petr Manchkha, the head of the CPSU African Section.)[112]

One more detail is relevant: the approval of Ponomarev's proposals given by his colleagues and superiors in the Party Secretariat was almost automatic. In the bureaucratic language of the day, the "CC secretaries agreed without recording in the minutes" – the least formal of the Secretariat's processes of decision. The claim appeared some time ago in the Johannesburg *Sunday Times* that "the all-powerful Central Committee of the Soviet Union Communist Party (CC SUCP) met for an important decision [on that matter]."[113] This is either incompetent journalism or a deliberate attempt to distort the truth: the Central Committee did not meet to discuss this issue at all.

The documents of the CPSU archives confirm, therefore, that Moscow neither instigated nor agitated for the armed struggle in South Africa but, rather, respected the decision taken by the South Africans themselves and agreed to render assistance, while warning against over-emphasis on armed forms of struggle. The Soviets did not rush to begin the military training of South Africans in the USSR, but favoured assisting their training in African countries.

Soviet support for the armed struggle may have been the cause of an increase of financial assistance to the SACP, from 50 000 dollars in 1961[114] to 112 445 dollars in 1962.[115]

There was activity in other areas of co-operation. On 16 September 1961 the CPSU Central Committee's Commission on Questions of Ideology, Culture and International Party Ties agreed to receive ten South African students for academic training and to cover their travel expenses from Johannesburg to Moscow. Vella Pillay's urgent request for this explained that these people had been "expelled [from school] for their political activities, especially for organisation of the strike in May." The leadership feared that they would be detained and banished to some remote area.[116]

Nine of the ten students, among them future ANC National Executive member Anthony Mongalo (now Deputy Director General of the South African Department of Foreign Affairs), managed to make their way to the Soviet Union in February 1962. Though they were six months late (the academic year had begun in September), they worked hard and completed the programme of the preparatory course in Kiev in five months instead of ten, and went on to various cities for full university training.[117]

Political students followed the academics. In 1962 three South Africans arrived, to attend the Institute of Social Sciences, better known by its "underground" name, the International Lenin School. The decision to resurrect this School (it had existed in Moscow in the 1930s and had been attended by Kotane) was taken on 19 December 1961 to meet an increasing number of requests from foreign communist parties and later from liberation movements.[118] Sixty countries were invited to send students for the first year of training; and four places were offered to South Africans.[119] The future of the three students who attended [120] is worth describing. Ruth Mompati remained very active in the liberation movement, enjoying high prestige as a member of the ANC National Executive Committee, later as a Member of Parliament, and then as Ambassador to Switzerland. Flag Boshielo, then known as William Marule or Magomane, died in 1969 while trying to return to South Africa. The third, Alfred Kgokong (Themba Mqota) joined the so-called "Gang of Eight" (to be described later).

In December 1962, the SACP requested a meeting in Moscow to discuss practical assistance for Umkhonto.[121] Representatives were Arthur Goldreich and Vella Pillay. Tom Lodge (perhaps the best-known writer on the history of the liberation movement in South Africa during the 1960s and 1970s) says Goldreich "visited Eastern Europe to arrange military assistance from the Soviet bloc ... at about the same time as Mandela's trip abroad." [122] In fact, the visit actually took place almost a year later. Mandela left the country in January 1962, whereas Goldreich arrived in Moscow in January 1963 with appeals that flowed from Mandela's mission. (Lodge also dates Mandela's visit inaccurately: January 1961 instead of January 1962. [123] This is worth noting, as Lodge's book is often considered as a Bible and the mistake has been repeated elsewhere.)

In a memorandum presented to the Soviets, the SACP described the efforts of the ANC and SACP to organise the training of Umkhonto cadres. "Negotiations are at present under way for the establishment of an all-South African training camp in friendly territory, where opportunities will exist for expanding the training programme both in scope and in effectiveness, by enabling recruits to be trained and supervised by designated representatives of UWS [Umkhonto we Sizwe] itself, rather than – as at present – by military personnel of other countries whose political orientation is not always identical with ours." [124]

The Soviets were told, however, that Mandela's trip to African countries in 1962 had shown that the large-scale training of cadres in Africa would be difficult to organise and therefore the Umkhonto High Command should seek assistance from the socialist countries. The original request was to train 20 cadres in the USSR, but numbers were soon dramatically increased. "Technical consultations" with relevant Soviet specialists were organised for Goldreich. It seems that this was the first time the Soviet Union gave assistance to Umkhonto.

Goldreich's travels to the "Eastern countries" (he also visited China) were widely publicised during the trial of the ANC and Umkhonto leaders; his notebook had been seized by the police. Security officials and pro-apartheid propagandists misunderstood some of the notes and, in fact, underestimated the degree of Soviet involvement. For example, first, the American author Nathaniel Weyl in a book entitled *Traitors' End. The Rise and Fall of the Communist Movement in Southern Africa* refers to Goldreich's discussion "with a certain Comrade Manshisha (possibly an Algerian)." [125] Second, Luritz Strydom's *Rivonia Unmasked!* reproduced a section of Goldreich's hand-written document, headed "C [Comrade] Manshisha on Problems of Transport."[126]

"C [Comrade] Manshisha" was, in fact, Petr Ivanovich Manchkha (well known in the late 1940s to communist guerrillas in Greece as Comrade Petrov). Quite why these authors, supposed "experts on terrorism and communism", thought that Soviet support would be discussed with an Algerian instead of with the Soviets is a mystery.

Arthur Goldreich recalls that his consultations in Moscow "were in a very practical sense influenced by the draft Operation Mayibuye plan," though this does not imply that the plan depended on the mission to Moscow. At that stage "the scope and scale of specific needs discussed in Moscow were of a very limited nature though [they] covered issues of wider significance and touched upon possibilities for continued assistance." [127]

Obviously the Soviet side was cautious. It became clear during the discussions that, despite the modesty of the requests, the implications for the Soviet Union were very complex and serious, particularly in its relations with other states, especially in Africa. The Soviet officials suggested that the supplies should go through independent African states. [128] In fact, these ideas put forward by "C Manshisha" and other Soviet officials were reflected in Goldreich's diary: "We [the Soviet Union] don't have any relations with Verwoerd Govt. in any way. So don't care what he say. Safest and surest way, transfer of arms through country where they have normal relations.- Govt. agreement. Willingness of this government to us [the liberation movement]. Govt. give us their armaments and Soviet compensates." [129]

It was during this visit that the South African representatives first raised the notion, which they entertained for many years to come, of acquiring a ship, perhaps a yacht, to transport goods for Umkhonto. But here, too, the Soviet side was cautious: "Transfer of armaments on high seas – difficult to speak of neutral waters," continues Goldreich in his diary. "We realise with techniques used to-day, reloading, on high seas are located very quickly. And here when discovered - serious entanglement, particularly for us and comrades involved." [130]

That the Soviet Union regarded the South African liberation struggle as important is clear from the fact that Ponomarev received the delegation, even though it did not consist of the movement's leading figures. The discussion "developed into theoretical issues of the national liberation struggle" and "the ideological dispute with China". The subject was "particularly expanded" after the delegation visited China, where it had been received by Deng Xiaoping. The South Africans were genuinely concerned about the growing split between the USSR and China. [131]

In welcoming the SACP representatives in Moscow, the Soviet officials – particularly those from the CP International Department – were anxious to establish direct contact with the ANC top leadership. One chance had already been missed: when Albert Luthuli was about to leave South Africa to receive the Nobel Peace Prize in December 1961, the SACP suggested that he and his wife be invited to Moscow, but this did not materialise, apparently owing to short notice.

A convenient channel for contacts with the ANC was the Afro-Asian Peoples' Solidarity Secretariat (later 'Organisation', AAPSO) in Cairo. On the eve of the 1959 ANC conference (the last to be held before it was banned), the Afro-Asian Solidarity Secretariat sent a circular letter to all of its committees requesting that a message of greetings be sent to the ANC. The lack of knowledge about the situation in South Africa is illustrated by the fact that the Soviet Solidarity Committee had to ask the African Department of the academic Institute of Oriental Studies for information about the ANC. A young researcher by the name of Appolon Davidson obliged by drafting a short paper on the ANC. [132] (Professor Davidson, who has done more than any Soviet/Russian academic to popularise the liberation struggle in South Africa, headed in 1994 - 1998 the Centre for Russian Studies at the University of Cape Town.)

Later the ANC representatives in Cairo, Mziwandile Piliso and Ambrose Makiwane, were in daily contact with the representative of the Soviet Afro-Asian Solidarity Committee, which gave political and material support to various liberation movements on the two continents. The Committee's premises in an old mansion (Kropotkinskaya 10) became the major reference point in Moscow for South Africans for the next three decades.

This body, founded in 1956 as the Asian Solidarity Committee, was reorganised and extended in 1958 after the First Conference of Afro-Asian Peoples' Solidarity, held in Cairo. It was procedure in those days for the Committee's leadership to be endorsed by the CPSU leadership. Browsing through the archive documents reveals, among its Presidium members, the name of Eduard Shevardnadze, then a Secretary of the Georgian "Leninist Communist Youth". [133]

The first representative of the ANC to come to Moscow, in the 1960s, was Tennyson Makiwane, who had left South Africa before Sharpeville and was resident in Accra and London. Incidentally, he and other ANC members often visited Moscow on their way to or from Beijing, China being very active in Africa in those days.

But the man most eagerly awaited in Moscow was the second most senior person in the ANC and head of the Congress External Mission: Deputy President General Oliver Tambo. On 22 December 1962 the Central Committee Secretariat decided to invite him, through the Soviet Embassy in Dar es Salaam, "to come to the USSR at any time convenient for him." The SACP was informed of the invitation through the Communist Party of Great Britain.[134]

It was not until three months later that Oliver Tambo arrived in Moscow, his delay explained by the fact that he had waited for Moses Kotane to leave South Africa. The ANC leadership insisted on Kotane's being involved in mobilising external support for the liberation struggle. Tom Lodge explains Kotane's departure from South Africa early in 1963 as being in "anticipation of the increased responsibilities the exile leadership would have in the context of a full blown guerrilla insurgency." [135] In fact, the Communist Party leadership initially acquiesced to the ANC's insistence on Kotane's involvement only on condition that he then returned to South Africa, though subsequent developments inside the country made that impossible.

Many years later Tambo was to recall how in the first years of exile he was in no hurry to visit Moscow. Perhaps his earlier prejudice against communists played a role, or perhaps he was trying to avoid siding with either camp in the Cold War, which intensified in the early 1960s. He spared no effort to obtain support for the ANC and Umkhonto from the West, but largely in vain.

When he tried to visit the USA in May 1960 as a key participant in the Emergency Action Conference on South Africa, convened by the American Committee on Africa, the State Department delayed the granting of his visa, causing him to miss the Conference. He went on a speaking tour afterwards.[136] George Hauser, who was for many years Secretary of the American Committee on Africa, wrote later that his organisation "was rather surprised to learn that the US government was giving Tambo problems with his visa. I called Washington and was at first told he was 'ineligible' for entry for undisclosed reasons." After "feverish protests ... finally in June the government decision was reversed. But it was too late. Tambo had missed our conference." [137]

If Tambo was somewhat cautious about visiting the Soviet Union, a similar caution can perhaps be detected in the formal details of his visit. Technically, he came on the invitation of the Soviet Afro-Asian Solidarity Committee for a rest, though the protocol arrangements of accommodation and so on were undertaken by the CPSU. Once in Moscow, Oliver Tambo found an attitude quite different from that encountered in the West. He was simply asked to present a memorandum explaining the situation in South Africa and the needs of the movement. Tambo described 5 April 1963, the day of his discussions in CPSU Headquarters, as a historic day in the life of the South African people. On that day direct contact between the CPSU and the ANC leadership was established.

In his testimony to the US Senate Sub-Committee on Security and Terrorism in 1982, Bartholomew Hlapane claimed that Umkhonto had been the brainchild of the SACP. He said that, after the decision to establish MK had been taken, Joe Slovo and J B Marks were sent by the Central Committee of the SACP to Moscow to organise arms and ammunition and raise funds.[138] Oliver Tambo had, however, been in Moscow to discuss assistance to Umkhonto long before Slovo and Marks left South Africa.

In his speech on the occasion of the SACP's 60th anniversary in July 1981, Tambo emphasised the fact that the relationship between the Party and the ANC was "not an accident of history", nor was it "a natural and inevitable development".[139] Equally, the fact that the SACP had initiated Soviet assistance to the South African liberation struggle was no accident. Moses Kotane accompanied Tambo on his first trip to Moscow. Later, it was Kotane who, as ANC Treasurer-General, forwarded many requests to the Soviet Union. The fact that they came from the SACP General Secretary doubtless gave them added importance in the eyes of the Soviets. The ANC became the first liberation movement in Southern Africa to have direct contact with the CPSU.

This is not to say that the assistance to the ANC would not otherwise have been forthcoming from Moscow. While the co-operation between the SACP and the ANC was an important factor for the Soviet decision makers, one should not forget that comparable assistance was provided to the people's struggles in countries which did not have Communist parties: Namibia, for example.

Reporting to the first National Conference of the ANC after its unbanning, in Durban in July 1991, Oliver Tambo said that the ANC leadership took a decision in 1959 to send him abroad, as well as Josiah (Joe) Matlou. His mission was "to rally international support for the isolation of the apartheid state" and also "to create a reliable rear base for our struggle."[140] He left the country a week after the Sharpeville massacre in 1960. Tambo recalled the aspirations and hardships of the first period of his exile: "Those were hopeful and exciting days. They were also particularly frugal ones when we often did not know where the next meal was coming from."[141]

In carrying out the first part of his mission, Oliver Tambo and his ANC comrades met with representatives of the PAC, the SAIC, and the South West African National Union (SWANU) and formed the South African United Front (SAUF). This was with the active encouragement of Kwame Nkrumah and some other African leaders.

At the meeting, held in Addis Ababa on 19 June 1960, it was decided to open offices for the Front in Accra, Cairo and London. (When the situation in what was then Tanganyika permitted it, an office in Dar es Salaam was also established.) At that meeting South West Africa (Namibia) was represented by SWANU and "an independent", Mburumba Kerina. In January 1961 the South West African People's Organisation (SWAPO) was admitted to the Front and Kerina became its representative. Some months later Kerina withdrew SWAPO from the SAUF.[142] His personal status in SWAPO had, however, been somewhat in dispute. In any event, SWANU soon lost its influence in Namibia and SWAPO became the undisputed leader of the liberation forces.

(In his report in Durban in 1991 Tambo spoke of the SACP as a participant in the talks, instead of the SAIC. The fact that Yusuf Dadoo, the SAIC representative in the SAUF, was a well-known communist leader could have caused this mistake. Also, the Namibian representation was not named entirely accurately: Tambo referred to "an organisation, which was later to be known as SWAPO of Namibia.")[143]

Though political support for the Front was provided (or at least promised) by a number of African governments, practical assistance was rather limited. In Ghana, for example, the authorities imposed "control on the money at the disposal of the Front," advanced earlier to the office from London, and required that a "government official be co-signatory."[144]

The SAUF opened its offices and sent delegations to the UN and to several Afro-Asian countries, particularly those who were members of the Commonwealth. "Much was achieved in the early stage of the United Front's existence," Dadoo wrote. "We succeeded in winning wide international support for our cause ... largely through our efforts, South Africa had to leave the Commonwealth." According to Dadoo, though, "behind the back of the United Front the PAC representatives worked for privileged contacts with governments and public organisations abroad." [145] Sharp contradictions between the ANC and PAC around the Pietermaritzburg All-in Conference and especially the May 1961 strike destroyed the basis for unity in South Africa and by the end of 1961 the Front was practically defunct. Its dissolution was officially announced on 13 March 1962 in London in a statement signed by Tambo, Dadoo, Mahomo of the PAC and Kozonguizi of SWANU. [146]

The second task of the ANC External Mission, that of creating a rear base, was carried out independently by the ANC. Tambo's visit to Moscow was an important part of that task. He came to the USSR soon after the ANC Consultative Conference in Lobatsi, a small town in Bechuanaland (Botswana) near the South African border, which allowed both the exiled and internal leadership to meet, the border being virtually open for all who had passes. The Bechuanaland police (the British colonial police force which kept close contact with its South African counterparts) were present, so naturally the subject of the armed struggle could not be discussed openly at the Conference. It was, of course, the main subject for discussion, together with the formation of the underground structures, and so most of the deliberations occurred outside the official sessions. The Conference decisions were not published, but the ANC statement issued after Lobatsi in April 1963 connected the organisation with the armed struggle for the first time. "In the changed South African conditions of struggle, we have the mass political wing, spearheaded by the ANC on the one hand, and the specialised military wing, represented by Umkhonto, on the other .... The political front gives substance to military operations." [147]

By that time the first casualties had been sustained, although most of the ANC leaders remaining inside the country were safe. In August 1962 Nelson Mandela was arrested soon after his return to the country and was sentenced to five years' imprisonment on 7 November. The repression of other leaders also intensified. Walter Sisulu was detained six times during 1962 and then sentenced to six years in prison, but on 20 April 1963, while out on bail, he went underground.

As Oliver Tambo told Moscow, the South African government declined to take the first Umkhonto actions with their limited use of violence as a warning that urgent changes were needed. In this situation the ANC leadership had to alter its plans and to start immediate preparation for guerrilla warfare. The need for this had been recognised earlier, but the ANC had been determined to avoid a civil war, which they saw as particularly dangerous in a country divided along racial lines.

Even at this stage Oliver Tambo urged the strengthening of political propaganda among the masses and the international campaign to isolate South Africa, in preference to military action. (His position coincided with that expressed by Ponomarev to Kotane on the eve of the Umkhonto actions.)

During discussions in Moscow in April 1963 the ANC leadership highlighted the sending of activists for military training abroad as an urgent task. They were worried that intensified controls at South African borders would make it increasingly difficult, perhaps impossible, to get people out of the country. At the same time, large-scale training of fighters inside South Africa had proved to be extremely difficult, though many efforts had been made.

By the beginning of 1963 the Umkhonto High Command was not merely planning isolated acts of sabotage, but was working on strategies and tactics for a revolutionary war, an armed uprising in reply to armed repression by the government. The overthrow of the government by armed struggle was the stated goal.

The ANC leadership recognised the strength of the enemy, but hoped the vast territory of South Africa would enable its guerrillas to manoeuvre freely. As a general strategy the "encirclement of cities from the countryside" was put forward: the influence of Mao Zedung's works on the experience of the Chinese revolution was evident. But this strategy was short-lived: emphasis on actions in the countryside proved unproductive in South Africa. The rigid security measures introduced by the South African government seriously limited the mobility of Umkhonto cadres.

At that time the role of the liberation army in the struggle was overemphasised. While the subordination of the military to the political was proclaimed and ANC bodies were to be created within the army units, in practice the army was expected to be "both the fighting force as well as a working force and an organiser of the ANC." [148]

Such ambitious plans required extensive support in cash and kind. The immediate requirement was 250,000 pounds sterling, a very substantial sum in 1963. This fund, to be accumulated from various sources in Africa, Asia and Europe, was needed for the transportation and maintenance of trainees abroad; the maintenance of the Umkhonto full-time cadres and underground workers inside South Africa; and the establishment and operation of ANC offices abroad. According to Nelson Mandela's notes later found by the security police, during his trip to various African countries 25,000 pounds sterling had been pledged. He concluded the section of his report headed "Funds" with the following: "Money collecting is a job which requires a lot of time. You must be prepared to wait. Visit to socialist countries has become imperative." [149]

The ANC leadership also requested training facilities, arms and equipment from friendly countries, including the USSR. The initial need was mainly for small arms and explosives, but heavy machine-guns, anti-tank and recoilless guns, anti-aircraft guns and other heavy weapons followed. The transportation plans were especially ambitious: from fishing boats and ships for bringing goods directly to South Africa or neighbouring states, to aircraft for cargo and trained combatants.

As the ANC prepared for its discussions in Moscow, it seems to have found it necessary to explain to the Soviets why Oliver Tambo had not visited the USSR sooner. (Perhaps Soviet unhappiness about this had been expressed in some way.) The ANC, they explained, had always regarded the Soviet Union as one of its closest friends and supporters, and was confident that large-scale Soviet assistance would be forthcoming when urgently required. Such a moment had obviously now arrived, and ANC requests put by Tambo included large-scale training facilities in the USSR, assistance in organisation and propaganda work and in the intensification of ANC activity internationally.

These requests were favourably received, although Ponomarev and other CPSU representatives were more interested in the political considerations: the state of the mass struggle; the people's readiness to respond to the ANC call for armed struggle; the attitude of the African states to the ANC, especially those which were geographically close to South Africa; and the degree of support for the ANC from democratic forces in other countries, particularly the USA. As in their dealings with the SACP, the Soviet Union did not urge ANC leaders to adopt armed struggle.

The approach of the Soviet leadership – to leave all important decision-making, such as the choice of forms of struggle, to the South Africans – impressed Oliver Tambo and his colleagues, particularly when compared to states and organisations which offered only conditional assistance. In 1956, for example, Albert Luthuli's representative had discussed financial assistance in publishing the ANC newspaper with George Hauser. Luthuli wrote in a confidential letter to Tambo that Hauser had raised "the question of the Editor … I suppose he wants to be sure that their money does not help leftist ascendancy in the African National Congress." Luthuli even suggested to Tambo: "Whatever we may do internally by way of editing the paper, could one not for their purpose say that you or I were Editors? This would dispel American fears and suspicion."[150] Assistance from the Soviet Union would hardly have been conditional on who was responsible for the implementation of an ANC project.

Tambo worked hard in Moscow to convince the Soviets that ANC supporters were prepared psychologically and politically for armed struggle. He claimed that not one operative had been arrested since the commencement of MK actions fifteen months before. But this situation was soon to take a dramatic turn.

The intensification of repression and the tightening grip of police on the ANC and Umkhonto leadership are well illustrated by the underground communication from the ANC London office entitled "A Circular Letter to All Our Offices", dated 23 April 1963. "As you will already have read from the Press, Walter [Sisulu] escaped from his home early in the month. He is now in hiding in the country, and we have no intention of sending him out of the country ....

"A little before Walter disappeared, Govan [Mbeki] who had been called away from P.E. [Port Elizabeth] to reinforce our depleted National Executive was caught by the S.B. [Special Branch] and served with three orders one of which provided a 12 hours house arrest at the address where he lived in P.E. before he came to Joburg in December last year ....

"He also disappeared a few hours before he was due to be taken to the train to P.E. Please note that we [should] make no reference to his disappearance as the police have not mentioned it themselves. He is also remaining in the country to carry on work from underground.

"The entire Executive ... is restricted in one way or another.

"We have no money at all to run the organisation, to say nothing of the campaign, and with the government increasing pressure internal sources have practically dried up.

Amandla! Ngawethu!

Thunder." (151)

This appeal from the internal leadership was heard. On 23 May 1963 "M.T.B." (Mendi Msimang, later to become South African High Commissioner in London and then Treasurer-general of the ANC) wrote to "Dear Booth" in South Africa: "Dar [ANC external leadership Headquarters] requested us to inform you that an amount of fifteen thousand pounds has been transmitted to Dr Letele [the ANC Treasurer General, then resident in Basutoland/Lesotho] and we should ask you to immediately contact him for same." (152)

However, the days of the internal leadership were numbered. The new Security Act permitted detention in strict isolation for 90 days (later increased to 180 days) and so allowed the security police to apply psychological and physical torture. Both political and military structures of the liberation movement suffered greatly. The heaviest blow came with the arrest in Rivonia, an outlying suburb of Johannesburg, of the top leadership of the ANC and Umkhonto. The famous Rivonia trial followed with Nelson Mandela as accused Number One.

After his release from prison 26 years later Walter Sisulu pointed out one of the ironies of the arrests at Rivonia: "Everybody had decided that we could no longer meet at Rivonia because there was already a lot of suspicion – this place was now becoming dangerous. But we said, let's go today for one day and finish ... We got arrested." [153]

State witness Number One, Bruno Mtolo (or "Mr X") was instrumental in securing the convictions. He was a member of the Umkhonto Regional Command in Natal and had spent just one night in Rivonia, but his evidence carried considerable weight. Ahmed Kathrada recalled later that Mtolo had seen him typing and cyclostyling a leaflet. "Now there was one sentence in this leaflet that put me into this conspiracy and which got me a life sentence." [154]

The police discovered several documents at Rivonia, the most incriminating of which was the plan for "Operation Mayibuye". The main argument of the defence, headed by Bram Fischer, was that the plan had not been approved and therefore the accused could not be held responsible for it. However, the statements of the Umkhonto leaders made after the trial contradicted this. Joe Slovo claimed that the plan had been prepared by the High Command and discussed both in the ANC and the SACP. The detailed description of the preparation for guerrilla warfare, followed by a general uprising, revealed an overestimation of foreign support.

Slovo wrote: "We had a rather euphoric expectation of what the African states would be prepared to do for us. We thought they could even provide aeroplanes to drop our personnel. We were a little naive." [155] Indeed, the document itself reads: "The political isolation of South Africa from the world community of nations and particularly the active hostility towards it from almost the whole of the African countries and the Socialist world may result in such massive assistance in various forms that the state structures will collapse far sooner that we can at the moment envisage." It spoke not only of "direct [foreign] military involvement in South West Africa" and "an effective economic and military boycott", but even the possibility of "armed international action at some more advanced stage of struggle." [156]

In addition, the ANC hoped to create a "political authority" in a friendly territory, "which in due course would develop into a Provisional Revolutionary Government" (an idea apparently borrowed from the Algerian experience). This would be capable of regular (weekly or bi-weekly) airlifting of recruits from South Africa and would maintain a reliable inflow of trained personnel. [157]

In the light of problems the ANC had to face later in supposedly friendly African countries, Operation Mayibuye now seems unrealistic, but it is important to remember the context in which it was drawn up. At the OAU inaugural conference in May 1963 several leaders of the independent African states had pledged their full support for the liberation of "all our brother Africans." Sekou Toure of Guinea had suggested fixing a date when any remaining white minority governments would have to face a joint military force of African states. Ben Bella of Algeria had volunteered to send ten thousand men to the assistance of the "fighting brothers". [158]

As early as December 1960, Alan Paton, President of the South African Liberal Party, whose views were hardly radical, had envisaged an "increase in unrest and conflict within the country" and "increasing aggressiveness from other African countries, who are determined they won't tolerate the state of affairs in South Africa. If that were to happen then I think you might find some intervention from United Nations, which might give some kind of interregnum." [159]

Some other internal aspects of Operation Mayibuye deserve critical examination. For example, 7 000 recruits into Umkhonto were to be mobilised in several regions of the country (with exact numbers prescribed for each region). [160] Over 20 years later the Umkhonto magazine *Dawn* argued that, although rural uprisings in the Transkei and Northern Transvaal had proved that the conditions for armed struggle were ripe, it had been wrong to assume that "congressists of non-violence" could be transformed and convinced overnight that the time had come to take up arms, and that 7 000 people could be mobilised in a prescribed period. It emphasised that the decision to join the liberation army was a highly personal one and required that a person be prepared to die if necessary. [161]

The proposed formation of combat groups, each comprising ten soldiers, was also criticised. Hindsight proved that smaller groups of three or four were more effective in the preparatory stage and the first phase of guerrilla warfare. [162]

Hopes of broad support from the African countries drew Slovo and Marks out of the country. According to Slovo, "a meeting of both the ANC and Party having examined Operation Mayibuye and having in principle adopted its main guidelines [exactly what the state failed to prove during the Rivonia trial] but still having to discuss details of its implementation, decided that it was urgent that this plan be taken to the external mission of the ANC so that our needs could be discussed further with the African governments."[163] To this end Slovo and Marks left South Africa at the end of May 1963. (The ANC Working Committee and the SACP Central Committee took the decision just three days before their departure.)

An interesting detail is worth noting here. When Slovo, Marks and some other South Africans were about to board a chartered Dakota to fly from Francistown to Dar es Salaam, two people asked for a lift. They were Samora Machel, future President of Mozambique, and Peter Nanyemba, future SWAPO Defence Secretary. The lift was given at the expense of two ANC members, who had to stay behind in Bechuanaland. [164]

After the discussion with the external leadership, "steps to send missions to Algeria and other places with the purpose of establishing what was possible and what not were immediately taken." Then, "Rivonia occurred. It became virtually useless to attempt to implement 'Operation Mayibuye' because of the destruction which had occurred," and Slovo, who was supposed to return to South Africa to work underground, had to remain in exile. [165]

In Slovo's opinion, one of the main reasons for Umkhonto failures at that stage was a mistaken belief that the security apparatus in South Africa remained as it had been in the 1950s. Then those who "were banned and subjected to all kinds of restrictions" nevertheless "committed three crimes every single day", for example attending meetings and leaving areas to which they were confined, and "were hardly ever caught." [166]

But as soon as armed activities commenced, South African security forces received training abroad which drew on the French experience in Algeria and the US experience in Korea and Vietnam. The security apparatus was "completely refashioned" and the struggle could no longer be "fought on a gentlemanly terrain", as had been the case prior to the isolation and torture of political prisoners. [167]

Among the Rivonia charges was conspiracy "to aid foreign military units when they invaded the Republic, thus furthering the aims of communism."[168] While Operation Mayibuye did not exclude foreign intervention in support of Umkhonto, units from "communist countries" were not mentioned in the plan.

Nevertheless the role of communists and relations between them and Nelson Mandela were central issues at the Rivonia trial. The degree of the "communist influence" in the ANC was to remain a headache, both for South African officials and for many academics. According to Tom Karis, Colonel Buys, "the Special Branch expert on communism", had told him that Mandela was a communist and this "became evident when Mandela became a member of the South African Peace Council and spoke on its behalf in 1948-1949."[169] There were, however, non-communist members of the Peace Council. And Mandela, along with some other leaders of the ANC Youth League, had argued for the expulsion of communists from the ANC.

More serious "evidence" was presented to Karis by Hendrik van der Bergh (Head of the Security Police and later of the notorious Bureau for State Security, BOSS). This was a document in Nelson Mandela's handwriting, introduced into the trial by the state, headed "How to be a good communist".[170] However, that document was dismissed by Mandela at the trial as not his original work, but an effort to demonstrate to an "old friend" (Moses Kotane) that these "lectures" could be rewritten to avoid "obtuse" language and "the usual communist clichés and jargon." [171]

In 1960 during the Treason Trial, Mandela had been asked directly if he had become a communist. He replied: "Well, I don't know if I did become a Communist. If by Communist you mean a member of the Communist Party and a person who believes in the theory of Marx, Engels, Lenin, and Stalin, and who adheres strictly to the discipline of the Party, I did not become a Communist." [172]

At the Rivonia trial Mandela resolutely rejected allegations by the State that the aims and objectives of the ANC and the SACP were the same. He compared their alliance in achieving "the removal of the white supremacy" with "the co-operation between Great Britain, United States of America and the Soviet Union in the fight against Hitler." He added: "It is perhaps difficult for white South Africans, with an ingrained prejudice against Communism, to understand why experienced African politicians so readily accept Communists as their friends. But to us the reason is obvious ... It is not only in internal politics that we count Communists as amongst those who support our cause. In the international field, Communist countries have always come to our aid." [173]

This controversial issue is not confined within the borders of South Africa. On 11 February 1977 *Pravda*, the official organ of the CPSU Central Committee, published an article about South African political prisoners, which spoke of "the leaders of the African National Congress, Govan Mbeki and Walter Sisulu and one of the South African Communist Party leaders, Nelson Mandela."[174] This article was attributed to Brian Bunting, who then worked in the London office of the Soviet TASS News Agency, covering mainly South African affairs. The mystery surrounding this utterance has never been solved. Firstly, Bunting himself denied writing about Mandela in this way. [175] Also, the article had never been discussed with the CPSU International Department officials. Unless the editor of *Pravda* mistakenly switched the names of Govan Mbeki and Mandela, a plausible explanation is that somebody at *Pravda* (or perhaps in TASS) decided to "improve" Bunting's article (in those days they could do this easily without an author's knowledge). Whoever this person was, his knowledge of South African personalities was rather limited: Bunting himself was introduced in the article as a "British journalist".

To add to the confusion, *Pravda*, not in the habit of publishing corrections or apologies, later in the same month published another article under the name of Brian Bunting, this time introducing Nelson Mandela as "one of the ANC leaders." [176]

Why were the South African authorities so determined to prove communist control over Umkhonto? And why did Mandela pay so much attention to this subject in his statement at the trial? Using the communist bogey, not for the first or the last time, the South African government wanted to justify its own repressive actions, and to confirm South Africa as an "indispensable defender" of Western interests against "the communist threat". Four days after the close of the Rivonia trial, in response to world outrage Prime Minister Verwoerd declared: "We are dealing here with a Communist attack which was directed not only against South Africa but against the West." [177]

The South African propagandists attempted to rally the white minority round the government, stirring up the "rooi gevaar" (red menace). Anti-communist propaganda was also used to dupe the black majority.

Michael Dingake (who himself later became an active member of the

SACP) recalled how in the early 1950s a friend tried to influence him politically by giving him a copy of the *Guardian*: "Whether through intuition or from information, I suspected the paper to be a Communist paper propagating Communism. My knowledge of Communism was zero except the injunction of the church: Communism is a Godless creed. Have nothing to do with it! ... As a result of this indoctrination I was extremely careful of what I read. Every time, after I had received this paper from my friend, I quickly dumped it into the rubbish bin the moment his back was turned, without even bothering to scan the paper headlines. The mere touching of the paper made me cringe from the sense of betrayal of my Christian principles, a sense of flirtation with the devil. I threw the *Guardian* into the rubbish bin, replaced the lid firmly and washed my hands in the tub." [178]

Exploiting anti-communism was a favourite ploy of police interrogators. When the notorious Captain (later Brigadier) Swanepoel demanded that Dingake testify against Bram Fischer, he said: "I am not asking you to give evidence against any Bantu and the ANC. Our fight is against white communists and Russian imperialism." [179]

The physical and psychological terror unleashed by the authorities after the arrests in Rivonia had a dramatic impact. The attendance by Africans at the Rivonia trial decreased. Special Branch agents took names and addresses of spectators and a police photographer was active. This intimidation, exacerbated by the threat of the death sentence for the trialists, engendered much bitterness and racial hostility. In a leaflet issued by the ANC in October 1963 there were explicit and unprecedented racial references: "If these leaders die in Vorster's hands you, white man, and all your family stand in mortal danger." [180]

The protests both inside South Africa and abroad had a restraining effect on the regime and the death sentence was not imposed. The Rivonia trial marked the beginning of an increase in political trials throughout the country in the period up to 1966. In fact, a trial of Umkhonto members was taking place in Natal at the same time as Rivonia. Before the Rivonia verdict was pronounced, the defendants, including future leaders of the United Democratic Front (and later Members of Parliament) Curnick Ndlovu and Billy Nair, were sentenced to long prison terms.

After the Rivonia arrests the second echelon of the internal leadership survived for more than a year, maintaining contact with the ANC External Mission. London was informed on 1 July 1964 (in an unsigned letter) that an amount of 1 400 pounds sterling was needed monthly by the ANC and Umkhonto "to help [keep] it going": approximately 250 for the ANC families, 250 for "MK wages, equipment etc., the balance on ANC Propaganda and wages." [181]

But soon the government delivered another heavy blow to Umkhonto: the Second High Command was uncovered and its members arrested.

Umkhonto we Sizwe was not alone in using violence against the apartheid regime. In the situation of brutal repression, the danger of inverse racism was growing. Poqo (meaning "clean" or "only") reflected a mood of African exclusiveness and the rejection of white participation in the struggle. The story of this movement and its relationship with the PAC, whose leaders claimed Poqo as its armed wing, are complicated and fall outside the scope of this book. Poqo actions, such as the indiscriminate killing of whites, in fact helped the government to mobilise the minority against the "swart gewaar" (black menace).

Nor will the history of the PAC in exile be dealt with here, except to note the number of quarrels and splits in its ranks, as well as the number of political somersaults. One example will serve. Potlako Leballo, the PAC Chairman (later expelled), who in the 1950s attacked "Eastern functionaries" and nicknamed Sisulu "Mao Tse-tung" after his trip to China, was later a great supporter of Beijing's line in the tragic years of "the Great Proletarian Cultural Revolution" in the late 1960s.

The National Liberation Committee, a small organisation which has largely been forgotten, was engaged in sabotage activities as early as September 1961, before the first operations of Umkhonto. In 1964 it was renamed the African Resistance Movement. The NLC/ARM membership was almost exclusively white, belonging to various leftist groupings or to the radical youth wing of the Liberal Party. [182] This organisation became notorious when a bomb, planted at the Johannesburg railway station by ARM member John Harris exploded, leaving one dead and many injured. The government used this incident, and the activities of Poqo, to whip up a psychosis of white fear and to intensify and broaden political repression.

THE EXTERNAL MISSION TAKES OVER

When attempts to restore the internal leadership structure of the ANC and Umkhonto failed, "the task of representing and leading" the movement as a whole was "imposed" on the External Mission of the ANC. [183] Notwithstanding Rivonia and the consequent disruption of internal communications, in the second half of 1963 Oliver Tambo and his colleagues in exile still expected that guerrilla warfare would be launched inside the country, and they continued to organise the training of cadres on a large scale.

A real breakthrough in relations between the USSR and the South African liberation movement occurred in 1963. The process, started earlier by the SACP, was greatly intensified after Oliver Tambo's visit to Moscow in April. He had further talks in Moscow on his way back from Beijing, where he had participated in marking the anniversary of the People's Republic of China. At his meetings with the CPSU officials on 9 and 10 October 1963 he confirmed the need to send new and larger groups of Umkhonto fighters (up to 300 at a time) for training in the USSR. He explained that it was not possible either to organise appropriate training in African countries, or to import Soviet military specialists to train ANC members in Africa.

The difficulties that the ANC faced were well understood in Moscow even before Tambo's second visit. Direct financial assistance to the ANC began in 1963 and was to continue for many years. The first allocation to the ANC was 300 000 dollars, a large sum in those days. By comparison the SACP received only 56 000 dollars. In fact, the ANC and the Indian Communist Party were placed ninth and tenth among 85 recipients of the financial support. The MPLA of Angola and ZAPU of Zimbabwe received 50 000 dollars each. In 1963 the newly established Communist Party of Lesotho received 52 000 dollars. [184]

Limited financial help had, in fact, been given to the ANC even earlier. In the archives there is a transcript of the Central Committee Secretariat's decision of March 1962 "on rendering assistance to the representatives of the African National Congress." It approved the Afro-Asian Solidarity Committee proposal to provide them with 100 Roubles in foreign currency (equivalent to $111). That request came through the Solidarity Committee's representative in Cairo. [185] The names of the "ANC representatives" did not feature in the transcript, but later Dr Sergey Mazov, while doing research in Soviet-African relations in the 1950s and early 1960s, uncovered the name of Nelson Mandela in the background papers (made public for a short period before being sealed again).

The Central Committee's decision on mass training of Umkhonto members was taken on the eve of Tambo's arrival. Special courses to train guerrilla commanders and various specialists were organised in Odessa, on the shores of the Black Sea. Odessa had been chosen for several reasons: facilities were available at the local military college; the "Hero City" was famous for its resistance to the German and Rumanian invasion in 1941; and from 1941-4 the catacombs were used as hideouts by guerrillas. A further reason was climatic: the military and academic training of Africans was generally organised in regions where (by Soviet standards) the climate was mild.

In organising courses for MK, the USSR Ministry of Defence needed to arrange for the translation of lectures and field exercises into English. Interpreters were conscripted and sent to Odessa in October in anticipation of the arrival of the ANC members. Among them was a young lieutenant, Alexei Makarov, a graduate of the Moscow Institute of Foreign Languages. (He could hardly have anticipated becoming Head of the Soviet Mission to Pretoria 27 years later.)

South Africans arrived at the Odessa camp in groups, beginning in November 1963. [186] In February 1964 a group of leaders arrived, which included commander Joe Modise (known for many years by his *nom de guerre*, Thabo More). Moses Mabhida was recalled by the ANC leadership from his position at the World Federation of Trade Unions Headquarters in Prague and became commissar of the group.

"Odessa" was to find a permanent and honourable place in the political geography and history of the South African liberation movement. For many ANC members, who later became prominent in the organisation, this city signified their first acquaintance with the Soviet Union. Many cadres flew direct from Africa to Odessa by Soviet Air Force Ilyushin-18 transport planes carrying an Aeroflot insignia. Among them in 1965 was Josiah Jele (now South African Ambassador to the UN), who as a member of the disciplinary commission had to sort out a number of problems, involving not so much South Africans as representatives of other countries, such as pro-Lumumba Congolese, who also studied there. [187]

Ronnie Kasrils, who trained there together with Modise and

Mabhida, happened to be the only white, and many years later recalled that he was sometimes asked: *"Pochemy byeli chelovek?"* (Why a white person?) [188]

The Umkhonto fighters were mostly young people, full of life and energy. Odessa, a historical city, provided an excellent opportunity to get acquainted with not only its rich culture, but also certain leisure activities. One of the trainees became known in the Umkhonto camps as *"Stakan Pozhaluista"* (A glass, please). Although there was strict prohibition at the college, vodka was cheaply available in the city, and trainees on leave would buy it in a bottle store and use borrowed glasses to drink it before returning to college. Many years later spectators at a soccer match in the ANC camp in Tanzania could be heard shouting: *"Stakan Pozhaluista,* shoot!"* – the fellow was a good player.

Liquor far stronger than vodka was also available. Mabhida, himself a very conscious abstainer, recalled an old Soviet bus driver who was contemptuous of vodka drinkers, insisting the real stuff was *"samogon"* (an illegally home-made brew). [189] Kasrils described how the camp was visited once by Moses Kotane: "Everybody was keyed up, but Moses Kotane gave a strict ten minutes' talk on discipline and then left. There had been serious lapses of discipline, a stabbing followed a drinking session." [190]

Two smaller groups, totalling about 40, were sent to other camps in the Soviet Union, one of them arrived in mid 1963, even earlier than Odessa. Among them were Mark Shope, who later served as General Secretary of the South African Congress of Trade Unions (Sactu) for several years, and Archibald Sibeko, known in Umkhonto as Zola Zembe, who was later active in ANC and Sactu structures in London.

A group went for training "in the environs of Moscow", known in the ANC as the "Northern Training Centre". A young university graduate, Martin Thembesile Hani, spent a year there in 1963-4. Like most trainees and Umkhonto cadres, he used false names; one of his was Chris Nkosana. He later became known by a combination of his real name and his *nom de guerre*, Chris Hani.

In an interview soon after his election to the post of SACP General Secretary in December 1991, Hani said: "How can the working class forget the Soviet Union? I went to Moscow when I was 21 for military training. I was accepted there and treated wonderfully." [191]

One of the groups was headed by Barney Desai, President of the Coloured People's Congress, part of the Congress Alliance. But he was soon withdrawn, or withdrew himself. It is not clear what was behind this. Some ANC members believed that the prospect of direct involvement in armed actions was not attractive to him. But perhaps political motives were more important: shortly thereafter, in 1966, Desai announced a merger of the CPC and the PAC, in the face of opposition from other prominent Coloured People's Congress activists.

The Desai experience was perhaps the first reflection of a real problem that existed only in exile. Non-ANC members of the Congress Alliance, divorced from their political structures inside South Africa, found themselves regarded as equals in Umkhonto and in the SACP, which had always been non-racial organisations, but not in the ANC.

After the first group completed its studies in Odessa, a second group followed. Later 49 cadres, including Josiah Jele, were sent to Tashkent in Uzbekistan, where advanced courses for high-level commanders were given at the local military college.

Military training was also organised in other countries outside Africa. In 1963-4 Czechoslovakia hosted seven activists, including Joe Modise and Raymond Mhlaba, who did a short course at Brno Military Academy. [192] Four cadres were trained in the handling of explosives in Cyprus, where a prominent politician and personal physician of President Makarios, Dr Vassos Lissarides, was a great friend of the ANC.

In 1964 the ANC was allowed to set up a military camp at Kongwa in Tanzania (other camps followed later). While the training there was organised on a much smaller scale, involving initially only nineteen people, what was significant was that at last the ANC had a safe and reliable place in Africa for Umkhonto members to return to after their training abroad.

By the mid 1960s the MK Command had about 500 well-trained fighters at its disposal. As indicated above, dozens of the first groups of trainees were infiltrated back into South Africa, but most of them were quickly arrested. Finding a suitable way back home for hundreds of fighters was a daunting task: a wide belt of territories controlled by Portugal and Great Britain separated and insulated South Africa from those states that were assisting the ANC.

The issue of infiltrating trained fighters into the country became even more critical after the arrest of the second Umkhonto Command. Speaking metaphorically Oliver Tambo commented, "by the end of 1964 ... it appeared as if the guns of MK had been silenced for all time ... the only cohesive organised force of our revolution that remained at the time was the comrades who had been sent out of the country to train in politics and in the art of modern warfare." [193]

Tambo admitted that the fighters hoped to return immediately to South Africa and believed that they "would be received by our leaders occupying the front trenches and guiding us into the battle." However, they had to deal "with the imponderable prospect of being cut off from the lifeblood of our revolution – our people." Nonetheless, various attempts to return to South Africa were made "by land, by sea and by air." [194]

In August 1965 an ANC delegation headed by Oliver Tambo visited Moscow. [195] This was to have consisted of three members (Tambo, Kotane, and the ANC Executive member James Hadebe), but an agreement was later made to include "ANC military leader Thabo More" [196] and to "entrust the USSR Defence Ministry [Comrade Zakharov, Chief of General Staff of the USSR Armed Forces] to discuss with Thabo More the questions of interest to him." [197]

The discussion at the Party Headquarters was at a high level. This time the delegation was received by the CPSU CC Presidium Member and Secretary Alexander Shelepin (at one stage tipped, together with Leonid Brezhnev, as a possible successor to Khrushchev, and later demoted by Brezhnev). Oliver Tambo and other members of the delegation described frankly the problems of the organisation.

While the ANC had to overcome serious obstacles in getting their cadres out of South Africa, they now faced even greater difficulties in organising their safe return home. Initial planning involved the return of around 300.

As it was not feasible to take the sea route, the only alternative was to travel overland through Zambia, Botswana and what was then Southern Rhodesia. Each of these countries presented its own set of problems. Zambia had attained independence just a few months earlier, in December 1964, and was favourably disposed towards the ANC, but it had inherited from the British colonial authority a civil service that included supporters and even agents of the South African government. In the circumstances, transportation of weapons through Zambian territory was likely to prove particularly difficult.

Seretse Khama, then Prime Minister of Bechuanaland, had also expressed himself as sympathetic towards the ANC, but the Botswana government, even after its independence in 1966, was not free to help.

The militarisation of the Caprivi Strip by South Africa and the construction of a huge military base there permanently threatened the route through Kazangula. Meanwhile Southern Rhodesia co-operated openly and actively with South Africa, and increasing numbers of Pretoria agents operated there.

The internal situation in South Africa was another focus of the Moscow discussions. The ANC delegation explained that, after the dismantling of the Umkhonto Headquarters in Rivonia and further repressions, the remnants of the old underground structures were maintained only for the purpose of misleading the enemy, while new underground structures were to be built.

Later Joe Slovo admitted: "On the one hand you cannot fight a people's war without the leadership of a political organisation. You need an underground, which is capable of providing both political and military leadership. On the other hand the post-Rivonia successes of the enemy had created such a demoralisation that without the beginnings of armed activity, without a demonstration of our capacity to hit at the enemy, it was difficult to conceive of people getting together in any large measure to reconstitute the political underground." [198]

The work of re-establishing the ANC underground, difficult enough in itself, was further complicated by the successful penetration of Congress structures by police agents. ANC security was practically non-existent at that time and, as the ANC delegation admitted, people drawn into underground work were not screened and the tactics and methods of the regime's security were not studied.

Shortage of finance was another major problem and Moscow was evidently the right place to raise it. Money was needed for everything: for organising underground, for transportation of fighters, for maintaining offices abroad, etc. In Tanzania, for example, the ANC had to cover the expenses of offices, accommodation and transport.

Sources of finance were extremely limited. No meaningful assistance came from the West (other than the assistance to political trialists, prisoners and their families organised by the International Defence and Aid Fund in London). The OAU Liberation Committee had taken over functions in support of the liberation movements which were previously carried out by the Pan African Freedom Movement for East, Central and Southern Africa (PAFMECSA). But, as distinct from PAFMECSA, of which the liberation movements were themselves members, they had to face the Liberation Committee officials as supplicants rather than as equals.

The Liberation Committee's support was extremely modest. In the first years of the OAU's existence the ANC received only 35 000 pounds, with 40 000 more promised for 1965-6, which the ANC leadership were not at all sure they would receive. Also, the Liberation Committee gave priority to the development of the armed struggle in the Portuguese colonies. The volume of assistance to the ANC decreased in the following years. In 1967-8, for example, of the $80 000 promised, the ANC received only $3 940. [199]

The extent of assistance that came to the ANC from "the East" in this period was $560 000 in 1965, which ranked it in seventh place among recipients of the International Fund. In addition, $112 000 went to the SACP and $41 833 to the Communist Party of Lesotho.[200] However, it is likely that these very large sums were intended to cover a two-year period, as no money was made available in 1966.

It is significant that at that time the CPSU contribution constituted almost 85% of the funding.[201] This helped the ANC to overcome the problems created by the sharp decline of support from China. On Oliver Tambo's visit to China in 1963 the ANC delegation was warmly received, but the relationship soured when the ANC and SACP failed to side with China in the growing Sino-Soviet dispute. This change of attitude was clearly felt by Mziwandile Piliso, who as the ANC representative in Cairo maintained cordial relations with the Chinese Embassy. When he visited China on his way to Japan for the commemoration of Hiroshima victims on 6 August 1963, he was given an extremely friendly reception. But on the way back, just a few weeks later, he was all but ignored.[202] The hope of receiving the substantial financial assistance promised earlier faded, and by 1965 all assistance from China had come to an end.

The ANC leadership preferred not to take sides in the Sino-Soviet dispute, certainly not publicly, even when China began actively supporting the PAC. The SACP was in no hurry to take sides, hoping for a rapprochement between Moscow and Beijing. Yusuf Dadoo, who represented the SACP at the GDR Party Congress in Berlin, reported to the Central Committee "Khrushchev's plea on behalf of the CC of the CPSU to call a halt to polemic between C. Parties, to stop criticising other parties inside one's own party and to allow some time for the passions to subside," and regretted that leaders of the Chinese delegation had not refrained from condemnation of the CPSU. [203]

The SACP understood and supported Oliver Tambo in his efforts to keep the ANC uncommitted. Tambo said later: "I recall he [Moses Kotane] addressed our cadres in Kongwa at one time. It was over the

Sino-Soviet dispute that was being debated there and developed into conflicts and we were to visit the camp and he addressed himself to this question and he was saying, very correctly, that we as comrades should not get involved in this, that this camp was the ANC camp and everybody belonged together there."[204] It was only in 1964 that criticism of Beijing's policy finally appeared in the pages of SACP publications, and then intensified during the years of the "Great Proletarian Cultural Revolution".

The ANC talks in Moscow in 1965 included three other issues. The first was the continuation of military training (fewer places were requested because of the decrease in volunteers after the destruction of the underground). The second was assistance in the establishment of safe communications between ANC Headquarters in Tanzania and the remaining underground cadres (this also involved the supply of radio equipment). The third was that consultations on "strategic issues" be organised for Joe Modise.

By that time Umkhonto we Sizwe was regarded as the armed wing of the ANC rather than as a separate organisation. This separate identity had become pointless because of the continued ban on the ANC, because of the imprisonment of many of its activists for participation in Umkhonto actions, and because the other Congresses had virtually ceased functioning. Later, in the 1980s Umkhonto was also called the ANC People's Army.

The earlier "disguising" of Umkhonto had often been controversial. During the Rivonia trial, when Nelson Mandela insisted on the independent status of Umkhonto, J B Marks was concerned that such a characterisation would diminish ANC prestige. He was convinced that the time was ripe to declare Umkhonto as the combat wing of the ANC. This was done only after the Rivonia trial.

At this time the internal and external situations of the ANC were extremely problematic. "Compared to the position in 1961-2 Africa has been shown to be an unstable factor as an aid and assistance to our struggle ... The material assistance that we expected from a united Africa has not been forthcoming." Tanzania and "to some extent" Zambia were regarded as rare exceptions.[205]

A Unilateral Declaration of Independence (UDI) by the minority white regime in Southern Rhodesia on 11 November 1965 had important repercussions in Southern Africa as a whole. It served to strengthen racist rule, but also freed the hands of the independent African states to act against the new Rhodesian regime, which was not recognised by either the UN or Britain. Britain regarded the UDI as tantamount to mutiny.

The ANC Planning Committee in November 1965 immediately decided to speed up the return to South Africa of MK fighters through Rhodesian territory. After UDI the position of the national liberation movement in Rhodesia/Zimbabwe was radicalised, and co-operation with the ANC became a real possibility. Many young Zimbabweans were leaving the country to join their liberation forces; there was also a large Zimbabwean community in independent African countries, mainly in Zambia, although most of them lacked adequate training. On the other hand, the ANC had well-trained cadres, which its leadership was unable to put into action in South Africa.

Talks took place in 1966 between the ANC and the Zimbabwean African People's Union with a view to forming a military alliance. The governments of Zambia and Tanzania were consulted and the initiative was supported by President Kaunda, whose party had links with the ANC. But during 1966 nothing happened in this regard. It was one of the most difficult years for the ANC, with no significant progress being achieved in any field.

The position of the ANC's External Mission had deteriorated after the transfer of its Headquarters from Dar es Salaam to Morogoro, a provincial town in Tanzania far from any international activity. The Tanzanian government ordered the move, and in November 1964 demanded that only four representatives of each liberation movement should remain in the capital. So all the ANC's top leaders – Oliver Tambo, Duma Nokwe (Secretary General), Moses Kotane (Treasurer General), and J B Marks (then Director of Transport and Communications) – had to reside permanently in Morogoro. [206]

The ANC (and SACP) leaders faced a range of problems at that time. "I have failed to attend the Solidarity Conference in Moscow on account of the fact that I am without a travel document at the moment," wrote J B Marks to Yusuf Dadoo from Morogoro in April 1964, adding, however, "Anyway this we shall overcome." [207]

Ahmed Kathrada's experience in 1966 illustrates the psychological fear that prevailed in South Africa. He and other political prisoners were brought from Robben Island to Pretoria as witnesses on behalf of a fellow political prisoner. Despite press information about their arrival, only a few relatives attended the court hearing. "Nobody else had come ... These people [the regime] had instilled tremendous fear," Kathrada recalled. [208]

The role of those who at a critical moment betrayed their comrades was evident in that period. Torture, mainly of African activists, often made it difficult to refuse to give evidence. The list of political activists murdered in detention was growing.

Robert Hepple was the first activist to agree to be a state witness in a political trial. Though he managed to avoid disgrace by leaving South Africa illegally before his day in court, his comrades did not forgive him. Even Walter Sisulu, a man of very fair judgement, said during the Rivonia trial: "He is a traitor. Anyone who gives information to the police is a traitor ... Hepple will be ostracised to such an extent that he can do no further harm."[209]

Helen Joseph wrote later with bitterness: "There have been many since Hepple, some tortured beyond endurance and for them there can be nothing but pity. There are others who have not been so tortured but have not kept silent." [210] For her, as for many others, the most shocking betrayal was that by Piet Beyleveld, President of the Congress of Democrats, especially because she had worked with him for many years as Secretary of that organisation: "I heard the rumours of his dishonour but I refused to believe them unless I saw him in the witness box, almost anyone else, but not Piet Beyleveld ... I was appalled at this betrayal and I could not bear to see him again. A year later, however, I saw him coming towards me in a city street. There was no time for me to cross to the other side. We passed each other in silence but our eyes met. I have seen that same look in the eyes of my dog after misbehaviour, but the difference is that I feel sorry for my dog." [211]

Piet Beyleveld became a state witness at the trial of Bram Fischer and his comrades in the underground, and he confessed that "My liberty became very important for me. I can think of nothing but my liberty and I am prepared to forsake my life-long principles for it. I have no other principle but to obtain my liberty." [212]

Something similar happened with Bartholomew Hlapane. Apparently he was unable to withstand psychological and physical torture, and after he had been released from his second term of 90-day detention, Hlapane "looked like a broken man." [213] "He was in the forefront of those who, in the very early days of violent methods of struggle, advocated elimination of sell-outs. He was to die a death of a sell-out," wrote Michael Dingake, who knew him well. [214] When Dingake returned illegally to South Africa, Hlapane travelled from one township to another, looking for him. [215] The South African Police often used him as a state witness in political trials, including Bram

71

Fischer's trial.

Poor selection of underground cadres was one of the problems. Bruno Mtolo, a key witness in the Rivonia trail, had been convicted for theft and fraud three times, but the ANC and SACP leadership discovered this only at their own trial. [216] Mtolo lied continually during that trial, not only betraying his comrades, but also inventing false evidence to satisfy the prosecution.

One clear reason for the destruction of the ANC and SACP underground machinery in the mid 1960s was betrayal by some members and even leaders, usually the result of torture. According to Helen Joseph, a quarter of those people detained became state witnesses. [217] This became a major concern for the liberation movement for many years. Mary Benson offered this explanation for such behaviour: "Perhaps the rot is inevitable in a sick society where it pays to lie and cheat and to fawn 'Ja, baas' to a man for whom only deadly contempt is felt. Today's informers are partly a reflection of all that has been done to a subject people in a century and a half." [218]

The activity of the SACP underground in the first half of the 1960s still needs to be researched. Its members were active in all four Congresses, those banned and those not banned. Many of them were members of the Congress of Democrats. Before its banning in 1962, COD membership grew in spite of police harassment. Eager to protest, many young people joined it.

After the banning some COD members formed a "volunteer corps", which specialised in illegal work such as painting slogans and distributing illegal leaflets and other literature. Their work finally fed into the underground SACP structures. [219] The security was initially good and nobody was captured while doing illegal work; but these structures were eventually smashed by the police.

By the second half of the 1960s the South African government had managed to "restore law and order". Mary Benson commented ironically: "South Africa 1965: a stable surface, a model of law and order: sunny, rich, inviting investors to enjoy phenomenally high, quick profits, and tourists to enjoy beaches, country clubs, flora and fauna with the titillating recollection that this is the country said to endanger world peace." [220]

But punitive measures alone, however drastic, would not have ensured such a sharp decline in the mass movement. The trend was greatly reinforced by the exceptional economic boom in South Africa that began in 1964 and continued well into the 1970s. The flight of capital after Sharpeville was halted, and opportunities for large profits in a country with rich natural resources and cheap labour ensured that capital investment increased by leaps and bounds. This meant the state could spend enormous sums of money on the army and the police to ensure "stability", which in turn attracted more investment. While the gap in income for whites and blacks was sustained and in some sectors even widened, the boom caused some easing in social tension through job creation and wage increases.

Although underground, the movement leadership inside South Africa understood the economic situation. Bram Fischer, in regular contact with his comrades in exile, said in a letter that, because of the economic boom, it was becoming more and more difficult to draw people into underground work. [221]

Then Chairman of the Communist Party inside the country, Fischer was the only major leader of the liberation movement who remained free. He went underground in January 1965 while on bail during his trial. At the time he wrote to his lawyer: "I owe it to the political prisoners, to the banished, to the silenced, and to those under house arrest, not to remain spectator, but to act." [222] Having changed his appearance and his identity papers, he managed to remain underground for months.

The forged documents found in Fischer's possession after his arrest caused much speculation. Henry Pike in his propagandist History of Communism in South Africa saw the documents as proof of Bram Fischer's contact with the KGB inside South Africa: "Word was sent from CPSA [read: SACP] in South Africa (probably, because of the urgency, by high-speed radio) to the KGB in Moscow. They, in turn, immediately notified their South African Residential Director, whoever he or she was at that time, of the plan. Through this Residential Director, moves were made to prepare false documentation." [223] All that was, in fact, needed was to send a photograph of Fischer in his disguise through SACP or ANC channels, even if it was done abroad, to be fitted into place in the documents.

Detective Warrant Officer Gerard Ludi of the Security Police, in a flight of imagination, wrote that Fischer's going underground "was a decision by a world-wide Communist network which had carefully weighed the pros and cons of such a move." This decision was then supposedly communicated to Fischer through the same Soviet KGB "South African Residential Director". [224] However, precisely the converse is true. The "communist network" (his comrades in the communist movement) in fact strongly advised Fischer not to return to South Africa after a visit to London on legal business, but he decided to ignore their advice.

The truth about the change in Fischer's appearance is very different from the inventions of Henry Pike and others. John Bizzel, an active member of the Congress of Democrats and Fischer's associate, recalls: "We had a cobbler alter Bram's shoes with insoles to eliminate his rolling gait derived from a sports injury. We built up some mouth inserts of false teeth gum material to alter his speech, compelled him to lose twenty pounds, procured some drug that would lower his ruddy complexion, plucked his hair to change the hair line ... On the day sentence was to be passed I picked Bram up at an agreed place and drove him to his destination. He went into hiding and proceeded with all the steps of changing to the underground as I prescribed."[225]

After his rearrest he was brought to trial again and sentenced to life imprisonment on 5 May 1966. Evidence at the trial of "Fischer and 14 others" was given by Piet Beyleveld, by Bartholomew Hlapane, and by Gerard Ludi, who had joined the Congress of Democrats and later penetrated Communist underground structures. The South African authorities afterwards used Ludi as well as Mtolo for propaganda purposes by publishing books supposedly written by them.

Before being sentenced, Fischer made a statement concerning his political credo and activities. "If one day it may help to establish a bridge across which white leaders and real leaders of the non-whites can meet to settle the destinies of all of us by negotiations and not by force of arms, I shall be able to bear with fortitude any sentence which this court may impose on me."[226]

Fischer's strength and commitment to his ideals won him world-wide sympathy. Though he visited Moscow only once, in the 1930s while a student in London, his name and his activities were well known in Soviet political circles. As a token of respect and admiration, the Lenin Peace Prize was awarded to him when he was incarcerated in Pretoria Central Prison.

By mid 1965 the SACP structures inside the country had been destroyed. The capture of Bram Fischer meant that the leadership of the SACP had to shift entirely to its external structures, as had been the case with the ANC earlier. Practically all those who remained in South Africa had been charged and sentenced. Nine of the seventeen Central Committee members were in exile. Moses Kotane and SACP National Chairman J B Marks lived in Tanzania, where they were concerned with ANC work at its headquarters. "We shall never forget," said Oliver Tambo later, "that during the three-year period ending in December 1968, two political giants of the South African struggle – J B Marks and Moses Kotane, comrades in arms for over 40 years – operated from a small room in Morogoro, sharing a small office and sleeping in two small adjacent rooms, which now deserve preservation as a national monument."[227]

Joe Slovo had been based in London for many years. He shared with Yusuf Dadoo a small office, which served as a kind of informal headquarters for the SACP. Brian Bunting was also in London, as was Michael Harmel before moving to Prague, where he represented the SACP on the Editorial Board of the international communist magazine *World Marxist Review*.

The external leadership did their best to reorganise the SACP. In the 1960s they managed to convene several meetings of the Central Committee, often annually. The first took place in Prague on 8-9 December 1963 and involved seven of the nine Central Committee members, including the General Secretary and the Chairman. The next meeting was held in Moscow during July 1964.[228]

At the meeting in January 1967, with the underground of the Party within South Africa in disarray, the mood was rather sombre. It was clear that the government had strengthened its position; its own brand of terrorism had practically destroyed the Congress Alliance. The meeting noted the growth of collaborationism, separatism and tribalism. The conclusions drawn were still too optimistic, however; the Central Committee hoped that the situation would change with the renewal of Umkhonto operations in South Africa.

The internal situation of the South African Communist Party was critically assessed. After Fischer's arrest, contact with members inside the country had all but ceased, and even between members in exile contact was very loose, to say nothing of the level of organisational work among them.

Tom Lodge, without reference to a source, writes that, "after some internal disagreement, in 1965 the SACP – at the insistence of Kotane – decided to refrain from building its own cadre group among the military trainees."[229] This issue was a complex one, and will be discussed in detail in the next chapter but, in summary, SACP organisational activity in most countries with exiled members (a notable exception being Britain) was virtually frozen; and much the same was true of MK units.

The Central Committee was concerned about signs of disunity among SACP members, particularly in Dar es Salaam. This was perhaps the very first indication of differences in the ranks in both the SACP and the ANC, something that later resulted in a splinter group, the so-called "Gang of Eight".

The Central Committee was also worried about the relationship between the Party and the ANC; they spoke of an absence of relations. Indeed, apart from the *African Communist* magazine and some international activity, the SACP appeared to be somewhat diluted in the ranks of the liberation movement. Not unrelated to these concerns was the fact that Umkhonto was no longer a "joint venture" with the SACP but had been consolidated as the armed wing of the ANC.

In particular, there were complaints that there was no contact with the leading bodies of the ANC and so complete ignorance of the politics and plans of Umkhonto, the most important sector of the liberation movement and the one that contained the greatest concentration of SACP members.[230]

But this was not the whole story. It may have reflected the mood of the London-based SACP, but leaders elsewhere (including the General Secretary and the Chairman, who were also members of the ANC's National Executive Committee) certainly participated in determining ANC and Umkhonto policy and activities.

The resolutions of the Central Committee's meeting, published in the SACP magazine, looked forward to the "opening up of a new front of struggle: the beginning of guerrilla actions by armed and trained freedom fighters, backed by revolutionary struggles of masses of workers and peasants."[231] This statement reflected the mood of the Umkhonto fighters, who were demanding a speedy return home.

Tom Lodge writes that "there was no evidence of any success in infiltrating trainees back into South Africa in 1964-7." By and large this is correct. But the number he gives of fighters in ANC camps in Africa – 2 000 in 1970[232] – is grossly exaggerated, and this may have led to the conclusion that "functioning ANC branches and Umkhonto cells must have continued the work of recruiting men for military training and dispatching them across the Botswana border."[233]

The truth is that the blows against underground structures in South Africa were so severe that the recruitment and transportation abroad of cadres for Umkhonto had ceased by the latter half of the 1960s.

As already indicated, the ANC leadership struggled without success to find a way to bring trained cadres home. In March 1967 two ANC activists were arrested in Botswana. In May a group of Umkhonto fighters, headed by Josiah Jele, was sent to Mozambique, to Nyassa province. They stayed there with Frelimo fighters for six weeks but when they attempted to move south they were ambushed and barely made it back to base. Another group spent five weeks in the Cabo-Delgado province but had to return to Tanzania, forcing the ANC leadership to conclude that it was impossible to return to South Africa through Mozambique.[234]

Indeed, the way to South Africa through Mozambique in the late 1960s was perhaps the least feasible of all potential routes. It required a lively imagination or real desperation to believe that a small group of fighters could travel several thousands of kilometres through territory controlled by colonial troops, particularly as they did not speak the languages of the local population. The Mozambican liberation movement could offer help only in the first stage of the journey; in 1967 Frelimo controlled only the northern areas of Mozambique close to the Tanzanian border.

The best-known attempt to reach home was by means of a military campaign in Zimbabwe in 1967-8. The decision to operate jointly with ZAPU was approved by the ANC Executive in June 1967. Chris Hani wrote later that the plan was "to build bridges, a Ho Chi Minh train [*sic*-trail] to South Africa."[235]

A communiqué, signed by Oliver Tambo and then Vice-President of ZAPU James Chickerema and published on 19 August 1967, announced the formation of a military alliance between the two organisations and the beginning of joint military actions. The operation had in fact begun earlier, and the statement, which went to press after hostilities had been reported by the Rhodesian authorities, was intended to explain (perhaps justify) what was happening. "We wish to declare that the fighting that is presently going on in the Wankie area is indeed being carried out by a Combined Force of ZAPU and ANC which marched into the country as Comrades-in-arms on a common route, each bound to its destination."[236]

A special group of ANC fighters, which became known as the Luthuli Detachment (Albert Luthuli had died earlier that year), was chosen. The group had an additional six weeks' training in Zambia before crossing the Zambezi River. (They had been preceded by a reconnaissance team, which had selected the best routes across.) Thomas Nkobi, who accompanied Oliver Tambo to the area, later wrote: "When we reached the river and were shown the places selected for crossing, we could not believe our eyes. The commander explained that those were the best points because they were hazardous and difficult and therefore the last places the enemy could suspect."[237]

The Wankie operation, named after the area where the first actions had taken place, was described by the ANC as the beginning of the armed struggle. Actions by Umkhonto in the earlier period, 1961-3, were exclusively sabotage operations.

Operations on the "Western front" – the Wankie area and further south – lasted from 14 August to mid September. The ANC-ZAPU units confronted not only Rhodesian security forces, but also South African Police (including SADF elements). The South African authorities officially announced their involvement as a limited "police action", but it also involved fighter planes.

At the end of 1967 preparations were made to open "the Eastern front" in Zimbabwe. Crossing the Zambezi was even more difficult there, and some arms and ammunition were lost. Fortunately no one was drowned, even though most of the fighters, including some Zimbabweans, could not swim.[238] The guerrillas on this front had no contact with the enemy for almost three months, and fighting began only on 18 March 1968. After fierce encounters the ANC-ZAPU units were forced to withdraw to Zambian territory.[239]

Among the equipment captured by joint South African-Rhodesian forces in this area was "excellent radio apparatus, including a Braun 12-band world-wide receiver", which was singled out by a Pretoria "expert on terrorism".[240] This receiver, while not of Soviet manufacture, was an example of Moscow's assistance to the ANC. It had been specifically requested by Moses Kotane on the eve of the operation.[241]

There is confusion about the overall number of casualties suffered by Umkhonto in the operations in Zimbabwe. The South African and Rhodesian governments were bound to inflate the guerrilla losses and diminish their own. In fact, Pretoria's statistics were contradictory in themselves. The head of South Africa's Security Police announced that, by August 1968, 29 of those killed in Zimbabwe had been identified as South African and 50 more were killed or died in the bush. The Minister of Police and the Interior announced later, in October, that 35 "ANC terrorists" had been killed. In Zimbabwe, nine South Africans were captured and sentenced to death (their sentences were later commuted).[242] The ANC leadership originally had different statistics: ten died on the Western Front, five on the Eastern Front, and seventeen were captured, apart, that is, from the group detained in Botswana.

The story of that last group needs some elaboration in order to understand the conditions in which the ANC had to operate in the independent African states. The group's commissar Chris Hani later recalled the high morale of the fighters, especially after the first encounters: "This was a virgin victory for us since we had never fought with modern weapons against the enemy. For us that day was a day of celebration because with our own eyes we had seen the enemy run. We had seen the enemy frozen with fear ... We had also seen and observed each other reacting to the enemy's attack. A feeling of faith in one another and recognition of the courage of the unit developed."[243]

After another successful encounter the group decided to retreat to Botswana. "This was no surrender to the paramilitary units of Botswana government. It was important for us to retreat to strategic areas of Botswana, refresh ourselves, heal those who were not well, acquire food supplies and proceed ... But by this time the South African regime had pressurised the Botswana government to prevent us from getting into Botswana."

From one side the Rhodesian and South African forces were pursuing the group, while from the other Botswana forces were mobilised to seal the border. As Hani put it, taking into account that "Botswana was a member of the OAU, and in theory it is committed to the struggle for the liberation of South Africa", the Umkhonto fighters did not regard Botswana as an enemy. Moreover, Botswana representatives who met them were "very conciliatory and friendly, saying they had not come to harm us ... and our fate would be discussed amicably." But, Hani continued, as soon as the MK group laid down their weapons, they discovered that the Botswana soldiers "were actually being commanded by white officers from Britain and South Africa." All of a sudden they were "manacled, handcuffed and abused ... sentenced to long terms of imprisonment: three, five to six years, and ended up in the maximum security prison in Gaborone."[244] The total number arrested was 35, of whom 29 were South African.[245]

Directly after the clashes on the "Eastern front" the mood of the ANC leadership remained positive. "For us here the ground is covered with thick thorny bush and we have to pick our way with meticulous care," Oliver Tambo wrote to Yusuf Dadoo from Lusaka in May 1968. "This does not facilitate a quick march forward, but we are by no means marking time, much less retreating. In fact, considering the circumstances, we are not doing very badly."

As to the future, Tambo was more circumspect: "The trouble is of course that we are but a chip off a monstrous block which has yet to roll forward, crushing and grinding everything in its path. This is what we are working for."[246]

In spite of their courage and commitment, the MK units did not cross into South Africa, nor did they succeed in establishing a base in Zimbabwe to facilitate new crossings. The ZAPU leaders wanted the ANC to continue joint actions, but Oliver Tambo refused, fearing that further commitment of the already weakened capacity of Umkhonto might lead to its destruction. Also, in early 1970 ZAPU suffered a destructive internal split and no further opportunities for joint actions in Zimbabwe arose.

The ANC-ZAPU operations caused a mixed reaction internationally. In the Soviet Union the response was very positive: the problems of Southern Africa were often considered as affecting the whole region, and the possibility of ANC involvement in the liberation process in Zimbabwe was regarded favourably, especially if it would also benefit the ANC. A positive reaction was also received from the OAU and its Liberation Committee.

Others were more critical. Of these, perhaps the most significant was a reaction from the Zimbabwean African National Union (ZANU), which believed that the ANC-ZAPU alliance made it "easy for Smith and Vorster to unite and concentrate their forces to slaughter Zimbabweans."[247] In fact, the ANC's alliance with ZAPU was for many years an inhibiting factor in its relationship with ZANU, which later became the strongest liberation organisation in Zimbabwe.

Criticism of the joint operation was later voiced in the ranks of the South African liberation movement itself, from so-called "ANC dissidents" as well as from leftist circles. For example, Karim Essac of the Non-European Unity Movement, who saw himself as something of a revolutionary theoretician, referred to the ANC-ZAPU alliance as "an exercise in adventurism and a glaring example of desperation."[248]

Chris Hani strongly rejected such criticism: "We disagree with that point of view. We believe that it was correct for our movement to be involved in actual practical steps in making preparations for MK to get back to the theatre of action in South Africa ... You never wait because no favourable conditions can come on their own without the participation of the subjective factor and the subjective factor in this case was our movement and its army, MK."[249]

Tactics used by the ANC fighters also came in for criticism. Some PAC representatives accused them of waging "a conventional style war", while claiming "to be waging guerrilla warfare".[250] Since so many Umkhonto cadres studied in the USSR, it is relevant to ask what kind of training they received there.

The ANC members and leaders who trained in Odessa – and in particular Moses Mabhida – attested that qualities of loyalty, resolution and decisiveness were instilled in them there.[251] Perhaps, however, training at a "conventional" military college, albeit in a special programme, created an impression of inflexibility. The need for a highly specific guerrilla training was evident and partly realised from the very beginning: many fighters, including Chris Hani, studied in a highly specialised centre, headed for several years by an ex-World War Two guerrilla brigade commander.

The Soviet political leadership closely observed the training of the first ANC cadres in Odessa. A special group, headed by Petr Manchkha, was sent from Moscow in June 1964, and its members were impressed. Equal in importance to the purely military training was the task of raising the morale of the trainees so that they gained the confidence and strength to form effective units, able to throw themselves out of armoured personnel carriers into attack, with assault rifles in hand.[252] These qualities were absent when the first small groups of South Africans huddled together to undergo training in special flats or houses in Moscow and its environs.

While Manchkha's group expressed satisfaction with the progress of the training, singling out the strict discipline and high morale of the ANC cadres, they did note the limitations of the college as far as the guerrilla training is concerned.

The need for a special training establishment suitable for large contingents of trainees became acute, particularly as more and more requests were being made by the liberation movements of the Portuguese colonies, Zimbabwe and Namibia. Such a centre was created in the Crimea, in Perevalnoye, near the city of Simferopol. There the training was specialised, and made good use of the World War Two experience of the Crimean guerrillas, who operated in mountains, forest and bush – in other words, in terrain not very different from Southern Africa.

In spite of their intelligence services, South African government officials and "experts" knew surprisingly little about the Crimean training facility. Even though a number of South Africans who trained there were later captured, the name of the camp was never correctly recorded. Harry Pitman of the Progressive Federal Party claimed in a speech in parliament that he knew "precisely" where the ANC members were trained. He mentioned two places in the USSR: "Jijinski in Northern Russia" and "Privali in Ukraine."[253] One can only guess what he meant by "Jijinski". The town "Dzerzhinsk" is close to Moscow, but no Umkhonto member has ever been trained there.

Later Pitman's spelling – "Privali" – was "improved" by *Africa Confidential*, which wrote: "The Soviet camps include Provolye in the Ukraine and Centre 26, near Moscow."[254] The South African special services fared no better: Major General F M A Steenkamp of the South African Police, in his press briefing for accredited foreign correspondents in 1984, spoke of "Prvolnye military camp" and (again) "Centre 26".[255] "Centre 26" is a phantom: it has never existed.

But perhaps we should not be too critical: even a recent Russian "expert on terrorism", journalist Vladimir Abarinov, refers to one of the ANC dissidents as having studied in "Pirivalye", assigning this name to Privolnoye in the Nikolaev region, several hundred kilometres from Simferopol.[256]

To put the matter to rest, all that needs to be said is that the road sign "Perevalnoye" was there for all to see, prominently displayed, on the road from Simferopol to Yalta. I saw it myself when I accompanied Joshua Nkomo, ZAPU leader and Co-President of the Zimbabwe Patriotic Front, to the training centre in 1978.

Specialised training in guerrilla warfare was organised also for the higher levels of the ANC and SACP leadership. One of the flats in the well-known apartment blocks of Moscow (close to the Kremlin) was occupied for several weeks in 1964 by a strange group: a number of black people of various ages, some even grey-haired, and a young-looking white man. Most of the time they remained indoors, but occasionally emerged and even visited the famous heated open-air swimming pool. Their faces were known to hardly anyone in Moscow, and even those dealing with African affairs would have had difficulty recognising them as the top ANC and Umkhonto leaders: Moses Kotane, Duma Nokwe, Joe Modise, Joe Slovo, and Ambrose Makiwane. They came to Moscow for "consultations" on the organisation of the armed struggle (the word "training" was not used for the leadership).

One final aspect of the Wankie campaign deserves attention. If one is to believe the source given by Tom Lodge, according to an alleged SACP Central Committee report on organisation, published by the so-called "ANC dissidents" in the *Ikwesi* magazine in London, the Communist Party leadership was "totally unaware" of the developments in Zimbabwe.[257] So Lodge concludes: "The decision to embark on the Rhodesian campaigns was apparently taken without consulting the ANC allies in the SACP."[258]

But even if *formal* consultations did not take place, "the ANC allies in the SACP" (including members of the Central Committee who were in the ANC leadership, and particularly Moses Kotane, who was in charge of all logistical matters) would have known in detail about the preparations. Not to mention Chris Hani, who was, of course, not the only communist among those engaged in the preparation and execution of the Zimbabwe operations.

"CHRIS'S MEMORANDUM" AND
A RETHINK IN MOROGORO

Initially the leadership of the liberation movement overestimated the impact of the clashes in Zimbabwe in 1967-8. The Political Report, presented to the SACP Central Committee in 1968, stated: "These first shots herald the opening of the South African revolution. Guerrilla clashes will spread in Zimbabwe together with increasing participation of the masses in their own liberation. They will spread South of the Limpopo, stimulating an ever-rising tide of mass revolution."[259]

Similar over-hopeful predictions were made about an expansion of SACP membership. "In the course of the struggle the best elements – that is, those that are most far-sighted, resolute and determined in the fight for liberation and social progress – are always drawn to the Communist Party."[260]

At the same meeting the Central Committee approved a special document on "The duty of a communist in the National Liberation Army – Umkhonto we Sizwe". This unequivocally stated: "It is the duty of Communists in Umkhonto we Sizwe to be an example of devotion and loyalty to the military command of Umkhonto we Sizwe and to the political leadership of the African National Congress."[261]

While the ANC attached great importance to actions in Zimbabwe, they also explored other routes for penetration into South Africa. One small group of activists was successfully transported home and managed to conduct important underground work before they were detained and put on trial in Pietermaritzburg in 1969 together with a group of ANC supporters. This trial was the first admission by the authorities of the existence of ANC underground activity. *New Africa*, a London magazine, made a somewhat extravagant claim that the trial proved that organised resistance in South Africa, destroyed in 1963, was flourishing again.[262]

After the Wankie operation South African security "experts" concluded that the "terrorists" had changed their tactics from aggression to "peaceful penetration", making use of a route through Botswana commonly used by migrant workers.[263] But the instances of such penetration were very rare.

The Wankie operation had forced the ANC to reconsider or at least to adjust its strategy. The problems of the relationship between the political and the military leadership and methods of mobilisation for the struggle were analysed by Joe Slovo in an article in the *African Communist*. He considered the relevance of Che Guevara's experience in Bolivia to the situation in South Africa and Zimbabwe. "The question which presents itself immediately upon reading [Che's] *Diaries* is: was there not too mechanical an application of the correct proposition that the subjective factor can help stimulate or create insurrectory conditions? Guerrilla warfare is above all a political struggle by means which include armed activities. It cannot be won by soldiers alone. Armed groups, however heroic, have not the slightest chance of surviving in isolation from the general stream of political ferment and organisation in the country."[264]

The situation after the Zimbabwe campaign demanded not only the reconsideration of theory, but also practical changes in organisational and cadre work of the ANC. The return to Zambia and Tanzania of the fighters from Zimbabwe, and, later, at the end of 1968, prisoners from Botswana sharply increased the tension in the ANC camps and in the exile movement as a whole. The foes of the ANC immediately exploited this. A group of deserters from Umkhonto, who found "an asylum" in Kenya, not only claimed that "there was widespread dissatisfaction within the camps" (which was true), but accused the ANC leadership of organising the "Rhodesian expedition" as "a suicide mission to eliminate dissenters".[265]

Much more serious and profound criticism was expressed by a group of Umkhonto commanders and commissars. The signature "M.T. Hani (Chris)" was the first of seven under a memorandum presented to the leadership. The strongly worded document expressed a lack of trust in the leadership and spoke in very dramatic terms of "the frightening depth reached by the rot in the ANC and disintegration of MK accompanying this rot."[266] In summary the main complaints were that the leadership "has created a machinery which is an end unto itself" and "completely divorced from the situation in South Africa. It is not in a position to give an account of the functioning branches inside the country. There has never been an attempt to send leadership inside since the Rivonia arrests." Whether these accusations reflected an unawareness among the authors or their unwillingness to come to terms with the fact that the organisational structures of the ANC inside the country were practically eliminated, the responsibility lay with the leadership, who had failed to admit this fact even to the membership.

The memorandum further spoke of "the careerism of the ANC

leadership abroad, who have, in every sense, become professional politicians rather than professional revolutionaries"; the writers objected to the payment of salaries to the full-timers working in the offices; and they called for equal treatment of "all members of the ANC, be they in MK or not."[267]

The memorandum demanded that the leadership be "committed to the resolution and programme of going home to lead the struggle there." A "leadership vacuum" there could result in a situation where "our people ... will be deceived by the opportunists of all shades." Those leaders attending international conferences and "other globe-trotting activities" had to be reduced "to a reasonable few" and "the remainder should work round [the] clock ... at [the] home front."

A serious accusation, difficult to sustain, was that Umkhonto was "being run independently of the political organisation" and that the political leadership abroad was "not aware of activities and the plans of MK." The authors concluded – unjustly, as later developments proved – that Umkhonto was "separate from the ANC" and that "the ANC has lost control over MK."

Complaints were also levelled against the "so-called Department of Security", headed at that time by the ANC Secretary General. Its "internally directed activities" were called "notorious", while it was said to be "doing nothing against the enemy". Its inability to provide information about "the fate of our most dedicated comrades in Zimbabwe" was underlined.[268]

While recognising the need for "execution and liquidation of traitors" the authors protested against "secret trials" and "extremely reactionary methods of punishment".[269]

Although the strategy of the Zimbabwe campaign was not questioned, the memorandum, regarded it as a "tragedy ... that we have been unable to analyse our operations so as to be able to assess and draw lessons that would make it possible for us to formulate a correct strategy and tactics vis-à-vis the enemy."[270] The alliance with ZAPU was not criticised, though the demand for "a full definition of the ANC/ZAPU alliance, its forms and content" was voiced.[271]

The lifestyle of some leaders was rejected as well. The fact that they had cars and received salaries was even regarded as building "a middle class" in the ANC. The authors were angered by the fact that leaders were not obliged to take the oath that rank and file Umkhonto members took, and they cited the "desertion" of James Hadebe as a consequence of this omission. (He had resigned from the External

Mission of the ANC and taken a job in Tanzania.) In the opinion of the authors such an oath could "deal with any leader harbouring right-wing designs of sabotaging our revolution."[272] (It is not clear whether Hadebe's action was of a personal or political nature. According to the ANC document, he had unsuccessfully tried to gather his supporters without the knowledge of the leadership. However, personal motives, such as complaints about lack of financial support, were also evident.)[273]

There were also more specific demands about the role of the youth organisation in the ANC and the need to consult conscientiously with the Umkhonto youth, who were the most revolutionary ("the youth of South Africa not located in London or in any European capital"). There was also an allegation about the "practice of nepotism". The fact that "virtually all the sons of the leaders" had been sent to universities in Europe was regarded as "a sign that these people are being groomed for leadership positions after the MK cadres have overthrown the fascists."[274] This complaint had an objective basis. The history of liberation movements generally shows that the cadres who spend years and decades in the ranks of military organisations often find themselves later with less advantageous career options than those who read for degrees in foreign universities but who were often out of touch with the movement and its politics.

The document insisted on "a renewal and rejuvenation" of those who were leading "the Revolution" and warned against "the fossilisation of the leadership".[275] The document concluded with the important demand that: "all these problems must be resolved by a conference between the ANC leadership and member[s] of MK and not just hand-picked individuals."[276]

It is no surprise that such an angry paper should meet with a very mixed reception in the ANC. Some even called it a "rebellion by Chris and others", though not necessarily in a negative sense as it was also described as an act of "tremendous courage".[277] But a part of the leadership regarded it as a violation of military discipline, even a betrayal. A tribunal was created to judge Hani and his co-signatories. The majority of this body favoured applying the most severe punishment, and only the firm objection from one member, the late Mziwandile Piliso, averted what would have been a tragedy.[278] (Later, in the 1990s, Piliso, who had been Head of ANC Security, was portrayed in some South African quarters as a kind of monster.) After a period of suspension Hani and his co-signatories were fully

87

reinstated in their positions.

Assessing the memorandum now, and taking into account the events which followed it, it is clear that, while it was written in excessively dramatic language, the problems raised in it had hampered ANC activity and threatened the very existence of its military wing. Some of these problems, such as those described in the memorandum as "reactionary methods of punishment" used by the ANC security service, remained unresolved for many years to come. But, significantly, in the opinion of Chris Hani himself, it was due mainly to this memorandum that the ANC conference, convened in April 1969, included the participation of not only leaders and high-ranking commanders but rank and file from the camps as well. The authors of the memorandum, however, were not allowed to be present because of their suspension.[279]

I have described this episode in ANC history in detail because the issue has already been grossly distorted by those who try to reconstruct the history of the struggle according to their own agendas. For example, Ellis and "Sechaba" ascribe Chris Hani's memorandum to 1966, prior to the Zimbabwe campaign, and try to prove that as a result he and other "disaffected" guerrillas were hastily "moved into actions" across the Zambezi.[280]

The decision to convene the ANC conference was taken by the National Executive Committee at its meeting on 14 February 1969.[281] The consultative status of the forthcoming conference was clearly stated in the directive, signed by Oliver Tambo, which stressed its special character: "The conference differs from previous consultations not only in its size, which will be swelled by the vastly increased youth contingent drawn mainly from the Army and students, but also in the large-scale pre-conference discussions now taking place at all levels in all our centres ... The Pre-conference discussions, criticism and recommendations are therefore vital for the success of the conference."[282]

The directive was sent to many countries, and within a short time the Secretary of the Preparatory Committee, Alfred Nzo, had "received 53 documents, of which 19 were the result of discussions at meetings of units of the movement and 34 were individual contributions." More were still to come.[283] But the disruption of communications between the ANC Headquarters and its members at home, as well as in the adjacent countries, was demonstrated by the fact that no responses came from South Africa, Lesotho and Botswana.

The responses received were an early indication of the main areas of concern and criticism at the conference in April. They ranged from "the consolidation of the national groups and progressive organisations – the SAIC, CPC, Sactu, the CP [SACP] – in the struggle as led by the ANC" to the "miniaturisation of the whole movement". There was to be "criticism of the NEC and allegations of various kinds directed at individuals or at the leadership as a whole."[284] Most of the concerns echoed the contents of "Chris's Memorandum".

About 60 people participated in the conference, which was held in Morogoro. Most were Africans, but there were eleven non-Africans, among them Yusuf Dadoo, Reginald September (a leader of the Coloured People's Congress) and Joe Slovo, representing the SACP and other groups. It was officially called a consultative conference (a full conference could take place only in South Africa with the proper election of delegates) but in reality it was much more important than that.[285]

The conference was crucial both to consolidate the ANC ranks after the failure in Zimbabwe and to determine the future prospects of the struggle. It confirmed the commitment to the Freedom Charter and adopted a special document, elaborating the Charter's main clauses. The ANC itself took an important step towards unity among the antiracist forces: "All South African patriots, irrespective of their race, must take a place in the revolution under the banner of the African National Congress."[286]

Another document – "Strategy and Tactics of the South African Revolution" – described the international situation, explained the decision to initiate the armed struggle, determined the main political forces participating in it, and outlined the social and political changes in South Africa to be made after "the seizure of state power".[287] Brian Bunting wrote: "Never before had the ANC produced such a sophisticated and progressive exposition of its nationalist philosophy ... The progressive nationalism was not being imposed from above, but thrust up by the ideologically enlightened rank and file cadres who had come to the conference straight from the bush."[288]

This last sentence should be underlined because some authors, such as Ellis and "Sechaba", choose to explain the adoption of this document as "setting the ANC upon the course originally charted by a mother organisation, the South African Communist Party."[289] Even if "Strategy and Tactics" was the most radical document in the ANC history, it adequately reflected views that prevailed in the ANC in exile at that stage, even if these views were later to change substantially, especially in regard to international issues. Few, if any, ANC documents describe, for example, the struggle in "an international context of transition to the socialist system."[290]

The document described "the national liberation of the largest and most oppressed group – the African people" as "the main content of the present stage of the South African revolution."[291] Particular attention was paid to the role of the working class, which was explained by "the special character of the South African social and economic structure." The organisational aspect was touched upon as well: "The independent expressions of the working class – the political organs [an indirect reference to the SACP] and trade unions – are very much part of the liberation front."[292]

A critical analysis was made of the role of South African whites: "The laager-minded White group as a whole moves more and more in the direction of a common defence of what is considered a common fate." This led to the alarming conclusion that the objective situation in South Africa brought about "a confrontation on the lines of colour at least at the early stages of the conflict." Though not of the ANC's but "of the enemy's making", it could have "tragic consequences".[293]

The document expressed the hope, however, that with the development of the struggle "the white working class or a substantial section of it" would understand that "their true long-term interest coincides with that of non-White workers."[294]

Fortunately, and to a large extent owing to the ANC policy and practical actions, a small but active part of the white population (though hardly the white workers) did come to understand that the elimination of apartheid was in their "true long-term interest" and either joined the revolutionary movement or at least refused to support the actions of the government.

The armed struggle was considered "the only method left open" to the ANC, and the prospects of guerrilla warfare in South Africa were outlined. The document expected that "superior forces can be harassed, weakened and, in the end, destroyed. The absence of the orthodox front, of fighting lines; the need of the enemy to attenuate his resources and lines of communication over vast areas; the need to protect the widely scattered installations on which his economy is dependent; these are among the features which serve in the long run to compensate in favour of the guerrilla and for disparity in the starting strength of the adversaries."[295]

With the benefit of hindsight one can say that the Morogoro document was an astute analysis of how things were developing. It is true that the struggle was to be even more protracted than expected, and the scale of guerrilla actions in South Africa did not ever reach the dimensions envisaged. But step by step the route was being mapped out for the ANC to persuade the government to start talks on dismantling apartheid.

The conference explicitly confirmed that "the primacy of the political leadership is unchallenged and supreme and all revolutionary formations and levels (whether armed or not)" are subordinate to it.[296]

The Morogoro Conference was perhaps the most critical moment in the history of the ANC after its banning. Its success was to a large extent due to the wisdom and flexibility of the most influential and respected ANC leaders. Joe Slovo wrote: "Looking back on it, comrades, it could be said that there were moments at that Morogoro Conference when the very future of our whole movement seemed to be in jeopardy. But it was J B [Marks]'s skill as chairman and the greatness of comrade President Oliver Tambo, who was then Acting President, which pulled us through and laid the basis for what we are today."[297]

A serious threat of a split between the leadership and the rank and file members, mainly the fighters of Umkhonto, was to a large extent avoided as a result of Oliver Tambo's unselfish stance. At the most critical moment, though the conference was only of a consultative nature, he surrendered all power to the delegates. He was reconfirmed as the Acting President General (the position he took after Luthuli's death), and after consultation he proposed a new National Executive Committee that was endorsed by the delegates.

The ANC National Executive Committee in exile was fairly large. It had eighteen members. Eight of them were based in Morogoro to "carry out and direct the day to day administration of the ANC": Oliver Tambo (Deputy President), Duma Nokwe (Secretary General), Moses Kotane (Treasurer General), J B Marks, Flag Boshielo, John Pule, Ruth Mompati, and Joe Matlou. Four were stationed in Dar es Salaam: Mziwandile Piliso (Chief Representative), Mendi Msimang (Administrative Secretary), Alfred Kgokong (Mqota), and James Hadebe. Other NEC members and representatives in various countries were Ambrose Makiwane and Alfred Nzo (Cairo), Johnny Makatini (Algiers), Raymond Kunene and Joe Matthews (London), Tennyson Makiwane, Thomas Nkobi and Memory Miya (Lusaka).[298] After

Morogoro the Committee was reduced to nine members: Tambo, Nzo, Kotane, Marks, Mabhida, Piliso, Matthews, Nkobi and Boshielo. It had a right to co-opt new members if necessary.[299] A number of prominent persons remained outside it, including Duma Nokwe, who was a target for criticism both in "Chris's memorandum" and at the conference itself. To his credit Nokwe was ready to serve the ANC in any capacity. After a period of heading Radio Freedom, the ANC broadcasts to South Africa, he was again elected in 1975 a member of the Executive, appointed Head of the International Department, and by the end of his life had become the ANC Deputy Secretary General. Ruth Mompati worked as a Secretary in the President's Office and then as Secretary of the ANC Working Committee. She was eventually re-elected to the National Executive Committee.

As part of the re-organisation the position of the Umkhonto Commander was abolished (to be restored almost 15 years later), and Joe Modise became Chief of Operations. He was then appointed to the National Executive Committee. A special body, the Revolutionary Council, accountable to the National Executive, was created to co-ordinate both the armed and the underground struggle. It was headed by Oliver Tambo, with Yusuf Dadoo as his deputy, and included, among others, Reginald September, Joe Slovo and Joe Matthews, who became its Secretary.

So for the first time non-Africans were included in ANC structures outside of Umkhonto. Their status in the ANC was one of the most controversial issues during the preparation for the conference and at the conference itself. Since it had been agreed in 1960 that the other congresses would not create external structures, non-Africans living in exile could not find any organised political home except in the SACP, where membership was almost totally secret. This was a cause for concern.

At a consultative meeting of members of the "Congress alliance" in Dar es Salaam in November 1966 an appeal was made to the ANC Executive Committee to improve co-operation and consultation with the non-ANC members of the Alliance. The meeting set up a Consultative Congress Committee (CCC).[300]

On the eve of the Morogoro Conference Joe Slovo noted that "for the first time members of the SACP were included officially" in this "internal non-public sub-committee of the ANC."[301] He urged the "integration of non-African revolutionaries both inside and outside the country into full ANC membership." This, he hoped, would ensure that "the tried and tested revolutionary leaders belonging to other groups [would] have a publicly acknowledged place at all levels (leadership and otherwise) of the ANC."[302].

The decision taken in Morogoro was a compromise: non-Africans could become members, but only in exile structures and could not be elected into the highest body, the National Executive Committee. These limitations to the ANC external structure were obviously aimed at satisfying those who thought that the most important decisions should be taken inside the country. The exclusion of non-Africans from the National Executive Committee also helped to ensure that overall control would be kept in the hands of Africans.

The general atmosphere of the conference was conveyed by Joe Slovo when he said: "In the first place Morogoro asserted the right of the rank and file to have a say as to who would lead them."[303]

In the National Executive Committee's political report to the next ANC Consultative Conference, convened in 1985, "the integration of all revolutionaries within the external mission of the ANC" was stated as the most important result of the Morogoro Conference. This was seen to have occurred side by side with the "reorientation of our movement towards the prosecution and intensification of our struggle inside South Africa" and the "restoration and reinforcement of unity within our ranks."[304]

In reality, the Morogoro conference signalled the intention to work decisively at home, in the underground. With almost total isolation of the external structures and the prevailing internal repression, many more years were required to put this intention into practice. While shortly after the conference statements appeared in ANC publications asserting that the period of restoration and reconstruction was over, this work had, in fact, just begun.

EVACUATING THE ARMY TO THE USSR

Soon after the Morogoro Conference the ANC leadership, supported by the SACP, requested that a delegation be received in Moscow. This request was granted,[305] and the delegation arrived. It was headed by Oliver Tambo and included Duma Nokwe and Joe Matthews.

By that time the relationship between the ANC and the Soviet Union had become more diversified. Contrary to the views of many writers,[306] Soviet military specialists did not train or advise the ANC in Tanzania or Zambia; this was done in the USSR. Moscow had also provided practical assistance in the operations in Zimbabwe, as well as appropriate back-up. This took many forms and included the supply of a powerful radio-receiver (mentioned above),[307] airlifting food and medicine,[308] a crash course for motor mechanics, [309] and a one-year training course for nurses.[310] This last was of special importance as the experience in Zimbabwe had revealed that the medical service available in Umkhonto was inadequate. Also, crucially, the provision of air tickets by the Soviet Union enabled the ANC to maintain international contacts, such as Tambo's visit to Algeria in 1968.[311]

The Soviet Union arranged trips for ANC and SACP leaders to visit their cadres studying in the USSR. For instance, in July 1968 the CPSU Central Committee agreed to receive "a member of the SACP CC Joe Slovo to conduct work among South Africans studying in the USSR."[312] I was astonished 24 years later to read in an article in the Johannesburg *Sunday Times* that "in the Party jargon of the times 'conducting work' meant nothing else but performance of special KGB assignments."[313] The author, Boris Pilyatskin of *Izvestiya*, "scoured the Kremlin archives" on a well-paid assignment for the *Sunday Times* trying – in vain – to find documents which would compromise Joe Slovo, Chris Hani and other prominent SACP and ANC members.[314] I am happy to inform Boris Pilyatskin that, in anyone's jargon, "conducting work" meant, in fact, meeting people, holding discussions with them, and canvassing their opinions. It is to the credit of the ANC and the SACP leadership that they maintained close contact with South Africans in the USSR and in other countries.

At that stage the presence of Umkhonto members in the USSR was secret, though sometimes secrets were not easy to keep. In June 1969 I visited Kiev, accompanying Mziwandile Piliso, who went there precisely "to conduct work among South Africans", that is, to see the students. The Principal of the local Nursery School explained that the attempt "to disguise" the ANC members as Zambians was hardly successful as the genuine Zambian students were surprised that their supposed compatriots could not speak their vernacular languages.

Piliso was the first member of the ANC leadership whom I met after joining the staff of the Soviet Afro-Asian Solidarity Committee in March 1969. I had earlier met rank and file members in Moscow, among them Joe Nhlanhla, now Deputy Minister of Intelligence Services, and Max Sisulu, Walter's son, now a member of the South African Parliament. Both of them were that year completing their Masters in Economics.

The first ANC delegation I met was the one that came to Moscow after the Morogoro Conference, in July 1969, a month after the SACP delegation that participated in the International Communist Meeting.

The SACP delegation was led by J B Marks, the Party Chairman, because Moses Kotane had suffered a severe stroke and had been brought to Moscow for treatment on the night of the year 1969. The members of the delegation were Yusuf Dadoo, Michael Harmel, and a young activist registered as J Jabulani.[315] Dadoo could stay for only a week as he was "wanted by the [ANC] Revolutionary Council".[316]

The international gathering in Moscow was a partially successful attempt to bring together representatives of the communist parties. Too many were absent, not only the Chinese, but those who did not want to quarrel with them, including the Vietnamese. A number of the participating parties refused to give full support to the documents of the meeting. But for the SACP the meeting was of the utmost importance: its delegation used the opportunity to develop bilateral ties with various parties. Part of the report of the delegation read:

"A meeting was held with the [Soviet] Prime Minister, A. Kosygin. He was especially interested in the conditions of the mine-workers in South Africa. A verbal report was given to him on the subject.

"He informed our delegation that the Soviet people are very interested in South Africa. He also said that they recognise that the South African struggle is probably the most difficult one in the world. He assured us of their total support of our struggle and invited us to ask for any support we may require whenever we need this."[317]

Mike Harmel took an active part in the preparation of the meeting, and made a preliminary draft of the speech delivered at the plenary session by J B Marks, who also chaired one of the sessions.[318] Joe

Matthews was also there, this time as a representative of the Communist Party of Lesotho. He made a strong anti-Beijing speech, comparing the Chinese Communist Party with a "mad elephant".[319] It was widely publicised in those days of Soviet-Chinese polemics, although the name of the "CPL representative" was not mentioned.

The ANC delegation discussed in Moscow the results of the Morogoro Conference, the renewed emphasis on the work inside South Africa, and the need to speed up the return home of Umkhonto fighters. New requests were presented, and new assistance was provided, particularly in training.[320]

In the period immediately before and after the Morogoro conference, which became known as "the era of the Lusaka Manifesto", the ANC was faced with a new and worrying development. Some independent African states proposed compromises with the Pretoria regime, at the expense of the ANC. The Lusaka Manifesto on South Africa was approved by the conference of the Eastern and Central African states in Lusaka in April 1969. The signatories confirmed that the liberation of Southern Africa was their aim, while stating their readiness to normalise relations with colonial and racist regimes. They would urge the liberation movements "to desist from their armed struggle" if those regimes recognised "the principle of human equality" and the right to self-determination.[321] The moderate tone of the Manifesto was used by collaborationists such as President Banda of Malawi to justify their policy of a so-called "dialogue" with South Africa.

It was perhaps ironic that the three members of the "Unholy Alliance" – Pretoria, Salisbury and Lisbon – felt themselves at that stage strong enough not to have to be concerned about concessions and compromises. The *African Communist* described the Manifesto as "insufferably patronising and even arrogant".[322] This sharp criticism was also a response to "perhaps the most sinister phrase" in the Manifesto, that steps against South Africa had to be taken "even if international law is held to exclude active assistance to the South African opponents of apartheid."[323] (That was an inexplicable mistake by the African leaders concerned, as the position of the international community, expressed by the UN, specifically prescribed assistance to those fighting against apartheid.)

However, the aspect of the Manifesto that most disturbed the ANC and other liberation movements was the fact that the decisions affecting the destiny of their countries and peoples were taken without their participation and without their knowledge.

At the same time ANC activities in African countries were faltering. After the failure in Zimbabwe, Umkhonto lost its capacity to operate from Zambian territory. Some of the Tanzanian leadership looked with suspicion at the presence of non-Africans and communists in the ANC. The influence of China is discernible at this stage as Beijing was very friendly not only with Tanzania but also with the PAC, headed by Potlako Leballo.

Tanzania preferred all assistance to be channelled through the OAU Liberation Committee (headed by a Tanzanian), but in fact not everything was reaching its destination. For example, there were consistent rumours that some arms, intended for liberation movements, were re-routed to Biafra, whose attempt to secede from Nigeria was actively supported by Tanzania. In 1972 King Hassan of Morocco allocated one million US dollars to the ANC. These funds were channelled through the Liberation Committee, and the ANC received only 5% of the promised sum. The same was true of assistance received by the OAU from US churches. Intended for the ANC, only 5% was actually passed on to South Africans, and then with the stipulation that it be equally decided between the ANC and the PAC.[324]

For many years the OAU Liberation Committee and many individual African states followed a strategy of attempting to impose unity on the ANC and the PAC and treating them as equally important. However, the position of these countries altered often, depending not only on their changes of government but even on the appointment of this or that government official. In these circumstances the ANC's approach was one of achieving "unity on the battlefield" – that is, inside South Africa – rather than in exile. The ANC insisted that this problem should be solved by the South African people and not be imposed from outside the country.[325]

The concerns of the ANC leadership were clearly expressed by Oliver Tambo and Alfred Nzo when they came to Moscow in April 1970 to participate in Lenin's centenary. They frankly described the growing difficulties, including the expulsion of ANC cadres from Lesotho and Swaziland and their detention in Botswana. Oliver Tambo was particularly concerned that many years of "inaction", of staying idle in the camps, were "breaking" the spirit of the activists.[326]

Tambo believed that the situation inside South Africa was explosive, but that Africans, without weapons for so long, were waiting for freedom fighters to return before starting the armed struggle. At the same time he was worried that the people's impatience might result in

97

a dangerous unplanned uprising.[327]

The degree of people's readiness to fight was clearly overestimated by the ANC leaders at that time, but they were correct in their concern about an uncontrolled uprising, even though it was not to occur until 1976.

In the wider context, the African continent was in a state of flux, with countries seesawing in their support for the liberation struggle in South Africa. When, for example, Tanzanian and Zambian relations with the ANC cooled, it received very resolute support from the new Sudanese government, formed after the military coup in May 1969. At some stage there was even an informal discussion between the CPSU and ANC representatives about the possibility of using the Sudan as a base from which Umkhonto units would move south, even in the face of lack of support from other governments in the region.[328]

The support from the Sudan, no doubt promoted by some influential ministers who were either members of the Communist Party or close to it, affected the responses to the Lusaka Manifesto at the regional conference convened in Khartoum in January 1970. It became clear that the colonial and racist regimes were not going to show any goodwill, and the Khartoum conference decided "to intensify by all adequate means" the national liberation struggle in Africa "by making available all necessary facilities to liberation movements as would enable them to carry out the struggle."[329] Resolutions of the OAU Assembly convened in August-September 1970 reflected this spirit as well.

The Soviet position on the Lusaka Manifesto was sceptical from the very beginning and the Soviet delegation to the United Nations registered a number of reservations. In its opinion the time had not come for dialogue with colonial and racist regimes. The eradication of the colonial and racist regimes in Southern Africa required not talks and persuasion, but concrete and effective action.[330]

However, in spite of the newly revised OAU position, the contacts between certain African countries and South Africa continued; others, like Zambia and Tanzania, started to feel increasingly isolated. This affected the activity of the liberation movements based in those countries.[331]

South African pressure was apparently one of the main reasons for a sudden decision to close the ANC camps in Tanzania. Many believed that a negative role was also played by Potlako Leballo, who was a state witness at the trial of the supporters of former Tanzanian Foreign

Minister (and former Chairman of the Liberation Committee) Oscar Kambona. Those in Tanzanian ruling circles who were hostile to the ANC used the suspicion that Umkhonto cadres would support the alleged coup attempt as a pretext to convince President Julius Nyerere to curtail ANC activity, even if only temporarily.

At this critical moment, when not a single African country was ready to house the remaining core of Umkhonto, the Soviet Union was again approached.[332] "In July 1969 our headquarters received a notice requiring that the ANC vacate its military cadres from the Kongwa Camp within a period of 14 days," explains the report presented to the ANC National Executive Committee session in 1971. "The reason given for this unprecedented notice was that our cadres in Kongwa had stayed so long that they had now become a security risk to the country."[333] The order was somewhat dramatic: if the ANC was unable to infiltrate its Umkhonto cadres into South Africa – within fourteen days – they would be sent to a refugee camp. "In other words this meant the liquidation of Umkhonto we Sizwe."[334]

According to the report, fighters were sent on "refresher courses" and, after these were completed, "we were able to obtain permission for their return to Kongwa."[335] This had been facilitated by a meeting between Oliver Tambo and Julius Nyerere.

But the reality was somewhat more complicated. Oliver Tambo at the Kabwe Conference was more straightforward: "In 1969 as a result of complications that our movement faced in this region, we had to evacuate [most of] our army to the Soviet Union at very short notice. Our Soviet comrades then worked with us to prepare the comrades who returned home in 1972."[336]

Their urgent transportation by "special flights" (Ilyushin-18 planes of the OKABON, the Independent Red Banner Special Purpose Air Brigade) relocated the Umkhonto fighters from Dar es Salaam to Simferopol and elsewhere in the USSR.

Initially it was planned that they would stay in the USSR for a short time, but it soon became clear that there was nowhere for them to go and the ANC leadership had to request that their course of "re-training" be extended. The situation was difficult for the Soviet Union as well: it is one thing to arrange for the training of military cadres and another to maintain them on an almost permanent basis. Here the SACP leadership again played an important role. At a later seminar in Tanzania in 1983 to commemorate the 80th birthday of J B Marks, Joe Slovo spoke of the "terrible hardships in the Tanzanian bush in

Kongwa ... there was a time when all seemed lost ... Those who lived through that period know that when things became really bad it was J B who was the one who came to face the music."[337]

J B had "to face the music" in the USSR as well – to face, that is, not very enthusiastic Soviets and even less enthusiastic South Africans. It was he who in 1970 had to explain to the Soviet political and military officials the need to prolong the stay of the Umkhonto cadres in the USSR. Further, it was he who had to fly from Moscow to Simferopol to explain to the fighters that the leadership was not in a position either to send them home or to redeploy them anywhere else in Africa.

The decision "to allow the Ministry of Defence to prolong to June 1, 1971 the training of the South African cadets who are in the Soviet Union according to the CC Central Committee decisions of 1 September 1969 ... and of 29 May 1970" was taken on 20 July 1970.[338]

J B Marks had to use all his moral authority and the high regard in which the Umkhonto fighters held him to convince them to accept the need to stay longer in Simferopol. Some time later the problem was solved: some of the fighters were enrolled in Soviet universities or vocational schools and others were finally returned to Africa. Algeria was the first to help the ANC. Also, as mentioned above, the attitude of the Tanzanian authorities improved.

"OPERATION J" AND OTHER ATTEMPTS TO COME HOME

JB Marks and his comrades had one more important issue to discuss in Moscow: the perennial one of returning Umkhonto cadres back home to South Africa. The closing of camps in Tanzania served to underscore the urgency of this issue.

One attempt after another was made. Soon after the Morogoro Conference Flag Boshielo led a group of Umkhonto fighters in a mission to cross into South Africa. The ANC believed that this group ran into an ambush in the Caprivi Strip because of a local agent provocateur. Speaking at the University of Lagos in 1971, Oliver Tambo said that Boshielo had been wounded and captured, and he called on Africa to spearhead a campaign to save the life of "this remarkable man".[339] But the South African security forces issued no official statement about Boshielo. Many believed that he died as a result of torture. Msebizi ("Castro"), who had recently been released from prison in Botswana, and Bob Zulu both died.[340] It seems that this mission was not properly planned. Apparently Boshielo himself had insisted on it, because he believed that leaders should return at any cost.

Even during this difficult period there were some signs of underground activity inside South Africa. As mentioned above, 22 Africans appeared in court on a number of charges relating to ANC activities. While all the accused were acquitted (Nelson Mandela's wife Winnie among them) a second trial of nineteen accused followed. With the exception of one person, they were also acquitted. Bannings and house arrests followed, resulting in protest from the English-speaking universities in particular.[341] In 1969, 1970[342] and 1971[343] ANC pamphlets were distributed in the major South African cities.

The SACP was engaged in the same kind of work (in practice SACP and ANC material was often duplicated and disseminated by the same people). In July 1971 the underground edition of the *Inkululeko-Freedom* paper was launched and, while it was far from regular, it had some impact on the developments in the country. For example, the *Sunday Express* stated on 2 September 1973 that this SACP paper "was widely distributed in Natal and other major centres just before the recent work stoppage of 500 workers at the Frame Wantex mill near

Durban."[344] A number of SACP publications, including the works of Marx and Lenin, were distributed under such innocent-looking covers as *Meet the Cape Wines*.

The South African authorities predictably attempted to portray all actions of the liberation forces as communist actions and at the same time to drive a wedge between communists and non-communists in the ANC. Brigadier P Venter, head of the South African Security Police, claimed in the Johannesburg *Sunday Times* in 1969 that the ANC leadership was divided. He identified a "pro-communist group ... actively supported by Russia", which included Kotane, Nokwe, Matthews, Marks, Robert Resha and Temba Alfred Mkota (Kgokong). This, he said, was "opposed mainly by Oliver Tambo". He further claimed that the ANC leaders received "R2 million a year from Russia alone."[345]

It is difficult to believe that a man in his position would regard Resha as "pro-communist", or that he would not be aware of the tensions between the ANC top leadership (communists and non-communists alike) and Kgokong at that stage. Either his sources were utterly unreliable or their information was deliberately distorted, but he certainly lost his way hopelessly when it came to figures, claiming Soviet assistance to the ANC to be several times more than it actually was at that time.

The same Venter two years later complained in an interview that the ANC was not only "brainwashing youth and students" and distributing "thousands of explosively worded pamphlets and literature", but that it was bringing into and taking out of the country "trained terrorists with forged passports".[346] He had reason to be worried. James April, now a Brigadier-General in the South African National Defence Force, who participated in the actions in Zimbabwe under the name of George Driver, crossed the South African border using another alias, that of Henry Marries, but was arrested some months later. He had the courage to say at his trial: "The African people will eventually win the victory over the fascist South African government. Time is on our side."[347] He was sentenced to fifteen years in prison.

On 27 October 1971 Ahmed Timol died in the Security Police Headquarters in Pretoria. They alleged that he jumped out of a window, but his comrades were sure that the police had killed him during interrogation. Timol, a very capable student in the Lenin School in Moscow in 1969-70, had returned to South Africa and for months had maintained regular contact with the exiled leadership, informing them of the build-up of the underground machinery.[348]

However tragic these setbacks were, when they were reported in the press, they helped to keep the flame of resistance flickering, not least among political prisoners.

Indres Naidoo, an MK member, recalled that during the period when radios and newspapers were banned on Robben Island, new arrivals proved to be important sources of information. "We met comrades who had gone for training in Ethiopia ... These comrades were a source of tremendous encouragement for us ... Then there followed a long spell of lull when nothing happened but we still had confidence in our MK. We then heard of the Wankie campaign and later some of the comrades who were involved landed on the Island. We questioned them at length about the nature of their training, what happened to them, how it was on the battlefield, etc. We kept on getting news of comrades infiltrating the country ... There was the case of James April and the case of the comrades who were picked up in 1976. All this gave us a lot of encouragement."[349]

As large-scale infiltration of trained fighters into South Africa proved unsuccessful overland, the ANC leadership again concentrated its attention on finding a sea route. As mentioned above, Arthur Goldreich in his discussions in Moscow in January 1963 suggested transporting Umkhonto personnel and arms by sea, and this idea was not discarded even after the commencement of the operations in Zimbabwe.

Joe Slovo specifically discussed this project in Moscow in July-August 1967. After persistent requests from the ANC and SACP leadership, the Soviet side, originally sceptical, agreed to support the plan "Operation J" but warned against any unprepared and hasty actions.[350]

It was agreed that, in the first instance, some "organisers of struggle" would be trained, as well as personnel who would study on site the possibilities of a coastal landing. Depending on the results of such a reconnaissance, the Soviet side would be prepared to assist in acquiring a vessel, supplying the necessary equipment, including radio equipment, and training the landing party.

The decision concerning preliminary arrangements, taken on 20 July 1970 by the CPSU Central Committee Secretariat, specifically enjoined the USSR Defence Ministry to discuss the issue with the South Africans and "to present to the CPSU CC concrete proposals on the results of the discussion."[351] In the bureaucratic language of the time, the use of the words "concrete proposals" implied a favourable attitude and would direct the interlocutors on the Soviet side (the Defence Ministry officials in this case) to look into the matter sympathetically.

The proposals were submitted and the decision of the Politbureau was taken on 20 October 1970, followed on the same day by the USSR Government order.[352]

The challenges in "Operation J" concerned not only training and equipment, but finding a country that would be ready to serve as a base for the operation. Naturally, among the independent African countries, Tanzanian ports were closest to South Africa, but, as has been mentioned, Tanzania's relations with the ANC were at a very low ebb. Fortunately, the new government of Somalia, which came to power in October 1969 as a result of the military coup, was a strong supporter of the ANC and offered its help. "Operation J" was to be assisted *in situ* by General Ali Samantar, who was at that time the right-hand man of the Somali leader Siad Barre.

Some of the facts of "Operation J" became known at the trial of ANC activists in 1972. The state claimed that the operation was planned directly by Tambo, Slovo and Mabhida. (This was correct.) An advance party, which included Alex Moumbaris, had made a reconnaissance of the seashore. Twenty-five trained fighters were to land from the appropriately named ship, *Adventurer*.[353]

More details were disclosed in the Umkhonto magazine *Dawn* in December 1986 by Joe Slovo. In his words, the group consisted of 45 fighters. The ANC leadership managed to buy a small ship in the Mediterranean. Owing to the closure of the Suez Canal after the Arab-Israeli war of 1967, she had to go around the Cape of Good Hope on her way to Somalia. In fact, she even docked in Cape Town and Durban to refuel. The crew was provided by "a friendly [Communist] party".[354]

During the preparations for the expedition ANC cadres received some specialised training, particularly in Baku at the naval base of the KKF (the Red Banner Caspian Flotilla) as well as in the base of the KChF (the Red Banner Black Sea Fleet) in Ismail on the Danube river. ("But we know nothing about the sea," said Kotane, when this project was discussed in Moscow earlier.) Their training was rigorous – for example, the trainees were required to jump from the ship into the sea and then clamber back by rope ladder.[355] The importance the top ANC leadership attached to this project was indicated by the fact that Oliver Tambo visited Baku.[356]

The Somali authorities were most helpful. When it was not on schedule, they sent an Air Force plane to spot the incoming ship at sea. But a day-and-a-half after the *Adventurer* left the Somali port she returned and the captain reported that the radar equipment was out of order. Within a week the ANC managed to fly in new equipment. However, by that time it had become clear that the captain and his crew were getting, as Slovo put it, "cold feet". When they started to look for other excuses to delay the operation, the ANC checked the ship and found both engines were not functioning. They suspected sabotage but could not prove it.

Another crew was recruited, "from another friendly party", and sent to Somalia within two weeks. They were quite different. They managed to repair one of the engines and decided to leave port, in spite of warnings that a ship with no sails could be smashed against the rocks in the event of her only engine failing. This time, a mere sixteen hours after leaving port, a radio signal was received that the only engine had collapsed. A Somali tug towed the ship back into port.[357] The information about the engine failure was relayed to the ANC leaders, present in Somalia at that time, directly by General Ali Samantar (who, reflecting political changes in Somalia, was later, in 1984, to have contacts with the South African military officials in Swaziland looking for arms).

The ship had to be abandoned, but the work already done inside South Africa to prepare for the expedition impelled the ANC leadership to try another way. A group of fighters, previously selected for "Operation J", were flown into Swaziland and Botswana; they then illegally crossed the borders into South Africa. But, as Ronnie Kasrils put it, "unfortunately one of the comrades who was infiltrated was caught and informed the enemy of Moumbaris's role and identified some of the others."[358] A number of people were arrested, all Umkhonto fighters, who had already reached different destinations inside South Africa. Also arrested, at the Botswana border, were Moumbaris and his wife, as well as John Hosey, a young Irishman, who had served as a courier.

The news of the failure of "Operation J" and of the subsequent arrests was greeted in Moscow with dismay. In spite of almost a decade of planning and some years of preparation (not to mention the high cost), the operation was a flop from the outset. Some of the Soviet officials, engaged in one way or another in assistance to the ANC, even started to suspect a betrayal in the high echelons of the ANC. The name of Joe Slovo was mentioned.

Twenty-five years later, information became public that allows one to look at the whole story in a new light.

In February 1992, soon after the USSR was dissolved, Boris Yeltsin, exercising his power as Russian President, pardoned ten people sentenced earlier for high treason and other crimes against the Soviet state. Among them was Nikolay Chernov.[359] Who was he? Where does he fit into the story of "Operation J"?

On 26 December 1990 Major-General Rastorguyev, Head of the Investigation Department of the KGB, sent a strictly confidential letter to Valentin Boldin, Head of the so-called General Department of the Communist Party Central Committee. (Boldin was for many years Gorbachev's trusted personal assistant, but fell out of favour in August 1991). Rastorguyev requested permission for his officers to look into CPSU archive papers concerning the trip abroad of Nikolay Chernov, "unmasked agent of American intelligence".[360] Chernov had been recruited by the Americans in 1963. At that time Chernov was stationed in New York with the USSR Mission to the United Nations as a "special technician", a junior officer of the GRU, the Soviet Military Intelligence Department. He embezzled some money while on official business, and was confronted by FBI operatives, who also showed him photographs of himself in dubious circumstances.

That was enough for him to cross over and to start working for the US special services. Before Chernov left for the USSR after completing his term in New York, the Americans paid him ten thousand roubles, a sufficient price for him to continue spying in Russia.

Apparently he was still trusted by his superiors because some years later, in 1969, he was seconded to the CPSU International Department. As a junior technical specialist he was far removed from any political matters, but his responsibility included keeping in order the passports and visas of the guests of the Communist Party. In this capacity he had access to their identity documents, particularly those of members of illegal parties who came to the USSR for political or "sensitive" training. In 1972, when he was on a short trip abroad, carrying a diplomatic passport and thus avoiding customs, he managed to "export" to the US handlers two containers of films.[361]

It is hard to believe that information concerning "Operation J", particularly names and photographs of the ANC members trained in the USSR for this purpose, were not passed on to the United States.

What remains to be found out is the degree of co-operation that existed at the time between the American and South African security services. There is good reason to suppose that before the ANC operatives found their way to South Africa, Pretoria already had their particulars, which made it easier to identify and detain them. It is also possible that information about Ahmed Timol was available to Chernov as well. Perhaps the South African archives will soon be opened to enable historians to find out the whole truth of the matter.

As for Chernov, in 1974 he was sent back to the Defence Ministry and later discharged.[362] For "almost thirty years, expecting retribution for his crimes, Chernov was drinking, trying somehow to stifle the fear of an inevitable exposure." He spent some time in a mental institution, and twice tried to commit suicide.[363]

According to the Moscow press, in 1987 another US spy, retired Major General Polyakov, under interrogation by the Soviet authorities revealed that his US handler had informed him of Chernov's collaboration.[364]

The trial of the "Pretoria Six" was used by the South African propagandists to prove the "international conspiracy against RSA". Though the main role both in "Operation J" and in the subsequent actions had been played by Africans, one of the accused was singled out: Alex Moumbaris. A Greek by origin, born in Egypt, a naturalised Australian, married to a French woman, living in Britain, he cut a plausible figure for those who tried to present the ANC as some kind of international terrorist organisation. But, as Ronnie Kasrils wrote, "instead the people everywhere were inspired and amazed. The imaginative episode really caught their minds."[365] (Moumbaris, whom the South African propaganda machine portrayed as a kind of James Bond, once again "caught their minds" when in 1979 he escaped from the Pretoria Central Prison, together with two other ANC and SACP activists, Stephen Lee and Timothy Jenkins.)

The trial of the "Pretoria Six" once again drew attention to the Soviet support of the liberation struggle in South Africa. The pro-government propaganda spoke of "black recruits smuggled out of South Africa to Russia and other Red states for all types of specialised training", and of "lessons in weaponry, topography, shooting, explosives, military engineering, sabotage, the doctrines of Marxism-Leninism and the ANC, trade unionism and socialist philosophy." One wonders why the "Red states" would need to teach ANC doctrine to members of the ANC.[366]

The South African authorities tried to use the "Pretoria Six" trial to demonstrate how dangerous the ANC was. But this boomeranged. For the first time after Rivonia people could read about the advanced military and political skills acquired by the ANC revolutionary cadres and about their readiness to use them to continue the struggle to overthrow the regime. After the courageous demonstrations on the black campuses had "reached a dead end", the Pretoria propaganda about the ANC activity helped the youth to see the way forward, to understand that "the ANC is a key."[367]

There was truth in the evidence presented by the state at the trial, but there were lies as well. The attempt to describe the relationship between the USSR and the ANC as purely military and "subversive" was clearly to be seen in the statements of the officials and in the media.

The truth of the matter is that from the very beginning, quite apart from assistance to Umkhonto we Sizwe, both the Soviet Government and non-governmental organisations provided substantial humanitarian assistance to the ANC. The mechanism of the assistance was somewhat double-tracked. The bulk of the assistance, including all "sensitive" issues, was discussed in advance between the ANC leaders and the Central Committee officials. Then the requests submitted by the ANC were processed by the relevant state departments, which were instructed to present their opinion and concrete proposals to the Central Committee (after they had been cleared by the Minister of Foreign Affairs or his Deputy). That served as a basis for the political decisions of the party leadership, the Politbureau in the most important cases or the Secretariat in others (to be ratified, as mentioned above, by the order of the USSR Council of Ministers when concrete directives to the state departments were needed).

Apart from this, the non-governmental organisations provided significant assistance, beyond the framework of the state budget. There was the Soviet Afro-Asian Solidarity Committee (SAASC), as well as the Soviet Women's Committee, the Youth and Trade Union organisations (corresponding to the ANC Women's Section, the Youth and Students' Section and Sactu). This channel provided the ANC with assistance to a lesser extent but usually more quickly than the government departments.

Some examples show how diverse that assistance was. In 1969 the SAASC sent to Dar es Salaam sportswear and equipment, musical instruments, film projectors; in 1970 food and clothes; in 1971 spare parts for trucks and cars; in 1972 four jeeps and two cars; in 1973 clothes, food, and another two cars; in 1974 25 tons of food, three cars, and radio receivers.[368] Though these statistics look rather small in comparison with the assistance the ANC received later, it should not be forgotten that until the mid 1970s assistance to the ANC from other sources was extremely limited. For instance, in 1972-3 the direct aid of the Swedish SIDA, which was government-funded, to four organisations (ANC, SWAPO, ZANU and ZAPU) totalled 22 000 pounds.[369]

In 1973 the OAU Liberation Committee had provided the ANC with 3 000 British pounds. In 1974, when the Committee's contribution was increased to 11 000, the ANC leadership considered this to be a major advance. A further aspect to be taken into account is this: in this period, 1973-4, the number of people in ANC care was much smaller than in the periods before or after: about 250 in the camps in Tanzania, 130 in Zambia, and about 100 in three other states, Botswana, Lesotho and Swaziland.[370]

Scholarships were also provided, though the call for them was rather limited. In 1971, for example, there were 21 ANC students in Soviet universities and five in vocational schools. These were made up of those who left the country as ANC members and those who were brought out by their ANC parents.

Another form of co-operation at this stage was the provision of air tickets to international conferences, particularly those organised by the Afro-Asian Peoples' Solidarity Organisation (AAPSO) and the World Peace Council. From the early 1960s the ANC had a representative in the AAPSO Secretariat, and in 1972 Josiah Jele was sent to Helsinki to represent the ANC on the World Peace Council Secretariat. In a number of cases at that time these were the only channels for the ANC to establish international contacts. For example, participation in the AAPSO delegation to Asian countries took Alfred Nzo to Nepal and both Western and Eastern Pakistan.

Apart from the annual quota detailed by the CPSU (ten places, later twenty), the Soviet Afro-Asian Solidarity Committee and other NGOs received South Africans for rest and medical treatment in the USSR. Then, on the initiative of the SAASC, wounded and sick ANC activists were admitted to the Soviet military hospitals as well. Oliver Tambo was not exaggerating when he said at the February 1974 meeting in Moscow: "Looking back I can't remember any request which the Soviet Solidarity Committee had not carried out."[371]

Summing up the efforts to return Umkhonto cadres to South Africa by sea, land and air, Joe Slovo wrote: "This went on till 1976 I would say with one project or another, with none of them really succeeding. But our failures, although one does not plan for them, have some kind of impact. It could be seen by everyone that the ANC was persisting in its efforts without end despite enormous difficulties. People were becoming aware that here was a committed and dedicated group which was just going to continue knocking their heads against the wall until somehow there was a crack in it. I think that was a very important side-product of the efforts most of which ended in failures. But one wonders where we would have been without these stubborn attempts to find the answer."[372]

Somewhat apart from all those attempts and efforts stands the so-called "Okhela" (or "Atlas"), an underground organisation whose existence came to light when a prominent self-exiled Afrikaner poet Breyten Breytenbach was arrested in 1975, having entered South Africa on a false passport. Apparently his mission was well known to the South African Police in advance. Though he pleaded guilty in court, he received a severe sentence: nine years in prison, of which he served seven.

After the trial the Security Police spokesman said that Breytenbach had acted according to the instructions of Tambo and Makatini. In his words, the operation was "an intention of Tambo and Makatini to break away from the Communist Party when the Okhela group was soundly established."[373]

This information was at best an exaggeration and at worst a deliberate attempt by the police to drive a wedge into the ranks of the ANC. Makatini himself told me that Breytenbach had been close to the ANC, and when he had decided to go to South Africa he had been advised to "carry out some missions". But, an excitable personality, he allowed himself to do more than was requested by the ANC. According to Makatini, nobody in the ANC leadership had ever heard the name "Okhela" before it was mentioned at Breytenbach's trial.[374]

Breytenbach himself admitted that the Okhela Manifesto contained false information on the organisation's origin when it said: "We derive our legitimacy from the African National Congress, who requested us to form this organisation." "That is not true," he confessed later. "In fact, the ANC office-bearers with whom we were in contact could not and did not encourage us in the name of the ANC," he said, though he claimed that Okhela was formed "in support of the faction within the

ANC."[375] The Okhela affair did not help the cause of unity in the ANC ranks, nor did it strengthen the relationship between the ANC and the SACP.

REDEFINING THE ROLE OF THE COMMUNIST PARTY

As mentioned above, while the Communist Party organisations inside South Africa had been virtually destroyed, a core of the communist leadership abroad was preserved. But, in spite of regular sessions of the Central Committee, the creation of the Central Executive Committee Headquarters in London, and the publication of a magazine and other materials, there were severe limitations to the Party activity, even abroad. Communication between members was a problem, one of several. At one of the first meetings of the Central Committee in the mid 1960s it was decided to set up Party organisations in countries outside South Africa where Party members happened to be, but the process proved to be very slow.

The main reason, apart from practical difficulties, was a certain hesitation, expressed by a part of the leadership, primarily by Moses Kotane. Chris Hani in an interview with Sonia Bunting in May 1974 said: "After coming out of prison [in Botswana] I made a serious attempt to organise party life. I saw Moses was keen on preserving the cohesion of the national liberation movement. He realised there were enemies and he felt the Party should never give them the excuse to destroy the good working relations between the two organisations [the ANC and the SACP]. Because of his credentials he felt that he himself was representing the Party in the ANC and that therefore there was no need for the Party itself. In a way he succeeded, he achieved the respect of OR [Oliver Tambo] and indirectly OR's recognition of the Party is mirrored in Moses. But Moses went too far."[376]

Chris Hani was not the only person who was worried about the prevailing situation. The motives for Kotane's actions (or inaction) were perhaps most pertinently explained by Joe Slovo: "Moses of all Communists I have known could not be described as a stereotype ... whereas a lot of us could in a general way go in for more or less profound theoretical political analysis in the last resort it was Moses who was the sort of link, not only with the ordinary people but with the organised national movement, particularly the ANC ... I think that he basically was driven in regard to his activities inside the Party by an endeavour to really assert the African personality both inside and outside the Movement and I think, to put it in a slightly different way, he more than anyone helped to indigenise [*sic*], if there were such a word, or to drive the Party to indigenise itself, to abandon the sort of flighty approach which the mechanical application of abstract theory often led leaders of the Party towards."[377]

Fortunately the SACP (and here it differed from a good number of Communist parties in other countries) did not have "a cult of personality". The faction struggles in the Party in the early and mid 1930s, and the damage they brought about, perhaps immunised the Party against splits and leader-worship. But Moses Kotane, the General Secretary from 1939, was held in very high regard, both as a man of integrity and as a person who, in Slovo's words, had "a wide and intimate contact with the people, a very profound almost peasant-like understanding (in the good sense of the term) of the needs, of the moods, the psychology and the real stuff of which his people were made."[378] It is not by chance that, as Chris Hani recalled, his father and uncle "were both party members in Stellenbosch and they would say they were members of Moses' party."[379]

Joe Slovo was of the opinion that Kotane maintained, "when he was stationed in Africa" (that is, in exile), the tactical approach to the relationship between the Party and the ANC which he had expressed earlier, resisting the public emergence of the SACP inside South Africa. "The sort of desire not to embarrass the ANC under very difficult conditions, it is true, but at the same time this overriding desire to maintain the cohesion and unity of the national movement, his conduct in furtherance of that approach, furtherance of that tactic objectively speaking presented at that period actually a very big danger to the historical survival of the Party."

If inside South Africa, even before the Communist Party emerged publicly, it had "organised collectives both at the top and down below", the situation outside the country was different, and Kotane's opposition to "the creation of organised party units in the difficult conditions of Africa ... created a danger of the disappearance of the Party as an organised political entity altogether."[380]

This position taken by Moses Kotane was supported by Oliver Tambo. "There were many Party people [in exile in Africa] who felt the Party should be organised as such outside and they should function as a Party does," said Tambo in 1973. "He [Kotane] would not have seen the need, I didn't see the need ... there was no reason why the Party should not be working underground in South Africa. But, as I say, in South Africa it is different [from the situation in the independent

African countries] .... We were all trying to get back to the country, we had to place ourselves in the countries like Tanzania and Zambia and we have done so as ANC."[381]

It is therefore hardly accidental that the practical steps to create SACP organisations in African countries were taken only after Kotane, bed-ridden in the Central Clinical Hospital in Moscow, severely limited his participation in everyday party activity. In the first months of his illness his hopes of recovery were shared by the Soviets. The message sent to him by the CPSU leadership on the occasion of his 65th birthday in 1970 expressed the hope that "the severe illness will retreat, [in the face of] the strength of your spirit and your commitment to the struggle for the cause you devoted yourself to."[382] After some improvement he was taken from the hospital to the Barvikha sanatorium near Moscow and later to Sochi, the Black Sea resort, as the last stage of his treatment before returning to Africa. But there his condition worsened again and his stay had to be prolonged.[383] Severe pain and lack of mobility persisted and he had to return to the Moscow hospital, to remain there for many more years.

Initially both SACP and ANC leaders tried to discuss all major issues with him. For example, Yusuf Dadoo asked to see Kotane in hospital in Moscow before travelling from London to Tanzania to participate in the Morogoro Conference.[384] I met Kotane for the first time when I accompanied Alfred Nzo to Barvikha. Notwithstanding these attempts, Kotane felt himself more and more isolated. "Cut away from everything for more than a year now, with nobody interested in informing me," he complained in a letter to Dadoo, inquiring incidentally about the plans to commemorate Lenin's centenary in April 1970.[385]

Owing to his illness, Moses Kotane was absent from the first official meeting between the delegations of the ANC and the SACP immediately after the Morogoro Conference. Because of the importance of this meeting and the issues discussed here, I have quoted at length from the statements of its participants, which included Tambo, Nzo, Marks, Dadoo, and Slovo.

The SACP delegation reported that the last session of its Central Committee had taken a decision to initiate discussions with the National Executive Committee of the ANC. Presenting its case, Joe Slovo stressed the impact each had on the other. "There was more than one occasion when the views, mood and arguments of ANC leaders radically influenced the formulation of Party policy and the other way as well. Indeed at the moment," Slovo continued with his typical sense of humour, "we have all been 'captured' by the ANC and it is right that this should be so. Only the vulgar or those who wish to make mischief see in our collaboration a white-anting process. They cannot understand how two political parties can work so closely together without stabbing each other in the back."[386]

Slovo acquainted the ANC representatives with the resolution of the SACP Central Committee, which had emphasised: "We have never considered that the way to play a 'vanguard' role is by 'proclaiming' it or by contesting for positions ... Leadership consists in each and every one of our members, in whatever field he may be working, at whatever level, setting an example of firmness and devotion in the common patriotic struggle against the common enemy. We maintain that our ideology of Marxism-Leninism enables our members to be better Congressists, better trade unionists, better fighters for the freedom of our country."[387]

He quoted from a directive adopted by the SACP Central Committee in 1968 "on the duties of a Communist in our National Army of Liberation", mentioned above. These included: "... to oppose all direct or indirect manifestations of racialism, tribalism and narrow nationalism ... to espouse the progressive nationalism" of the ANC "as enshrined in the Freedom Charter."[388]

Recognising "many objective difficulties" which the ANC faced in Africa, he admitted: "At this stage an open association between our two bodies would be exploited by our enemies at a time when we are vulnerable and when so much depends upon the courtesy of not-so-advanced friends. This is why we are not talking of the creation of any sort of public alliance." Slovo proposed, however, that the leaders of the SACP and the ANC "as two collectives" should "regularly discuss and consult on all the fundamental problems."

The other point raised by Slovo was the situation in the SACP that required "the strengthening of our organisation." He said that the Party "also suffered from the disease of exile" and that the "major difficulty has stemmed from our failure to maintain adequate contact with our members scattered in so many parts of the world."[389]

In his opinion the absence of "organised contact" brought about "many examples of backward political postures (including tribalism)" and "encouraged all sorts of so-called revolutionaries or so-called Marxist-Leninists to fill the gap and to use the mantle of revolutionary doctrine for intrigues etc. In this sense the almost complete isolation of individual members from the Party collective has weakened the movement as a whole."

The SACP leadership was eager "to re-establish some form of organised conduct" with its members, wherever they might be, ensuring at the same time that "nothing must be done in such a way that it can be exploited by the enemy or the wedgedriver," and being ready to "be very much influenced" in its methods by the ANC views.[390]

On behalf of the SACP Slovo proposed "regular non-public contact" between the two leaderships "as collective bodies on common problems and policy", and urged that steps to improve contacts between the SACP Central Committee and its membership should be "decided upon in consultation with the NEC of the ANC."[391]

Oliver Tambo called the ANC and the SACP the "two pillars" of the struggle. He recalled that "there was a time when anti-communism reared its head in the ANC and there were often moves for the removal of Communists" from the ANC ranks, but, after rapidly moving forward, the two organisations "to all intents and purposes" were "running a common struggle together." He underlined that the leading members of the Party were also leading members of the ANC. "And from my experience, you could not have asked for more loyalty."

He explained this by emphasising "the special character of the SACP which in many respects is also unique. It has shown the sort of flexibility which one does not always see in the other organisations claiming to be Communist. It has not stuck to narrow and orthodox ways of working. It has always paid strict regard to the realistic position during the struggle."[392] Tambo supported the idea of "regular discussions on the common problems facing us in bringing our revolution to its successful conclusion." At the same time he expressed surprise that the SACP did not operate as a collective, and questioned the difficulties it faced in maintaining effective contact with its leadership group and its members.

On the latter point Tambo was more circumspect: "It depends what is precisely meant [by effective contact]. I must be frank and say that on odd occasions when the question of SACP members in the army meeting as separate groups was raised, my reaction was to express disapproval." Despite his criticism, Tambo indicated his readiness to "look at the problem afresh and attempt to find some other answer."[393]

He saw several "obstacles". They did not want to provide "the evidence which our enemies so badly want, to show (which is of course quite untrue) that the SACP runs the ANC." In his opinion it was "good politics and good tactics to separate the two organisations even if in practice we work intimately and closely together." Tambo further explained his political position: "Amongst other reasons it is also good tactics because the masses of our people have not yet been mobilised into a socialist way of thinking."[394]

He was especially worried about the possible consequences of the new arrangements for the Army: "To have Party meetings at this present stage of a crisis situation as a regular pattern of activity, could produce the same sort of result as meetings of members who come from a specific province or a tribe – it could precipitate its counterpart although the motivation is, of course, quite different." Tambo was also worried that setting up "two levels of discipline ... might if not done discreetly and carefully undermine the authority of the ANC."[395]

J B Marks addressed the problem of leaders of the SACP who were at the same time leaders of the ANC: "I cannot hide and have never hidden the fact that I am a leading member of the SACP. As such I have in the past years been under ceaseless fire from our [SACP] members in the ANC who have accused us of abandoning them. If this problem is not tackled it could lead to an unhealthy situation." On how to solve the problem, Marks believed that "it should not be public; yet it should also not be of such a conspiratorial nature that it created suspicion and resentment."[396]

After the discussion a small sub-committee was formed and its recommendations were unanimously accepted. The two leaderships were to maintain regular non-public contact on common problems and major policy questions, and the SACP Central Committee was to appoint "two or three [SACP] members in each major centre to maintain discrete [discreet?] contact with the CC." At the same time these members were "themselves to maintain *individual* contact" with all SACP members, "or, where necessary, appoint one or more ... members to do [this] under them."[397]

As far as the collective organisation of the SACP members was concerned, the agreement did not go very far: "Outside the army where it is possible and can be done discreetly and without the sort of complications of which we are all conscious, members may meet from time to time in small groups." In addition one of the leading SACP members in the ANC was to be "appointed by the CC as a liaison man between it and the Acting President." This person would also keep in touch with the members appointed in various centres.[398]

Decisive steps towards the reorganisation of the SACP were taken a year later, at the meeting of the SACP Central Committee in 1970 in Moscow. The idea to convene an enlarged meeting of the Central Committee had been forwarded much earlier. In one of the internal SACP papers, "Aide Memoire" of 1966, it was suggested that the meeting "include additional comrades who are not members of the CC." Among a dozen or so names proposed were Moses Mabhida, Chris Hani (only 24 years old), Flag Boshielo, Ray Simons, Dan Tloome, and Tennyson Makiwane.[399]

The 1970 meeting decided to take concrete steps to reorganise (not to say resurrect) the SACP. It was the first session of the SACP Central Committee after Kotane had suffered a stroke, though the participants met with him in Moscow. But the meeting was different in more ways than one. Michael Harmel noted: "The particularly difficult conditions facing the Party, especially the widespread dispersion of cadres, made it impossible to convene meetings sufficiently representative in character." For the first time an "augmented meeting" of the Central Committee was convened, "comprising a majority of non-members of the Executive, including a number of Party members who had already participated in armed struggle."[400]

A distinct feature of the meeting was the greater number of participants. Facilities for twenty people, instead of the more usual ten, were requested and provided by the CPSU.[401] Apart from the members elected at the SACP Congress in 1962, a group of younger Party members participated, mostly from the Umkhonto camps.

This meeting was as important for the SACP as the Morogoro Conference had been for the ANC. It focused on the democratic process and accountability in the SACP. Through an irony of history it took place at Joseph Stalin's dacha, a villa in the environs of Moscow in the Volynskoye area. He lived there almost permanently during his last years and, contrary to the official report, died there and not in his Kremlin apartment. Later, for almost four decades it functioned as a CPSU guest house.

The group photograph of the session participants – old and young, Africans, whites, Indians, and one Coloured person – taken against the background of this dacha was impressive. The meeting was, in fact, a party conference: it analysed the experience of the SACP after 1962, the developments in South Africa and worldwide, elaborated plans to rebuild the party inside South Africa, and to "re-integrate" party members abroad into organisational structures.

The activity of the SACP in the years from 1963 onwards was critically assessed: "The Party failed to play its leading role within the national movement and its independent role as the vanguard Party." Several reasons were given: "The failure of the Party to re-establish a working Central Committee collective in which the members in leading positions in the national movement [read: Moses Kotane and J B Marks] were an integrated and functioning part," as well as "the inability of the CC to resolve the issue of the reconstruction of the Party in the most crucial area of operation, namely in Mkhonto and among our members in Africa."[402] It was stated that "leading members of the Party, however strategically placed in the national movement or Mkhonto or in any other sector of our struggle, do not function as party cadres unless they take part in continuous collective Party life and policy-making."[403]

The meeting decided: "Where two or more members are situated in the same area, units should be created which are either in direct touch with the CC, or, where the number of units warrants it, a regional committee appointed by the CC."[404]

At that stage the SACP would repeat the formula, used in other parts of the world, of a Communist Party being "a vanguard force within the national liberation movement." But the way to achieve it was projected more realistically (and modestly) than in some other cases: "Experience has shown that the Party can fulfil its vanguard role without 'being at the head' of the movement in the physical or public sense. Our leadership must rather depend on the correctness of our political line, on our ability to win non-Party comrades to supporting our line, and on our cohesiveness as an organisation."[405]

Special attention was paid to the "democratisation" of Umkhonto we Sizwe. "High standards of discipline are vital but they must be instilled by understanding rather than drill, by respect rather than fear, and by conviction rather than by arbitrary punishment."[406]

Oliver Tambo's response to these developments in the SACP indicated that, initially, he was still worried about their impact on relations with the ANC. "First on the organisation of the Party I received this with some reserve because I had to think in a new way, a new form of reference. I must learn to identify the people which I hated to have to do." Nevertheless he added: "It's quite possible, quite possible that this was inevitable and we mustn't look at the situation just for the immediate things, which had to be sacrificed in order to achieve long-term objectives and in sacrificing them we minimize the damage as best as we can ... I say we had to start thinking in terms of ANC and Party and one had stopped thinking in these terms for a whole decade. As I was saying for more that one and half decades one had not thought in terms of Party and ANC although these were very different. But it was such a pleasant thing not to have to make this distinction, that I still have not taken to thinking in these terms."[407]

Fortunately Tambo's worries proved to be unfounded: the developments in the South African liberation movement in the 1970s and beyond proved that the SACP reorganisation brought about cohesion rather than division in the ranks of the ANC. For example, a number of communists worked in the ANC camps as commissars or political instructors, such as the Party veteran Professor Jack Simons, and did their best to educate the youth – new recruits from South Africa – as loyal ANC members.

The CC session in 1970 re-elected Moses Kotane and J B Marks to the highest positions in the Party, though in practice Kotane was unable to carry out his official duties. The composition of the party Central Committee was enlarged and underwent serious changes. Several "old" members, mostly whites, did not stand for re-election, and a number of new, mostly African, members were elected. Some of them, including Chris Hani (elected in his absence), were under thirty.

The sessions of the Central Committee were as a rule convened annually.[408] In the early 1970s the problem of the top leadership in the party became quite acute. Two and a half years after Kotane's stroke, in August 1971 Marks too became seriously ill and, accompanied by a Soviet doctor specially sent to Dar es Salaam, had to be transported to Moscow for "lengthy treatment".[409]

Incidentally, a security police author of a book, published in 1971 and claiming to be "the first full account in detail of terrorism and insurgency in South Africa", insisted that Marks had "taken up residence in Red China".[410].

In the last year of his life Marks resided, once again, next door to Kotane in the Central Clinical Hospital in the environs of Moscow. These two men had often been on opposing sides during the factional struggles in the SACP three and a half decades earlier. They had both suffered as a result of the prevailing intolerance at the time, Kotane being removed from the top positions and Marks expelled for revealing his real name to the police after losing some of his luggage. They became close friends for the last decades of their life.

Uncle JB was a very good-natured personality who kept his sense of humour through everything. I once heard him say, as he entered Kotane's room for a visit, "Moses, I don't know what you communists are saying, but we Christians say ..." and he started quoting from the Bible.

Marks's health deteriorated considerably after he received news of his mother's death. "I am afraid," he wrote to Dadoo two weeks before his death, "we might have to make the land of the proletariat our sleeping place."[(411)] Uncle JB found his last resting-place in the Novodevichye cemetery, traditionally reserved for the most prominent figures in the Soviet political, academic and cultural life. Two years later, on 16 December 1974, his tombstone, a bust made of black stone, was unveiled on the left side of the main aisle. Some years later, on the right side of the same aisle, another monument was raised, on the grave of Nikita Khrushchev. And in 1979, further to the right, near the wall separating the cemetery from the Moskva river embankment, one more grave appeared, that of Moses Kotane.

Almost fifteen years later, the International Department of the CPSU received a message from the South African Communist Party, informing them that Marks's widow Gladys wanted to visit Moscow. Her request was immediately granted. It was an emotional moment when the ANC students in Moscow, with clinched fists raised, sang "Nkosi Sikelel' iAfrika" together with her at the graveside. I was happy to pass on to Gladys a few memorabilia that had remained in our safekeeping all those years: Uncle JB's Tanzanian travel document, driving licence, and a small photograph of herself. She was very moved and said, "Look, I am wearing the same necklace as in the picture."

In the 1980s one more grave, that of Ivon Jones, one of the founders of the Communist Party of South Africa, was discovered in the same cemetery. The tombstone bearing his name and a hammer and a sickle had been there for many decades, but earlier attempts to locate it had perhaps not been sufficiently persistent.

The archive of another cemetery, Donskoye, confirms that it holds the ashes of the first black Secretary of the SACP, Albert Nzula (registered as Tom Jackson), who died and was cremated in Moscow, but the exact spot has not been found.

At the Central Committee session at the end of 1972 Yusuf Dadoo was elected SACP Chairman. In addition, since it became clear that there was no realistic hope of recovery for Kotane, the new post of Assistant General Secretary was created and Chris Hani was elected to this post. The fact of the election (though without the name of the office-bearer) was announced in the *African Communist*[412], but for some reason this did not attract the attention of the numerous so-called experts on the SACP.

The same may be said about a very significant phrase in the CC session statement: "They ['the liberation alliance headed by the African National Congress and embracing the SACP'] have never had a 'putschist' approach to our revolution, we recognise that the South African revolution must be seen as a process accompanied by an ever-rising combination of forms of resistance, action and organisation, violent and non-violent, illegal and legal, spontaneous and planned."[413]

Building the underground machinery and launching the struggle from abroad were viewed in an increasingly "sober" light, and this was reflected in the Central Committee's call to the membership to take their own initiatives to create "illegal units [to] plan and generate day-to-day organisation, resistance, and struggle [not waiting] until they have made formal contact with the existing apparatus of our revolutionary front."[414]

The next session of the SACP Central Committee took place again in Moscow in November 1973. Apart from discussing the internal difficulties in the ANC (to be described later), this meeting paid attention mainly to the prospects of the struggle inside South Africa. The party leadership, perhaps for the first time, faced the reality that the prospects for the return to South Africa of the "old" Umkhonto cadres were very remote. Their number had shrunk after ten and more years in the camps: some had been killed in action or arrested, others took on more civilian duties within ANC structures or took jobs. There were deserters as well. To be confined within the camps for many years with no clear future and not become demoralised was not easy, even for the most committed freedom fighters. Those who remained full-time in Umkhonto were almost all over thirty, and had left home a decade before. This meant that, if they were successful in returning home, adapting to the changing realities inside South Africa would be problematic.

In addition, such projects demanded generous material resources. At this time financial aid to the ANC from most of its traditional sources had been reduced, owing to both the unpromising prospects of the struggle within South Africa and the understandable focus on the liberation movements in the Portuguese colonies, where successes were more tangible in the early 1970s.

That was true as far as Moscow was concerned as well: in 1973, for example, the ANC received from the International Fund 150 000 dollars (and the SACP 50 000) in comparison with 220 000 for MPLA and 150 000 for PAIGC in the tiny Guinea-Bissau. Frelimo's share was smaller, 85 000,[415] most probably because its new leader Samora Machel was regarded as being too close to Beijing at that time.

In these circumstances the SACP leadership saw a way forward in the careful selection of small numbers of activists to be sent home, while at the same time recruiting Umkhonto cadres inside the country to conduct limited military actions, in the way that SWAPO was doing in Namibia. Such actions were intended to stimulate political activity in South Africa, raise the international prestige of the ANC, and so attract more support to it.

The need to foster co-operation with other liberation movements in Southern Africa was also noted. Contrary to Pretoria's claims of a "common terrorist Command", and with the exception of the operations in Zimbabwe, the interaction between other movements and the ANC was extremely limited. There were several reasons for this. It seems that in the early 1960s some ANC leaders felt themselves to be "elder brothers" towards the "younger" political organisations in neighbouring countries. The fact that the world had diverted its attention and its material assistance to those liberation movements proved painful and irritating.

The following example is indicative of the attitude of most of the Western governments to the ANC in the early 1970s. When Anthony Mongalo was sent to represent the ANC in Italy in 1970, his status was initially "semi-legal". An Italian non-governmental organisation "MOLISV" (Movement for Liberation and Development) provided accommodation, but he could not obtain a long-term visa. It was necessary for Mongalo to enlist the help of Johnny Makatini (the ANC representative in Algiers) and so acquire an Algerian passport that entitled him to stay in Italy without a visa for 90 days at a time. The result was that he had to leave the country periodically for a short time and then return.[416]

In spite of a genuine and prevailing spirit of solidarity with the ANC, some leaders of the liberation movements in Mozambique, Angola and other colonies felt that their own clear-cut classical anti-colonial struggle could more easily attract the support of the international community. The same view prevailed among a section of the SWAPO leadership, who were suspicious that, even if the ANC came to power in South Africa, it would try to keep Namibia under South Africa's control. They felt Namibia had to be liberated first.

This mood was manifest at the UN-OAU International Conference of Experts in Support of Victims of Colonialism and Apartheid, held in April 1973 in Oslo. Its name was unfortunate. First, it reflected the lack of enthusiasm in some UN quarters for the anti-colonial and anti-racist struggle. Second, the representatives of the liberation movements refused to regard themselves as victims, while most of the participants were unhappy to be reduced to the level of "experts".

The treatment accorded by the official convenors and the Scandinavian hosts to the ANC delegation, headed by Tambo, was palpably different from that given to the delegations from the Portuguese colonies.

Oslo was the first time an ANC delegation to an International Conference included Chris Hani, though he was not registered under his real name or under his *nom de guerre*. It was in Oslo that I met first him. "Hello, Comrade Manchkha," said a young African, approaching the only member of the Soviet delegation he knew personally. "Who is that?" I asked Manchkha later. "Chris Nkosana, Kotane's assistant," he replied.

And as it turned out, it was Chris who was most directly affected by the deliberations and decisions of the 1973 SACP Central Committee meeting. The SACP leadership assessed the state of the struggle in South Africa and came to the conclusion (correct and overdue) that it was high time to stop speaking as if the liberation movement was already engaged in the armed struggle. Preparations were continuing into a second decade, but Umkhonto had not fired a single shot on South African soil. At the same time, the South African authorities started arming black policemen and recruiting black soldiers. On top of this, long-held hopes that the independent African states would participate actively in the armed liberation of South Africa had faded altogether.

The prevailing view of the meeting was that people in South Africa should no longer pin their hopes on the intervention of some external liberation force. They needed to understand that they themselves had to create such a force. This was in striking contrast to the position held only a few years before by the SACP (and by the ANC for that matter). Umkhonto could most effectively contribute to the political mobilisation and preparation for the armed struggle by sending cadres back to South Africa as political and military organisers and not as armed groups to act on their own. It was conceded that some selected military actions should be conducted as well.

After the Central Committee session the SACP delegation was received by Mikhail Suslov, the second man in the CPSU leadership, whom many "Kremlinologists" used to call the *éminence grise* behind Leonid Brezhnev. The SACP delegation then visited several Eastern European countries, including the German Democratic Republic. The GDR's contribution to the South African liberation struggle should not be overlooked, despite later events. It is, of course, up to the South African and German *"genossen"* to describe it, but at least one fact should be recorded here. It was in the GDR where Chris Hani prepared for his trip home, and the pretext of continuing his studies there was intended to explain his absence from Africa.[417]

Hani's return to South Africa was the first successful step in creating a permanent underground structure within the country. His illegal work in South Africa and then for a much longer period in Lesotho is well known nowadays, but strangely enough even after his tragic death his coming home was referred to as a mission by a newly elected member of the ANC National Executive Committee. In fact, he was elected to the NEC later, in 1975[418], though when he crossed the border he did so in his dual capacity as a designated head of the ANC underground and as Assistant General Secretary of the SACP.

Many years later he said: "I arrived at Johannesburg and found that the conditions for survival were not ideal. It was a question of safe places. Friends and relatives were very scared to accommodate me. They just stopped short of kicking me out because I was a relative."[419] But even before that things had not been easy. After jumping over a fence of the Botswana-South African border he had to make his own way for two nights, using a compass and the stars to reach Zeerust, where he took a train to Johannesburg.[420]

In South Africa at that time the prevailing mood was "a feeling of hopelessness, of surrender.... You had a feeling that you had to look over your shoulder whenever you uttered anything political."[421] After spending four months in South Africa, he crossed to Lesotho, where he remained for almost eight years.

Chris and his comrades started "to turn Lesotho into a temporary base from which to carry out our activities. We would cross into the country and meet with comrades to build units. By this time we had structures in the Free State, Transkei, Western Cape, Eastern Cape and Border."[422]

But why did this happen so late, more than ten years after Rivonia? Why in the first decade after Rivonia could the ANC "External Mission" not manage to organise a viable underground structure? What was behind it?

First, the geographic conditions were unfavourable. No other liberation movement in Africa (perhaps with the exception of the Algerian FLN in the first years of its struggle) had succeeded without a secure rear base in a neighbouring territory. But it was only in the late 1970s that Mozambique provided such a base for the ANC, and then for only a short time.

Another reason was the belief, cherished for too long, that the suppressed majority of people would give immediate support as soon as the freedom fighters came home. Worse, the ANC and SACP propaganda for many years suggested that this was imminent. While the Umkhonto external contingent, limited from the very beginning to several hundreds, was sweltering in the hot sun of tropical Africa (only the attitude of some African governments could be described as "cool"), the *African Communist* wrote: "The fully trained and equipped guerrilla units of Umkhonto, already tried in battle before the [Morogoro] Conference, now stand ready for bigger battles nearer home."[423] This was written when most of the fighters were based a further five or six thousand kilometres from home, having been forced to leave Tanzania.

But step by step the reality of the situation was becoming evident both to the leaders and the rank and file of the liberation movement. Michael Morris wrote in his "anti-terrorist" book: "The insurgent, of course, is a living tragedy. His role in Africa is increasingly becoming one of stateless and aimless fugitive wanderer with no end in sight to his personal homelessness."[424] Though his assessment was not entirely fair, these words reflected the aim of the Pretoria regime: to make the ANC activists unwanted and uninvited in Southern Africa. This aim was very nearly achieved, even if only temporarily.

The Umkhonto fighters had been separated for years, and later for decades, from home. They were completely cut off from contact with their families by the structures of military discipline. They were deprived of reliable support from the countries they had to reside in, and sometimes even harassed by officials. They were therefore understandably eager to hear any encouraging news from South Africa, in much the same way that political prisoners on Robben Island and in Pretoria Central Prison were eager to hear anything about the activities of the ANC and especially of Umkhonto.

It was at precisely this time, when the liberation movement abroad was at its lowest ebb, that the first rays of hope appeared inside South Africa after the gloom and dark of the late 1960s.

CLASS AND COLOUR IN THE STRUGGLE

The processes which were slowly maturing under conditions of repression and political apathy came to a head at the very beginning of the 1970s.

With the ANC and other progressive organisations banned and their leaders and activists imprisoned, exiled or banished, the protests against the racist order found expression in the Black Consciousness Movement. The creation and activities of that Movement are beyond the scope of this book and so I will limit myself to the assessment given by Oliver Tambo in Moscow in February 1974: "We played and play a role in all this [the developments in South Africa] but it is not a decisive role."[425] The approach of the ANC to the South African Students Organisation (SASO) and other structures of the BCM was one of constructive criticism with the purpose of winning them over and achieving unity.

In his report to the ANC National Consultative Conference in Kabwe in June 1985 Oliver Tambo said: "Our enemies entertained hopes that the BCM would emerge, survive and grow as the organised representation of the 'nationalist tendency' within the national democratic revolution, independent of the ANC."[426]

The process of achieving unity or at least mutual understanding was, of course, hampered by the actions of Pretoria, which did its best to sabotage contacts between the BCM and the ANC. Also certain forces in Africa and, especially, in Western Europe tried to play off the internal young BCM leaders against the "exiled and aged" leadership of the ANC. They hoped to encourage the BCM leaders to play an independent role in South Africa at the expense of the anti-racist movement as a whole.

Moses Kotane wrote in 1974: "Maybe the Black Consciousness people don't want to state their aims because the Government will act against them. But the Government will act against them anyhow."[427] History proved him right. Even though the BCM leaders continued to adhere to non-violence, as soon as they started talking about the formation of a broad political movement and to support the efforts of the emerging black trade unions, they were repressed. This came to a head with the rallies, organised by SASO and the Black People's Convention on 24 September 1974, on the eve of the installation of the

Transitional Government in Mozambique, which transferred power to Frelimo.

The mid 1970s witnessed another development in South Africa, the growth of the workers' movement, signalled by the Durban strike of 1973. This caused Oliver Tambo in 1975 to refer to "a revolutionary ferment manifested by a series of mass strikes by Black workers," along with "the growing militancy of the youth," as being among the developments which had "radically shifted the balance of forces in our subcontinent."[428]

Tambo's reference to the "subcontinent" was not accidental. The need for joint actions by the liberation movements in various Southern Africa countries was constantly advanced by the ANC leadership. This idea had an objective basis: the Pretoria regime gave active and often quite open support to Salisbury and Lisbon. But another factor was perhaps even more important. At a time when the ANC (and the SACP) could not claim any tangible success inside South Africa, in the context of the whole region things looked much more positive. In Mozambique and Angola (and later in Zimbabwe and Namibia as well) the armed liberation struggle was on the upswing. Perhaps this was one of the reasons why the ANC leadership was somewhat critical of the domino theory, which envisaged the countries of the region being liberated one by one, with apartheid South Africa the last one to fall.

One more phenomenon in South African political life required the attention of the ANC, and that was the formation of the bantustans. When the government started implementing its plans, the liberation movement condemned these steps, and at the same time expressed the hope that popular movements would arise in those rural areas, which could link up with the organised protests of the urban workers.[429] This excessive optimism was perhaps caused by the dearth of opposition work in the "white" areas; as it happened, up to the late 1980s the opposition in the bantustans was suppressed as well.

Of all the bantustan leaders, the attitude of the ANC leadership was quite specific towards Gatsha Buthelezi, appointed by Pretoria to the post of Chief Minister of KwaZulu. In Tambo's opinion, Buthelezi's position was ambivalent. On the one hand, Buthelezi helped the government to strengthen its bantustan policy and "in this he was a counter-revolutionary". On the other hand, he used his official position against the regime, helping to raise the political consciousness of the people, and in this way he indirectly helped the ANC. When he attacked racism he stirred up the population in other bantustans as well, making them pressurise local leaders such as Lucas Mangope in Bophuthatswana and Kaiser Matanzima in Transkei to alter their positions.[430]

The ANC leadership was ready to support any "progressive" moves by bantustan leaders. As Oliver Tambo admitted later, it encouraged the creation (or, rather, re-creation) of the Inkatha movement in KwaZulu.[431] Apparently the fact that Buthelezi himself had been a member of the ANC Youth League in the 1950s played a significant role. As early as 1954 Joe Matthews, then a member of the leadership of the ANC Youth League, called Buthelezi "one of the most loyal sons of this land".[432] Did he anticipate then that he would one day become one of his lieutenants?

But the ANC leaders underestimated Buthelezi's personal ambitions. Oliver Tambo and other Congress leaders, who were older and much more prominent in South African politics in the 1950s and 1960s than Buthelezi, would not have expected him to play his role independently of the ANC, let alone claim to be a major national leader. The first warning was sounded when Buthelezi visited Ethiopia and Tanzania in December 1973 and met a number of African leaders.

Students' and workers' frustrations were coming to the boil in South Africa. The US and some of the Western European governments, particularly West Germany, feared revolution in South Africa and started looking for reformist alternatives. As Oliver Tambo put it: "The USA wants to destroy the liberation movement." His concern was that, by meeting Buthelezi, the African leaders (including even Julius Nyerere) were in a sense collaborating with Washington.[433]

Buthelezi's policies and to some extent those of the BCM can be regarded, in ANC vocabulary, as expressions of "narrow nationalism". In South Africa this had co-existed for several decades, though often in confrontation, with "revolutionary nationalism". Towards the mid 1970s a "narrow nationalist" tendency became manifest in the ANC itself.

The results of the Morogoro Conference elections had left some ex-Executive members disgruntled. The top ANC leadership, and Oliver Tambo in particular, were concerned to preserve the unity of the organisation at all costs. At the first meeting of the new National Executive Committee, which took place in the bush near Morogoro at the end of August 1971,[434] it was decided to give those ex-Executive members other important positions. Some were appointed to the Secretariat, a new body complementing the Executive in carrying out the daily work of the movement. Tennyson Makiwane was appointed head of the ANC International Department. Alfred Kgokong was put in charge of the Committee to plan the commemoration of the ANC 60th anniversary. Ambrose Makiwane was sent to Pyongyang as a member of the important delegation headed by Nzo.

Tambo did his best to keep these members within ANC ranks even at the expense of his relationship with the SACP leadership, who were unhappy that the SACP had not been invited to the "meeting in the bush".

The meeting was said to have taken place in a spirit of unity, but this spirit quickly evaporated. The Secretariat failed to function (according to Alfred Nzo, its appointees sabotaged its work),[435] and at the next meeting, in October 1972, it was replaced by a Working Committee. This consisted of all Executive members present in Lusaka. (By that time the Zambian capital had become the unofficial venue of the ANC Headquarters and only the Women's and Youth Sections remained in Morogoro.)

Among the international issues discussed at the next meeting in May 1974 particular attention was paid to the improvement of ANC relations with the countries bordering South Africa (later known in the ANC as "forward areas"). The first official ANC delegation visited Botswana in 1973;[436] others followed, though all of them avoided publicity and travelled there in secrecy.

The discernible downgrading of the ANC by the OAU Liberation Committee was a point of serious concern.[437] In the context of the high regard in which the independent African countries later held the ANC and its leaders, it is difficult to accept that, twenty years before, even acquiring a travel document was a major problem. Most of those countries, with the exception of Tanzania, Algeria, and sometimes Somalia and Ghana, refused to provide even this minimal assistance.

As in the 1960s the ANC leadership had to look elsewhere for assistance. At the end of 1972 an ANC delegation visited Czechoslovakia, the GDR, Hungary, Romania and Bulgaria. In the meantime co-operation with the Soviet Union continued on a regular basis. As a rule, towards the end of each year an ANC delegation, headed by Oliver Tambo or Alfred Nzo, would discuss international developments and the situation in both South Africa and the USSR.[438] Contact between the ANC and Eastern Europe resulted "in a tremendous increase of assistance".[439]

As mentioned above, some help, initially rather limited, was

131

provided by the Scandinavian countries as well. An ANC office was opened in Stockholm.

A report presented to the ANC Executive Committee meeting in 1974 referred to a successful consolidation of the ANC membership.[440] It had to admit, however, that most of the ANC members living abroad were not involved in the political life of the organisation, and suitable structures to facilitate this were not available. The majority, it stated, were "spectators", becoming "victims of desperation" and its consequences.[441]

Such a situation provided fertile soil for those who set themselves against the leadership. For years after Morogoro, Oliver Tambo did his best to avoid a split by embracing the opposition. Other members of the leadership, even started to accuse him of being too zealous a conciliator.

But, despite his efforts, members of the dissident faction soon started to attack him personally. Ten years later, in his report to the ANC conference in 1985, Oliver Tambo said: "By the policies of vilification and outright lies it [the faction] tried to discredit the leadership of our movement and to foment a rebellion from within the ANC in the hope that it would regain the positions it had lost at the Morogoro conference. For its activities this faction won the public recognition of the Pretoria regime which showered praises on it as the genuine leadership of the ANC and of our people."[442] They failed, however, to win support from the rank and file members of the ANC in Africa, and gradually their activity was concentrated on London. By 1975 it became clear that all attempts to keep them in the ANC fold had failed.

That year an important step was taken to strengthen the ANC's leading structures. In the words of Oliver Tambo, 1975 was the first year of the "Period of Consolidation and Advance" after the previous 1969-74 "Period of Regrouping and Recovery".[443] But it was difficult to start consolidation when in the highest ANC body – the National Executive Committee – only five or six people continued to function: Flag Boshielo and J B Marks had died, Moses Kotane was incapacitated, Joe Matthews had left for Botswana. M B Yengwa, who had been co-opted on to the Executive in 1971, soon suffered a stroke and could no longer participate in its work. Dr Zami Conco, also co-opted, left to live and work in Canada.

The need for by-elections to the Executive was discussed at the Executive meeting in 1974. These were held at its next session, in

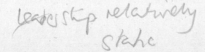
leadership relatively stable

March 1975. This meeting was enlarged to about fifty people. All delegates submitted six names of people they wanted added to the Executive. The highest number of votes was received by Josiah Jele (then the ANC representative in the World Peace Council in Helsinki), Johnny Makatini (the representative in Algeria), Thabo Mbeki (the representative in Swaziland and later in Nigeria), Florence Moposho (the head of the Women's Section), and John Pule (Motshabi), who became the head of the department dealing with reconstruction of the ANC structures in South Africa.[444] They were all required to work in Lusaka, but in practice this happened only much later.

The meeting had once again to face the problem of the opposition within the ANC, which had by then organised its supporters and begun openly to criticise the decisions taken in Morogoro. In 1969 Raymond (Mazisi) Kunene had been replaced as the ANC Chief Representative in London by Reginald September. The opposition used this as a pretext to encourage the ANC African members to distance themselves from the new representative and his office. Kunene, who left for the USA to lecture, complained later: "I was said to be in cahoots with the dissidents. I think one must avoid a damaging labelling of people because it doesn't build an organisation." However, in the same interview he advocated the "rehabilitation" of Tennyson Makiwane, a leader of the dissidents.[445]

In January 1975 a "meeting of African members of the ANC resident in the United Kingdom" was convened, which called for "a comprehensive review of the 1969 Morogoro decisions in particular with regard to opening membership of the ANC (externally) to non-Africans", as well as "a comprehensive review of the relations between the ANC and the South African Communist Party". The SACP, it was claimed, "appears to exercise undue influence upon the policy and the decision-making organs of the ANC."[446]

Some of the dissident group were present at the ANC Executive meeting in March, which not only rejected their position but also elected an enlarged Executive which did not include those identified with the dissidents. Their next opportunity to defy the ANC leadership (and not only the Morogoro decisions) was presented at the ceremony to unveil the tombstone on the grave of Robert Resha in September 1975.

Robert Resha, a prominent ANC leader in the 1950s and early 1960s, Deputy Volunteer-in-Chief during the Defiance Campaign of 1952 (Deputy, that is, to Nelson Mandela), was well known both in South

Africa and among South African exiles. Helen Joseph, who was close to him, especially during the Treason Trial, wrote: "Resha lost his fight against this new policy ("of admitting non-Africans to membership") and died a tragic, lonely and embittered man, rejected by many of those who for nearly thirty years had been his leaders and his colleagues in the struggle to which he had devoted his life."[447]

She was right. Persisting in his position, Resha veered away from the mainstream of the struggle. It should be mentioned that taking extreme positions was typical of him. For instance, the most harmful evidence presented against the accused at the Treason Trial had been a speech by Resha, secretly taped by the police at an ANC meeting on 23 November 1956, in which he had said: "If you are disciplined and you are told by your organisation not to be violent, you must not be violent; if you are a true volunteer and you are called upon to be violent, you must be absolutely violent, you must murder! Murder! That is all."[448] This statement was manna from heaven for the authorities, and two weeks later the Congress Alliance leaders, including Resha, were detained.

In 1975 a special committee was created, headed by Joe Matlou, another ex-Executive member. (In the early 1970s Matlou came to Simferopol as head of one of the Umkhonto groups but was soon withdrawn because of misbehaviour and indiscipline). It published a booklet, written by Alfred Kgokong, which contained direct attacks against the ANC leadership and a "non-African group in London".[449] An open revolt by the "African Nationalists" (as the group started to call themselves) was immediately highlighted by some of the Western media as a "declaration of war" by rank and file Africans in the ANC against the "non-African and communist-controlled" leadership. The allegation that "the ANC has been hijacked by communists and Africans will regain it" received wide publicity both outside and inside South Africa.

The reaction of the ANC leadership was both rapid and balanced. Under threat of expulsion, the Makiwanes, Kgokong, and their supporters were requested to renounce in writing their factional activity within three weeks. They failed to do so and the ANC Executive published a statement which said: "Every effort was made to try and persuade these ringleaders to desist from their acts of subverting the struggle but the tolerance and constructive approach of the movement was mistaken for weakness on its part and rewarded by these conspirators by an intensification on their part of attempts to sow division and confusion." The list of the expelled ANC members ("a small conspiratorial group of dissidents") contained eight names, including those mentioned above.[(450)] The group became known as "the Gang of Eight" by analogy with China's "Gang of Four".

The SACP leadership reacted strongly as well. Its statement, headed (in the words of Samora Machel) "The enemy hidden under the same colour", pointed to similarities between the position taken by the Gang of Eight and that of the PAC's Potlako Leballo in the late 1950s. The statement characterised members of the group as opportunists. "Most of them have made many somersaults in their chequered political careers, always following what seemed to serve their ambitions at the given moment. Some of them were communists at one time and anti-communists at others, tribalists and African nationalists, strongly pro-Soviet and equally strongly anti-Soviet and pro-China."[(451)]

They were accused of deliberately distorting the nature of the SACP's relationship with the liberation movement. "In the case of at least two of them (Kgokong and Makiwane) they were both members of the SACP ... but were expelled ... when outside the country they attempted to use the party as a base for their tribalist and factionist activity against the ANC."[(452)]

After their expulsion the dissidents announced the creation of a new organisation, "the ANC (African Nationalists)" or "the ANC – Luthuli", as distinct from "the ANC – Tambo". They tried to entrench themselves in African countries – Tennyson Makiwane in Dar es Salaam, Ambrose Makiwane in Lusaka – and even managed to convene a meeting in the Tanzanian capital, which they called "a session of the ANC (African Nationalists) Executive Committee". They planned to call a conference to create a "proper leadership" with the participation of "people from home". Some of them managed (using Zairean passports) to go to Port-Louis, the capital of Mauritius, where they tried, unsuccessfully, to attend the OAU Assembly.

They were given a platform by some of the Western media, mainly right-wing (often connected with Pretoria), but leftist as well. The West German "solidarity" magazine Sudlische Afrika published a lengthy article by Tennyson Makiwane, criticising "Tambo's group" and "the reformist Communist Party" as politicians who were beating "the drums of war from a safe distance". Makiwane called for "the continuation of the revolution"[(453)], but this was short-lived. When he found that "the ANC (African Nationalists)" was not viable, he changed both his language and his residence and settled in the newly "independent" Transkei (with the permission of Pretoria?) to serve in the bantustan's "diplomatic service". Not long after, he was killed by an unidentified gunman. Many years later I asked a member of the ANC Executive, "Who killed Makiwane?" "*Narod* (the people)," he answered in Russian.

While the group was openly anti-communist, Ambrose Makiwane boasted in Dar es Salaam that he would soon be going to Moscow to arrange that all Soviet assistance should be divided equally between the ANC and his organisation. He was aware that ANC members held the Soviet Union in high esteem and may have been trying to win their support by leading them to believe that he himself was well known in Moscow.[454]

However, neither the veterans nor the youth who left the country in 1976 were drawn to the side of the Gang of Eight in any substantial numbers. Soon they started to quarrel among themselves and splits occurred in their own ranks.[455] Apparently this disintegration was caused not so much by political differences as by personal interests. As Thomas Nkobi stated, Kgokong, Makiwane, Matlou and some others disapproved of Moses Kotane "because he [was] strict in Treasury, not so much because he was a Communist Party [*sic*]. They did not like the austerity because he stopped them doing as they pleased."[456]

On the eve of the Soweto uprising, the ANC and the SACP leadership had to handle another problem: Joe Matthews's public renunciation of his revolutionary past in an article in the Johannesburg *Sunday Times*, published under the headline "I believed".[457]

The story of Vincent Joseph Matthews, known to everybody as Joe Matthews, perhaps deserves special mention as he is once again endeavouring to play an important role in South African political life. Tom Karis and Gail Gerhart wrote that Matthews "gained a wide reputation over the course of the 1950s as an independent-minded and articulate radical, attracted both to Marxism and to western concepts of the rule of law."[458].

Criticising the future PAC leader Robert Sobukwe, who suggested that Africa should "borrow the best from the East and West", Joe Matthews wrote in 1959: "He is inviting the Africans to ride astride two horses going in opposite directions. The whole world is marching to socialism and the only argument is on how to carry out the re-organisation of society on the basis of socialism."[459]

Karis and Gerhart state that Matthews left South Africa in 1960 for Basutoland (Lesotho) and then, having been banned from that country in 1965, moved to London, where "he served as managing editor of *Sechaba*. After 1970, when he moved to Botswana, he gave up his active involvement in the ANC. He has since worked in the office of the President and as an assistant Attorney-General in Botswana, and has also acquired substantial business interests there."[460]

This is true, but is not the whole truth. Matthews joined the illegal SACP in the 1950s and in 1960, as has already been noted, became a member of its Central Committee and was sent as a delegate to the International Communist Meeting in Moscow.

His highest position in the ANC was as the Secretary of the Revolutionary Council (the importance of this office is underlined by the fact that his successor was Moses Mabhida). After this appointment at the Morogoro Conference, he became very active. During his visit to Moscow he discussed a variety of questions and even forwarded a request to have designed and minted "Luthuli Medals" for three levels of Umkhonto cadres, and received some samples of designs for these.

But a year later, in 1970, he left for Botswana with the permission of both the ANC and the SACP. Naturally the South African authorities were worried: *Newscheck* magazine, close to Pretoria, wrote about "anxiety in top South African circles" that Matthews's advice "could be only detrimental to good relations between the Republic and Botswana."[461]

The liberation movement did hope that Matthews could be useful in his new position as assistant to the Permanent Secretary of the President's office in a country which had been "forbidden territory" for ANC political and military cadres.

Initially Joe Matthews (at least on paper) seemed a devoted revolutionary. He wrote in July 1971 from Gaborone to Yusuf Dadoo: "I hope people are resisting any wild dreams or hopes about what is happening in the Bantustans. The nearer one is to a mirage the more you recognise it for what it is, namely, waterless desert.... What there is in SA is a Tsarist Russia apparently immune from all the changes that shook Europe in 1879 [read: 1789], 1830 and 1848. Yet everyone feels in their bones that something will take place there bigger and more significant than any thus far!" He made an emotional appeal to his comrades: "Friends! Do not let winds of the current reformist atmosphere cause the slightest shift in what is and has been a basically correct line."[462]

In August 1971 he continued: "No reforms initiated by the rulers can bring about change in this part of the world. They [the people] will have to fight for even the slightest morsel of a concession. Only revolution will bring about the change.... It does not require more than a few months back in this atmosphere to realise that in broad historical terms if not in details of execution the approach of yourself and your closest colleagues is absolutely correct. Therefore I would urge that there be no concessions made to doubt on broad strategy."[463] In 1972 he was still corresponding with Yusuf Dadoo, though with less enthusiasm: "I hope to pass through London early October and will make it a point to see you."[464]

But before long Matthews severed all his ties with the ANC and the SACP. Later, when the ANC resumed contacts with the Botswana government, it found that Matthews had not been invited by the President of Botswana, as he had claimed, but had himself applied to Seretse Khama, a disciple of his late father Z K Matthews, asking for a job. After his father's death he became the most senior member of the family clan and had to administer the family estate. When his former colleagues finally had a chance to meet him in Botswana, his attitude was reserved and even hostile. Some of his old friends in Moscow were also worried. When *Izvestiya* correspondent Boris Pilyatskin went on assignment to Botswana, Petr Manchkha specifically asked him to visit Joe Matthews.

On 18 April 1976, soon after resigning from his job in the government and just two months before the Soweto uprising, Matthews published his "I believed" article in the *Sunday Times*. It contained a call for the creation of a capitalist class among Africans, a rejection of the armed struggle, and the acceptance of a policy of reform.

Did it represent sincere disillusionment with socialism and the revolutionary struggle? Was Matthews a forerunner of those prominent communists in the USSR and elsewhere who, often at pensionable age, suddenly discovered that they were heading in the wrong direction? It seems as if the reason in both cases is much more mundane. It is no accident that Matthews published this article shortly before the proclamation of the "independence" of Transkei, and called for it to be recognised. His former comrades were sure that his approaches to Transkei were connected with his business plans.

What caused the greatest indignation was this unequivocal statement: "Throughout history the ANC had in its ranks African members of the Communist Party ... I never was a member."[465] The SACP Central Committee promptly expelled him from the party. In a notice, published in the *African Communist* under the title "A renegade

138

expelled", it said: "He has chosen the path of opportunism and personal advancement in preference to that of struggle, and history has already passed judgement on him ... The Communist Party has no room in its ranks for opportunists and renegades."[466]

Luck was not on Matthews's side. The events in Soweto changed the situation not only for South Africa, but also for him and his position in Botswana. Some time afterwards students in Gaborone openly protested against him, so he had to leave not only his job but later, after the collapse of his commercial venture, the country as well.

After spending some years in the West, Matthews came back to South Africa. He tried to register as a veteran at the ANC Conference in Durban in July 1991. Again, he was unlucky. Those responsible for registration reminded him that he had been expelled from the ANC.[467] A new somersault brought him to Inkatha, to become its Chief Executive Officer, and from there to the post of Deputy Minister for Safety and Security in May 1994. At the time of his Ministerial appointment he was still wanted in Botswana for fraud and theft.

REFERENCES

1. *Argus*, Cape Town, 9 July 1991.
2. Dadoo Y. and Pillay V. *The Political Situation in the Union of South Africa.* 14 July 1960, (Moscow), p.5.
3. Karis T. and Carter G. *From Protest to Challenge. A Documentary History of African Politics in South Africa. 1887-1964. Vol.3.* Karis T. and Gerhart G. *Challenge and Violence.* 1953-1964. Hoover Institution Press, Stanford. 1977. p.649.
4. Mayibuye Centre Historical Papers Archive, Brian Bunting's Collection, Interview with Moses Kotane, 17 April 1972.
5. Quoted in: Bunting B. *Moses Kotane. South African Revolutionary. A Political Biography.* Inkululeko Publications. London, 1975, p.231.
6. *Report* (s.a.e.l,), p.2.
7. Ibid. p.10.
8. Ibid. p.12.
9. Ibid. p.13.
10. Dadoo Y. and Pillay V. *The Situation in the South African Communist Party.* 14 July 1960 (Moscow) p. 3.
11. Harmel M. *Some Notes on the Communist Party in South Africa.* (Moscow, 1960), pp. 14-16.
12. Ibid. p.17.
13. Dingake M. *My Fight Against Apartheid.* Kliptown Books, London, 1987, p.64.
14. Karis M. and Gerhart G. *Challenge and Violence*, p.355.
15. Joseph H. *Side by Side. The Autobiography of Helen Joseph.* Zed Books Ltd, London, 1986, p.103.
16. Quoted in: Karis T. and Gerhart G. *Challenge and Violence*, p.364.
17. Quoted in: Ibid.
18. *African Communist*, Johannesburg-London, 1961, N 6, p.5.
19. Lodge T. *Black Politics in South Africa from 1945*, Longman, London and New York, 1983, p. 234.
19. Ludi G. *Operation Q-018*, Nasionale Boekhandel, Cape Town, 1969, p.30
21. *African Communist*, 1961, N 6, p.4.
22. Lambett R. *Resistance in South Africa 1950-1961: an assessment*

of the political strike campaigns. University of London, Institute of Commonwealth Studies, Seminar paper, 25 August 1987, p.17.

23. Lodge T. *Black Politics*, p.233.
24. Ibid.
25. Bunting B. *Moses Kotane.* p. 268.
26. Ibid. p. 269.
27. Benson M. *Nelson Mandela.* Penguin Books, Harmondsworth, 1986, p.116.
28. *Dawn.* Journal of Umkhonto we Sizwe. Souvenir Issue. 25th Anniversary of MK. p.21.
29. Ibid. p.25.
30. Ibid. p.10.
31. *African Communist.* October-December 1962, pp. 5-6.
32. Ibid. N 9. p.51.
33. *South Africa - What Next. Draft statement of the South African Communist Party circulated to members for comments and criticism before being issued to the people of South Africa.* August 1960. p.13.
34. MCHP, ANC London Collection, *Bulletin N 2.* Political Report. (s.a.e.l.), p.3.
35. Ibid. p.8.
36. Ibid. p.9.
37. Ibid. p.11.
38. Ibid. pp. 11-12.
39. Ibid. p.12.
40. Ibid. p.15.
41. Ibid.
42. Kotane M. *Notes on some aspects of the political situation in the Republic of South Africa,* 9 November 1961, (Moscow), p.12.
43. MCPH, BBC, Interview with M.B.Yengwa, 30 August 1973.
44. Ibid. Interview with a SACP and Umkhonto member (name withheld for ethical reasons). Typed October 1973.
45. Mandela N. *The Struggle is My Life,* International Defence and Aid Fund, London, 1986, p.165.
46. Ibid. p.174.
47. Karis T. and Gerhart G. *Challenge and Violence,* p.648
48. MCHP, Yusuf Dadoo's Collection, Notes on the discussions between a delegation from the C.C. of the S.A.C.P. and the N.E.C. of the ANC p.1.
49. *Dawn.* Souvenir Issue, p.24.

50. MCHP, BBC, Interview with J. Slovo, September 1973.
51. Mbeki G. *The Struggle for Liberation in South Africa: A Short History.* Mayibuye Centre, Bellville, David Phillip, Cape Town, 1992, p.91.
52. *Memorandum* (s.a.e.l.). p.2
53. *Dawn.* Souvenir Issue. p.24.
54. Ibid.
55. *Pravda*, Moscow, 29 July 1971.
56. Slovo J. *Slovo. The Unfinished Autobiography.* Ravan Press, Randburg, 1995, p.151.
57. Mandela N. *Long Walk to Freedom. The Autobiography of Nelson Mandela.* Abacus, London, 1995, p.322.
58. Ibid. pp. 342-343
59. Ibid. p.325.
60. Slovo J. *Slovo*, p.148.
61. Mandela N. *The Struggle is My Life,* p.167.
62. Slovo J. *No Middle Road.* In: Davidson B., Slovo J., Wilkinson A. *Southern Africa. The New Politics of Revolution.* Penguin Books, Harmondsworth, 1976, p.185.
63. *Dawn.* Souvenir Issue, p.24.
64. Ibid.
65. Benson M. *Nelson Mandela,* p.116.
66. Dingake M. *My Fight Against Apartheid*, p.68.
67. *New Nation.* Johannesburg, 27 October - 2 November, 1989.
68. *Dawn.* Souvenir Issue, p.13.
69. Ibid. p.12
70. Ibid. pp. 12-13.
71. Discussion with J. Makatini, Moscow, 10 January 1987.
72. Discussion with E. Mtshali, Moscow, 5 March 1986.
73, *Dawn.* Souvenir Issue, p.12.
74. Ellis S. and Sechaba T. *Comrades against Apartheid: the ANC and the South African Communist Party in exile.* J. Currey, Bloomington, Indiana University Press, Indianapolis, 1992, p.27.
75. *New Bridge,* Moscow, N 2, 1992.
76. Centre for Storage of Contemporary Documentation. Minutes of the Secretariat of the CPSU Central Committee, N 54, item 341g, 27 March 1954.
77. CSCD, Minutes of the Secretariat, N 59, item 333gs, 4 June 1954.
78. Discussion with B. and S. Bunting, Cape Town, 20 May 1993.
79. CSCD, Minutes of the Secretariat, N 54, item 1433g, 27 March

1954.

80. Discussion with W. Sisulu, Moscow, 1 December 1990.
81. Joseph H. *Side by Side,* p.18.
82. CSCD, Minutes of the Secretariat, N 79, item 160g, 7 June 1955.
83. Ibid. N 31, item 3g, 6 June 1959.
84. MCHP, BBC, Kotane M. *Meet the fighters for a new South Africa.* p.2.
85. MCHP, YDC, (Yusuf Dadoo's autobiographical notes), p.2.
86. CSCD, Minutes of the Secretariat, N 56, item 22 gs, 5 July 1960.
87. MCHP, YDC, Pahad E. *Yusuf Dadoo. A political biography* (unpublished manuscript), p.211.
88. Dadoo Y. and Pillay V. *The Political Situation.*
89. Dadoo Y. and Pillay V. *The Situation in the South African Communist Party.*
90. Ibid. p.4.
91. Ibid. p.6.
92. MCHP, YDC, Y. Dadoo's interview with B.R. Nanda, 15 October 1971.
93. CSCD, Head of the CPSU CC International Department B.N. Pomomarev's report on expenditures of the "International Trade Union Fund for Assistance to Left Workers' Organisations attached to the Romanian Council of Trade Unions", 2 November 1960.
94. CSCD, Extract from the Minutes of the Politbureau of the AUCP (b) Central Committee N 76/12, 19 July 1950.
95. Ibid.
96. CSCD, Decision of the CPSU CC Politbureau P 76/XXXVI, 7 January 1963.
97. Pahad E. *Yusuf Dadoo,* p.211.
98. Ibid. p.217.
99. Ibid. p.218.
100. *African Communist,* 1964, N 16, p.46.
101. Quoted in: Campbell K. *Soviet Policy Towards South Africa.* The Macmillan Press Ltd, Houndmills, Basingstoke, Hampshire, 1986, p.102.
102. CSCD, Minutes of the Commission of the CPSU Central Committee on Ideology, Culture and International Party Ties, N 55, item 100g, 30 March 1961.
103. CSCD, Minutes of the Secretariat, N 190, item 20 gs, 29 July 1961.

104. *Bulletin* N 2, (s.a.e.l.) p. 3.
105. Ibid. p.2.
106. Discussion with V. Shemyatenkov, Moscow, 6 January 1997.
107. Discussion with R. Mhlaba, Moscow, 6 August 1992.
108. CSCD, Minutes of the Secretariat, N 1, item 3g, 2 November 1961.
109. Ibid.
110. CSCD, Decisions taken by the instruction of the Secretaries of the CPSU Central Committee without recording in the minutes, N 478, 28 November 1961.
111. Ibid.
112. Ibid.
113. *Sunday Times*, Johannesburg, 16 August 1992.
114. CSCD, Head of the CPSU Central Committee International Department B.N. Ponomarev's report, 1 November 1961.
115. CSCD, Head of the CPSU Central Committee International Department B.N. Ponomarev's report, 3 January 1963
116. CSCD, Minutes of the Commission, N 59, item 69g, 16 September 1991.
117. Discussion with A. Mongalo. Cape Town, 3 June 1993.
118. CSCD, Minutes of the Secretariat, N 6, item 38g, 19 December 1961.
119. Ibid. N 16, item 13, 27 February 1962.
120. Discussion with R. Mompati, Johannesburg, 21 February 1993.
121. CSCD, Minutes of the Secretariat, N 50, item 46g, 11 December 1962.
122. Lodge T. *Black Politics,* pp. 234-235.
123. Ibid. p.235.
124. *Memorandum*, p.3.
125. Quoted in: Weyl N., *Traitors' End. The Rise and Fall of the Communist Movement in Southern Africa.* Tafelberg Uitgewers. Cape Town and Johannesburg, 1970, p. 163.
126. Strydom L., *Rivonia Unmasked!* Voortrekker Pers. Johannesburg 1965, pp. 113-114.
127. A. Goldreich to the author, 24 August 1993.
128. Ibid.
129. Quoted in: Strydom L. *Rivonia Unmasked!* p. 113.
130. Ibid.
131. A. Goldreich to the author.
132. Archive of the Soviet Afro-Asian Solidarity Committee. South

African Collection.

133. CSCD, Minutes of the Secretariat, N 61, item 35g, 24 March 1958.

134. Ibid. Minutes of the Secretariat, N 52, item 10 g, 22 December 1962.

135. Lodge T. *Black Politics,* p.292.

136. *Meeting the Challenge. The Story of American Committee on Africa.* New York, 1981, p.9.

137. Houser G. *No one can stop the rain. Glimpses of Africa's liberation struggle.* The Pilgrim Press, New York, 1989, p.129.

138. *The role of the Soviet Union, Cuba and East Germany in fomenting terrorism in Southern Africa.* Vol. 1, US Government Press, Washington, 1982, p.553.

139. *African Communist.* 1981, N 87, p.22.

140. *ANC National Conference July 1991, Report.* Johannesburg. (s.a.e.l.), p.2.

141. Ibid. p.3.

142. MCHP, ANCLonC, Minutes of the South Africa United Front Conference held in London from 25 August to 4 September 1961, p.11.

143. *ANC National Conference July 1991, Report,* p.3.

144. MCHP, ANCLonC, Minutes of the South Africa United Front Conference, p.7.

145. *Spearhead.* Dar es Salaam. April 1962, pp. 21-22.

146. Ibid. p.21.

147. Karis T. and Gerhart G. *Challenge and Violence*, p.762.

148. *Our Immediate Task* ANC (s.a.e.l.) p.3.

149. Quoted in: Strydom L. *Rivonia Unmasked!* p.108.

150. Karis T. and Gerhart G. *Challenge and Violence*, p. 91.

151. MCHP, ANCLonC, Thunder to OR, 23 April 1963.

152. Ibid. M.T.B. to Booth, 23 May 1963.

153. *New Nation.* 27 October - 2 November , 1989.

154. Ibid.

155. *Dawn*, Souvenir Issue, p.24.

156. Karis T. and Gerhart G. *Challenge and Violence,* p.762.

157. Ibid. p.764.

158. Quoted in: Morris M. Terrorism. *The first full account in detail of terrorism and insurgency in Southern Africa.* Howard Timmins, Cape Town, 1971, p.3.

159. Quoted in: Strydom L. *Rivonia Unmasked!* p.152.

160. Karis M. and Gerhart G. *Challenge and Violence,* p.765.

161. *Dawn*, October/November/December 1982. pp. 37-38.

162. Ibid. p.38.

163. *Dawn*, Souvenir Issue. p.24.

164. *African Communist*, 1983, N 95, p.81.

165. *Dawn*, Souvenir Issue. pp. 24-25.

166. Ibid. p.25.

167. Ibid.

168. Benson M. *Nelson Mandela*, p.138.

169. Karis M. and Gerhart G. *Challenge and Violence*, p.696.

170. Ibid.

171. Ibid.

172. Mandela N. *The Struggle is My Life*, pp. 91-92.

173. Ibid. pp. 174-175.

174. *Pravda*. Moscow, 11 February 1977.

175. Discussion with B. Bunting, Moscow, 25 June 1988.

176. *Pravda*. 28 February 1977.

177. Quoted in: Strydom L. *Rivonia Unmasked!* p.163.

178 Dingake M. *My Fight Against Apartheid*, pp. 35-36.

179. Ibid. p.116.

180. Karis T. and Gerhart G. *Challenge and Violence,* p.769.

181. MCHP, ANCLonC, Unsigned letter, 1 July 1964.

182. Lodge T. *Black Politics*, p.240.

183. *African National Congress. National Consultative Conference. June 1985. NEC Reports. President's Statement to Conference,* p.7.

184. CSCD, Head of the CPSU Central Committee International Department B. N. Ponomarev's report, 29 December 1963.

185. CSCD, Decisions of the Secretariat, N 17, item 37g, 10 March 1962.

186. Discussion with A. Makarov, Pretoria, 21 November 1993.

187. Discussion with J. Jele, Moscow, 1 May 1985.

188. Discussion with R. Kasrils, Moscow, 25 November 1984.

189. Discussion with M. Mabhida, Moscow, 15 November 1982.

190. MHPC, BBC, Interview with R. Kasrils. London. September 1971.

191. *Star*, Johannesburg, 11 September 1991

192. Discussion with R. Mhlaba, Moscow, 6 August 1992.

193. *Dawn*. Souvenir Issue. p.2.

194. Ibid.

195. CSCD, Minutes of the Secretariat, N 123, item 217g, 20 July 1965.

196. Ibid. N 125, item 83g, 23 August 1965.

197. Ibid.

198. *Dawn*, Souvenir Issue, p.33.

199. Lodge T. *Black Politics*, p.300

200. CSCD, Head of the CPSU Central Committee International Department B. N. Ponomarev's report, 16 December 1965.

201. Ibid.

202. Discussion with M. Piliso, Moscow, 20 July 1973.

203. MCHP, YDC, Mota's Report, p.2.

204. MCHP, BBC, Interview with O. Tambo. Typed October 1973.

205. MCHP, ANCLonC, Problems of the Congress Movement. (s.a.e.l.)

206. MCHP, YDC, Summary of the Events in Connection with Mr. James Jobe Hadebe and his Resignation from the External Mission of the African National Congress, p.1.

207. MCHP, ANCLonC, John Marks to Yusuf Dadoo, 9 April 1964.

208. *New Nation*, Johannesburg, 27 October - 2 November 1989.

209. Joseph H. *Side by Side*, p.159.

210. Ibid.

211. Ibid.

212. Quoted in: Mitchison N. *A Life for Africa. The Story of Bram Fischer*, Merlin Press, London, 1973, p.140.

213. Dingake M. *My Fight Against Apartheid*, p.73

214. Ibid. p.118.

215. Ibid. p.84

216. Benson M. *Nelson Mandela*, p.141.

217. Joseph H. *Side by Side*, p.155.

218. Benson M. *South Africa. The Struggle For A Birthright.* International Defence and Aid Fund for Southern Africa, London, 1985, pp. 280-281.

219. J. Middleton to the author, 11 December 1995.

220. Benson M. *South Africa*, p. 268.

221. Discussion with Y. Dadoo, Moscow, 23 February 1981.

222. Quoted in: Joseph H. *Side by Side*, p.160.

223. Pike H. *History of Communism in South Africa. Christian Mission International of South Africa,* Germiston, 1988, p.430.

224. Ludi G. and Grobbelaar B. *The Amazing Mr. Fischer.* Nasionale Boekhandel, Cape Town, 1966, p.84.

225. MCHP, YDC, Bizzel J. Background to my political involvement in South Africa. 1982, p.5.
226. Quoted in: Mitchison N. *A Life for Africa*, p.173.
227. *African Communist*, 1978, N 75, p.40.
228. CSCD, Minutes of the Secretariat, N 103, item 13g, 17 June 1964.
229. Lodge T. *Black Politics*, p.301.
230. MCHP, YDC, Problems and Prospects. Discussion Statement, p.15.
231. *African Communist*. N 29, 1967, p.11.
232. Lodge T. *Black Politics*, p.298. Lodge refers to Kenneth Grundy's *Guerrilla Struggle in Africa*. Grossman. New York. 1971. p.195, but this reference is a mistake.
233. Ibid. pp. 298-299.
234. Discussion with J. Jele, Moscow, 1 May 1985.
235. *Dawn*. Souvenir Issue, p.35.
236. Quoted in: *International Defence and Aid Fund. Information Service.* London, N 2, p.63
237. *Dawn*, Souvenir issue, p.39.
238. Ibid. p. 42.
239. *Guerrilla Warfare.* ANC. (s.a.e.l.) pp. 72-73.
240. Morris M. *Terrorism*, p.54.
241. CSCD, Decisions of the CPSU Central Committee taken by voting of the CC Secretaries without recording in the minutes, 21 April 1967.
242. *A Survey of Race Relations in South Africa.* 1968. South African Institute of Race Relations, Johannesburg, 1969, pp. 66, 68.
243. *Dawn*, Souvenir Issue, p.36.
244. Ibid. p.37. According to the Botswana authorities, refereed to in: *A Survey of Race Relations in South Africa.* 1967. Johannesburg, 1968, p.69, the maximum penalty was three years plus R 750 or 18 months.
245. *A Survey of Race Relations in South Africa.* 1967. Johannesburg, 1968, p.69.
246. MCHP, ANCLonC, Oliver Tambo to Yusuf Dadoo, 6 May 1968.
247. Quoted in: Slovo J. *No Middle Road*, p. 235.
248. Quoted in: *Dawn*, Souvenir Issue, p. 37.
249. Ibid. p. 38.
250. Quoted in: Slovo J,. *No Middle Road*, pp. 235-236.
251. Discussion with M. Mabhida, Moscow, 15 November 1982.
252. Discussion with V. Shemyatenkov, Moscow, 6 January 1997.

253. *Rand Daily Mail*, Johannesburg, 21 May 1982.

254. *Africa Confidential*, London, 10 December 1986.

255. *Press briefing for accredited foreign correspondents on the history, aims, activities and the level of threat posed by the African National Congress (ANC)*. By - Maj Gen FMA Steenkamp - SA Police. In - The Auditorium, HF Verwoerd Building, Cape Town, 8 February 1984, p.30.

256. *Segodnya*, Moscow, N 5, 1993.

257. Quoted in: Lodge T. *Black Politics*, p.299.

258. Ibid.

259. MCHP, ANCLonC, Central Committee. Internal Circular, p.2.

260. Ibid. p.8

261. Ibid. p.9.

262. *New Africa*. London. 1969, N 3/4, p.4.

263. Ibid.

264. The *African Communist*. 1969, N 38, p.51.

265. Lodge T. *Black Politics*, p.300.

266. (*Chris Hani's memorandum*), (1969), s.l. p.1

267. Ibid.

268. Ibid. p.2.

269. Ibid. p.4.

270. Ibid. p.3.

271. Ibid. p.5.

272. Ibid. p.4.

273. MCHP, YDC, Summary of the Events, p.5.

274. (Chris Hani's memorandum), p.5.

275. Ibid. p.4.

276. Ibid. p.5.

277. MCHP, BBC, Interview with B. Turok, typed October 1970.

278. Discussion with C. Hani. Moscow. 27 April 1992.

279. Ibid.

280. Ellis S. and Sechaba T. *Comrades*, p.48.

281. MCHP, ANCLonC, Report of the preparatory committee on the pre-conference discussion, p.1.

282. MCHP, ANCLonC, African National Congress (S.A.). Directive on the nature of the forthcoming conference. March 1969.

283. MCHP, ANCLonC, Report of the preparatory committee, p.1.

284. Ibid. pp 1-2.

285. T*he Enemy Hidden under the Same Colour.* Inkululeko Publications, London. p.15.

286. Quoted in: *Apartheid. Collection of writings on South African racism by South Africans.* International Publishers. New York. p.231.
287. *Forward to Freedom. Documents on the National Policies of the African National Congress of South Africa.* African National Congress of South Africa, Morogoro, (s.a.), pp. 3-17.
288. Bunting B.*Moses Kotane*, p.282.
289. Ellis S. and Sechaba T. *Comrades*, p. 59.
290. *Forward to Freedom*, p.3.
291. Ibid. p.13.
292. Ibid. p.14.
293. Ibid. p.13
294. Ibid.
295. Ibid. p.10.
296. Ibid. p.9.
297. *African Communist.* N 95, 1983, p.89.
298. (Notes by Duma Nokwe), Moscow, June 1967, pp. 1-2.
299   MCHP, ANCLonC, (Yusuf Dadoo's notes at the Morogoro Conference).
300. MCHP, ANCLonC, Recommendations. (1966, Dar es Salaam), p.1.
301. MCHP, ANCLonC, Thoughts on the future of the alliance: J.S. April 1969, p.2.
302. Ibid. pp. 4-5.
303. *African Communist*, N 95. 1983, p.89.
304. MCHP, ANC Lusaka Collection, African National Congress. National Consultative Conference. June 1985. NEC Reports.
305. CSCD, Minutes of the Secretariat, N 73, item 342s, 11 June 1969.
306. See, for example: Nel P. *Soviet Embassy in Pretoria? The Changing Approach to South Africa.* Tafelberg, Cape Town, 1990, p.43, Campbell K. Soviet Policy, p.43.
307. CSCD, The decisions of the CPSU Central Committee, taken by voting, 21 April 1967.
308. CSCD, Minutes of the Secretariat, N 55, item 299g, 25 July 1968.
309. Ibid. N 52, item 60g, 24 May 1968.
310. Ibid. N 53, item 40g, 6 June 1968.
311. CSCD, The decisions of the CPSU Central Committee, taken by voting, 10 September 1968.
312. Ibid. 24 July 1968.

313. *Sunday Times*, Johannesburg, 16 August 1992.

314. *African Communist*. N 132. 1993, pp. 67-69.

315. MCHP, YDC, List of members of delegations of Communist and Workers Parties, taking part in the work of the Meeting, p.16.

316. Ibid. Meeting of the delegation. 4 June 1969, p.4.

317. MCHP, ANCLonC, Report of the work of the delegation of the SACP to the International Conference of Communist and Workers' Parties. Moscow/1969, p.2.

318. MCHP, YDC, Meeting of the delegation, p.2.

319 *Mezhdunarodnoye soveshchaniye kommunisticheskih i rabochikh partii, Moskva,* 1969, (International Meeting of Communist and Workers' Parties, Moscow. 1969), Mir i Socialism, Prague, 1969, p.815.

320. The Decision of the Politbureau of the CPSU Central Committee P 135/19, 1 September 1969, referred to in: CSCD, Minutes of the Secretariat, N 103, item 24g, 20 July 1970.

321. Quoted in: *African Communist*, N 40, 1969, p.8

322. Ibid.

323. Ibid. p.9

324. Discussion with O. Tambo, Moscow, 12 February 1974.

325. Discussion with O. Tambo and A. Nzo, Moscow, 24 April 1970.

326. Ibid.

327. Ibid.

328. Discussion of R. Ulyanovsky, Deputy Head of the International Department, CPSU Central Committee, with M. Piliso, Alma-Ata, 2 October 1969.

329. Quoted in: *African Communist*, N 41, 1970, p. 69.

330. Urnov A. *South Africa Against Africa.* Progress Publishers, Moscow, 1988, p.83.

331. Discussion with O. Tambo and A. Nzo, Moscow, 24 April 1970.

332. CSCD, Minutes of the Secretariat, N 99, item 128gs, 28 May 1970.

333. MCHP, ANCLusC, The report of the Secretariat covering the last two years (1971), p.5.

334. Ibid.

335. Ibid.

336. MCHP, ANCLusC, African National Congress National Consultative Conference. President's Statement, p.19.

337. *African Communist*, N 95, 1983, p.80.

338. CSCD, Minutes of the Secretariat, N 103,N 24g, 20 July 1970.

339. *Pravda*, 18 August 1971.
340. Mabhida M. *An article for the journal "Party Life"*, (s.a.e.l.) p.7.
341. *A Survey of Race Relations in South Africa.* 1970. South African Institute of Race Relations. Johannesburg, 1971, pp. 57-63.
342. Ibid. 1969, p.10, 1970, p.14.
343. *Rand Daily Mail.* Johannesburg, 11 August 1971.
344. Quoted in: *African Communist*, N 42, 1970, p.123.
345. *Sunday Times*, Johannesburg, 2 February 1969.
346. *Southern Africa Information Service*, IDAF, London, N 11, p.449.
347. Ibid. p.452.
348. MCHP, ANCLonC. (Messages from A. Timol)
349. *Dawn*. Souvenir Issue. p.33.
350. The decision of the Politbureau of the CPSU Central Committee P 58/52 of 18 October 1967, item 1, referred to in: CSCD, Minutes of the Secretariat, N 193, item 24g, 20 July 1970.
351. CSCD, Minutes of the Secretariat, N 103, item 24g, 20 July 1970.
352. The decision of the Politbureau of the CPSU Central Committee P 183/13 of 20 October 1970 and the order of the USSR Council of Ministers 2217s of 20 October 1970, referred to in: CSCD, Minutes of the Secretariat, N 103, item 24g, 20 July 1970 as a proof of fulfilment of the latter.
353. *Dawn*. Souvenir Issue, p.43.
354. Ibid. p.33.
355. Discussion with P. Tshikare, Cape Town, 15 October 1993.
356. Discussion with S. Makana, Cape Town, 3 June 1993.
357. *Dawn*. Souvenir Issue. pp. 33-34.
358. Ibid. p.43.
359. *Izvestiya*, Moscow, 6 March 1992.
360. CSCD, Major-General V.N. Rastorguyev to V.I. Boldin, 26 December 1990.
361. *Izvestiya*, 6 March 1992.
362. Ibid.
363. *Pravda*, 11 February 1994.
364. Izvestiya, 6 March 1992.
365. *Dawn*. Souvenir Issue, p.43.
366. Pike H. *History of Communism*, p.474.
367. A brief report on the activities during the period from September 1971 - April 1974, (s.a.e.l.) p.17.
368. Archive of the SAASC.
369. *Africa Bureau Fact Sheet,* London, 1977, N 52.

370. Discussion with T. Nkobi, Moscow, 1 October 1974.

371. Discussion with O. Tambo, Moscow, 13 December 1974.

372. *Dawn*, Souvenir Issue, p.34.

373. *Rand Daily Mail*, 28 November 1975.

374. Discussion with J. Makatini, Moscow, 11 February 1976.

375. Breytenbach B. True *Confessions of an Albino Terrorist*. Faber and Faber, London, 1984. pp. 389, 62.

376. MCHP, BBC, Interview with C. Hani, Berlin, 27 May 1974.

377. Ibid. Interview with J. Slovo, typed October 1973.

378. Ibid.

379. MCHP, BBC, Interview with C. Hani.

380. Ibid. Interview with J. Slovo.

381. Ibid. Interview with O. Tambo.

382. CSCD, Minutes of the Secretariat, N 103, item 91 g, 14 July 1970.

383. CSCD, Decisions of the CPSU Central Committee Secretariat, taken by voting, 15 July 1970.

384. CSCD, Decisions of the CPSU Central Committee Secretariat, 11 April 1969.

385. MCHP, YDC, M. Kotane to Y. Dadoo, 13 January 1970.

386. MCHP, YDC, Notes of the discussions between a delegation from the C.C. of the S.A.C.P. and the N.E.C. of the A.N.C. p.2.

387. Ibid. pp. 2-3.

388. Ibid. pp. 3-4.

389 bid. p.6.

390. Ibid. p.7.

391. Ibid. pp. 7-8.

392. Ibid. p.8.

393. Ibid. p.9.

394. Ibid. pp. 9-10.

395. Ibid. p.10.

396. Ibid. p.11.

397. Ibid. p.12.

398. Ibid. p.13.

399. MCHP, ANCLonC, Aide Memoire, p 3.

400. Lerumo A. (Harmel M.). *Fifty Fighting Years. The Communist Party of South Africa. 1921-1971.* Inkululeko Publications, London, 1971, p.109.

401. CSCD, Minutes of the Secretariat, N 94, item 89g, 18 March 1970.

402. MCHP, ANCLonC, (SACP Internal Bulletin, no number)), p.14.

403. Ibid.
404. Ibid. p.13.
405. Ibid. pp. 14-15.
406. p.17.
407. MCHP, BBC, Interview with O. Tambo.
408. CSCD, Minutes of the Secretariat, N 23, item 78g, 6 February 1971.
409. Ibid. N 13, item 112g, 23 August 1971.
410. Morris M. *Terrorism,* p. 8.
411. MCHP, ANCLonC, J. Marks to Y. Dadoo, 18 July 1972.
412. *African Communist,* N 52, 1973, p.10.
413. Ibid. pp 11-12.
414. Ibid. pp. 31-32.
415. CSCD, Head of the CPSU Central Committee International Department B.N. Ponomarev's report, 17 December 1973.
416. Discussion with A, Mongalo, Johannesburg, 26 November 1993.
417. Discussion with C. Hani, Moscow. 27 April 1992.
418. *Echo,* 21 February 1990.
419. *New Nation.* 30 March - 4 April, 1990.
420. *Echo.* Op.cit.
421. Ibid.
422. *New Nation.* 30 March - 4 April, 1990.
423. *African Communist,* N 46, 1971, p.61.
424. Morris M. *Terrorism,* p.124.
425. Discussion with O. Tambo, Moscow, 12 December 1974.
426. MCHP, ANCLusC, African National Congress. National Consultative Conference. June 1985. NEC Reports. President's Statement to Conference, p.6.
427. Quoted in: Bunting B. *Moses Kotane,* p.278.
428. *Sechaba,* London, N 6-7, 1975, p.4.
429. Karis T. and Gerhart G. *Challenge and Violence.* p.661.
430. Discussion with O. Tambo, Moscow, 12 February 1974.
431. Documents of the Kabwe Conference, Lusaka, (sa) pp. 20-21.
432. Karis T. and Gerhart G. *Challenge and Violence,* p.688.
433. Discussion with O. Tambo, Moscow, 12 February 1974.
434. *A brief report,* p.6.
435. Discussion with A. Nzo, Moscow, 6 September 1973.
436. *A brief report,* p 2.
437. Ibid. p.4.
438. CSCD, Minutes of the Secretariat, N 102, item 66g, 23 October

1973, Decision of the Politbureau P 87/34g of 16 July 1973, referred to in: CSCD, Minutes of the Secretariat, N 144, item 69g, 28 October 1974, CSCD, Minutes of the Secretariat, N 151, item 52g, 11 December 1974.

439. *A brief report*, p.14.

440. Ibid. p.27.

441. Ibid. p.34.

442. *African National Congress. National Consultative Conference. President's Statement to Conference,* p.5.

443. Ibid. p.7.

444. Discussion with M.P. Naicker, Moscow, 14 April 1975.

445. Bernstein. H. *The Rift. The Exile Experience of South Africans.* London, Jonathan Cape, 1994, p.356

446. MCHP, YDC, Draft Resolution of the meeting of African Members of the ANC resident in the UK, held on 4 January 1975.

447. Joseph H. *Side by Side*, p.73.

448. Karis T. and Gerhart G. *Challenge and Violence,* p.80.

449. *Invitation and programme for unveiling of the tombstone of the late Robert M. Resha.* London.

450. *Sechaba*, 2nd Quarter 1976, pp. 40-43.

451. *African Communist*, 1976, N 65, p.20.

452. Ibid. p.36.

453. *Sudlische Afrika,* N 5, 1976.

454. Discussion with E. Mtshali, Moscow, 12 May 1976.

455. MCHP, YDC, African National Congress of SA. African Nationalists. 18th July 1977. Statement of the National Executive Committee.

456. MCHP, BBC, Interview with T. Nkobi. 21 November 1973.

457. *Sunday Times*, Johannesburg, 18 April 1976.

458. Karis T. and Gerhart G. *Challenge and Violence,* p.79.

459. Ibid. p.539.

460. Karis T. and Carter G. *From Protest to Challenge. A Documentary History of African Politics in South Africa. 1887-1964,* vol. 4. Karis T. and Gerhart G. *Political Profiles.* Goover Institution Press, Stanford, 1977, p.79.

461. *Newscheck*, Johannesburg, N 26, 1970, p.9.

462. MCHP, ANCLonC, J. Matthews to Y. Dadoo, 14 July 1971.

463. Ibid. J. Matthews to Y. Dadoo, 11 August 1971.

464. Ibid. J. Matthews to Y. Dadoo, 5 August 1972.

465. *Sunday Times*, Johannesburg, 18 April 1976.

466. *African Communist*, N 67, 1976, pp. 15-16.
467. Discussion with J. Jele, Johannesburg, 2 May 1993.

PART TWO
CHANGING BALANCE OF POWER
(1974-1985)

INDEPENDENCE FOR ANGOLA AND MOZAMBIQUE

The Soweto uprising in June 1976 proved to be a turning point in the liberation struggle in South Africa: from this moment, in a strategic sense the anti-racist forces went on the offensive. Also of major significance were the political changes in the Southern African region as a whole in the early 1970s.

After the April 1974 Portuguese revolution it became clear that independence for Mozambique and Angola was imminent. This led South African Prime Minister John Vorster to promise a dramatic revision of his policy. He called on Pretoria's critics to "give us six months or a year", and added: "They will be amazed at where we stand then."[1] At the same time, however, South Africa was pouring more and more money into its military.

The combination of South Africa's pressures and promises affected some independent African countries, especially Zambia, where the ANC had its Headquarters. Kenneth Kaunda spoke of "the voice of reason for which Africa and the whole world were waiting."[2] The Zambian leadership did not expect real change in South Africa, but hoped for Pretoria's assistance in bringing about a political settlement in Zimbabwe, something which became more promising after the changes in Mozambique. But it felt Pretoria's big stick as well: several armed attacks were carried out in Zambia by Pretoria's agents, including the parcel bomb explosion which killed the ANC Deputy Chief Representative and prominent Umkhonto commander John Dube (Adolfus Mvemve). Two other activists, including Walter Sisulu's son Max, were wounded and subsequently received treatment in the Burdenko Military Hospital in Moscow.

The ANC position in Zambia became uncertain. At the end of 1974 the ANC was requested to curtail its activities and not to undertake any actions against South Africa from Zambian soil for at least three months.

No explanation was given for these restrictions. A meeting planned between Kenneth Kaunda and Oliver Tambo was cancelled at thirty minutes' notice. The number of ANC officials at the so-called African Liberation Centre in Lusaka was cut down to six and even the right of the ANC Secretary General to stay in Lusaka was limited to not more than 90 days a year. It seemed highly likely at the time that Umkhonto members would be withdrawn from Zambia.

It was clear that the contacts of the independent African states with Pretoria aimed at achieving a settlement in Zimbabwe and Namibia were made at the expense of the ANC. The ANC's concern was made clear at its Morogoro Executive Committee meeting in March 1975. "The fascist enemy, under the smoke-screen of ... peaceful solution talks - this talk of 'development', 'co-operation', 'financial aid' and 'détente' to mention but a few of its newly found slogans, is feverishly and rapidly strengthening its defences of the status quo in our country, recruiting allies from among our own anti-imperialist ranks and moving out in a determined bid to break up or sow confusion in the international solidarity movement."[3]

The ANC Revolutionary Council, meeting a few days earlier in March, "gave a general directive to all its units to go into action." That was done "to channel the militancy of our people in the interest of our struggle for liberation and for the movement to live up to the expectations of our people who have placed boundless confidence in the African National Congress."[4]

The Revolutionary Council, with limited personnel at its disposal, created a special Sub-Committee on recruitment and training, which had "to co-ordinate its work closely with the Operations Committee" (OPCO).[5] One further significant development was occurring. Reports from South Africa indicated that "comrades have now been released [from prison and] are ready to work regardless of the consequences." The Revolutionary Council resolved to "establish and maintain contacts with them" as well as to "look into the question of their support and welfare."[6]

The OAU Council of Ministers session in Dar es Salaam in April 1975 was crucial. Much depended on the direction to be decided upon. The ANC had good reason to be worried. Vorster himself had declared: "The forthcoming OAU conference in Dar es Salaam could influence the course of events in Africa for a long time to come."[7] But the ANC was well prepared. To counter the campaign for so-called dialogue with Pretoria, the ANC broadened its contacts with a number of African states, including those which were already talking to Pretoria. (When Alfred Nzo visited Monrovia the Liberian officials pointed out that he was sitting in the same armchair that Vorster had sat in some months earlier.)

The ANC drafted a special declaration criticising the covert contacts with the Pretoria regime and giving notice of its intention to declare the Pretoria regime a product of colonial plunder, whose independence, sovereignty and membership of the United Nations were a violation of the principles of the UN Charter.[8]

The ANC position at the meeting was strengthened by Julius Nyerere, President of the host country Tanzania. In his opening speech he made the point that the OAU meeting had been convened not to discuss so-called dialogue with Pretoria, but to promote the liberation of South Africa, following the successes in Angola and Mozambique.[9] The results of the session could not have been better for the ANC. The sovereignty of the liberation movements was endorsed as well as their right to choose their own forms of struggle. The OAU role was to support this struggle, not to make decisions for the liberation movements.[10]

The ANC expected that the situation would change in its favour as soon as Mozambique and Angola were independent, though it was ready to exercise restraint (at least initially) in using these territories. On 18 September 1974, immediately after the installation of the Transitional Government in Mozambique, its head, Prime Minister Joachim Chissano, stated that Frelimo did not want to start a new war and did not pretend to be a reformer of South African policy: "This job belongs to the people of South Africa."[11]

But the very fact of the creation of a government headed by a liberation movement on South Africa's doorstep had a great impact. The student rallies in September 1974 were not simply an expression of solidarity with Frelimo but an affirmation that the new state would be born as a result of revolutionary struggle. This helped people realise the need to participate actively in the struggle, to create illegal structures, rather than to wait passively for the arrival of "liberators". The ANC leadership even became concerned that spontaneity and impatience could provoke massive state retaliation if the organisational work was not done in time and properly.

The changes in Mozambique helped the ANC to establish direct contact with the Swaziland authorities. King Sobhuza II was strongly sympathetic to the ANC, and, in fact, he considered himself a lifetime member (his uncle and regent had participated in the Inaugural Conference of the ANC in 1912). Initially Thabo Mbeki and Max Sisulu participated in a UN-sponsored meeting in Swaziland, and soon Mbeki became the ANC's informal representative there.

The presence of ANC representatives in Swaziland was one of the issues raised by my Mozambican hosts when I visited Maputo (then still called Lourenco Marques) in April-May 1975. Pretoria was shocked by the developments in Mozambique, which included Soviets travelling there. When I switched on Radio South Africa one morning, there were three main news items: the communist capture of Saigon, the visit of a top-ranking delegation from Moscow to Lourenco Marques, and a South African sportswoman refused the right to participate in a competition somewhere in Latin America. Switching over to the local Mozambican radio brought a further surprise: the Internationale in Russian.

At the Mozambique independence ceremony on 25 June 1975, support for the ANC was expressed openly and strongly, and the ANC delegation was warmly welcomed. It was headed by Oliver Tambo, and included Joe Modise among other Executive members. On the day of the delegation's departure, thousands of Mozambicans came to see the visitors off, chanting "Viva ANC" and carrying banners that read: "ANC = Frelimo".

Thousands of South Africans tried to visit the Mozambican capital, and the Frelimo leadership was forced to close the border for fear of provocation.[12] The ANC members and its supporters inside South Africa were inspired by the words of Samora Machel, who introduced Oliver Tambo as his friend, his comrade, and his brother in arms, and declared that "the Mozambican people and the People's Republic of Mozambique under the leadership of Frelimo will always assume their duty of solidarity with the interests of the South African masses and of all mankind, whatever difficulties they may face."[13] Machel could hardly have imagined the difficulties the newly born state was soon to encounter.

The ANC leadership was perfectly aware of the need to be extremely cautious in Mozambique, especially now that Pretoria was doing all it could to monitor the ANC presence in neighbouring countries. The most the ANC could hope for was a free passage through Mozambican territory, not directly to South Africa, but to Swaziland. Apart from this, an ANC office was established, at best semi-official. It was kept busy sorting out the people who were coming to Mozambique from South Africa in an attempt to contact the ANC.

The ANC's relations with the other countries of the region also began to improve. The first clear signs of a change in the Lesotho government's attitude was the ceremony at which the OAU prize was presented to Albert Luthuli's widow in Maseru in the presence of the

ANC representative. But in 1975 the ANC had to contend with the detention and manhandling of Chris Hani and his assistants by the Lesotho security services. By that time Hani was actively engaged in creating underground structures inside South Africa. "We started by making individual contacts," he recalled later. "We had undergone a course in the Soviet Union on the principles of forming an underground movement, that was our training: the formation of the underground movement, then the building of guerrilla detachments. The Soviets put a lot of emphasis on the building of these underground structures, comprising at the beginning very few people."[14]

Finance for the needs of the underground machinery in Lesotho and for the needs of the emerging structures inside South Africa was supplied, particularly by transactions through Canada to "H. Timbisile", facilitated by Yusuf Saloojee, who lived in Canada.[15] (The alteration to Chris's real name was intended to confuse those who might monitor transactions.)

But the Lesotho authorities suspected that the money at Hani's disposal was intended for the opposition Basutoland Congress Party. Also, the then Foreign Minister C D Molapo complained to the ANC that Hani and his comrades used forged Lesotho papers. Hani later admitted that this was so, and asked, "But how else could we ensure transportation of ANC recruits from Lesotho to outside?"[16]

The danger of deportation to South Africa was averted and the ANC secured Hani's right to stay in Lesotho. Later, with relations between the government and the ANC further improved, he even became its official representative in Maseru. When the first Soviet delegation of the Afro-Asian Solidarity Committee, including Andrei Urnov of the CPSU International Department, visited Maseru in 1980, its members were pleasantly surprised when the Lesotho officials on their own initiative organised a meeting with Hani.

ANC contacts with Swaziland also developed successfully, especially after a secret visit by Oliver Tambo later in 1975. But the situation there was more difficult. While the King himself was very friendly, many officials of the Prime Minister's office did not share his sympathy with the liberation movement. This created a host of problems, including the detention of Thabo Mbeki. A very important role in building ANC structures in Swaziland and, through Swaziland, in South Africa itself was played by Stanley Mabizela, who lived there for many years. (Mabizela is currently South African High Commissioner in Namibia.)

Interest in the ANC was also developing in other regions and other continents. In 1975 an ANC delegation composed of Oliver Tambo and Johnny Makatini visited China at the invitation of the Chinese Association for Friendship with Foreign Countries. Some assistance, both financial and military, was promised to the ANC. However, the circumstances of the visit raised some criticism in ANC ranks. At the time the Chinese would not welcome SACP members as their guests, and so insisted on the right to veto the composition of the delegation. Beijing's support of FNLA and UNITA in the conflict in Angola further hampered relations with the ANC.

A significant victory for ANC diplomacy was the refusal of the United Nations General Assembly in 1974 (under the chairmanship of the Algerian Foreign Minister) to recognise the credentials of the South African government delegation.

All these developments as well as South Africa's internal situation were discussed in Moscow in August 1975 when a group of top ANC and SACP leaders, including Tambo, Nzo, Dadoo, Nkobi, Slovo, Mabhida and Modise, visited to mark Moses Kotane's 70th birthday. All hope of recovery by now lost, the CPSU's message to Kotane was not as optimistic as its previous message. Instead, it looked back on his life: "The example of many years of your fruitful activity convincingly testify that the communists carry out selfless struggle together with the democratic forces of Africa."[17]

In their discussions in Moscow the South Africans emphasised that the rapid changes in Southern Africa which followed the Portuguese revolution had caught Pretoria unprepared. In trying to adapt to the situation, the regime had made some small concessions such as the removal of so-called "petty apartheid" legislation. An important new development was that many workers and students, former supporters of the Black Consciousness Movement, were now finding a new home in the ANC. The freeing of a number of political prisoners who had completed sentences imposed in the early 1960s had presented new opportunities for building the ANC underground.

Perhaps for the first time since Rivonia opportunities (that were real and not imaginary) arose for relaunching Umkhonto operations inside South Africa. These plans were discussed at the ANC National Executive meeting in December 1975. Oliver Tambo, while exhorting the military structures to carry the struggle forward, at the same time demanded proper preparation to avoid failures that would be demoralising. He underlined the need to start military operations in the

163

heart of South African territory, far away from the Mozambican border. Also, training centres were urgently needed to accommodate new recruits.

The discussions were dominated by the situation in Angola. Even the anticipated actions by Umkhonto inside South Africa were seen as indirect support for the MPLA, distracting Pretoria's attention away from Angola. An ANC Statement on 31 October 1975 condemned South Africa's covert and later open aggression against Angola, actions intended to prevent the MPLA from coming to power and to ensure the installation of a government friendly to Pretoria.[18] In the opinion of Oliver Tambo, Pretoria intervened in Angola not only to protect its buffer zone but also to use its "assistance in the struggle against communism" to mobilise support from international imperialism and to demoralise the opposition in South Africa.[19]

The ANC and MPLA had a good relationship from the early 1960s and as soon as the MPLA created legal structures inside Angola, the ANC initiated contact with them. An ANC delegation was sent to Luanda to participate in the commemoration of the anniversary of the armed struggle on 4 February 1975, the day when Agostinho Neto returned triumphant to Luanda. Another delegation, headed by Alfred Nzo, was supposed to be present at the Independence Day celebration in November, but travel arrangements could not be made in time. ANC Executive Committee member Josiah Jele was in Luanda during the festivities as a member of an international delegation.

Measures to support Angola were also discussed at the SACP Central Committee meeting late in 1975 in Moscow.[20] After the session the SACP delegation met Boris Ponomarev.[21] At this meeting, possibly for the first and last time, the Soviet side intervened in the practical activities of the South African liberation movement. Deeply concerned about South Africa's aggression in Angola, Ponomarev asked if the SACP and the ANC were able to render practical support to the MPLA, such as sending an Umkhonto contingent to participate in actions against the SADF. This question, though apparently unexpected, received a positive response from both the SACP and, later, from the ANC. However, in practical terms the existing Umkhonto core was too small to make more than a token contribution to the actual fighting in Angola.

Nevertheless, this overture by Moscow encouraged the ANC to pursue its contacts with Luanda. In January 1976, Moses Mabhida, then Secretary of the Revolutionary Council, was sent to Angola as a special envoy. Earlier, at the end of 1975, several ANC members were dispatched to assist the Angolans in the interrogation of South African prisoners of war.

The growing demands for material assistance, including military hardware, in a situation where the changes in Angola and in Mozambique were favourable to the ANC, led to an ANC delegation, headed by Alfred Nzo, visiting Moscow in January-February 1976. The purpose was not just "to discuss inter-party relations", as in previous years, but also to seek military assistance.[22] More discussions followed when Oliver Tambo came to Moscow to participate in the Soviet Communist Party Congress at the end of February.

The ANC played a very active role in the international campaign in support of the MPLA and the People's Republic of Angola, particularly in organising an International Solidarity Conference in Luanda on 4 February 1976. This was done on the initiative of the AAPSO. By that time the direct threat of an attack by South African and Zairean troops against the Angolan capital had been rebuffed, but military actions continued in many areas of the country.

Johnny Makatini headed the ANC delegation to the Luanda conference. In fact its journey was a lesson in "political geography": delegates from Lusaka had to go via Dar es Salaam to Moscow by Aeroflot, the Soviet Airline, then to Berlin and further to Luanda by Interflug plane, chartered by the GDR Solidarity Committee. The problem was that, at that stage, the Zambian government sided with UNITA and no direct connection between Luanda and Lusaka existed. En route he visited Moscow, and I met him. It was the start of a long friendship with this charismatic and independent-thinking leader of the ANC. I was to have many more meetings with him, and every discussion was productive, whether it concerned the formation of an ANC cultural group (well before the famous Amandla was founded), or the methods of the armed struggle inside South Africa.

Makatini believed that, having acted as the aggressor in Angola, Pretoria had forfeited its claim to the role of peace-maker in the Southern African region. A situation, therefore, that had been fraught with danger for the ANC when even its main allies in Africa, especially Zambia, started to call for détente with Pretoria, was no more.[23]

However, for a short period at the end of 1975 and the beginning of 1976 the ANC position in Lusaka had been far from secure. Its support for Luanda met with a hostile reaction from the Zambian government, who at that time supported UNITA. They demanded from the ANC information regarding all its members currently in Zambia. In the opinion of the ANC leadership, since Lusaka had become a "nest" for the South African intelligence, this information could find its way to Pretoria. To describe the situation as peculiar is understating the case: the ANC Headquarters located in a country whose government had, in the Angolan conflict, virtually sided with the ANC's arch-enemy, the Pretoria regime. As a consequence some practical difficulties ensued. The ANC "Radio Freedom" broadcasts from Lusaka were suspended, and ANC activists were put under surveillance by Zambian security.

The failure of the South African intervention in Angola brought about the changes anticipated by Makatini. The ANC was now in a better position, particularly at the OAU Liberation Committee meeting on 19-20 January 1976, to request military assistance from the African countries. The need for this was evident after the SADF intervention in Angola.[24] Military actions inside South Africa planned by the ANC were now regarded as an important contribution to the liberation of Namibia and Zimbabwe as well.

After the events in Angola, Africa took a much more positive view of the international position of the ANC and, in particular, its ties with the USSR. The Angolan government naturally saw the ANC as its ally in struggle against present and possible future South African intervention. It expressed its readiness to host an ANC office (initially it even proposed the premises of the former South African Consulate). Mutual co-operation got under way in a number of fields, including the organisation of the military training of Umkhonto cadres.

From the very beginning the ANC and Umkhonto leadership wanted training to be organised independently of the Liberation Committee, a position well understood by the Angolans. The MPLA, too, had had its share of troubles from the Committee (particularly when some of the Committee members tried to impose unity with the FNLA and sided with malcontents inside the MPLA). An ANC training camp was set up, followed by a transit camp. By February 1976 it was clear that Angola could become a reliable base, and the ANC leadership took a decision that Umkhonto fighters would be trained in Angola, and that only specialised and advanced courses would be organised in the USSR and other friendly countries. This was successfully implemented.[25]

While giving the ANC a virtually free hand in organising the training, the Angolan leadership was not in a position to provide solid material support. It advised the ANC to approach the Socialist

166

countries for arms and other military equipment and provisions. This was extremely urgent: the recruits expected in Angola had to be immediately and properly cared for. Practical difficulties were considerable. Things had developed rapidly in Angola, and this had not been foreseen by the ANC. Some supplies from the USSR, previously requested and sent to the ANC in Tanzania and independent Mozambique, had to be re-routed to Angola. To speed up the deliveries, the ANC leadership appealed direct to the Soviet Afro-Asian Solidarity Committee, rather than using the usual government channels, which were reliable but somewhat slow. They urgently requested that all the necessary equipment for 400 trainees – from binoculars to socks and shoes – be sent to Angola.[26]

During his visit to Moscow Oliver Tambo not only described the situation as promising, but indicated that, as a result of previous Soviet support, "desperation had not broken our people. Even when our struggle was forgotten, the initiatives, in particular by the Soviet Afro-Asian Solidarity Committee, helped to keep some focus on the South African situation."[27]

At the end of the same month, in March 1976, when the SADF was leaving Angolan territory in disgrace, Tambo himself visited the country, including its southern region. In an interview with *Sechaba* he identified one specific feature of the Angolan Army which made it different from many other African armies: "The significant aspect of the MPLA [and Cuban for that matter] forces which defeated the racists is that they are not divided racially according to whether the person is white, brown or black – they are simply Angolans. This is the kind of South Africa we are going to have."[28]

THE 1976 SOWETO UPRISING

Apart from the military setback, Pretoria's failure in Angola had a major psychological impact in South Africa. For many blacks the SADF ceased to be regarded as invincible, and a considerable number of whites openly criticised the intervention. The economic situation in the country deteriorated too: the world economic crisis of the mid 1970s, provoked by the oil price rise after the Arab-Israeli war of 1973, hit South Africa hard. Pretoria's debacle resulted in a new militancy among South African blacks, especially the youth. One reflection of this was the campaign of resistance against Afrikaans as a medium of instruction in all so-called Bantu Education Department schools, culminating in the famous Soweto uprising, which started on 16 June 1976.

The events of 1976 are well covered in a number of books such as *Whirlwind before the Storm* by Alan Brooks and Jeremy Brickhill.[29] So I will try to answer just one question: What role did the ANC play in the June events and in the unfolding developments?

From the outset Pretoria's propaganda levelled various accusations against the ANC, but these charges contradicted one other. On the one hand, they tried to prove that the ANC forced school children to face police bullets. The National Party MP Hennie van der Walt, for example, stated: "Communists abroad have been planning the Soweto riots through local agitators for two years." He further claimed that "the African National Congress, the Black People's Convention and SASO had turned Black Nationalism into Black Power and Black Power is an agent of international communism."[30]. But, on the other hand, the same propaganda machinery tried to present the unrest as purely accidental.

The events in Soweto represented, as Chris Hani was to put it later, "a spontaneous outbreak of anger and frustration" and the ANC underground structures "were not responsible for it."[31] However, they did contribute to it. Presenting an Organisational Report on behalf of the National Executive Committee to the ANC Consultative Conference in 1985, Alfred Nzo said: "Our political underground, though small had taken a palpable role, and its influence – by means of direct organisation, propaganda etc. – was clearly manifest within the workers' and students' movements." He stressed the role of "a few leading cadres and stalwarts within the country, many of them ex-Robben Islanders, who, in liaison with External Mission, revived the underground network."[32]

On the eve of the uprising the South African authorities began a propaganda campaign, claiming that the ANC underground had been destroyed. On 14 May 1976 the trial of ex-political prisoner and SACP veteran Harry Gwala and nine other ANC members started in Pietermaritzburg. It was no accident that six of the accused were ex-Robben Island prisoners. The trial continued for a year, followed by other trials of ANC members as well as BCM activists. The public galleries at all the trials were packed: the psychological intimidation of the mid 1960s was no longer effective. While the damage to the ANC structures, especially in Natal, that resulted from the arrest and sentencing of Harry Gwala and his comrades was extensive, the government actions again boomeranged.

Hani confirmed that the ANC structures in the underground were rather limited at this time and were controlled from outside, particularly from Maseru.[33] But their work inside the country was supplemented with increasing effectiveness by the broad political work outside South Africa – by meetings with South Africans, who were legally visiting Britain and other foreign countries, broadcasts by Radio Freedom, and international solidarity campaigns. In addition, ANC announcers worked and broadcast for Radio Moscow and Radio Berlin International. By the end of 1974 ANC political material was being sent regularly to over 500 addresses inside South Africa.[34]

After the Soweto massacre the ANC put out a new slogan: "Don't mourn! Mobilise!" The ANC underground paper *Amandla-Matla* called on the youth to join Umkhonto, to study the art of guerrilla warfare. It advised against actions involving a large number of activists but enjoined the new recruits to strike at the enemy in small groups.[35]

Pretoria's "dirty tricks department", in an attempt to discredit the ANC, printed strong "anti-Western" and "pro-Communist" statements under forged ANC letterheads. Some supposedly independent academics were used as "agents of influence" and as sources of information and advice by government agencies.

For many years the Pretoria propagandists had tried to play down the importance of the ANC and its influence in South African political life. *The Communist Strategy*, the brainchild of the Department of Information published in 1975, claimed: "The leaders of the African National Congress were never the leaders of the people and the organisation was never a truly 'national' one, as its name implies, but developments within South Africa in the past 10 years have stripped the ANC of any pretence it had of representing anyone in South Africa."[36]

Initially Pretoria tried to follow the same line after Soweto. Paul (Jimmy) Kruger, Minister of Justice and Prisons, claimed in August 1976 that "the ANC Secretary General [sic] Oliver Tambo" tried in vain to recruit the youth.[37] But very soon their language changed. In July 1977 the Commissioner of Police stated that "black unrest" in the previous year "brought a considerable number of recruits into the terrorist movements."[38] Pretoria started complaining that black youths, smuggled out of the country for training in terrorist warfare, were returning to South Africa to commit acts of terrorism, using strategy and tactics similar to that uncovered in the Rivonia trial.

The developments which followed the Soweto uprising confirmed the validity of Oliver Tambo's statement, made in Algiers on 6 August 1976, that the situation in South Africa was ripe for the resumption of armed operations and that the confrontation between the people and the oppressors would undoubtedly grow.[39]

DEALING WITH THE EXODUS

The Soweto uprising radically changed the situation in South Africa. For the first time in a decade and a half the government was faced with mass resistance. The conditions were now favourable for launching and sustaining armed resistance.

For the armed struggle to be effective, there were two major prerequisites. Firstly, it was necessary to establish a relevant political presence inside South Africa which could capitalise on the mood of young people no longer cowed by guns or ruled by fear. Secondly, it was imperative to organise proper training for hundreds (and later thousands) of young South Africans who left the country.

Tom Lodge is of the view that the ability of the "nationalistic and revolutionary" organisations "to affect the course of black resistance in South Africa in the dramatically altered conditions of the late 1970s was more a result of the extent to which they had succeeded in overcoming the inherent difficulties of the exile environment than their relative degree of influence within the country at the point when internal circumstances began to change in their favour."[40] This statement is only partially correct. Naturally, the ability of organisations to deal with the exodus of black youth, yearning to be trained and to come back to fight the regime, was extremely important. But the ability of the exiled groups to cope was to a large extent conditioned by the capacity of these organisations to obtain external support for training programmes from African and other countries. This support in turn depended both on the historical record of the organisations and their actual or potential influence inside the country.

In responding to the dramatic developments in the sub-continent, Oliver Tambo had posed a critical question to the ANC in 1975: "Do we belong to the past? Are we properly marching with the time?"[41] Even before the Soweto uprisings, it was becoming clear that the political expectations of the oppressed in South Africa were rising rapidly. The situation inside South Africa resembled in many respects that of the early 1960s. When deciding on the formation of Umkhonto the ANC leaders had to take into consideration the fact that unless they acted swiftly other more extremist forces could capture the moment. They were again worried that the emerging situation "could be used by somebody else, who would ignite the fire."

There was a real danger of a "third force" coming into the equation. Johnny Makatini told us in Moscow in February 1976 that he was particularly worried about the possibility of adventurist actions by the PAC leadership. He feared that having been discredited by co-operating with the FNLA in the Angolan conflict, the PAC might try to retrieve lost ground (with the assistance, ironically, of the Ugandan dictator Idi Amin). Under an agreement with the Basutoland Congress Party, the PAC had at that stage already sent several groups of Lesotho PAC supporters to Uganda and Libya for military training.[(42)]

The logistical problems faced by the ANC leadership were enormous. Within weeks of the Soweto events, and with very limited resources, the ANC was required to charter planes to transport first 100 and later another 300 recruits to Luanda. By the end of July 1976 the ANC was already accommodating several hundred young people from within South Africa. Strenuous efforts were necessary to place them either in Umkhonto or (for the minority who preferred to continue their academic studies) in training institutions in Africa or overseas.

The problems in dealing with the new wave of recruits were perhaps more daunting than those experienced at the beginning of the armed struggle in the early 1960s. Then the people leaving the country were as a rule operating under the aegis of the ANC, Sactu or the SACP. This time the exodus was much more spontaneous. This resulted in a myriad of problems, such as a relative lack of commitment to the ANC, poor discipline, as well as errors in selection for the various kinds of training available.

After Soweto many students fled South Africa without proper education certificates. This was understandable, given the conditions at the time. However, in practice it afforded the opportunity for some students arbitrarily and unscrupulously to upgrade their education levels or qualifications. Taken together with the prevailing low "Bantu Education" standards and the cultural shock accompanying the flight into exile, such opportunism led to what one ANC figure described as "heavy losses".

At this stage assistance from the Soviet Union was invaluable to the ANC. Dozens of recruits wanting to pursue the academic route were sent to the USSR. Almost half of them did not complete their courses of study, either because of academic failure or because of violations of discipline.

The situation within the South African student community was a cause of concern to the ANC leadership. In a letter to the Secretary of the Students Union in the USSR, Alfred Nzo deplored the fact that some students were abandoning any commitment to the ANC as soon as they reached their places of study. He warned of harsh measures, including the withdrawal of scholarships.[43]

It is worth noting in passing that, although the ANC did not regard itself as a political party in those days, it was often referred to as such in the Soviet press and sometimes even in official documents[44]. Under the one-party system in the USSR, the word "party" usually meant "the Communist Party" to the Soviets. As a result there was often confusion. Officials would report, for example, that "six members of the SACP" were studying in Odessa, when all of them were, in fact, ANC members and none belonged to the SACP.

During one of his visits to Moscow Oliver Tambo called the post-1976 group of students a "non-typical" generation of ANC cadres. They had been in ANC ranks for too short a time to be sufficiently disciplined. But he expected the situation to improve when the first students emerged from the new school established by the ANC in Tanzania.[45]

In 1977 the government of Tanzania granted to the ANC about 600 acres in the area of Morogoro for this purpose. Opened in 1979, the school was named the Solomon Mahlangu Freedom College (SOMAFCO) in honour of a slain guerrilla. Designed to admit some 300 pupils into the primary division and some 400 into the secondary school, SOMAFCO became an important centre in the ANC's exile network. Later a vocational training centre was set up in nearby Dakawa.[46]

There were also problems in the military training programmes in the Soviet Union at this time. ANC Headquarters was sometimes prone to dispatch for training people it was itself unable to accommodate. For example, some cadres sent for sophisticated courses in the "Northern Training Centre" (intended for the best Umkhonto cadres) fell far below the standard expected, especially in respect of discipline. For years a story was told in that Centre about the peculiar way a graduate expressed his gratitude to the instructors at a farewell party. They could hardly believe their ears when he said, "Thank you, comrades. Now we know how to rob a bank."

The recruits from South Africa had one significant advantage over members of some other liberation movements. They generally had a reasonable knowledge of English, which obviated the need for "double translation". When I went to tropical Africa for the first time in 1967, our mission was to bring Frelimo fighters from Dar es Salaam to Simferopol, and I will never forget how on the long journey to the USSR some Frelimo cadres were reading big-lettered ABC books in Portuguese. In these cases it was often very difficult for Soviet instructors to communicate effectively.

Obviously, apart from the logistical problems of accommodating new recruits, the ANC also needed to provide a psychological and organisational sanctuary if it was to become a permanent home for them. Various means were used to influence the new exiles politically. These included the distribution of ANC literature, greater emphasis on political education and lectures on ANC history, and visits by leaders to the places where they were based. Soviet assistance in this respect was channelled mainly through the Committee of the Youth Organisations and the Students' Council (virtually the International Department of the Komsomol). In August 1977 this body helped the ANC organise a student summer school in Moscow. This was the first conference to bring together exiled South African students.

The exodus after Soweto, therefore, both stimulated and severely taxed the ANC, and the first generation of Umkhonto cadres were called on to play the role of "elder brothers and uncles". As Oliver Tambo put it, "Had it not been for the steadfast commitment and loyalty of these comrades to our organisation and our revolution, there might very well have been no ANC to join when the young poured out of the country after the Soweto uprising."[47]

Newly released political prisoners, who had spent a decade or more on Robben Island, also played an important part in strengthening ANC structures both inside and outside South Africa during the mid 1970s. One of these people was Andrew Masondo. After being freed and banished to a remote area, Masondo managed to establish contacts with the ANC leadership and left the country soon after the start of the Soweto uprising. In October 1976 he was already in Moscow. After a short rest he started a course of specialised military training.

Edward Delinga (Masondo's *nom de guerre*) had to undergo his own "crash course", to make up for the twelve years he had missed while in prison. In the evenings, after his studies were over, he would often come to Kropotkinskaya 10 – the premises of the Soviet Solidarity Committee – to seek out literature, to talk about issues and to become acquainted with the previous decade's world events. It was interesting for us to meet with him because he was the first South African in many years to come to Moscow straight from inside the country and, in fact, from the very place where the ANC leaders were incarcerated.

After his time in Moscow Masondo was appointed the National Commissar of the ANC. In 1977 he was elected to the ANC Executive, together with two other recently released political prisoners, trade unionists Steven Dlamini and John Nkadimeng (who is now the South African Ambassador to Cuba). Joe Modise, the head of Umkhonto, Masondo and Mziwandile Piliso played a very important role in reorganising and rapidly expanding the ANC's military structures. Piliso, for several years Head of the Department of Personnel and Training, was able to draw on the military training he received in the USSR in the early 1970s.

At the same time as a new leadership was emerging, some of the old ANC cadres were departing. M P Naicker died suddenly on 29 April 1977. Comrade M P was at that stage Head of Publicity for the ANC External Mission and editor of *Sechaba*. Ronnie Kasrils (his pen name was A N C Kumalo) wrote fondly in a "Farewell to M P": "It was as natural and sweet as mountain water to call him *qabane* [comrade] and *mfowetu* [brother], as natural as it was for him to place a friendly arm around our shoulders and join in our joyous round of songs."[48]

It was difficult to find a more warm-hearted person than M P. Easy to communicate with, he was at the same time a popular and somewhat controversial figure in the ANC and the SACP. At the Rivonia trial in 1964 Bruno Mtolo (state witness "Mr X") claimed that "suspicions had been expressed" about Naicker. Though Nelson Mandela said he did not have "any recollections" of this,[49] a cloud of doubt followed Naicker into exile. Limitations were imposed on his role in the SACP leadership, something about which he was particularly bitter.

It was Naicker who was the first to draw my attention to the Black Consciousness Movement, assessing it more positively than did most of the ANC leaders at that time. M P was terribly homesick. After one long friendly dinner in Moscow he virtually begged his Soviet friends to help him reach Natal; he was sure he could survive and operate on his home turf. He was deeply proud of South Africa and everything it produced. "When you come to London next time," he told me during his last visit to Moscow in the autumn of 1976, "I will violate the boycott and buy a bottle of KWV brandy."

When the telephone rang in my flat and the recognisable delayed-clicktones of an international call brought Yusuf Dadoo on the line from London, I was shocked to hear him say, "Bad news. Please, find

Prem [M P's son who was studying medicine in Moscow]. MP died on his way from London to Berlin."

This period witnessed the resumption of Umkhonto actions at home. Towards the end of 1975 and at the beginning of 1976, one or two sabotage actions were carried out.[50] However, regular infiltration of Umkhonto cadres into South Africa started later, after Soweto.

The most publicised event was an explosion in the well-known Carlton Centre in the heart of the Johannesburg business district. The target was civilian, violating ANC rules. We were told by ANC people that the decision to act in this way had been taken on the spot by the fighters themselves. Although they were operating successfully in the area, blowing up railways and disrupting traffic, there had been no reports of these actions in the media. The fighters decided to do something "spectacular", and indeed when the Carlton Centre was targeted a great deal of publicity resulted. Another feature of this period was the execution of notorious policemen as well as traitors who had crossed over to the regime's side.

These actions helped consolidate what was later referred to as the phase of "armed propaganda" in the ANC's struggle. Its primary objective was "to announce once again the presence of MK in the only way the army announces its presence: action."[51] Step by step the Umkhonto fighters and underground activists mastered the art of taking on an experienced, highly trained and vicious enemy, while paying a high price for each mistake. For example, by 1978 it had apparently become routine procedure on the South African side of the Lesotho border to speak to Africans crossing the border in the specific language which their papers indicated they could speak. Activists trying to cross the border using forged Lesotho passports but unable to speak Sesotho found themselves arrested.[52]

After the ANC re-launched its armed actions inside the country, the South African authorities tried to dismiss them as insignificant failures. A triumphant Minister of Police, Jimmy Kruger, waved "a Czech-made gun" at MPs on 24 January 1977 and "elatedly told the assembly: Urban terrorism is totally finished."[53] But eight months later the selfsame Jimmy Kruger was warning the public "to be very cautious, because the terrorists are returning to the country in big numbers."[54] The chief of the Security Police, Brigadier Zietsman, estimated in June 1978 that 4 000 people were "currently undergoing training outside South Africa as 'terrorists', and that 75 per cent of them had been recruited by the ANC."[55] In reality, the percentage of

176

those joining the ANC was higher. For example, of the first 500 South Africans who arrived in Tanzania via Botswana and Swaziland in June-December 1976, 400 joined the ANC. In addition, some of those who initially joined the PAC later crossed over to the ANC.

Even if the direct adversaries of the regime during the so-called disturbances in 1976-7 were mainly young people supporting the Black Consciousness Movement, Pretoria understood that the ANC was its main enemy. On the eve of the banning on 19 October 1977 of 17 opposition organisations, mostly BCM-inclined, Kruger said: "The Black Consciousness Movement in South Africa has turned into the black power movement which has been infiltrated by members of the ANC."[56]

There clearly was an inter-connection between the ANC and the BCM, though the level of this still needs to be ascertained. The involvement in ANC activities of Nkosasana Dlamini, Vice President of the South African Students Organisation, provided one example of this. Dlamini, who as Dr Nkosasana Zuma became Minister of Health in South Africa's first democratically elected government in 1994, was in contact with the ANC inside the country and was part of the ANC delegation to the Emergency International Conference Against Apartheid held in Addis-Ababa on 30-31 October 1976.

Oliver Tambo claimed that by 1976 the ANC "arrived at the point where the time had come for us to meet the leading representative of the BCM, the late Steve Biko." According to Tambo, Biko and his colleagues recognised that the ANC was the leader of the revolution and that they should function "within the context of the broad strategy of our movement." But the attempts "to bring Steve out of the country failed."[57]

In July 1977, shortly before the death of Biko and the banning of the next generation of resistance groups, the National Executive Committee of the ANC met in Lusaka for ten days to discuss the unfolding events in South Africa and the prospects for its own armed struggle. Surprisingly, this was the first time the NEC had held this kind of meeting since the Soweto uprising the year before. The NEC concluded that the Military Command had outpaced political organisation at home. Umkhonto cadres often acted independently of the political underground. It was decided to establish "flying squads" which could penetrate South Africa, attack and then return to the "forward areas", that is, the countries adjacent to South Africa. Most of these began to operate in the Transvaal, with some in Natal and in the Cape.

SOWETO INFLUENCES INTERNATIONAL DEVELOPMENTS

The Soweto uprising significantly influenced international attitudes towards South Africa, and the ANC in particular. In order to capitalise on the rising political temperature at home and on the independence of Mozambique and Angola, the ANC made it a priority to improve relations with countries bordering South Africa. But some of South Africa's neighbours were either vulnerable to pressure by the regime or unsympathetic to the ANC. While the organisation could count on Mozambique as a rear base, and was expecting the newly independent Angola to become a firm ally, it could not rely on countries like Zambia and Swaziland for the support it sought. ANC activities there had been paralysed.

In Swaziland South African special services kidnapped several people. Efforts to organise the recruitment and screening of cadres from South Africa were being hindered both in Swaziland and in other neighbouring countries by pressure from the South African regime and the host countries.

Although long dependent on Zambia, the ANC could not count on it. Certain ANC members were refused entry to Zambia even when they had valid visas. The situation there improved slightly towards the end of 1976 when leading Zambian officials met with the ANC. They agreed to the continued presence of the ANC in Zambia and requested the organisation not to make public the harassment experienced by ANC members. Nonetheless, it remained unclear whether the ANC Headquarters could remain in Lusaka. In practice, the ANC leadership was to a large extent locating itself in Luanda, where the Revolutionary Council had established its Headquarters.[58]

Countries such as Botswana and Lesotho were more positive. Lesotho Prime Minister Leabua Jonathan personally promised some assistance to the ANC.[59] The American-African Dialogue conference held in Maseru in 1976 provided an opportunity for the ANC leadership to liaise directly with the Lesotho government and its cadres there. The flight to Lesotho over South African territory required some courage on the part of Alfred Nzo, who represented the ANC at the meeting, but one of the benefits was that he was able to meet on four consecutive days with the ANC group in Maseru led by Chris Hani.

The dialogue in Maseru once again showed the desire of the US government and its agencies to find an alternative to the ANC in South Africa. Attempts were made there to introduce bantustan leaders as international figures, and, when this failed, the Black Consciousness Movement was put forward, once again without success.[60].

In Botswana, too, the government was more sympathetic towards the ANC. Although the ANC had to operate covertly for many years, the authorities turned a blind eye, their attitude being: "Do what you want but don't put the country in danger."[61]

The relationships with the governments of the Front Line States was part of a broader network of international activities and alliances pursued by the ANC. Apart from sending groups of selected cadres to South Africa, it once again involved its fighters in conflicts in other countries of the sub-continent. Joshua Nkomo's wing of the Zimbabwe Patriotic Front (ZAPU) agreed to the participation of Umkhonto cadres in its operations in the Matabeleland region of south-western Zimbabwe. ANC instructors also helped train ZAPU cadres in Angola, where both organisations had established bases, as, too, had SWAPO. ANC fighters were now mainly deployed in guarding actions in Southern Angola by the Angolan army.

The above activities were, in turn, part of a broader network of international alliances. For example, after the victory of the Vietnamese patriots in 1975, the ANC leadership closely assessed the international solidarity movement with the Vietnamese people in the 1960s and the first half of the 1970s, and tried to win over those solidarity groups to the South African cause. Previously, this had been a rather difficult task because the impression had been gained that "nothing was happening" in South Africa.[62] But after the independence of Mozambique and Angola and, especially, after the Soweto uprising, international solidarity increased significantly. The Emergency International Anti-Apartheid Conference held in Addis Ababa in October 1976 was particularly important in this respect. It helped the anti-apartheid and solidarity groups in various European countries to understand the reality of South Africa and the position of the ANC more fully. Two leading ANC members, Josiah Jele and Joseph Nhlanhla, played a major role in organising this conference.

In spite of the fact that Western support for Pretoria's actions in Angola in 1975-6 proved to be limited and sometimes reluctant, the South African government still hoped to consolidate its support. This it did by using the bogey of "Marxist total onslaught". At the same time it claimed to be ready to go it alone. "If need be, small as we are, but if we are to fight alone against the Russian aggression and imperialism in my part of the world, we will fight for South Africa and we will fight for mankind," declared Pik Botha in parliament on 27 May 1977.[63]

After Steve Biko's death in detention on 12 September 1977 and the banning of even non-violent organisations, Pretoria's old friends in the West had no option but to agree to the mandatory arms embargo against South Africa. The Security Council resolution was a heavy political blow to the regime. Shortly afterwards, on 26 October 1977, for the first time the ANC was given the opportunity to address the UN General Assembly, through its representative Johnny Makatini. The position of the Soviet Union, expressed by the USSR Ambassador to the UN Oleg Troyanovsky, was strongly supportive of the embargo actions adopted: "This decision can serve as a point of departure for application of the regime of effective sanctions against Pretoria."[64]

Several international non-governmental organisations began to display a more supportive attitude to the ANC. In August 1976 the World Council of Churches donated 50 000 dollars (an equal amount was assigned to the PAC). It was emphasised, however, that the money had to be spent for humanitarian purposes and could not be used to support military activities in any way.[65]

There were also favourable developments within the Socialist International. The entire speech of the Socialist International Vice President, Swedish Prime Minister Olaf Palme, at its 13th Congress in Geneva in November 1976 dealt with the Social Democrats' approach to the Southern African liberation struggle. He rejected Vorster's claim that Pretoria was defending the interests of the free world, emphasising that it was precisely the racist regimes that were to blame for the escalation of the struggle in the region.[66] In September 1977 a special mission of the Socialist International visited Angola, Zambia, Botswana, Mozambique and Tanzania, where it met leaders of those countries, the liberation movements and the OAU Liberation Committee. The proposals contained in the report of the mission were unanimously approved in October by the Socialist International Bureau as its Programme of Action on Southern Africa.[67]

However, members of the Socialist International often differed with each other in their responses. Many Social Democrats, mainly representatives of the left wing, participated in the preparation and deliberations of the World Conference Against Apartheid, Racism and Colonialism in Southern Africa, held in Lisbon from 16 to 19 June

1977. It was attended by Oliver Tambo as well as by the leaders of SWAPO and the Zimbabwe Patriotic Front. At the same time the government of Portugal, led by the Socialist Party of Mario Soares, declined at the last moment to participate in the conference in any way, refusing to meet the delegations of the liberation movements.

That Conference, which was the most representative and the broadest of its kind, attracted the attention of various forces, not only of friends but also of foes. "Look, the rats are '*mnogo*' [Russian for 'many'']," one of the ANC Executive members told me, looking at the guests at the Penta Hotel, where delegates stayed. He laughed when I replied, "But the cats are also '*mnogo*'."

A positive shift in the position of the Socialist International towards the ANC was reflected in the decision of the mainly Social Democrat-sponsored International University Exchange Fund (IUEF) in June 1978 to recognise the ANC as "the leader of the National Liberation Movement" in South Africa. In its support for the liberation movement the IUEF pledged to "work in closest possible consultation with the ANC."[68]

In March 1978 an ANC delegation headed by Oliver Tambo had a "successful official visit" to Finland, Norway and Denmark.[69] In Denmark it participated in the Hearing on South Africa opened by the Social Democratic Prime Minister Anker Jørgensen. But some days later Josiah Jele, who was a member of that delegation, had great difficulty in obtaining a visa to Britain, where another member of the Socialist International, the Labour Party, was in power.

Jele, who had been on his way to participate in the meeting of the Continuation Committee of the Lisbon Conference, was not the only member of the ANC leadership who had problems with British immigration. Delays in issuing visas, straight refusal and even body searches were not uncommon in Britain. Once an immigration officer asked an ANC Executive member, "Why do you go to the Eastern countries so often?" "Because they never treat me this way," he replied.

Soviet delegations to anti-apartheid meetings received similar treatment from the British authorities. In January 1978 a member of the USSR Parliament, Izvestiya columnist Vladimir Kudryavtsev, obtained a British visa on the very day of the meeting he was due to attend. Two other delegates, one of them the Solidarity Committee official (and later a staff member of the ANC Mission in Moscow) Eduard Samoylov, were refused visas because they were not considered "to be conducive to the public good".[70]

A year later, still under the Labour government, the same treatment was meted out to me: I was barred from attending an international anti-apartheid meeting in London. I was informed by the British organisers that the Home Secretary "personally refused a visa" and "no reason was given". I was surprised. A few months earlier I had visited London for the AGM of the British Anti-Apartheid Movement and the only conceivable crime I can recall committing was strolling along London streets and visiting a pub in the company of Aziz Pahad of the ANC office. Pahad is now the South African Deputy Minister of Foreign Affairs.

It is ironic that, soon after Labour's defeat in the general elections in 1979, Samoylov was freely admitted to Britain by the Tories, and I, too, had no difficulty being granted a British visa.

Oliver Tambo had good reason to state that, while some Social Democrats were rendering the ANC practical assistance, some others were "intolerable". [71]

RE-ORGANISATION OF THE ANC AND SACP

The increased role of the Soviet Union in Southern Africa was highlighted during the visit to the region in March-April 1977 by Nikolay Podgorny, the Chairman of the Presidium of the Supreme Soviet (often called "the USSR collective President") and number three in the Soviet hierarchy. In Lusaka he met Oliver Tambo, together with Sam Nujoma and Joshua Nkomo.

But the benefits of that visit were negated by his dismissal in May of the same year: his position was taken by Brezhnev himself, who at this stage, although practically incapacitated by illness, had begun to acquire a number of new posts, titles and awards. This development in Moscow brought about the postponement of the visit of the ANC delegation from May to June 1977.

The ANC leaders regarded the situation in South Africa as not only extremely promising but, at the same time, fraught with dangers. Talking in Moscow about Umkhonto's actions, Oliver Tambo explained: "The ANC should give the masses a chance to express their feelings, especially when imperialist countries (and perhaps the regime itself) are trying to create an alternative to the ANC that can take over the initiative." [72]

Joe Slovo, who was introduced by Tambo to the Soviets as a Member of the Revolutionary Council and Deputy Chief of Operations, characterised the situation in South Africa as extremely favourable for carrying out ANC strategy and tactics. There were no more "client states" adjacent to South Africa, and the people inside the country were no longer demoralised. Despite the killings in Soweto and the resulting national uprising during which many more people were killed than at Sharpeville in 1960, the unrest continued. For the first time in many years three mass political stay-aways took place.

The ANC delegation, however, soberly assessed the situation and concluded that victory was "not around the corner", as the enemy was still strong and the neighbouring African countries, which could provide a rearguard for the ANC, had suffered great difficulties. Some of them, in fact, had asked the ANC "to wait a bit." But, as Slovo put it, "the historic moment could be missed." By making some concessions, Pretoria was trying to create so-called "responsible black leadership", in particular in the bantustans, where some elements of the population were gaining material advantages from the new arrangements. The people had to see a clear alternative to subjugation to the regime in return for some concessions. [73]

At the subsequent July 1977 Executive Committee meeting, Oliver Tambo was finally "confirmed as President of the ANC."[74] The fact that Tambo had been acting head of the ANC for ten years caused some speculation. In particular, Ellis and "Sechaba" wrote: "The [Morogoro] conference voted merely to confirm Tambo as acting President-general of the ANC without making his position permanent. He was not in fact confirmed in this post until 1977. It is appropriate to observe that it suited the Party to have a relatively weak non-communist president of the ANC serving as symbolic leader of the triple [ANC-SACP-Sactu] Alliance."[75]

The assessment of Oliver Tambo as "relatively weak" or a "symbolic leader" can be made only by those who did not know him. As far as the SACP was concerned, exactly the opposite was true. Tambo himself had been hesitant about accepting this post outside the country without adhering strictly to the procedure of the ANC Constitution, and it took a long time for his comrades to convince him. Apparently the fact that the ANC ranks were swelling and that it was no longer isolated from home encouraged him to agree to their request in 1977.

The fact that the ANC managed to publicise his election only six months later in the first issue of *Sechaba* in 1978 shows the difficulties the organisation faced in disseminating information.[76] Fortunately in 1977 it began to publish the *Weekly News Briefing* compiled and edited in London by Gill Marcus (now South African Deputy Minister of Finance). For the first time ANC activists and supporters all over the world were able to get speedy and concise information about developments in South Africa. Because the ANC's other publications – *Sechaba* and (to a lesser extent) *Mayibuye* – were subject to a lengthy production process, the *Weekly News Briefing* became a source of more up-to-the-minute information about ANC positions on major issues.

The July 1977 ANC NEC meeting discussed prospects for the struggle inside the country. As mentioned above, "flying squads" were created, which were able to penetrate South Africa, attack, and then to return to the forward areas in countries adjacent to South Africa. The NEC was concerned, however, that the Military Command was moving ahead of the political organisation at home and that the Umkhonto fighters often acted on their own initiative.

The escalation of ANC activities after the Soweto uprising made it necessary to undertake major structural re-organisation. The next NEC meeting in Lusaka at the end of January 1978 was devoted to "a complete review of every aspect and department of the movement".[77] The meeting confirmed the traditional structure of the top positions – President, Secretary General and Treasurer General – each of which presided over one of three main departments. An important position was allocated to Thabo Mbeki, that of Political Secretary in the President's Office and Head of the Political Commission. That new structure had considerable responsibilities, including studies of the overall political situation internally and internationally, recommendation of new political initiatives, and training of political cadres. Since then, Thabo Mbeki, serving in various positions, has been at the centre of the political life of the ANC.

The President himself led the Information Department, which included the Research Division, headed by Pallo Jordan. The Secretary General had under him the International Department (with Jele as Head and Makatini as his Deputy), the Women's Section, the Youth and Students' Section, the Control Commission, and the Internal Political and Reconstruction Department (sometimes called the Department of Political Internal Reconstruction), headed by John Pule (Motshabi).

The Regional Political Committees (RPC), subordinate to the Secretary General, were new structures, the highest political organs of the movement (apart from conferences) in those countries where ANC members resided. They had the task of ensuring that "all members of the organisation are integrated in functioning branches, and that members are actively involved in the work of the movement."[78] The election of the Regional Political Committees was a step towards democracy, which was very hard to maintain in the conditions of exile and semi-legality. The growing spirit of non-racialism in the ANC was demonstrated by the election of veteran revolutionary Eli Weinberg to the post of the RPC Chairman in Tanzania.

The next annual visit of the ANC delegation to Moscow took place in October 1978. In these discussions with the Soviets Oliver Tambo concentrated on the upsurge of the national liberation struggle in South Africa, and the ANC's efforts to rally all opponents of apartheid in a united democratic front.[79] A new feature of the situation in South Africa was the "arming of the people". For the first time since the colonial conquest, actual armed combat was taking place in South Africa.

Aware of the sources of assistance to the ANC, the imperialist forces were trying to cut them off. According to Tambo, that explained "the noise" about the Soviet and Cuban presence in Southern Africa. Simultaneously, the US administration was doing its best to isolate the ANC from the struggle inside South Africa, and to make it difficult for the ANC to operate in neighbouring countries.

In Tambo's opinion some forces in the West understood the inevitability of "some kind of majority rule" in South Africa. For this reason they wanted to have organisations in the country which would use revolutionary and anti-imperialist rhetoric but would in fact collaborate in the government's reforms and ultimately in a puppet regime. They tried to sell those organisations to the international public.[80]

The usual practical requirements of the ANC were also discussed, including the provision of all essentials, from food to stationery, for SOMAFCO. However, this visit resulted in a change in the kind of support the Soviets would give to the ANC. The delegation requested not only increased supplies of military hardware and training facilities in the USSR, but the assistance of the Soviets in the actual organisation of training of Umkhonto cadres in Angola.

The initiative to involve the Soviets came originally from Havana. The matter had been raised with ANC leaders by Jorje Riskyet, at that stage head of the Cuban contingent in Angola and later actively involved in talks on the Angolan-Namibian settlement. The Cubans had become involved in training ANC cadres as soon as they arrived in Angola. By the end of 1977 two detachments of Umkhonto fighters had been trained there. The first was named "16th of June" and the second "Moncada" (the name of the military barracks attacked by Fidel Castro and his followers) in appreciation of the Cuban assistance. "Cadres of the ANC, of Umkhonto we Sizwe, have completed their course, taken under guidance and instruction by members of the Revolutionary Armed Forces of Cuba, on ground made available by the Angolan Government and under the security of the People's Armed Forces for Liberation of Angola," said Oliver Tambo at the second graduation ceremony.[81] When they raised this new issue the Cubans either wanted to lighten their own burden, or to have the Soviets more deeply involved. Or – the most likely option – they wanted a combination of both.

So, seventeen years after the first discussions in Moscow in 1961, the participation of Soviet instructors in the training of Umkhonto fighters on African soil was at last possible. The first group came to

Angola in 1979. Others followed, replacing each other in two- or three-year shifts.[82] Their number gradually increased from the three that were initially requested by the ANC to several dozen. There can be no doubt that the direct involvement of Soviet officers helped to raise the level of combat readiness of ANC armed units and, especially, of the organisers of the armed underground.

The ANC was unique among liberation movements in that it managed to preserve its unity over more than three decades of exile. The defection and later expulsion of the Gang of Eight was the sole exception, and even in their case the ANC leaders made every effort to keep them within the organisation.

"I am very impressed by Oliver's action + all others," Nelson Mandela wrote in a letter smuggled from Robben Island Prison in 1976. At the same time he continued, "Does Oliver think I should write to Tennyson Makiwane; would this have a reuniting effect? The letter would ask Tennyson to rejoin the group and would be sent to him via Oliver."[83] Mandela was ready to make a personal effort to bring the dissidents back in, but he would do it only through Tambo.

This message is interesting also because it reflects the staunch spirit of the political prisoners and in particular of Mandela himself: "We are still very solid here .... In RIP [Robben Island Prison] we are sharply divided on what actions should be taken inside the country [prison] by our members:

some think that time come to act as politicians so as to improve the conditions.

some are thinking of open defiance to authorities.

my own view is that all possible means of negotiation have been used and that therefore open defiance is the only way out.

I personally favour this attitude, but the majority of colleagues think we should be more conscious [cautious].

The matter is still being discussed."[84]

Mandela was worried about the absence of regular contacts between the prisoners and the leadership outside South Africa, and urged: "Oliver should see that people (respectable English MP or journalist) still come to RIP." He was clearly happy that a person he trusted was leaving the island: "Mac Maharaj is one of the most reliable boys who has gone out from here; he is bringing a lot of messages for Oliver."[85]

Satyandranath (Mac) Maharaj (at present South African Minister of Transport) was released from Robben Island on 17 December 1976 and sent to Durban under a banning order. In July 1977 he fled to

Maputo and immediately became active in the ANC in exile. He was soon appointed to the Revolutionary Council.

Nelson Mandela's message was especially important in the light of a report that was smuggled out from Robben Island about the political and personal differences which existed, over a long period from 1969, in the top leadership in the prison – the "original High Organ" of the Congress Movement – in particular between Madiba (Nelson Mandela) and Xhamela (Walter Sisulu) on the one hand, and Govan Mbeki and Ndobe (Raymond Mhlaba) on the other.

The final findings of the new High Organ held "the four original High Organ men ... primarily responsible for disunity through maladministration and incorrect attitude towards one another." While an "immediate cause of misunderstanding was the proposal for discussion on separate development institutions ... personal relations and clash of personalities between Madiba and Govan contributed to the discord. ... Power struggle in jail was a factor in the dispute [and] questions of tactics were elevated to questions of principle in discussions."

It was decided to "reinstall the four persons" (mentioned above) in the High Organ "partly as a practical test of the effect of the unity discussion." "Madiba's status" was referred to the general membership and "by an overwhelming majority the meeting reaffirmed Madiba's leadership of the Congress Movement on Robben Island Prison."[86]

The SACP leadership was realistic in its approach to developments in South Africa. The Central Committee meeting was convened in April 1977 in the GDR, even though the airfares for the fifteen participants had been provided by the Soviets. Their geographic spread is worth mentioning. Yusuf Dadoo and Brian Bunting flew from London, Joe Slovo from Luanda, Moses Mabhida and John Nkadimeng from Maputo, Ray Simons and Dan Tloome from Lusaka.[87] The meeting adopted a document, "The Way Forward from Soweto", which stressed that "Soweto closed the debate about the legitimacy of the armed struggle."[88] Nevertheless, the document emphasised that the 1976 events could not in themselves have been transformed into a successful general armed uprising even if adequate stocks of weapons had been available. "We must not play with the idea of an armed uprising by treating it as a question only of logistics and organisation."[89]

This first CC meeting after Soweto had special significance and its decisions had long-term effects on the SACP activity. Several people who had recently left South Africa were elected to the SACP Central Committee. It was decided to dissolve the Executive Secretariat, which had operated in London, and to replace it with a Politbureau, consisting (initially) of five members. It became the Party's supreme organ between the sessions of the Central Committee, and was charged with all the responsibilities of guiding the SACP both politically and organisationally.

At that stage the Politbureau had its Headquarters in Luanda, but it was soon moved to Maputo and later, in 1984, to Lusaka. The Politbureau was to have a full-time administrative officer. Francis Meli was proposed for this post but in practice he did not work in that capacity.

There was to be a Secretariat, to consist of the full-time functionary, the members of the Politbureau present in Angola, and at least three members of the Central Committee stationed in Angola. In fact, this body began to function on a regular basis only in 1982 and in Maputo.

It was decided also to create sub-committees of the Politbureau in designated regions for SACP activities in exile: London, Dar es Salaam, Lusaka, Angola, Lesotho, Botswana, Mozambique and Swaziland. These subcommittees were instructed to create organised Party units in their areas. Each region had a Central Committee member as its head. The Party structures in Lesotho were headed by Chris Hani, in London by Yusuf Dadoo, in Lusaka by Ray Simons, in Botswana by Dan Tloome, in Swaziland and Mozambique by Moses Mabhida. Two structures were created in Angola, one in Luanda and another in the South of the country, where most Umkhonto fighters were based at that time.

Two of the main functions of the regions were the creation of "internal units" of the Party (that is, units within South Africa), and ensuring a flow of SACP educational, organisational and propaganda material to them.

A strict procedure was established for the recruitment of new Party members, which was to be by the unanimous decision of the regions; in cases of disagreement, the matter had to be referred to the Politbureau for a final decision. New recruits had to accept the SACP policy and programme, be ready to carry out all Party directives, pay Party dues, conform to high standards of personal conduct, and be prepared, if called upon, to become full-time professional revolutionaries either inside or outside South Africa. In such cases the Party had no obligation to make provision for economic losses or for

189

the maintenance of dependants.

The international activity of the SACP was to be conducted from London under the direction of the Politbureau. All the Party's financial matters became the responsibility of Yusuf Dadoo and Joe Slovo.

After discussing a proposed meeting between the leadership of the SACP and the ANC it was decided to suggest to the ANC leadership the creation of permanent liaison machinery.[90]

Politically at that stage both the ANC and the SACP tried to temper the enthusiasm of the Umkhonto youth, anxious to get back home quickly and win victory over the enemy. "People's armed conflict is a protracted process," the SACP statement said. "Even though the conditions now exist for the struggle to be extended enormously, we must not be tempted by the passion and excitement of the moment to spread a dangerous and damaging illusion that it will be short and swift."[91]

The regime did its best to destroy the ANC and the SACP underground. On 29 July 1977 a number of activists were arrested in Cape Town: Jeremy Cronin, a lecturer in political science, David Rabkin, of the *Cape Times*, David's wife Sue Rabkin, and Anthony Holliday of the *Cape Argus*. Their trial highlighted the methods and the scope of the propaganda work executed by the SACP and the ANC. The judge named the garage where leaflets and papers were produced a "propaganda factory". A Special Branch "expert" complained: "The SACP and the ANC literally bombarded the country with pamphlets, which are inflammatory and attempted to prepare people for an armed struggle to remove the government by force and to install a new regime."[92]

The new upsurge in the struggle was accompanied by the radicalisation of its participants. A number of new recruits to the ANC expressed their intention to join the Communist Party as well, and at the bilateral ANC-SACP meeting held in 1977 Oliver Tambo raised no objection to this. The SACP delegation also raised the question of releasing the names of two members of the SACP (apart from Yusuf Dadoo and Moses Kotane). It was agreed in principle but not carried out in practice. However, from time to time leaks occurred. For example, while Essop Pahad (now Deputy Minister in Deputy President's office) usually signed his articles in the *World Marxist Review* with a pen name or as "South African journalist", he was once accidentally referred to by his real position as a member of the Editorial Council.[93] And, some years later, when Brian Bunting participated in a conference in the GDR, his position as Editor of the *African Communist* was announced.

THE MAIN TASK: POLITICAL MOBILISATION

As the SACP structures and membership expanded, the Politbureau drafted "Guidelines", a broad outline of Party policy and required standards of conduct. While the document was a directive from the leadership and had to be observed, Party units were encouraged to forward comments and criticism for consideration at the next plenary session of the Central Committee. Even in conditions of illegality the SACP leadership tried to combine strict discipline with the proper involvement of members in decision-making.

A particular paragraph of this document is worth mentioning. "Whilst it is the duty of Communists to work together collectively wherever they find themselves, they must not do it in such a way that they act, or are seen to act, as cliques or as groups which caucus and impose decisions by conspiracies and factionalism. Communists who are activists in other organisations have no special rights or privileges and are totally subject to the democratic processes and authority of the superior organs of such organisations. They are not to 'impose' the party line but rather to strengthen unity and revolutionary policy by example and open persuasion."[94]

The next plenary session of the SACP Central Committee took place in August 1978, in the Party Guest House in the resort area Serebryany Bor (Silver Pine Forest) on the outskirts of Moscow. Transportation and accommodation for seventeen participants was provided.[95] Though this was an ordinary meeting, the increased number of participants reflected the development of the SACP structures. One of the major problems discussed there was the state of the labour movement in South Africa, based on a report prepared by Ray Alexander (Simons).[96]

It realistically stated that Sactu as an organised federation had ceased to exist in practice in the mid 1960s as a result of repression, although some activities continued under the guise of burial societies and other advisory committees. After the Morogoro Conference in 1969 Sactu surfaced again but mainly as an exile group. Only in 1975 did the external leadership of Sactu manage to meet activists from inside the country.[97]

The sharper focus on the armed struggle brought many trade union activists into MK's ranks. Because the liberation movement did not pay enough attention to the structures (work committees etc.), created at that time by the regime, when workers started to organise themselves, after the wave of strikes in 1973, reformist trade unions enjoying considerable financial support from the West, especially from the African-American Labour Centre and its competitor, the ICFTU, began to fill the vacuum.

Sactu was by that time a considerable bureaucracy in exile. But, of the existing 29 African trade unions with about 60 000 members it exercised an influence in only five of those unions, with about 10 000 members, as well as in one "Coloured" trade union. Apart from noting that the membership of the unions had to be strengthened by bringing in people from Umkhonto, Ray Alexander's report concluded that strong and politically motivated trade unions could not be built with financial assistance from external forces, and that in the long run the expenses of the movement should be covered by the workers themselves.[98]

In the aftermath of Soweto the ANC and the SACP had to combat the efforts of those who were trying to stem the flow of new recruits to the ANC. "Our adversaries tried to use the great contribution of our youth and students in the struggle to ascribe to the students the role of the vanguard force in the struggle," Oliver Tambo said later. "On the basis of this wrong thesis, desperate attempts had been made by elements in the USA, independent Africa and Western Europe to form some youth political organisation specifically as a counterweight to our movement, taking advantage of the political immaturity of some of the youth ... It was from these manoeuvres that the so-called South African Revolutionary Youth Council was born."

Attempts were made to form an anti-ANC coalition, composed of "SARYCO [South African Revolutionary Youth Council], remnants of the BCM, the PAC, the Unity Movement, and the Gang of Eight.[99]

Efforts hostile to the ANC to find or to form a "third force" worried the ANC rank and file as well. A paper prepared by ANC students in Scandinavia pointed out that Buthelezi was the first bantustan leader invited to the USA within the framework of the USSALEP "leadership exchange programme".[100] They claimed that a "second army" was being formed and that some African countries were helping to train "an army of traitors" to sow more chaos in South Africa than the alliance of "UNITA/FNLA/Zaire/USA/RSA" had achieved in Angola.[101]

A dubious role was played by the military rulers of Nigeria. The Nigerian authorities started to organise military training for young

South Africans without the knowledge of the ANC. They took an ambivalent position during the UN Conference on Apartheid, convened in August 1977 in Lagos, and tried to have a critique of the major Western powers excluded from its proceedings.[102] It required a major effort by the ANC and particularly by Thabo Mbeki, who was sent to Lagos as the ANC Chief Representative, to overcome the anti-ANC tendency in the Nigerian government.

On 4 July 1979 the ANC issued a special statement in response to an attempt to set up the Black Consciousness Movement as an organisation in exile. It stated: "In the recent past attempts have been made to form the new organisations outside South Africa, detached from masses of our people and from the realities of practical struggle ... These organisations have in the main sought to attract the youth which left South Africa after the heroic uprising that began in Soweto on June 16th, 1976, claiming to be a continuation, in one form or another, of the black [consciousness] organisations." Confirming "direct links" between the ANC and the organisations of the BCM inside the country, the statement criticised "a campaign of lies ... and distortion against the ANC" conducted by the BCM representatives outside South Africa.[103]

Joe Slovo wrote of the period of the early 1960s: "The energy and resources devoted to planning and execution of acts of sabotage and to the military apparatus and its auxiliary requirements began to affect the pace of political work amongst the people."[104] Towards the end of the 1970s this situation was virtually repeated. Once again, "political work" suffered, because of too strong a concentration on military affairs.

The intention to develop the armed struggle was underlined by declaring 1979 "The Year of the Spear". At the same time, the trip to Vietnam by an ANC delegation headed by Oliver Tambo in October 1978 encouraged the ANC (and the SACP) leadership to give greater attention to the mass political struggle inside the country.

This was not the first contact with the Vietnamese. Yusuf Dadoo had visited Hanoi earlier, in December 1976, and, judging by his notes, he met both political and military figures, including the Chief of Staff.[105] However, it is difficult to overestimate the importance of the 1978 visit. Tambo's trip was not widely publicised, but he, Slovo and other delegates were deeply impressed by the Vietnamese methods of underground armed struggle during the many years of the US occupation, especially the co-ordination between illegal and mass activities.

Soon after the return of the delegation to Africa its impressions were discussed at a special joint meeting of the Revolutionary Council and some members of the National Executive, which took place in Luanda at the end of 1978.

The ANC Secretary General Alfred Nzo was not present at the meeting; he had gone to Moscow for a short course of military training. The previous meeting of the ANC Executive had insisted on the compulsory training of all NEC members who had not gone through it before. In a matter of months almost all fulfilled that requirement, usually in small groups.

Those of the ANC cadres who had many months of barracks and field exercises behind them were somewhat sceptical about these courses. They jokingly called them "kitchen training" (very often the trainees stayed in special flats and their classroom might indeed be next to a kitchen). Nevertheless, the courses were important in that they gave the ANC political leadership a basic knowledge of military science and helped them understand the capacity of Umkhonto and the needs of its members. One of the larger groups, on an earlier course in 1978, included prominent ANC members who had recently left South Africa: Joe Gqabi, John Nkadimeng, and Henry Makgothi.[106]

The meeting of the Revolutionary Council adopted important documents, necessitated by the growth of the movement: "The Code of Conduct", "Rules and Regulations Governing Handling Weapons and Explosives of Our Movement", as well as "The Military Code".

"The Code of Conduct" was both a legal and political document. It spoke of the creation of a new man and woman, of a non-exploitative system, new laws and a new people's state, and about the liberation of the human being. For some reason it started with a section on drinking and drugs. It forbade the excessive consumption of liquor, drunken behaviour in public places and on public occasions, the consumption of liquor while driving and in areas declared "dry" by the competent ANC authority, and the habit of frequenting bars or other drinking places.[107]

"The Code" was especially important in the first post-Soweto years. Lapses in commitment and dedication occurred. For example, when one of the ANC members was sent to Swaziland as head of the "Operational Machinery", he disappeared after three days. His comrades feared that he had been kidnapped but in reality he was just drinking and womanising. After wasting R2 000, he surrendered himself to the Royal Swaziland Police. Discotheques, drink and other "forbidden fruits" which were difficult to get in Maputo were drawing some ANC members away from Mozambique and to Swaziland.

A special Politico-Military Strategy Commission was formed at that meeting to work out a document on ANC strategy (and tactics). It was approved at the next meeting of the ANC Executive Committee and became known in the ANC as the "Green Book".[108]

This meeting was important for ANC tactics, and the materials presented to it deserve detailed study. The Executive discussed the state of the ANC organisation in various fields. In spite of severe difficulties, an elaborate system of military training was developed, with five camps in Angola. The main training base was a camp near the town of Novo Catengue, opened in May 1977, administratively run by the Cubans. Earlier another camp of a more special nature was created, not far from the coastal town of Benguela. Cubans led the training, and in December 1978 a group of 60 specialists in sabotage completed their studies.

The third camp, near Quibaxe, was a main transit point for those who came from South Africa. They were kept there for some period before being sent on to training camps. The fourth camp was created nearby and hosted the fighters who had completed their basic training. Here they received additional training for terrain conditions. One more camp – Funda – was under the direct control of the ANC Department of Operations. It was used as a transit camp for fighters being sent into South Africa, as well as for short-term training of people who had managed to leave the country for a brief time.

By the beginning of 1978 the total number of Umkhonto fighters outside South Africa was 1 167, the majority of them new arrivals. Expectations of an even greater increase in recruit numbers is seen from the fact that in 1978 the ANC leadership forwarded to the Soviet Afro-Asian Solidarity Committee a request for goods and equipment for the camps in Angola sufficient for 10 000 people.[109]

A rapid swelling of the ranks of the ANC combat formations and the need for greater skills demanded the organisation of training not only in Angola, but overseas as well. Again, as in the 1960s, a stream of cadres went to the Soviet Union. In 1976-8 140 were trained there, apart from about a hundred in the GDR, 10 in Bulgaria and 12 in Cuba.

The growth of Umkhonto's strength and of its actions brought about the formation of one more Department within the Revolutionary Council, that of Ordnance. The task of providing the fighters with arms for training and for operations was a difficult one. Originally the ANC had virtually no arms in Angola or anywhere close to South Africa, the exception being a limited stock in Tanzania. The training camps in Angola were supplied with arms from several sources. The SWAPO leadership rendered valuable assistance: 10 pistols and 30 sub-machine guns, as well as some ammunition, were provided to the ANC, and more at a later stage. The Angolan government supplied some arms. Compared to what was to be made available in the future, those quantities – 2 AKM, 8 Uzi, 12 Sterling, 30 pistols, 50 grenades – were small, almost symbolic, but they made it possible to start training and to give at least elementary protection to the camps. Soon hand sub-machine guns and cartridges were sent from the ANC stock in Tanzania.

A large part of this limited stock was sent to Mozambique for the needs of the Department of Operations (mostly to be sent into South Africa) and the rest to the camp in Funda. Fortunately the Cubans, who were conducting training, also provided some arms for this purpose.

In December 1976 a considerable quantity of arms arrived in Maputo from "Malome's place". In the ANC language of the time the USSR was sometimes called that, the place of Moses Kotane ("malome" is "uncle" in Setswana). A group of specially selected Umkhonto cadres in Angola were put through a course in covert storage and transportation of weapons.

By 1979 the Umkhonto Headquarters consisted of its Head, Joe Modise, his Deputy, Joe Slovo, and five members. While in 1977 the Head, his Deputy and the Revolutionary Council were stationed in Angola, in March 1978 Joe Modise was transferred to Lusaka to lead the operations from there, especially those operating in the Western Transvaal and the Eastern Cape, as well as the groups sent to Zimbabwean territory. The attitude of the Zambian government towards the ANC had improved by this time. Radio communications were established between the ANC structures in Angola and Zambia, agreed to by the governments of both countries and with equipment supplied by the USSR.

Joe Slovo went to Maputo, with particular responsibility for operations in the Eastern Transvaal, Northern Natal and Central "urban" Transvaal. Some areas of the country, including the Orange Free State, were the responsibility of the group in Lesotho, headed by Chris Hani. Later a new structure dealing with "special operations" was created under Slovo's command.

During 1977 and 1978 about a hundred fighters were sent into South Africa; 23 of these were killed or captured. According to a police spokesperson, from October 1976 to September 1979, 170 "trained terrorists" had been "captured".[110] This figure was a gross exaggeration. The "naturalisation" of the fighters in South Africa in order to have a permanent presence there proved extremely difficult, and of those who survived arrests and clashes, practically all had left the country again by the end of 1978.

The planning of operations inside South Africa at the end of the 1970s was much more realistic than that envisaged by Operation Mayibuye. About 90 people in small groups were to be sent to one of five selected areas over six months, with smaller numbers to other areas. It was intended that they should stay inside the country for a long time.

Very small groups of two or three fighters with grenade launchers were to be sent into the urban areas to carry out attacks under the direction of the internal political leadership; the targets were to be selected jointly with the external Headquarters. In addition, some groups were to be sent for "special operations", such as attacks against police stations. After the completion of their missions they were to leave the country until the political structures inside the country became strong enough to support them.

Speaking at the NEC meeting about the state of Umkhonto, Oliver Tambo expressed his concern about its social composition. He referred to a glaring absence in the ANC camps of cadres of working-class and peasant origin, the very people whom the ANC had always regarded as the decisive moving force of the revolution. Tambo refused to believe that they were not to be found in the camps because they were cowards or not interested in their own liberation. In his opinion their absence could be explained by the fact that, in building up Umkhonto, the ANC leadership randomly accepted people coming out of the country rather than recruiting selectively, and so ensuring a strong component of workers.

Tambo believed that, to improve the situation in Umkhonto and to fight reactionary ideas, a vigorous, questioning political education was needed, with open debates taking the place of lectures. The youth, straining to confront "the fascist regime" face-to-face, were giving vent to their impatience, sometimes to the point of desperation. This worried Tambo greatly, and he ascribed to this the increasing number of suicides within Umkhonto's ranks.

On leaving South Africa, the youth wanted, in short order, to obtain guns, to receive some military training, and then to return home. But, as the figures show, in a year and a half fewer than 10% of them were actually sent back into South Africa, and then in the main for a short time. Apart from their new Umkhonto experience, most of these young men had not worked in the structures of illegal organisations before and were not accustomed to strict discipline. Tambo felt that an honest approach to the cadres was needed. It had to be explained to them why they could not be sent to fight as soon as they felt they were ready. Military actions at that stage had to be planned in such as way as to have maximum political effect, as in the case of the attack on the Moroka police station in Soweto.

As early as 1979 Tambo thought about the training of the officers of a regular army, who would be taught the skills of modern regular military actions and at the same time would develop political loyalty to the ANC leadership. Tambo was also worried that little or nothing was done to infiltrate the enemy's army, security forces and the "puppet" armies of the bantustans. (Some successes by the ANC in this field were to come much later.)

Apart from the problems of the armed struggle, the ANC Executive Committee discussed several organisational questions. Oliver Tambo's report to the NEC meeting confirmed the decision taken five months earlier to start a process involving all members of the ANC in a major reviewing and re-formulating of ANC policy. Unfortunately, this process was slow and took too long: the Second Consultative Conference was convened only six years later.

Another very important problem raised by the ANC President was ANC membership for non-Africans. His approach was cautious: he regarded it as a full departure from past practice, from the traditional wisdom of the leaders and the people, who had limited the membership mainly to Africans for several decades. In Tambo's opinion it was not enough for the ANC outside South Africa simply to take a decision and behave as though nothing had happened. He thought that if the mass of the membership was not prepared, the ANC could become an *émigré* organisation, and the people inside South Africa could form another organisation, corresponding more closely to what they understood the ANC to be.

This did not mean that Tambo was against the lifting of the limitations. In his annual message in January 1979 the ANC President expressed the hope that the 25th anniversary of the adoption of the

Freedom Charter in 1980 would be observed "under the banners of a people united in the declaration of the Freedom Charter, which says 'South Africa belongs to all who live there, black and white'."[111] He expected that membership of the ANC, and all offices in its structures, would be open to all South Africans who accepted its programme and policy. This did not happen until the next ANC conference in 1985.

Oliver Tambo was worried about the ethical side of his and his colleagues' position in the ANC leadership. Always tactful, he was not happy that, as he put it, an ANC official could remain in the same post for 21 years without periodic renewals of his mandate. The last election at a National Conference of the ANC had taken place 21 years earlier, in 1958. He wanted the internal structure of the ANC to be strengthened so that it became in fact a people's revolutionary movement as distinct from a group of friends who reserved leadership positions for themselves.

Tambo himself would have preferred to receive confirmation of his position as the leader of the organisation from the ANC members in South Africa. He mentioned in his report that there was better access to the people than ever before in the previous fifteen years (that is, since Rivonia) and hoped to get a chance to seek and receive a mandate.

But he was being unduly sensitive: firstly, the ANC Constitution was written for conditions of legality, and its drafters could not have imagined that the ANC leadership would be forced to live in exile for decades. Besides, when the opportunity arose, at the Morogoro Conference, Tambo announced his resignation, and his mandate was renewed, or confirmed, by the delegates.

The meeting critically reviewed underground work inside South Africa. The decision to concentrate on internal activities had been taken, as mentioned earlier, in Morogoro. But in practice in the following years the political work was not separated from the military, and the main emphasis was on the establishment of contacts inside the country which would ensure the safe reception of fighters from outside, and the reliable storage of arms. There was a contacts committee in the ANC Headquarters and each member was responsible for contacts with one of the regions. For security reasons, only these individual members knew the number and names of contacts inside South Africa, and the committee as a body discussed only general problems.

The need for re-organisation and reconstruction of the political underground machinery in South Africa became evident after Soweto. The Internal Political and Reconstruction Department had its first meeting in December 1977, but in practice it became operational only in March 1978.

A radical decision was taken from the outset, to start from scratch, as if no mechanism existed inside South Africa. The structures which survived in the forward areas (that is, countries adjacent to South Africa) were completely reshuffled. The Department was given considerable clout: the ANC Secretary General, Treasurer General, the Women's and Youth Sections were represented on it ex-officio.

The South African territory was zoned by the regional committees in the forward areas and by the end of 1977 underground organisations of the ANC were created in almost all areas, though their liaison was rather uneven. For example, in the Transvaal, where the efforts were concentrated in the Reef area, contacts were established by the Department structures with 22 Africans, four whites and two Indians, mostly activists in the trade union, student and youth structures. On the other hand, in the Western Cape only three people were contacted, an African, a Coloured person, and a white. However, a separate committee existed in Cape Town that was already able to carry out some underground activity. When one activist was sent there from Lesotho, he was safely passed from one group to another during a month's stay. Traditionally the weakest link was the Orange Free State.

The total number of underground operatives mentioned in the report of the Internal Policy and Reconstruction Department in April 1979 was still small, about 70, although this figure was perhaps an underestimation: the forward areas did not always pass on information about their newly established contacts in time. Also, these 70 people were genuine operatives and not simply people who had been contacted by the ANC. In most cases, they were not known as ANC sympathisers – a valuable asset for underground work. Over 50% of them were Africans; among the others most were Indians, and the smallest number were Coloured people. The remoteness of the Western Cape from the external borders and, comparatively speaking, a lack of Congress Movement traditions in that area were cited as the reasons.

The main goals of the IPRD at that stage were to impress the ANC presence upon the minds of the people, and at the same time to maintain, however tenuously, a national underground network. Preference was given to the creation of underground organisations rather than to mass mobilisation. However, attention was paid to the

201

establishment of links with legal organisations, including sports, cultural, community, rent payers', and self-help groups. Contacts were established with underground groups not only in the black universities, but also in the white University of the Witwatersrand.

Special importance was attached to the reception groups, which were to accommodate and ensure jobs for political and trade union organisers as well as for Umkhonto fighters after their training abroad.

The improvement of contacts with home made even more acute the question of the criteria for membership in the ANC. That problem as it affected those in exile had been solved (at least partially) in Morogoro. But inside the country the paradoxical situation continued that non-Africans could not find a place in any ANC structure except for Umkhonto. For example, some radical White and Indian students inside South Africa wanted to join the ANC. Unable to get a reply from the internal underground ANC structures, they tried to establish contact directly with the ANC in exile. By raising the matter of their membership in the ANC, these supporters were putting themselves at risk; they would have to keep it secret from their families. Some did not concern themselves with normalising their status; they simply regarded themselves as members.

In spite of the limitations imposed by illegality, it would be wrong to see the relationship between the ANC leadership and the underground groups in South Africa as a top-down formation. For example, the underground groups criticised the leadership for concentrating on military matters to the detriment of political work among the people.

A deep and sober (and therefore critical) analysis of the situation inside South Africa – ANC actions and problems – was contained in the report submitted to the NEC by Joe Gqabi, who after his release from Robben Island was actively organising inside the country. He underscored the need to clarify the relationship between the underground structures and the fighters sent into the country from abroad. At that stage these fighters very often felt responsible only to the Revolutionary Council and even dismissed underground operatives as "ordinary welfare workers" who should provide them with accommodation, transport etc., but who had no right to interfere in their activity.

Gqabi was worried by the impatience of the cadres and at the same time by their desire to stay inside South Africa, come what may. This was very much the attitude of the post-Soweto recruits. When one of the unit leaders disappeared, the commander of a group was told to cross immediately into Swaziland, but he ignored the instruction. When a second resident of the house where the group was staying also disappeared, they were ordered to change their refuge immediately, but, again, the commander did not carry out the order. All the members of the unit were arrested. When he himself was arrested, he revealed the location of their hideouts.

Joe Gqabi made a number of important recommendations based on the experience acquired by the underground. In particular, he emphasised the need for the ANC structures inside the country to be entirely self-reliant. For example, the underground leadership in Soweto divided their region into several zones and, having initially provided activists with a small sum of money, left it to them to organise all further collection of funds. This had a very important mobilising effect. New recruits for the underground could be selected from people who participated in the collection of funds.

The social composition of the underground activists was diverse: trade unionists, agricultural workers, teachers, students, nurses, a taxi-driver and a shopkeeper. A number of them worked in national and local legal and religious organisations.

A measure of the success in building up the underground machinery was the fact that the number of the ANC publications sent to the forward areas for distribution at home proved to be insufficient. Orders for copies of *Mayibuye* and *Sechaba* to be sent to Botswana and Swaziland had to be substantially increased.

The attitudes to the ANC changed inside South Africa in the years immediately after Soweto. The feeling of apathy and even bitterness which many youth had shared, accusing the ANC of being out of touch and not giving clear guidance, almost completely disappeared. It is worth noting, however, that many in the black community thought that the ANC placed too great an emphasis on military strategy and neglected political strategy. The experience of Vietnam and the opinion of Joe Gqabi and other activists inside the country coincided to a remarkable degree.

On the other hand, the people did expect some resolute actions from Umkhonto. This was clear from their reaction to the execution of the Umkhonto fighter Solomon Mahlangu in April 1979. He was arrested after a skirmish in the centre of Johannesburg in June 1977 when three Umkhonto fighters opened fire while being apprehended, killing two white civilians. Solomon Mahlangu's case became international news. In spite of the protests, he was hanged, and many in the black community were disappointed by the lack of ANC military operations around this event. ANC leaflets were distributed, but, as one activist said, "It is not enough to call people to join MK when it is doing nothing that warrants joining it."

The ANC had earlier tried to encourage the formation of the mass democratic organisations in the bantustans and urged the mobilisation and strengthening of those organisations that did exist. Contacts were maintained for this purpose in Transkei, Lebowa, Venda, Bophuthatswana and other bantustans. In particular, the ANC established regular contact with Gatsha Buthelezi, who headed the administration of the Kwazulu bantustan.

However, controversy arose between the delegations of the ANC and Inkatha at a meeting in 1979. In his report to the ANC National Consultative Conference in 1985, Oliver Tambo explained in retrospect: "Unfortunately we failed to mobilise our own people to take the task of resurrecting Inkatha as the kind of organisation we wanted, owing to the understandable apathy of many our comrades towards what they considered as working within the bantustan system. The task of reconstituting Inkatha therefore fell on Gatsha Buthelezi himself who then built Inkatha as a personal power base far removed from the kind of organisation we had visualised, as an instrument for the mobilisation of our people in the countryside into an active and conscious force for revolutionary change."[112]

Tambo confirmed that the ANC Executive had agreed to meet a delegation of Inkatha in 1979, when differences between the two organisations were becoming evident on such questions as armed struggle and disinvestment. The meeting was to take place in London and it was agreed that it be secret and its deliberations confidential. "However, Gatsha announced that we had met and explained the purpose, the contents and the results of the meeting to suit his own objectives."[113] The ANC leader admitted later: "In a way Gatsha is our fault."

In Lusaka in March 1979 Alfred Nzo, John Pule and Mac Maharaj met with Dr Sibusiso Bhengu (now South African Minister of Education). A prominent educationalist and a nephew of Albert Luthuli, Bhengu had resigned from the post of Secretary-General of Inkatha as a result of conflict with Buthelezi. At that meeting it was confirmed that many people in Natal had regarded Inkatha as a continuation of, if not a legal cover for, the ANC. For example, Luthuli's widow was elected an honorary patron of its local branch.

At the NEC meeting Oliver Tambo also drew attention to the security situation in the ANC. At that time major Western intelligence services held the view that the only way to defeat the revolutionary forces in South Africa was to infiltrate the ANC and transform it from within. They were coming to the conclusion that it was impossible to create a viable third force, although the attempts to do this did not stop.

In Tambo's opinion at that stage such a force could only be created, however shakily, on the basis of two ideological platforms. The first was an ultra-left position, which claimed that the immediate goal of the struggle was socialism; in his opinion that tendency had not done much harm to the ANC. The second platform, adopted by the PAC, the Gang of Eight and some groups before them, was called by Tambo nationalistic and chauvinistic. Some elements of the Black Consciousness Movement used that platform as well. This second platform had to be countered by the patriotic and revolutionary programme of the ANC, which considered the process of national liberation to be inextricably connected with social liberation.

The ANC President was looking at the security situation mainly from the political point of view. However, practical steps in this direction were taken as well: the Department of Intelligence and Security (or NAT as it became known in the ANC) had to be virtually reconstructed.

In February 1979 its core structure was appointed and consisted of just three people. The Department was to have operated from Angola, where the Revolutionary Council was stationed, but it soon moved to Lusaka. The Department was subordinate to the Office of the ANC President and, like some others created after Soweto, it had to start its work from scratch. Though there were still some (small and weak) comparable structures in the ANC, they did not transfer to the new Department experience or documentation or personnel: the remaining staff were redeployed to different departments and some had even left the ANC.

During the mass exodus of the youth from South Africa which started in June 1976, there was no special security machinery in place. What screening there was was carried out by the Department of Personnel and Training. Step by step the evolving department took over this function. During the first two years 932 new recruits were interviewed, 291 of them twice. Sixty-one people, those in some way suspect, were interrogated, and 26 confessed to being enemy agents. Interrogation continued with the 35 remaining. 2.8% of the total number confessed, and 3.7% were suspected to be moles of the regime. Correct or not, that figure was not too high, if one remembers that the South African Minister of Police boasted in 1976 that "of every ten who cross the border to join the ANC, five are mine."[114] The lack of security was clear from the fact that five suspects managed to abscond from the ANC camps.

The government of Angola demanded from the ANC that suspects be charged and stand trial. As a consequence, the creation of a Tribunal within the ANC framework became an urgent issue. Unfortunately this problem of detentions, fair trials and fair punishment was never successfully solved by the ANC in exile, to a large extent precisely because of the specific conditions in which it had to operate.

The ANC Security came to the conclusion that the regime had started sending large numbers of agents to obtain both short- and long-term results. Some of them were expected to insinuate themselves into "strategic positions" in the ANC. As a rule the agents were told by their handlers to join Umkhonto and, if unsuccessful, then to switch to the "student front". To recruit the youth, Pretoria's agents exploited their economic dependence and political naivety, as well as using intimidation. Very often youth detained by the police in South Africa for ordinary crimes were recruited as agents. The economic rewards were attractive: from R299 to R500 a month, and R1 000 if their information led to the arrest of "terrorists" or the seizure of arms. Later, in the mid 1980s, these sums were raised to R5 000 and even R7 000. More experienced agents who had already served in the Special Branch were also infiltrated into the ANC.

The spies were ordered to find out the location of ANC houses and camps in the forward areas, their daily routine, the identity of the people who lived there, and the system of protection and defence. Special attention was given to finding out the names and location of the leadership.

THE ANC'S GROWING INTERNATIONAL TIES

Despite the international ties with the ANC growing rapidly at the end of the 1970s, they were not easy to maintain, because, as Tambo put it, the ANC International Department consisted of virtually "one man". According to Tambo, the ANC had for decades sought to identify itself with the world's progressive forces as active fighters "for the liberation of all oppressed peoples, for democracy, peace and social progress." In this endeavour the ANC was guided not only by national interests, but also by what it saw as its international duties.

Reasonably good relations were established by the ANC with all countries of the Southern African region (with the exception of Malawi and Zaire), as well as with SWAPO and the ZAPU wing of the Zimbabwe Patriotic Front. Unfortunately, however, the ANC was still hesitant to broaden relations with ZANU-PF. Its leadership, headed by Robert Mugabe, proposed taking Umkhonto fighters into its Army, ZANLA (as had already been done in the case of ZAPU's Army, ZIPRA). But this proposal was ultimately not accepted by the ANC, presumably because ZANU maintained traditionally close relations with the PAC. In any event, the ANC wanted first to discuss this issue with ZAPU, whose leadership was apparently opposed to it.

Excellent relations had developed by that time with the government of Lesotho. Mutual understanding was reached on a number of points, including the issuing of Lesotho passports to ANC members, ANC representation in Lesotho, co-operation in the field of intelligence and security, some training for South African refugees in Lesotho, and co-operation in international affairs. Tambo characterised as "sterling" the work carried out in Lesotho by Chris Hani and his ANC comrades.

With regard to Swaziland it seemed that, while the most difficult period was over, Pretoria would continue putting pressure on the government of Swaziland. The South African Police tried to monitor the movements of the top ANC members in Swaziland, in particular Moses Mabhida and Stanley Mabizela. The latter's car, for example, was stolen in October 1976 and spotted later at John Vorster Square, Police Headquarters in Johannesburg.

Positive developments in relations with Botswana followed the visit of an ANC delegation in December 1978, headed by Tambo. For the entire day, a single theme was discussed with President Seretse

Khama: activating the struggle in South Africa. Botswana emphasised the importance of the mass political struggle and assessed the military actions of Umkhonto as poorly prepared. It was clear that Botswana was still too dependent on South Africa. The situation became problematic on 14 March 1979 when the Botswana police carried out a raid on the houses of ANC activists. Four were arrested and sentenced to imprisonment for illegal possession of war materials. Those actions were regarded as a consequence of pressure from Pretoria.

The ANC position in Zambia was strengthened, despite there being elements in Zambian ruling circles who were sympathetic to South Africa. Goods for the ANC were delayed at Lusaka airport for up to three months. The route from the African Liberation Centre to the Defence Ministry, the Ministry of Trade, and the Ministry of Finance, which finally approved import licences, was long and circuitous, with many a pothole along the way.

The security situation was very delicate. New information about South African agents in Lusaka was received almost daily. Even the Zambian authorities admitted that there was co-operation between some Zambian citizens and the Rhodesian and South African secret services. As a result many ANC members raised doubts about Lusaka's suitability as a venue for the ANC Headquarters. It was also very difficult to obtain any assistance from the sub-regional committee of the OAU Liberation Committee in Lusaka.

Good relations between the ANC and Tanzania had finally been re-established after Julius Nyerere received an ANC delegation headed by Oliver Tambo on 20 September 1978. The Tanzanian President expressed his willingness to strengthen ties with the ANC and promised to use his influence in the OAU and its Liberation Committee to strengthen their support. He agreed to assist the ANC in the accommodation of its activists, to provide travel documents for them, as well as to help in the creation of the training complex near Morogoro. He indicated that, as Tanzania was also giving support to the Patriotic Front of Zimbabwe, her resources were limited.

As Oliver Tambo put it, the ANC was again in contact with the people and the ruling party in Tanzania and the page of history relating to strained relations between the ANC and Tanzania could be torn out. The fact that Julius Nyerere became the Chairman of the Front Line States strengthened the importance of Tanzania for the liberation movements. Although the Tanzanian government continued its support

208

of the PAC, it had stopped putting pressure on the ANC to create a united front.

The ANC tried to consolidate its relations with "vanguard parties", the MPLA- Party of Labour in Angola and Frelimo Party in Mozambique. In Tambo's opinion they and the ANC shared a common vision of the future of the Southern African region, but had not set up adequate machinery to consult with one another.

The ANC Office in Mozambique was from the outset only semi-legal, though from time to time its representatives were officially invited to public occasions. Later a special organ –*Nucleo de Opoio* (Nucleus of Assistance) – was created to channel communications with the liberation movements, though in practice many problems were solved by direct consultation with the Ministry of Foreign Affairs and other Mozambican Ministries. Mozambicans also facilitated contacts between the ANC and South African political refugees

Tambo advocated various foreign policy strategies beyond the Southern African region. On the African continent, the songs and dances of the ANC cultural group were often more effective than political speeches. In the Middle East, contacts with Iraq, South Yemen and especially the PLO were developed, with the added intention of convincing Libya (who supported the PAC at that stage) to adopt a more positive stance towards the ANC.

After the Islamic Revolution, the ANC tried to develop contacts with the new Iranian authorities. Two goals were obvious: to stop Iranian oil supplies to South Africa, and to obtain material assistance. The first aim, at least officially, was achieved. But the second one remained a distant goal even after Alfred Nzo's visit to Teheran in November 1979.

Latin America and the Caribbean were regarded as virgin soil for the ANC, and its recently opened office in Havana needed to be strengthened.

The socialist countries were considered to be solid allies of the ANC cause, but a more active engagement was required with some of those countries where relations were underdeveloped. Those countries were to receive literature, exhibitions, and cultural groups to assist the ruling parties in their work of strengthening internationalist feelings among their people.

China was a special case. Tambo said later: "I think that in the 1960s and early 1970s this [the Sino-Soviet conflict] was a factor but in 1975 we resolved that question. The Chinese accepted the fact that we have nothing against the Soviet Union, that the Soviets were close friends of ours, and that friendship with anyone else was not condition[al] upon our weakening of relations with the Soviet Union."[115] But the armed conflict between China and Vietnam early in 1979, soon after Tambo's visit to Hanoi, froze ANC relations with Beijing for several years. For the first time the ANC leadership (whatever its assessment of the Chinese policy had been before) openly criticised it.

The "Statement of the National Executive Committee of the ANC of South Africa on China" of 22 February 1979 noted that, only weeks earlier, the ANC representatives had met Chinese Vice-Premier Li Hsien Nien in Lusaka. "The Chinese side expressed the readiness of China to normalise relations with the African National Congress on the basis of their support for our struggle and the policy of the ANC and a common hostility to imperialist domination." But "the naked aggression against Vietnam had however shown that this was not a genuine approach but constituted an attempt to organise the ANC into a reactionary front spearheaded against the world progressive forces." Nevertheless, the ANC Executive declared "its readiness to normalise relations with the People's Republic of China as and when China rejoins the forces genuinely fighting for the liberation of all oppressed people, against imperialism, for national independence, democracy, peace and social progress."[116]

The Working Committee of the ANC had developed a strategy of winning over smaller Western countries to the side of its struggle, and that strategy was beginning to bear fruit. In addition to the Scandinavian countries and Holland, Italy and Ireland started to give some small assistance to the ANC. At the same time there was increased pressure on the imperialist states to endorse the demand for the complete isolation of Pretoria. The growing anti-apartheid movement in the USA showed that the South African question could become an important issue in any country.

The ANC information and publicity machinery had always known that it faced an adversary that was very experienced, well-equipped, and utterly cynical. However, an exposé of some of Pretoria's corruption, manipulation and bribing of foreign and local journalists during the "Muldergate" scandal forced Vorster to move across to what was then the ceremonial post of State President, and in 1979 to resign.

210

RESISTANCE TO APARTHEID GROWS

The armed actions of the ANC were becoming more effective in 1979, especially the attacks on police stations. When Umkhonto staged a raid on the Moroka police station in Soweto, the policemen were unable to respond with even a single shot. Some months later more than 60 policemen in the Orlando police station hid under their beds or fled during an Umkhonto attack.

After the attacks on the police, Bill Sutton, MP from the (supposedly liberal) New Republican Party said: "The next step is the attacks on payrolls and banks. The revolutionaries need money."[117] He was both right and entirely wrong: the South African revolutionaries did need money, but the ANC refrained from such activity, typical of armed movements in other parts of the world.

An armed action did take place against the Silverton branch of the Volkskas Bank on 25 January 1980, but its purpose was not "money for revolutionaries". Having taken hostages, the Umkhonto fighters demanded the release of their leaders. Whatever their intentions were, this action was definitely not authorised by the ANC leadership and was an isolated incident. To the best of my knowledge, apart from what became known as "the Silverton siege", ANC fighters have never taken hostages. Notwithstanding the ANC's policy on hostages, in the eyes of its supporters the Umkhonto members killed in that action were not terrorists but heroes.

In an effort to stop the increase of ANC armed actions inside South Africa, Pretoria unleashed an aggressive campaign early in 1979. In a special (internal) ANC document, published on 26 March, Pretoria's actions were described as a campaign to physically liquidate ANC members. On 15 February four explosions took place near the ANC residence in Maputo and one member was killed. On 14 March five jets bombed the ANC camp in Angola. According to the statement, three ANC members were killed and eight wounded.[118] (Ronnie Kasrils in his book puts it at two ANC members and one Cuban killed.)[119]

An ANC delegation visited the USSR in December 1979. Its composition confirms that the main purpose of the mission was support for the struggle: Joe Modise, Mziwandile Piliso, Thomas Nkobi, and Cassius Make (Job Tlhabane), who was Assistant Secretary

211

of the Revolutionary Council. At that time a political settlement in Zimbabwe was pending and the ANC leadership was worried that it could bring not only new prospects, but also new problems for the movement. It was anticipated that one consequence of Zimbabwean independence would be that the Botswana government would try to improve its relations with Pretoria at the expense of the ANC by banning it.

Oliver Tambo was concerned that the ANC could not rely on African countries to satisfy its growing needs. However, he undertook that the ANC would continue to try to solve the problems itself and would appeal to the Soviet Union (and other socialist countries) only when unable to do so. He was particularly concerned that the Rhodesian settlement had been reached through the Commonwealth and that the OAU had been excluded. But he was sure that, even if neo-colonialist regimes were established in Zimbabwe and Namibia, Southern Africa would never be the same again.[120]

In the circumstances the ANC was anxious to increase its presence within South Africa and to broaden contacts there with legal organisations. It was also trying to establish contacts between itself and those with whom it could not always agree. The ANC leadership expected that this process would bring those forces into the ANC fold, and this often proved to be the case.

The combat units of Umkhonto inside South Africa went on the offensive, but they still had to vanish into thin air after their attacks and this was not easy to do because there were no ANC bases inside the country and the position in the forward areas was complicated. The continuing exodus of young people created many problems, including security, transport, logistics, and food.[121]

Thomas Nkobi, the Treasurer General, was satisfied with the growing humanitarian assistance from some Western countries, in particular that channelled into the building of SOMAFCO. He recalled how in the 1960s the Soviets recommended that the ANC look in the West for financial assistance for humanitarian purposes, initially for the legal defence of the opponents of the apartheid regime and assistance to the families of political prisoners. Nkobi was glad that the ANC had done this and had succeeded.[122]

Like the ANC, the SACP in exile grew in numbers. This was shown during the preparations for the enlarged meeting of the Central Committee, which took place in late 1979 in the GDR. Dozens of responses were received to a draft document, circulated beforehand

212

and titled: "Forward to People's Power – the Challenge of the 1980s". The sources of these responses show that the SACP had a broad network, at least outside South Africa. For instance, the responses from Angola, apart from the Regional Committee, came from District Committees in Quibaxe, Catengue and Novo Catengue, Villa Rosa, Funda, (places where Umkhonto camps were situated), and from two units in Luanda as well as from some individuals.

Several units existed in Lusaka, three in Mozambique, two in Botswana, and one in Dar es Salaam. From outside Africa the responses came from the GDR, Cuba, and the USSR (the students in the International Lenin School). However, the Regional Committee in the "Island" (the ANC and SACP name for Lesotho) stated: "Unfortunately, the internal units will not be in a position to submit their comments on time."[123]

The South African Communist Party continued working in conditions of great secrecy. At that meeting Moses Mabhida was elected General Secretary, although this was not announced for more than a year. One of the reasons for the delay was apparently the need first of all to relieve him of his everyday ANC work as Secretary of the Revolutionary Council. In the biography of Mabhida published on this occasion, his membership of "the Political Bureau" and therefore the existence of that body were made public for the first time since its creation four years earlier.[124]

Speaking in London at the 60th anniversary of the SACP on 30 June 1981, Oliver Tambo used the election of Mabhida to describe the character of the relationship between the ANC and the Party: "It is often claimed by our detractors that the ANC's association with the SACP means that the ANC is being influenced by the SACP. That is not our experience. Our experience is that the two influence each other. The ANC is quite capable of influencing, and is liable to be influenced by others. There has been the evolution of strategy which reflects this two-way process. In fact the ANC was quite within its rights to tell the SACP that we are sorry we cannot release Comrade Moses Mabhida from his tasks in the ANC – find another comrade to be General Secretary. Yet we agreed he would be a good General Secretary for the SACP. He was not grabbed."[125]

Soon after the announcement of Moses Mabhida's election, an article by him, devoted to the 60th anniversary of the SACP, was published in the *Kommunist* magazine in Moscow. One paragraph deserves quoting: "It should be emphasised ... that the communists do

213

not reject the possibility of the peaceful development of the revolution in South Africa. To achieve it the power, in their opinion, should be transferred 'to the representatives of the oppressed majority of the people peacefully, by negotiations.' However, such a prospect was unlikely from the very beginning. After the authorities took new, even more rigid repressive laws it became 'virtually impossible'."[126]

1980 was proclaimed by the ANC "The Year of the Charter". The ANC leadership tried to achieve maximum unity among the opponents of Pretoria and to re-adopt the Freedom Charter as a model of the South Africa the masses of the people were fighting for.[127]

For the first time in two decades a public discussion started in South Africa on whether the Freedom Charter was a legal document. At the 25th anniversary of its adoption, in June, the Johannesburg *Sunday Post*, a paper read mostly by Africans, published it, even as the police were detaining people for distributing leaflets which contained the text of the Charter.

A morale boost to ANC members and supporters was the publication in 1980 of a message from Nelson Mandela. As Oliver Tambo indicated, it took over two years for the message to reach the ANC leadership, but it remained "fresh and valid".[128] "Between the anvil of united mass action and the hammer of the armed struggle we shall crush apartheid and white minority racist rule," Mandela wrote.[129]

The independence of Zimbabwe and the crushing defeat of the neo-colonialist forces, in particular the defeat of Bishop Abel Muzorewa's party, forced Pretoria to take some urgent steps. On 9 March 1980 Prime Minister P W Botha announced the government's intention to convene a conference of representatives of all races to "deliberate about matters affecting South Africa."[130] He admitted that the results of the elections in Zimbabwe had strategically changed the situation for South Africa. But at the same time he reiterated his opposition to the "One man, one vote" principle. The ANC sharply criticised Botha's statement and exhorted: "Attack and attack once more without giving the enemy the respite he seeks!"[131]

The determination of the South African authorities to find a way to draw the ANC into talks on their terms was confirmed when Victor Matlou (his real name was Zenjiwe Nkondo) was detained on the South African-Lesotho border. (The Lesotho plane he was travelling in landed in Bloemfontein instead of Maseru. He was later released, after international pressure.) His interrogators wanted to know the political orientation of the liberation movement, its attitude to the South African

214

state, and its strategy. They asked Matlou, "What is the ANC's political line? Why does the ANC not negotiate?"[132] For those in Moscow who were watching the developments in South Africa, this was the very first sign of what many saw as inevitable, the fact that sooner or later Pretoria would have to start talking to the ANC.

The frequency of attacks on police stations did not mean that Umkhonto was capable of only actions against small targets. Those attacks were aimed at showing that the police were vulnerable and not to be feared.[133] The beginning of the decade of the 1980s was characterised by a qualitative shift in anti-racist activities in South Africa. At long last, the masses were no longer spectators, applauding the actions of the favourite team – Umkhonto – but were beginning to participate themselves; they were becoming increasingly involved in active and resolute protests.

Also, the social composition of the protesters had changed. As distinct from 1976, now the workers were not only supporting the actions of the students, they were taking action themselves. The ANC tried to bring together all forms of resistance. A new feature was the mass struggle in the Western Cape, with the largest concentration of Coloured people, and, as described by Oliver Tambo, "historically, the main stronghold of [anti-ANC] Trotskyism in our country."[134]

A new success in uniting the broad anti-racist forces was registered on 3 December 1980. Sabata Dalindyebo was a prominent Xhosa chief who was regarded as a king and who had been deposed by the Transkeian authorities and forced to go into exile in Lusaka. He now announced that he had "formed an alliance with the ANC."[135]

The same year witnessed new spectacular actions by Umkhonto. As was traditional, on 31 May 1980 military parades took place in several South African cities to commemorate the anniversary of the Republic and to demonstrate the might of Pretoria's armed forces. On the very next day, 1 June, Umkhonto fighters attacked several targets at SASOL, a state-owned company producing liquid fuel from coal, and set them on fire.

The *Rand Daily Mail* in an editorial was unequivocal: "We must recognise that there can be no military solution to a revolutionary war ... there can be only a political solution."[136] But Pretoria again tried to put the blame on external forces. The Minister of Police Louis le Grange stated: "The Russian Ambassador in Lusaka, Dr Solodovnikov, played an important role in the planning of ANC and communist strategy and he was assisted by a South African refugee woman Frene

Ginwala."[137]

On the other hand, Oliver Tambo made the point that these attacks had peaceful purposes. Referring to the claim of the South African authorities, Tambo said: "One must pity the South African government for they are going to be misled into suicidal positions. These actions are done by blacks within the country ... No one outside South Africa – not even the Soviet Ambassador – has got a way of reaching into South Africa and telling the people exactly what to do."[138]

After the SASOL operation the term "armed propaganda" came into the political vocabulary of the ANC and the SACP. The operation against SASOL had a great psychological impact. This was the first time that limpet mines were used in South Africa. It would not be an exaggeration to compare their use with that of Soviet-made Strela ("Arrow") anti-aircraft missiles in Guinea-Bissau and in Mozambique in the early 1970s against the Portuguese Air Force. Those weapons could not in themselves change the course of the armed actions, but their effectiveness, psychological as much as anything else, could not be overestimated.

Occasionally a new type of weapon influenced ANC tactics. Limpet mines were quite new to South Africa. Joe Slovo recalled that when they were first supplied to the ANC in Mozambique, nobody knew how to handle them. The Soviet military experts stationed there were unable to help: their field was conventional warfare, not sabotage equipment. Fortunately someone in the ANC managed to figure out the mechanism; otherwise the whole lot would have been sent into South Africa without fuses.[139] That story is reminiscent of Kasrils's description of stealing dynamite and throwing the fuses away twenty years earlier.[140]

The ANC leadership did its best to co-ordinate military and political actions. For this reason, the attacks against SASOL coincided with the international campaign for the oil embargo against South Africa. A series of operations in May 1981 was carried out during nation-wide protests against the celebration of the 20th anniversary of the "White Republic of Black Misery". The explosion in the office of the South African Indian Council on 3 November 1981 was organised on the eve of the elections to that puppet body.

PROPAGANDA AND INTELLIGENCE GAMES

Despite the claim by the Minister of Police Louis le Grange that the police "knew all about the activities of the ANC, PAC and SACP in the country,"[141] regular attacks by Umkhonto against strategic installations occurred.

In January 1980 the Security Branch of the South African Police lost the services of a valuable agent, Captain Craig Williamson, who for a number of years held a senior position in the International University Exchange Fund. In an effort to save his agent, General Johan Coetzee, Head of the Security Police, flew to Switzerland to convince the Director of the IUEF, Swedish social-democrat Lars-Gunnar Eriksson, that there was only "one common enemy. Craig's target all along has been Communists."[142] His attempt failed.

Earlier in his address to the IUEF Assembly, Thomas Nkobi had called for "the closest co-operation" between the ANC and the IUEF "in actually setting up the assistance programme inside South Africa."[143] How pertinent his caution was became evident when Williamson was exposed. It was revealed that a secret account in Lichtenstein channelled IUEF money to the PAC and the Gang of Eight. Not surprisingly, the ANC later pleaded for "closer and honest co-operation" on the part of organisations assisting the liberation movement.[144]

Some members of the ANC were taken in by Williamson in his position with the IUEF. Confidential police documents made public in 1994 by Mac Maharaj show that agents of the South African security forces served as couriers for a section of the ANC underground and semi-legal structures in Southern Africa.[145] But, notwithstanding this, Williamson's successes were exaggerated. Many people in the ANC suspected him of being an agent, especially as it was known that he had been a police officer before enrolling at the University of the Witwatersrand.

Pretoria tried to disguise its defeat as a propaganda victory. A series of articles, written by Williamson, appeared in *Servamus*, the South African Police magazine, in which he highlighted his supposed successes. "S.A.P. penetrates Moscow" was the headline on the cover of *Servamus* under the picture of Williamson in Red Square.[146] But, how had he got there?

The Johannesburg *Sunday Times* claimed that Williamson "even had the audacity to spy on the mighty Russian KGB," and visited Moscow "as an official guest."[147] The truth is different. One day a member of the Soviet Peace Committee came to my office (we shared the building in Kropotkinskaya Street) and told me about a message they had received from Geneva. A top official of the IUEF, one Craig Williamson, had applied for a tourist visa to pay a private visit to Moscow during the Christmas holidays. As a reference he used the Soviet Peace Committee, an organisation with connections to the IUEF in the international peace structures.

I suggested that we should not commit ourselves in any way, though the chance to meet Williamson and make up my own mind about him was rather attractive. As an ordinary tourist, in possession of a valid travel document (*not* a South African passport), Williamson was granted a visa at the discretion of the Soviet consul in Switzerland.

It is of interest to note that, on the previous occasion when a Pretoria agent, Gerard Ludi, had "penetrated" Moscow in 1962, this was also achieved through the structures of the peace movement. Neither agent was exactly precise in his reports. Ludi referred to "Paliso" instead of Piliso.[148] While strolling about in Red Square, Williamson claimed that he "monitored the Communist Party of the Soviet Union ... I also infiltrated several other anti-South African organisations such as the Soviet Afro-Asian Friendship [read: Solidarity] Committee."[149]

If the correct name of the organisation he supposedly infiltrated slipped his mind, it is hardly surprising that Williamson wrote nothing of any substance about his "penetration" into Moscow in his *Servamus* articles. Needless to say, he never so much as knocked on the doors of No. 10 Kropotkinskaya, nor had the slightest contact of any sort with the Communist Party structures. It was enough to send his bosses a photograph taken in Moscow.

His subsequent promotion to the rank of major and later of lieutenant-colonel, his appointment to the President's Council, his supposed resignation to disguise his transfer from the Security Police to Military Intelligence, his "reconciliation" letter to some prominent ANC members, and his disclosure of Pik Botha's involvement in Pretoria's terrorism ... all of this lies outside the scope of this book. Perhaps one final point is worth mentioning. Either this so-called expert on "ANC clandestine operations" was hopelessly ill-informed about the ANC and its relationship with the Soviet Union or he was deliberately deceiving his audience. As late as 1989 he claimed that

Nelson Mandela "was appointed [to lead Umkhonto we Sizwe] on the recommendation of Moscow, a decision of which Andrei Gromyko remains proud to this day."[150]

The contacts between Craig Williamson and ANC officials in Gaborone and London served as a basis for a number of papers prepared by the South African National Intelligence Service (NIS) on the underground operations of the ANC ("ANC/CP" in their terminology). One of the documents put its position bluntly: "This memorandum helps to emphasise the lack of knowledge we have of ANC/CP networks operating from neighbouring states in terms of methodology, couriers, contents of letters, agents within the RSA etc."[151] At least Pretoria's special services got that right: the contents of the documents prove their lack of knowledge.

Having boasted of acquiring through Williamson information that was "ultra top secret, even within the ANC [about] a new A.N.C. committee ... called the Internal Reconstruction and Development Department",[152] they then proceeded to get names, composition and functions of this body wrong. They placed the name of "John Matshobi" [Motshabi], officially the Head of the Department, last in the list of the "committee" members. The political side of the Department's activity was virtually non-existent, according to the reports. In addition, this Department was identified as "the Intelligence Service of the ANC/CP",[153] despite the obvious fact that the ANC had a specifically-named Department of Security and Intelligence.

The future prospects of the liberation movement they got right: "The ANC/CP can only go from strength to strength under the present condition of growth, and correspondingly its support groups and manpower also gather strength in their onslaught against the RSA ... The political lobbying has badly damaged the Republic's political and economic position, and has led to a degree of international isolation. The RSA can no longer pretend that it has not been affected by the insidious efforts of the ANC/CP."[154]

Their information about the strength of Umkhonto was rather limited. They referred to "between five and ten thousand ... trained ANC/CP terrorists," adding the qualification "if the figures ... are true."[155] They managed to multiply the actual figure of Umkhonto fighters by several times. The relationship between the USSR and the ANC and SACP was grossly distorted. The NIS report stated: "To a large extent one can say that the onslaught against the RSA is an operation of the C.P.S.U."[156] The NIS, supposedly a think tank of the

219

South African establishment, became a hostage of its own propaganda.

The successes of the Umkhonto actions in the early 1980s caused a furore in South African ruling circles. The blame was again put on Moscow. P W Botha called the ANC "a small clique of blacks and whites, controlled by the Kremlin."[157]

General Constand Viljoen, then Head of the SADF, claimed that the Kremlin in 1981 formed a Co-ordination Committee on Southern Africa to undermine the region, and named the USSR Ambassador in Botswana, Nikolay Petrov, as the co-ordinator of the revolutionary onslaught against South Africa.[158] One cannot but wonder open-mouthed at the appalling paucity of the general's knowledge. The irony is that in Gaborone, as distinct from Lusaka, Luanda or Dar es Salaam, the Soviet Union did not have so much as one single person specifically in contact with the ANC. For many years Ambassador to Zambia Solodovnikov was portrayed as a "mastermind" of "terrorist attacks". When he left Zambia, the new Ambassador, Vladimir Cherednik, was immediately elevated by the pro-Pretoria press to the rank of "General in the KGB".

The South African authorities did their best to convince the leading Western countries of the "communist threat" to their country. An outstanding feature of this long campaign was the hearing on "the role of the Soviet Union, Cuba and East Germany in fomenting terrorism in Southern Africa", organised in the US Senate in 1982. The then South African Ambassador to Washington D B Sole wrote in his memoirs about the supervision of "an interesting exercise initiated by the Embassy to present black South African and Namibian witnesses to a special Congressional Committee on Terrorism in South West Africa set up by Senator Denton from Alabama. We had engineered the establishment of the Committee," he admitted.[159]

I experienced the quality of that "presentation of witnesses" somewhat indirectly. In May 1982 I was completing my PhD dissertation in the Academy of Social Sciences, and had scarcely been involved in any practical sense in Southern African affairs for almost three years, though naturally I maintained contacts with friends from the region.

One day at the end of May my telephone rang. "Have you seen the latest issue of *Sechaba*?" asked Eduard Samoylov, an old colleague from the Solidarity Committee. When I looked through the magazine, I had to laugh. *Sechaba* quoted one of the "witnesses" of "Denton's hearing", Nokokono Kave, a niece of Ciskei's "President" Lennox

Sebe, who claimed that "she was ... introduced to a Russian named Shubin who she was told headed the armed struggle in Southern Africa."[160]

As silly as such a statement was, it was printed in *Sechaba* along with her complaint about "sexual abuse" by the Soviets. When I later saw Francis Meli, the then editor of *Sechaba*, I asked why he had quoted that part of Kave's so-called evidence. He replied that his intention was satirical, but for me it was, as we say in Russian, "laughter through tears". I read the whole text of her statement many years later in Cape Town.

In spite of several months of preparation, the staged performance at the Senate hearing was rather weak. Apart from resurrecting Bartholomew Hlapane, a state witness in a number of the political trials of the 1960s, Nokokono Kave was the star turn among the witnesses. Nimrod Mkele wrote in the Johannesburg *Star*: "Nokokono Kave, Sebe's niece, has become something of a star performer in this regard, but her performance was marred by disclosures that she is far from the innocent and dedicated freedom fighter she claims to have been and is suspected of being a South African government plant."[161] I do not know whether she was an agent of Pretoria or not, but what is quite clear from her "evidence" in the Senate Subcommittee[162] is that she was mentally unbalanced.

The story has a tragic end. Almost five years later, in January 1987, Johnny Makatini came to Moscow. I phoned him at the Rossiya Hotel and he told me shocking news: "Your friend has been necklaced." Who could that be? I wondered. He continued, "Kave, when she returned to South Africa, was killed as a traitor." I do not know the circumstances of this occurrence, but whatever happened, the major responsibility for it lies with those South African and American officials who arranged for a mentally sick person to be a witness in the US Senate.

The same hearing was revealing in terms of the US attitude to the ANC. Speaking as a witness, Chester Crocker, the Assistant Secretary of State for African Affairs (and the father of the US "constructive engagement" programme in Southern Africa), on behalf of the US Administration "categorically condemned all terrorist and other violent acts" undertaken by SWAPO and the ANC "to bring about change in Namibia and South Africa."[163] He estimated that SWAPO received "90% of its military support and some 60% of its overall support from communist sources," and the ANC received "a comparable percentage of its military and other support from communist and other sources."[164]

The ANC reacted with this statement: "The derogatory reference by Dr Crocker to the just struggle for national liberation as 'terrorist' is but a feeble attempt by the Reagan administration at concealing its role as the mainstay of terrorist regimes throughout the world ... Neither the ANC nor the Soviet Union made any secret of the selfless support that the Soviet Union, the Socialist community and the progressive forces the world over are granting to the people fighting against oppression, exploitation and human degradation."[165]

While Denton's report did not make much impact internationally, inside South Africa it served its purpose. The (mis)information supplied by the South African security services had now been filtered through the mesh of the US Senate.

The summary of the hearing under the heading "Report of the Chairman"[166] was widely publicised by the US and South African media. But the information it contained cannot be read without a wry smile. For example, it stated that Joe Slovo was "still a member of the National Executive Committee of the ANC" even though at that time only Africans could be members; Slovo was elected to the Executive some three years later. Yusuf Dadoo was made "vice-president" of that body, despite his not even being a member, for the same reason.[167]

The Report's revelations about the membership of leading ANC figures in the SACP, on the basis of "South African intelligence sources", was also far from the truth. Some non-communists were recorded as SACP members, but others, such as Sizakele Sigxashe, then an active communist, soon to be a member of the SACP Politbureau, were not included.[168]

The White Paper on Defence and Armaments Supply placed before parliament by Magnus Malan in May 1982 emphasised the threat of the "total onslaught" against South Africa. It described "Soviet intentions" to tie down South African forces in SWA [Namibia] while giving increasing support to the insurgency in South Africa itself.[169]

Such a plan (perhaps, unfortunately) simply did not exist. The support to this or that country of the region, to this or that liberation movement, was rendered by the USSR in a piecemeal way, on a bilateral basis, taking into account their requests. Though there was some co-operation between the progressive forces of the region, its level was far below what was desired.

As to the "Soviet intentions", unfortunately the Soviet ruling bodies, especially government departments, paid much more attention to the wishes and official requests of Presidents and Prime Ministers than to those of the leaders of the liberation movements. For example, the Angolan government certainly needed a considerable amount of support, but I have no doubt that if a significant part of the aid supplied to it had been re-directed to the ANC, the pressure of the SADF and Pretoria's surrogates in Luanda would have been considerably reduced. Suffice it to say that the whole volume of Soviet support to the ANC over thirty years did not amount to more than two per cent of the assistance given to Angola after independence.

In its propaganda war Pretoria tried to exploit each and every instance when visas were granted to South African participants of international conferences convened in Moscow. While the academic boycott of South Africa by the USSR was strictly observed, in several cases international scientific organisations insisted on the participation of South Africans, especially when they were members of their governing bodies. In particular, the convening of the International Congress of Cardiologists in Moscow afforded an opportunity for Helen Suzman to visit the USSR, accompanying her husband in July 1982.

Unfortunately, those Soviet diplomats who issued the visas had not heard of her and treated the matter as routine. But Suzman's visit, highlighted in the South African and international press, caused serious concern in the ANC and SACP leadership. That might seem strange now, when she is regarded as a universally respected political figure, but in those days her record was not considered so positively. "Vorster, Suzman and lesser agents of colonialism have turned Africa into a veritable hunting ground for stooges and indigenous agents of racism," said Oliver Tambo in his New Year address in 1971. "Mrs Suzman deserves special mention. This sweet bird from the bloodstained south flew into Zambia and sang a singularly sweet song:

"I am opposed to apartheid;
I am opposed to the isolation of South Africa;
I am opposed to violence;
I am opposed to guerrillas;
I am opposed to Lusaka Manifesto;
I am opposed to the decision of the World Council of Churches;
I know the Africans can do nothing to cause political change in South Africa;
I am in favour of change;
I am clearly in favour of change, but determined to prevent change."[170]

Helen Suzman's role in improving the plight of political prisoners and her visits to Robben Island are lauded today. However, it is worth recalling what Mac Maharaj wrote soon after his release. When Nelson Mandela reminded Helen Suzman that "white political prisoners who had taken to arms [Afrikaners in 1914] ... had been released before they had even served as much as a third of their sentence and we demanded the same," Suzman, according to Maharaj, replied: "The difference, Nelson, is: are you prepared to say you'll abandon violence and the armed struggle? ... True, the rebels of 1918 [read: 1914?] were released ... but their struggle had been defeated, now yours is ongoing, it weakens your case and I cannot demand your release."[171]

Apart from the open terrorist activity in the neighbouring countries, the South African special services were supplying the international media (and conservative political circles) with deliberately distorted information about the ANC. Among the Western magazines specialising in (mis)information about the ANC and its allies, a specific role was played by the journal *Africa Confidential* in London. Speculation about the internal situation in the ANC and especially its leadership was one of its hardy perennials. Some obvious inaccuracies and gross mistakes could perhaps be explained by the difficulty in obtaining information about an organisation waging an underground and armed struggle (despite the magazine's claim to be "confidential"), but self-evident blunders with regard to prominent ANC leaders could not but amaze.

The magazine claimed in 1981 that Thabo Mbeki was "a US-trained economist in his early thirties." He graduated in Britain and was born in 1942. It called Joe Slovo the ANC "military *supremo*", while in fact Joe Modise was the top military commander. It further claimed that Slovo might soon be removed from his post because of ANC sensitivity "to the wishes of thousands of young black South Africans who have swelled the guerrilla ranks since the Soweto upheaval" and expected Thabo Mbeki to be "promoted to the key military job".[172] In reality, of course, Slovo was extremely popular among "young black South Africans", while Thabo Mbeki, though he underwent sophisticated military training in the USSR, concentrated his energies on political activity.

The shift of the major Western powers towards the ANC was slow and painful. The attempts to uncover – or to create – a "third force" in South Africa continued in the 1980s. Young South Africans were encouraged to accept scholarships in the USA on condition they left the ANC. Even the top leadership of the South African liberation movement were sometimes subject to hostility. In June 1981 Oliver Tambo was issued with a US visa to participate in a seminar at Howard University. His programme included meetings with senators and congressmen as well as with the Mayor of Washington and the US companies involved in South Africa. But it took him much time and effort to obtain entry into the USA.

The State Department stated that, while Tambo had received a visa, "it was given improperly." "Proper procedures were not followed and the department was not informed that a visa was issued. An error was made in not referring his application to the department for review." Although the ANC was not officially named by the State Department as a "terrorist" organisation, its representative said: "There is little question that elements in the ANC engaged in terrorism."[173]

Later, at a diplomatic function in Lusaka, Oliver Tambo walked past the US Ambassador, declining to greet him. This indicates how deeply the actions of the US authorities had offended the supremely polite and considerate ANC President.

The USSR reacted to the growth of the political and military resistance to the apartheid regime in two ways. First, it steadily increased its assistance to ANC military operations. Second and parallel to this, an important decision was taken by the CPSU Central Committee in 1981 on the initiative of the Ministry of Foreign Affairs, supported by the ruling Party's International Department. It envisaged the establishment of contacts with legal anti-racist forces inside South Africa (obviously, with the full knowledge of the ANC and the SACP). Sensing that the general trend of developments would force Pretoria sooner or later to change its policy and to negotiate with the liberation movement, some future contacts between Moscow and Pretoria were hinted at, though the formulation of these was very cautious and limited, so as not to prevent "normal" protocol contacts with South African government representatives.

Though correct in its essence, this decision was premature. At that stage the legal anti-racist opposition inside South Africa was still weak and vulnerable. As to the potential interaction with Pretoria, the sharp escalation of South African aggression against Angola and other states of the region made this more problematic. Among the victims of those aggressive actions, both direct and indirect, were Soviet citizens in Angola and Mozambique.

Paradoxically, it was events such as the capture of Soviet citizens that made some kind of contact between the Soviet Union and South Africa unavoidable. Ambassador Yury Yukalov, the Head of the African Department of the USSR Ministry of Foreign Affairs, admitted in 1988: "Closed contacts took place several years ago. But they were aimed at releasing Soviet geologists captured by Renamo units in Mozambique [and other citizens as well]. Then we had to be cautious and avoid publicity."[174] However, the South African side, which faced the problem of international isolation, tried to use each such contact to its political advantage. More often than not, the nature of the contact was distorted or blown out of proportion.

The growth of international attention to South Africa was demonstrated by the convening of the International Conference on Sanctions against South Africa by the UN and the OAU in Paris in May 1981. Though the major Western powers boycotted the conference (with the exception of France, where the left came to power and Socialist Party leader Francois Mitterand was elected President), its message was clear: the sanctions against Pretoria were to become increasingly comprehensive. I was impressed in Paris by the firm stand taken by Oliver Tambo: he made it clear that Pretoria's partners should be made to choose between ties with apartheid and ties with Africa.

1981 was a year when ANC security managed to uncover a number of Pretoria's agents. Some of them had long-term assignments spread over five or more years and were supposed to work their way up into the ANC leadership. The story of one man, known in the movement as "Piper", was typical of such actions. After spending some time in the ANC camps in Angola, where he performed well enough to be recruited into the SACP, "Piper" was sent to the International Lenin School in Moscow for political studies. He was so highly regarded by some SACP and ANC leaders that he was invited to an enlarged meeting of the Central Committee, which took place in the GDR. But after his return to Moscow he suddenly started behaving oddly, was recalled, tried to run away to South Africa, but was detained by the Botswana authorities and returned to the ANC.

During interrogation he confessed that his nerve started to crack when one of the Soviet lecturers asked him, "Why are you so perfect? You don't make any mistakes. Behave naturally." He imagined he was under suspicion, and started violating discipline in order to leave Moscow as soon as possible.

These disclosures caused a wave of detentions in the ANC which became known as "shishita" ("clean-up" in one of the Zambian vernaculars). As a result of this about 60 people confessed to contacts with the South African special services, and an even greater number came under suspicion.

APARTHEID STATE TERRORISM AND POWER DIPLOMACY

Pretoria continued to rely on repression inside the country, coupled with an increase in SADF raids against ANC targets in neighbouring countries. The attack against ANC houses in Matola, a suburb of Maputo, in January 1981 caused the loss of fifteen lives. Three ANC activists were kidnapped and taken to South Africa. One of the victims was a trade union activist and SACP member, William Kanyile, who went into exile after thirteen years on Robben Island. In 1978-9 he spent several months in Moscow in the Higher Trade Union School.

At least initially, the Mozambican government was not intimidated by the attack on Matola. On the contrary, a mass protest rally was organised in Maputo. At the end of his speech Samora Machel embraced Oliver Tambo.

Attempts on the lives of ANC leaders and members outside South Africa intensified. In February 1981 an explosive device was found at the home of Joe Gqabi, who by that time had become an ANC Executive member and its representative in Zimbabwe. Several months later he was killed by an unknown gunman outside his house. As heavy as this blow was for the ANC, it had the effect of improving relations between the ANC and the Zimbabwe government. Speaking at his funeral in the presence of Oliver Tambo, Prime Minister Robert Mugabe declared that Zimbabwe and the people of South Africa were united by the death of Joe Gqabi in their just common cause and would remain united until the final victory. Turning to Tambo, he added: "Have no fear, therefore, Comrade President Tambo, that this act might deter the people of Zimbabwe from their noble duty to render assistance to the people of South Africa."[175]

To justify its aggressive actions against Mozambique and other states, the South African military hierarchy, and especially the Defence Minister General Magnus Malan, referred again and again to the threat of the "total onslaught" against South Africa. In his first speech in parliament Malan announced that "more than five hundred Russian tanks" were poised close to South Africa's borders, ready to launch a conventional attack. *The Times* of London, not exactly known to be a supporter of the ANC or the Soviet Union, openly ridiculed him, calling his speech "pretty hot stuff even by South African standards ... Nobody [in parliament] challenged General Malan's figures, for instance nobody asked the general about the range of a Russian tank, how it will get from Angola to South Africa through Namibia. Still generals are not accustomed to having their opinions questioned."[176]

The ANC intensified its armed actions inside South Africa, especially with sabotage of railways and other economic structures. One operation against an electrical substation in Durban on 21 April 1981 caused damage of about two and half million Rands.[177] Perhaps the most spectacular of Umkhonto's achievements was an attack against the South African Army base at Voortrekkerhoogte. It took place on 16 June 1981, on the anniversary of the Soweto uprising. For the first time the ANC used rockets (in previous attacks what were described by the press as rockets were, at least in Soviet military terminology, grenades from RPG launchers). The *Grad P* ("*Grad*" means "Hail" in Russian and *P* stands for "portable") rocket launcher was widely used in Vietnam and other liberation wars, and proved to be an easily portable and effective weapon.

According to SADF information, four rockets hit the base but only one of them caused any damage. The Umkhonto Command, on the other hand, felt sure that the damage, both in manpower and equipment, was more extensive. What was important was that another blow had been dealt to the myth of SADF invincibility.

On 25 August 1981 the SADF launched Operation Protea, a new large-scale incursion into Angola. It coincided with a seminar convened in East Berlin by the UN Committee Against Apartheid. Having switched on the radio in the Berlin Stadt Hotel on the morning of 1 September I heard: "A Soviet non-commissioned officer Nikolay Pestretsov was captured by South African troops miles inside ... (Namibia? I thought for a second. What the hell was he doing there?) ... Angola."

Pestretsov's wife, two senior officers, and the wife of one of the officers were killed while trying to retreat to safety. The same day Magnus Malan made a statement in Cape Town describing this as "indisputable evidence of Russian involvement with SWAPO."[178] Again, the top South African military hierarchy was ready to twist the facts. From the documents captured and later made public by the South African authorities,[179] they were fully aware that the Soviet officers were attached to an Angolan Infantry Brigade and had nothing to do with SWAPO. Truth is easily disregarded for propaganda purposes.

(We did have experts with the SWAPO military headquarters in Lubango for many years, but none of them had ever been captured or killed.)

A statement by TASS, the Soviet official news agency, made the point that the activity of these Soviet citizens in Angola did not go beyond "the framework of technical consultations and training of Angolan national cadres ... The Soviet side places full responsibility for the death of the Soviet citizens on the Government of the RSA and demands the immediate return of the captured Soviet citizen and of the bodies of the deceased."[180]

The 70th anniversary of the ANC in January 1982 was marked widely by ANC communities and its supporters in many countries around the world under the slogan, "Unity in Action". A special committee headed by Joe Nhlanhla prepared the jubilee programme, which was designed and used by the ANC leadership to raise the profile of the ANC abroad. Oliver Tambo participated in the celebrations in Tanzania, Alfred Nzo in London, Thomas Nkobi in Stockholm, and Moses Mabhida in Luanda. The delegation to Moscow was headed by Thabo Mbeki.

There was good reason to celebrate. 1981 witnessed the highest level of Umkhonto's military actions, and that, in turn, inspired mass political activity. The protests against the celebration of the 20th anniversary of the Republic of South Africa were used to advance the issues of wages, rents, and education.[181]

The ANC leadership closely followed the growth of the trade union movement. In August 1981 a preliminary meeting took place in Cape Town to form a national trade union federation. Difficulties arose as a result of interference by foreign organisations. The International Confederation of Free Trade Unions, the American AFL-CIO, the British Trade Union Congress, and Swedish trade unions, while giving considerable financial assistance, insisted that the newly emerging South African trade unions should deal exclusively with economic and not political problems. The ANC for its part was trying to support workers' strikes by taking armed actions against the relevant companies. It appealed for the creation of combat units at the factories.[182]

A new feature of the situation inside South Africa was the appearance of a legal leadership of the struggle for the first time in many years. A united leadership was essential to overcome the tendency shown by, for example, trade unions and youth organisations

230

to act independently. The ANC was extremely popular, and was able to assist the unity of the legal opposition, bringing together trade union, youth, women's, church and other organisations.

An important political victory was won by the ANC when it was invited to participate in the summit meeting of the Front Line States in Maputo on 6 and 7 March 1982. That meeting decided, in particular, "to increase their material and diplomatic support for the liberation movements of SWAPO of Namibia and ANC of South Africa, so that they can intensify the armed struggle for attainment of national independence of their peoples."[183] The African leaders went on record as supporting the ANC and its armed struggle and promised their assistance in this field. The notion of "attaining independence" was stated to mean the non-recognition of the Pretoria regime.

Unfortunately the reality was far removed from the conference declaration. *Sechaba* published a picture of Joe Modise at the venue in Maputo.[184] He had participated in the meeting together with the Presidents of the Front Line States, including Botswana. Only months later he and Cassius Make, Assistant Secretary of the ANC Revolutionary Council, were arrested, charged and sentenced in Botswana for illegal possession of arms. Instead of "intensifying the armed struggle", they had to serve a years sentence in the Gaborone gaol.

Under pressure from Pretoria the government of Swaziland asked the ANC representatives to leave the country. That request was made by the Swazi Prime Minister at a meeting in Lusaka with Oliver Tambo and the Presidents of Zambia and Kenya. He complained that the use of Swazi territory by the ANC for the transit of personnel and weapons to South Africa created increased pressure from Pretoria. This threatened to transform Swaziland into an operational zone, the implication being that South Africa might intervene directly inside Swaziland as it had in the operational zone in Angola.

In these circumstances the ANC tried to create strong structures inside the country as soon as possible, to continue the struggle even if their contacts with Headquarters were weakened.[185]

When an ANC delegation headed by Alfred Nzo visited Moscow in mid May 1982, one of the issues raised was the increase of Pretoria's state terrorism, which had spread far beyond the African continent.

On 14 March 1982, on the day when 15 000 people demonstrated against apartheid in London, an explosion partially destroyed the ANC London office. On 17 August 1982 a parcel bomb killed Ruth First, a prominent South African intellectual, who worked in the Centre of African Studies of the Eduardo Mondlane University in Maputo. Pallo Jordan, who was in the same room at the time, was injured.

Why did they kill her? Were they afraid of Ruth First's intellectual influence on the Mozambican leadership and were they trying to clear the way for a separate deal with Mozambique? The recently published documents of the NIS, mentioned above, add one more dimension to the tragedy. Pretoria's security establishment thought that Ruth First was "the co-ordinator" of the "IRDD" machinery in Mozambique, just as they believed that it was Phyllis Naidoo and not Chris Hani who headed the underground structures in Lesotho, despite his being named "a known trained terrorist". Their logic was simple: it was Whites, "at worst" Indians, but never "Bantu" (after 1976, "Blacks"), that could mastermind "the ANC/SACP" activities.[186]

Sechaba completed its obituary to Ruth First with this warning: "There may yet well come a time when the murders and assassinations of the opponents of apartheid will provoke similar assassinations of establishment politicians, police and military chiefs."[187] Fortunately, that time did not come in South Africa, at least as far as the ANC was concerned. But armed actions were becoming more risky.

After a rather long sabbatical term – three years of studies and research – I was again in Africa in October 1982 to attend the Congress of the CCM, the Tanzanian ruling party. Apart from having the usual discussions with friends in the liberation movement, I was able to visit the newly established Solomon Mahlangu Freedom College (SOMAFCO). The stream of refugees from South Africa into the ANC camps continued. The Tanzanian government allocated 10 000 hectares of land in Dakawa, not far from Mazimbu to the ANC. A vocational training centre and a centre for permanent accommodation of the refugees was to be built there.[188] It was good to see many veterans of the South African revolutionary movement in Mazimbu, people who had come to help the young ANC members. Among them were Rica Hodgson, Jack Hodgson's widow, and George Ponen, the trade union veteran.

There were some people at the CCM congress whom the Soviets did not meet often, such as the PAC delegates. The allegation was often made that the Soviet Union discriminated against the PAC. Perhaps we were really "more Catholic than the Pope himself", strictly following ANC advice on the matter. But the activities of the PAC leadership in exile also contributed to the estrangement. For many years, including the tragic period of the "Great Proletarian Cultural Revolution" in China, the PAC was ready to support any statement against "social-imperialism" (read: the USSR) coming out of Beijing. However, the almost total absence of PAC political and military activity inside South Africa was the main reason for our lack of contact.

But this does not mean that we avoided the PAC at international meetings. On the contrary, during that very CCM Congress, for example, I spent an evening in discussion with one of the then PAC leaders, who had for many years worked for the Coca-Cola company in Swaziland. In introducing himself to me, he said, without so much as a wink, "My name is Joseph, like Joseph Stalin."

Oliver Tambo came to Moscow in mid November that year to attend Leonid Brezhnev's funeral. During his stay a disturbing event took place. As was common practice among ANC and SACP leaders, Oliver Tambo went to visit the Umkhonto cadres in one of the small camps not far from Moscow. While there he received a message that President Samora Machel urgently wanted to speak to him. Later, when Tambo emerged from Machel's suite in the Moskva Hotel, he was visibly worried.

That conversation was perhaps the first warning of a possible change in Mozambique's relations with Pretoria. As Tambo related it to us, Machel was extremely worried about the situation in Mozambique, and complained about the lack of Soviet support. Aware of the longstanding close relations between the USSR and the ANC, he perhaps hoped the ANC could influence the situation. He was successful, at least in part: before Tambo left Moscow we were able to tell him that the Defence Minister Marshal Dmitry Ustinov had already met with Machel.

Although the SACP was represented at Brezhnev's funeral by Moses Mabhida, the original purpose of his journey was quite different. A shift in the Chinese policy had opened the way for their having contact not only with the ANC but with the SACP as well. The first approach, transmitted to the SACP leadership by Vella Pillay, who worked in the London branch of the Chinese Bank, was received with mixed feelings. It was decided to seek more information about China's internal and external policies from the Soviets.

When I came to the airport to meet Mabhida, who had arrived on an Aeroflot flight from Maputo, I found that the plane had been diverted some distance from the main terminal. I felt something was wrong. I saw a group of Soviet officers, and among them was Colonel Nikolay

Olshannikov, a senior colleague of mine during military service in the late 1960s. The old man could hardly hold back his tears: the plane had brought back the remains of his son, a young interpreter killed in a helicopter shot down by Renamo.

By mid 1982 most of the SACP leadership was concentrated in Maputo. Apart from the meetings of its seven-member Politbureau (four of whom – Moses Mabhida, Joe Slovo, John Nkadimeng and Chris Hani – stayed mostly in the Mozambican capital), a permanent executive body, the Secretariat, was operating there as well. The change of leadership in the USSR overshadowed the original aim of Mabhida's visit. However, the "Chinese question" was not forgotten, and Mabhida's report was discussed by the Secretariat and then by the Politbureau: "G.S. [General Secretary] reported on consultations with CPSU ... CPSU of the opinion that we should be cautious but should not reject the overtures [by the Chinese]."[189]

The document is a good example of the relationship that existed between the CPSU and the SACP. The Soviets did not dictate their position to the SACP, nor did they prevent the SACP from developing relations with Beijing.

The same approach was typical of the Soviet Union's relations with the ANC. In his interview with the US magazine *Africa Report* Oliver Tambo made this clear: "We stood together with the Soviet Union and the allied forces in fighting Nazism during the Second World War. True to these positions the Soviet Union and other socialist countries stand with us to this day fighting the apartheid system itself and its leaders .... of Nazi ideology and practice."[190]

These words resembled (and were an ironic response to) the statement by President Ronald Reagan in 1981 about US relations with South Africa: "Can we abandon a country that has stood behind us in every war we have fought, a country that strategically is essential to the free world in its production of minerals we all must have and so forth?"[191]

Oliver Tambo was expected in Moscow again in December 1982, when the USSR celebrated its 60th anniversary. But events required that he travel to Maseru instead. In the early hours of 10 December Pretoria's commandos attacked twelve residences in the capital of Lesotho. Forty-two people were massacred. Of the 33 South Africans killed in Maseru, only six were trained fighters; the others were either new recruits or civilians; some prominent commanders were among the victims.

Oliver Tambo decided to fly to Maseru from Maputo, even though the Mozambican authorities tried to convince him not to. The risk was great, but the ANC President was resolute: "They can kill me somewhere else if they wish," he said.

The effect of his presence in Maseru was enormous. "Tambo flies in for the ANC funeral" was a headline in one of the South African papers. The flight to Maseru was, of course, a flight over South African territory. As the *Rand Daily Mail* put it, the appearance of the man "most wanted by the SA Security Police" at a time "when most of the South African refugees were expecting fresh attacks from across the border came as a complete surprise to all but the highest ranks of the Lesotho government."[(192)]

The initial reaction of the South African press to the SADF invasion, including so-called liberal papers, was positive. Even the avowedly anti-apartheid *Rand Daily Mail* wrote on 10 December: "While this paper has consistently deplored the use of violence as an alternative to political negotiation, it remains difficult to censure the defence force for what is a natural military response to a situation, which, if General Constand Viljoen ... is to be believed, would have seen guerrilla incursions across the Lesotho border during the Festive season. No efficient army can be blamed for acting to paralyse that kind of plan."[(193)]

When all the details of the Maseru massacre became known, the tone of such papers changed. As for the ANC, the reply came soon. The explosions that occurred at the building site of the Koeberg atomic power station near Cape Town on 19 December 1982, the day of the funeral in Maseru, were a stern warning to the regime and its supporters.

Another, quite separate, Umkhonto action took the lives of the traitor Bartholomew Hlapane and his wife, no doubt caused partly by Hlapane's appearance at the US Senate hearing. He might have expected such an outcome, as his name was mentioned in the leaflet *Traitors*, distributed illegally in South Africa fifteen years earlier: "We swear that every traitor will be punished – each will pay with his life for destroying the lives of others."[(194)] After his killing, *Sechaba* wrote: "The ANC like an African elephant has demonstrated a long historical memory in such cases."[(195)]

SACP RELATIONS WITH THE ANC IN THE 1980s

The relationship between the ANC and the SACP has often been at best misunderstood, at worst deliberately distorted. At different stages of the struggle different aspects of this relationship have come to the fore. In the early 1980s the ANC leadership believed that its members should not be discouraged from discussing socialism, despite its absence from the policy of the ANC. Some communists in the ANC, for example the late Mzala, felt that socialism as an aim should be debated within the ANC: "The transition to socialism is a logical development of the present revolutionary process in our country and this proposition in my view should be raised to the level of debates even within the African National Congress."[196]

But this position was not supported by the top SACP leadership. Moses Mabhida said at the ANC Youth Conference: "Some of our people think that the party and ANC have come to an unwritten agreement amounting to which the ANC will head the struggle for a democratic revolution, the so-called February phase, while the party will be responsible for leading the advance to socialism. This impression ought to be corrected. There is no such agreement."[197]

In South Africa knowledge of the SACP was at an appallingly low level, even in those institutions which purported to possess "expertise" on the subject. For example, one of the papers of the Institute of Strategic Studies, written in 1983, claimed that the SACP consisted of 85% white intellectuals. In fact, at that stage the great majority of SACP members were African, and some units, as Chris Hani confirmed in a discussion with me in Moscow, consisted entirely of Africans.[198]

Even in conditions of strict illegality, the SACP leadership did its best to be in contact with its regions; every report from them received a response. As the archive documents show, the local Party committees tried to influence some decisions concerning the ANC by appealing to the SACP Central Committee. For example, the London regional committee was concerned about the plan to replace Ruth Mompati with Solly Smith (Samuel Khunieli) as the ANC Chief Representative there, referring to it as "a disaster".[199] They were proved correct. Not only did the misbehaviour of Solly Smith not help the movement's prestige (he appeared at public ceremonies drunk), but he later confessed to having been recruited by Pretoria.[200]

One of the issues discussed by the SACP Secretariat in September 1982 was a letter from Ray Simons "proposing a document that would clearly formulate the policy of the party on Trade Unions."[201] It was decided to organise a "joint meeting of the P. B. with selected comrades involved in T.U. [trade union] work."[202] This meeting took place in Moscow in May 1983 in the CPSU Guest House estate named Volynskoe 2 (a few hundred metres away from Volynskoe 1, Stalin's dacha.)

The meeting discussed steps to encourage trade union unity inside South Africa, as well as the work of communists in Sactu, by this time practically leaderless. Its President Stephen Dlamini had never fully recovered after being tortured in prison and was often sick; its Vice President Moses Mabhida concentrated on SACP affairs; and its Secretary General John Gaetsewe, who was also sick, left London for Francistown in Botswana, where his work effectively came to an end.

It was perfectly clear to the leaders of the SACP (and the ANC) that Sactu could not be a co-ordinator of the trade union movement inside the country. While it had no industrial trade unions as members, it did have a certain influence in the workers' movement and it was therefore considered a mistake to dissolve it at that stage.

The exchanges in Moscow helped to activate Sactu to some extent. In August at the enlarged meeting of the Sactu Executive John Nkadimeng was elected its Secretary General and Thozamile Botha its Administrative Secretary.

The Politbureau meeting in Moscow was remarkable for a number of reasons. Some prominent activists of the liberation and trade union movement of South Africa came to Moscow for the first time, including Thozamile Botha, a well-known leader of the African civic organisation in Port Elizabeth (PEBCO), who had to leave the country to avoid arrest. Another person new to us was Ivan Pillay, who was later to play a key role in Operation Vula.

It was during the meeting, on 20 May 1983, that the news came of an explosion in Church Street in Pretoria, at the entrance to the South African Air Force Headquarters and opposite the building which housed Military Intelligence.

That action was perhaps the most spectacular of many carried out by Umkhonto. Magnus Malan stated in parliament in 1983 that "bombings" over five years had caused damage of about 508 million Rands.[203]

The Johannesburg *Sunday Times* reacted to the Church Street explosion under the heading: "'Colonel' Slovo lies low in London".[204] It quoted Louis le Grange, Minister of Police, who dubbed Slovo the "country's enemy No 1 ... He prefers London, it seems, to Moscow ... Slovo is thought to have gone to London immediately after the Pretoria explosion – apparently anticipating the SADF retaliatory raid on Maputo ... It seems," the newspaper continued, "his every move is monitored by the South African agents and informers." But apparently those agents were tracking the wrong man: Slovo was in Moscow when the explosion in Church Street took place. Besides, the *Sunday Times* (apparently on the basis of the police reports) wrote that Slovo "had no military background",[205] discounting his service during World War Two, to say nothing of his "consultations" in Moscow.

Slovo was planning to fly from Moscow to London via Berlin and Amsterdam. We thought that it was rather risky in the circumstances, but he insisted; in Amsterdam he managed to get an earlier connection.

The *Sunday Times* elaborated: "He is a Moscow communist, KGB colonel, who has a dacha on Lake Baikal – and he is a leading ideologue in the ANC-SACP alliance."[206] Four years later, when for the first time his purpose in coming to the Soviet Union was a short holiday, I suggested to Joe Slovo that he should go to Lake Baikal to sleuth out that dacha, but he was, as usual too pressed for time.

However, strange as it may seem, that tale became an urban legend in South Africa. In a rather warm "tribute to the white man black South Africa loved", Shaun Johnson wrote about Joe Slovo's "impressionability in a Soviet dacha".[207]

There was much speculation in South Africa and in the West about a change in the ANC strategy after the Church Street explosion. But Oliver Tambo commented in an interview with a Mozambican journalist at that time: "There has been no change in strategy at all. I think that perhaps the idea of a change in strategy arose from the fact that the headquarters of the South African Air Force was an unfamiliar target: unfamiliar because it has been the policy of the regime to conceal the casualties they suffer in the conflicts we have had with them over a period of years now."[208]

One person was missing at the SACP meeting in Moscow: the Party Chairman Yusuf Dadoo. His condition had been reported to the SACP Secretariat the previous September: he had to undergo an operation for the removal of a cancerous growth. Unfortunately, the operation did not help to any great degree and his health continued to deteriorate. By

May it became clear that the disease was terminal.

South African comrades were deeply concerned. Joe Slovo, who for some years shared a small office in London with Dadoo, told us how Dadoo might have become rich as the eldest son of a prominent businessman, and how he lived in very modest circumstances in London. "But he has lived a much happier life," Slovo concluded.

The admiration which many South African revolutionaries felt for Dadoo was shared by Nelson Mandela. In a letter smuggled out by Mac Maharaj, he wrote to Dadoo about his experience in the prison: "I think much of the days to come, the problems of adjustment, picking up old threads. It is mainly in this regard that I never really live on this island. My thoughts are ever travelling up and down the country most of the time and the Oxford Atlas, in spite of its old age, having acquired it in 1963, is one of my greatest companions. In the process I have come to know the world and my country far better than when I was free.

"But the purpose of this letter is not to talk about correspondence, past memories or atlases, but to tell you that I don't forget 5/9 [Dadoo's birthday] and to wish you many happy returns; to let you know that we think of you with far more pride that words can express ... We hope that you, 2 Reggies [Oliver Reginald Tambo and Reginald September] and Toni's Pa ["Rusty" Bernstein] are keeping together like quadruplets..." (No doubt Mandela was alluding to the four organisations of the Congress Alliance.)

"I look forward to seeing you some day. I never forget ties of a personal nature which link you and I and which may help cement the fond memories of 3 decades."[209]

Dadoo sought treatment for his condition, originally in Czechoslovakia and then in Britain. It was only in July 1983, when his condition had deteriorated further, that he decided to go to Moscow.

The Soviet doctors as a rule do not inform a patient about an illness such as cancer. But in this case they did not hide the truth from Dadoo. I heard that he was upset, just for a moment, when they told him, but immediately braced himself and started thanking the doctors and nurses for all they had done for him.

When he was leaving the hospital, comrades informally asked a nurse how long Dadoo would live. "A month," she replied. And he lived exactly a month. His death, or how he "turned this moment of irreversible defeat into a victory", was well described by Joe Slovo in an article in the *African Communist*.[210] His death coincided with the

239

last days of preparation for the SACP Central Committee meeting in Prague and I had the sad duty of telling Moses Mabhida and his other comrades about Dadoo's death soon after they landed in Sheremetyevo on their way from Africa to Czechoslovakia.

Information about the deterioration of Dadoo's health reached South Africa. "*The great coolie vrek*" [is dead] was the reaction doing the rounds in police circles.[211] In a letter to his supporters at home Dadoo wrote: "These small minds tout [*sic*] our people with the question of my dying, in particular the Indian people ... But this should not worry you unduly. None of us is immortal, but the cause for which we live and fight is."[212]

The Pretoria regime could indeed celebrate the departure of Dadoo. His role had been well known for more than 40 years. The confidential document of the National Intelligence Service described him as "the co-ordinator and brains behind much of the organising against the RSA in Europe."[213]

Dadoo's testament, in a letter to the Central Committee meeting, deserves to be included in the history books of the liberation struggle. I record only a fragment from it. Dadoo quoted from the then Soviet leader Yury Andropov: "In politics one pays for one's errors. When the guiding role of a Communist Party weakens, there arises the danger of sliding back to a bourgeois-reformist way of development. If a Party loses touch with the people, self-proclaimed aspirants to the role of those who express the interests of the working people emerge in the ensuing vacuum."[214] That is exactly what was to happen in the Soviet Union.

During their Politbureau meeting in Moscow the SACP leadership asked if the USSR would host Chris Hani and his family for a holiday. His wife Limpho had been wrongly listed as one of the victims of the Maseru massacre. When the SADF released the names of "four ANC exiles killed in the raid", they included "Limpho Sekamane, who is the wife of a top ANC man Mr Temi Hani."[215]

General Johan Coetzee even claimed that the woman who had been killed was not a civilian, but a person trained as a terrorist in Russia. In fact, the person killed was a daughter of a former Lesotho Minister. Apparently a night watchman, who knew Hani's family, deliberately pointed to a wrong apartment in an effort to save Limpho and her children. The police lie became evident when Limpho appeared "back at work in Maseru at the Lesotho Tourist Corporation offices where she has worked for a long time."[216]

Again, information coming from the boss of Pretoria's security makes one think: either the South African intelligence was hopelessly weak, or its chiefs were ready to use any lie to justify their criminal actions. Limpho had not ever visited the USSR before 1983.

That was the third attack on Chris and his family. Two unsuccessful attempts to blow up his car and his house had taken place earlier. When Limpho Hani, a Lesotho citizen, was arrested on South African territory (she had gone there for family reasons), the authorities tried to blackmail her father, proposing to release her only if Chris surrendered himself.

But all this did not prevent Hani from coming secretly to Lesotho again on an ANC mission and at the same time "to attend to [SACP] cell question of re-organisation."[217] The Lesotho authorities were not officially informed and he encountered some difficulties when his stay was discovered, but members of the Lesotho cabinet, including Vincent Makhele, helped him.

Chris and his family came to Moscow by two different routes: his wife and two small daughters arrived via Lusaka, and a couple of days later he came from Maputo. The morning after her arrival Limpho Hani told us: "This is the first quiet night I have spent, without fear, for many years."

Chris grieved over the death of his friends in Maseru. "Do you remember Uncle Gene? [Gungushe]?" he asked his little daughter. "Do you remember how he used to sing 'Bourgeoisie can kiss my arse'?"

Of course, apart from having a holiday, Chris had a busy time in Moscow. Both political discussions and some practical problems were waiting for him. He met a group of selected cadres who were in Moscow on their way to Simferopol for training in "Malyutka", wire-guided rocket launchers. (Originally developed as an anti-tank weapon, "Malyutka" could be used for sabotage activities. However, it was not, apparently, ever used inside South Africa.)

I accompanied Chris to one of the camps (little more than a house) outside Moscow where another group of Umkhonto cadres was taking a course in military combat work. Chris had studied there twelve or thirteen years earlier, and most of the staff were still there. They were excited to see Chris again, especially as he had arrived in a black official limo as an honoured guest.

A spirit of defiance and high expectations dominated the SACP Congress, which took place in Moscow at the end of 1984. In those years the SACP held "ordinary" Central Committee meetings

241

annually; once every three or four years an enlarged meeting would take place. With more participants attending, the enlarged meetings elected the Central Committee and then the new Central Committee would elect the Politbureau.

Supposed experts on the SACP claim that this or that person was either "expelled" or "dropped" from its Politbureau or Central Committee. There was no question of expulsion: if members were not re-elected, it was because others were not fully satisfied with their work performance or moral behaviour, and not for political differences. In some cases those not re-elected would be returned to the leading bodies at the next enlarged meeting of the Central Committee. In addition, these changes often reflected the arrival of new cadres from South Africa, including veterans finally forced to leave the country.

The meeting in Volynskoe 2 in November 1984 was attended by delegates from Africa – Lusaka, Luanda, Harare, Dar es Salaam, Maputo (in a clandestine transit from Swaziland and Lesotho) – and from Europe, mainly from London. Some "Muscovites", South African students in the International Lenin School, joined them. Apart from the veterans of the struggle, many delegates were military and political cadres of the Soweto generation.

Some details of this meeting, particularly the circumstances of transforming it into a Party Congress, are described in Kasrils's book.[218] What came to be called the Sixth Congress approved the new Constitution of the SACP and several resolutions: on party work, on ideological work, on mobilising and organising the working class, on armed struggle and the Pretoria "peace offensive", and on the SACP periodical *Inkululeko* (renamed *Umsebenzi*).

It was envisaged that all the SACP members would work in collectives; in cases where some were heavily involved in the activities of the ANC, Sactu or other organisations, the Central Committee would check their activity directly or through the regional committees. (In practice such an arrangement increased the secrecy of the membership of certain people in the SACP.)

The SACP Congress documents confirmed that the Party would conduct its work in Umkhonto through Party collectives at all levels of the army structures.

It should be emphasised that the SACP organisational efforts were made with Oliver Tambo's agreement. His new attitude was influenced by a radical shift in Southern African politics. If in the 1960s and early

1970s the presence of communists in the ranks of the ANC was as something negative by its host countries, Tanzania and Zambia in particular, by the 1980s the situation had been transformed. The ruling parties in both Angola and Mozambique proclaimed scientific socialism as their ideology (Mozambican leaders claimed that their country was already socialist and called themselves communists), so an alliance between the ANC and the SACP now strengthened the ANC's position in these countries.

Frelimo and MPLA established bilateral relations with the SACP and jointly played a leading role in persistent attempts to bring together twelve "Marxist-Leninist" parties in Africa.

The SACP Congress documents spoke (prematurely?) about incipient civil war in South Africa and the readiness of the people to take up arms. The Central Committee was asked to work out the Party position on "people's war". The CC was to inform the liberation movement of this position in order to reach consensus with its allies in struggle.

By that time preparations for the ANC National Conference had started and the Central Committee was to supply the Party members with a set of guidelines to facilitate the Conference. The guidelines were designed to improve the capacity of the ANC to carry out its historic mission of leading the national struggle and to strengthen the ANC as an anti-imperialist formation. Thus in the most important (and most confidential) SACP documents the leading role of the ANC was recognised and encouraged.

These decisions were not imposed from above but were the result of pre-Congress discussions and lively debates at the Moscow meeting. The opinions expressed were mostly sober. They covered such aspects as the strength of the enemy and the weakness of the internal organisations of the liberation movement, which was at odds with its popularity.

Apart from "people's war", the prospect of a crippling general strike, combined with the actions of communities, was envisaged. However, it was underlined that to encourage the people into unsustainable actions would be adventurist.[219]

We spent most of the days of the Congress at Volynskoe-2, but obviously not in the conference room, where the sessions took place. Finally, the sounds of the "Internationale", clearly heard in the lobby, signalled the end of the proceedings. The delegates emerged, and soon I saw Mabhida and Slovo conferring on a sofa in the lobby. It became

243

clear that, as expected, they had been elected to the highest Party positions. Moses Mabhida again became the SACP General Secretary and Joe Slovo took the second highest post, that of National Chairman, vacant for a year after Yusuf Dadoo's death.

Unfortunately some academics, though they profess non-racism, cannot rid themselves of the notion that only whites can lead political organisations. "Take the case of the late Moses Mabhida: he may have been the official Secretary General [read: General Secretary] of the party, but when pressed for a decision he used to say that he had first to refer the matter to Bunting or Slovo," writes Oxford-based R W Johnson.[220] As is often the case, he does not disclose his source, but it is certainly unreliable. Moses Mabhida was not a man to be "pushed ... into a symbolic front seat"[221]; he had enough self-confidence to take all decisions relating to his position as leader of the SACP and as an Executive member of the ANC. And if in some cases he decided to refer the matter to Bunting, Slovo or other comrades, that kind of collective leadership was standard practice in the SACP.

The procedure for the election of other Central Committee members was rather unusual, but democratic in its own way. All the delegates were required to write down the names of those they wanted to see elected. The two names with the highest number of votes were announced, and they, together with the General Secretary and Chairman, constituted a kind of Electoral Commission mandated to finalise the list of the CC members.

Some adjustments could be made for two reasons: security considerations (understandable for an underground organisation), and balance among various groups: ethnic, gender, age. I heard for example that, during the previous election Ronnie Kasrils received a sufficient number of votes but the place on the CC was given to someone else. In Moscow only one amendment was made: an exile veteran was dropped in favour of a representative of the Soweto generation.

The full composition of the Central Committee was kept secret even from the delegates at the Congress. Subsequent events justified this secrecy. Ellis and "*Sechaba*" wrote that Chris Hani had been "re-elected to the Politburo in triumph, receiving the highest number of votes jointly with the veteran trade unionist Ray Simons."[222] Apparently their source (either a person with a loose tongue or an agent planted in the SACP) was present at the Congress and took it for granted that both Hani and Simons, as members of the Central

Committee, also became members of the Politbureau. In fact, Ray Simons did not accept that position, vacating it in favour of one of the younger Black candidates.

The informal closing ceremony of the Congress was always a farewell reception (a "comradely supper", as it used to be called in the CPSU bureaucratic papers). This one was rather moving. One after another the delegates – veterans, middle-aged, young – stood up to propose their toasts (this was six months before "Gorbachev's prohibition"). "When I was in South Africa, I wondered what kind of animal a communist is," joked one of them. "But when I came out, I found out that everybody is a communist. Uncle Dan [Dan Tloome] is a communist, Bra So-and-so is a communist ..."

Ray Simons spoke about the Soviet Union as an anchor, but did not fail to mention tragic events in the USSR in the thirties: Kirov's murder, the political trials.

A young Black woman (let us call her Rose), who had completed the International Lenin School course six months earlier, stood up and started singing, in good Russian, "Do Russians want a war?" That song, based on one of Yevgeny Yevtushenko's poems, was popular in the Soviet Union in the 1960s. But I suddenly sensed an amendment to the text: she sang not about the wife but about the sister of the author. The reason was clear: Yevtushenko was at that stage married to an English woman, and Soviet teachers in the Lenin School had carefully edited the text. Some of us listening to this young Black woman singing in Russian found ourselves hardly able to hold back our tears, the moment was so moving. (We will have to return to the fate of this young woman later.)

While the SACP delegates were conducting their deliberations in Volynskoe, the ANC President Oliver Tambo was scarcely twenty kilometres away in the Barvikha Sanatorium. After the elections, the top leadership of the Party, including Mabhida and Slovo, visited Tambo and informed him of the deliberations and resolutions of the Congress.

That night I heard from Slovo that Tambo was not happy about Joe's election to so high a Party post. Perhaps the main reason was his concern for Umkhonto: it was clear that sooner or later Slovo would have to give up his post as its Chief of Staff. Slovo explained that he had been "recruited" to the SACP position. Tambo invited Slovo to visit him again the next day, and they had a very warm and fruitful meeting. "You are stepping in the shoes of great men – Marks and

245

...e ANC President told him.

...decided not to announce the fact of Slovo's election for some ...ven when he came to Moscow in May the following year to participate in the celebration of the fortieth anniversary of victory over Nazi Germany, he was introduced simply as "a member of the SACP leadership" (before that, even the fact of his membership of the illegal SACP had never been publicly confirmed). It was only in February 1986 at the 27th Congress of the CPSU that Slovo was named openly as the National Chairman of the Party.

Following the Congress decision, the SACP Politbureau re-organised the Party machinery (it was run by part-timers). The heads of several departments were appointed: propaganda, research and education, industrial, internal reconstruction, work in mass organisations, military affairs, international affairs, and security. But perhaps this development was too ambitious, and many of those departments did not function. The Politbureau itself, whose members were mostly concentrated in Lusaka, started regular meetings twice a month.

Public information about the SACP Congress was distributed in London on 12 January 1985. But by that date the Party had suffered a heavy blow: Moses Mabhida had had a stroke while he was in Havana on his way to Nicaragua.

Mabhida had not been well for several years. Suffering from diabetes, he was able to control his disease through strict discipline: diet, medicine, no alcohol, etc. The Soviet doctors were helpful. He was supposed to come back to them immediately after the Party Congress, but he decided to visit Latin America, Sandinist Nicaragua and Cuba; and promised to return on the first flight from Havana in January.

Mabhida had to stay in Cuba for an extended period. The Cuban health system was perfect, not only in primary health but in sophisticated treatment as well. Still, Mabhida was eager to return to the Soviet Union. The Soviets were, of course, ready to receive him for treatment, but requested confirmation that he could safely make the journey.

He finally arrived six months later, accompanied by a Cuban doctor, who informed us at the airport that his health had recovered "by 85%". He spent some weeks more in the Moscow hospital and then left for a sanatorium in the Soviet South on the Black Sea coast. This time he went to Yalta in the Crimea and not to his favourite Gagra resort in Abkhazia.

He was very popular and loved by the local staff there, who used to call him "Chapayev", after the hero of the Russian civil war who had a long moustache just like Mabhida's. Apparently he was embarrassed to tell his friends among the staff about his health problems.

Back in Moscow Mabhida had a final medical examination and the doctors pronounced him fit for work. But he never fully recovered. The Frelimo government provided him with a house and other facilities in Maputo. Soviet doctors were available there, as well, but nothing could prevent the fatal heart attack on 8 March 1986.

THE NKOMATI DRAMA

Chris Hani came to Moscow in 1983 not only as a political leader, but also as the Commissar of Umkhonto. He was appointed to this position during the re-organisation of the ANC structures. And this step was to a large extent prompted by the development of relations between the ANC and the Front Line States.

The military delegation of the ANC, headed by Joe Modise, which visited Maputo at the end of 1982 was the first of its kind. It was offered red-carpet treatment, and was housed in the luxurious Polana Hotel. With high praise for the actions of Umkhonto inside South Africa, the Mozambicans created the impression that they would be ready to lift the restrictions on armed activity across the border. Further, they would support the intensification of the ANC armed struggle in general. The only proviso was that the burden be shared among the Front Line States.

In January 1983 another delegation, led by Mziwandile Piliso, who at that stage headed the ANC Department of Intelligence and Security, held talks with the Zimbabweans, including the Army Commander Rex Ngongo (Solomon Majuru). The Zimbabweans promised to give some limited assistance to ANC actions – in particular, the movement of ANC cadres into South Africa; but at the same time they asked a number of questions about the ANC structures. They wanted to know who the Commander of Umkhonto was, who the Chief of Staff was, etc.

It seems these questions prompted the ANC leadership to undertake a major re-organisation of its structures. In anticipation of a new positive attitude to its armed actions, the ANC National Executive Committee decided in March 1983 to create two Headquarters: Political and Military. The post of the Umkhonto Commander was re-established, and Joe Modise was again appointed. Chris Hani became Umkhonto Commissar (and Second-in-Command), Joe Slovo became Chief of Staff. Several new departments, including the Department of Military Intelligence, headed by Ronnie Kasrils, were created.

According to the new structures, two co-ordinating bodies "with executive powers between meetings of the National Working Committee" were established. The first was the Political Military Council (PMC), which was "charged with the task of handling and directing the internal work of the movement." (This body replaced the Revolutionary Council.) The second new body was the External Co-ordinating Council, which was "charged with the task of handling and directing the work of the movement externally."[223]

The PMC initially consisted of Oliver Tambo, Alfred Nzo, Thomas Nkobi, Moses Mabhida, Yusuf Dadoo (they constituted "the Chairmanship"), three representatives of the Military Headquarters (Thabo More [Joe Modise], Chris Hani and Joe Slovo), four representatives of the Political Headquarters (John Nkadimeng, Mac Maharaj, Josiah Jele and Jacob Zuma), the Director of Information and Publicity (Thabo Mbeki), the Head of the NAT (Mziwandile Piliso), the Sactu President and General Secretary (Stephen Dlamini and John Gaetsewe respectively), as well as the members of its Permanent Secretariat (Joseph Nhlanhla, John Pule and Reginald September).[224]

The effect of the ANC re-organisation was varied. The new military structures helped to broaden the scope of Umkhonto actions. But the dangers inherent in the separation of the two types of activities, which had always been there, now became greater.

The reshuffling of the Umkhonto Command and especially the creation of the new departments required additional training of its members. One of the groups which came to Moscow was headed by Ronnie Kasrils. (It may come as a surprise to some, but the first time I met Ronnie was in March 1977 when, together with Keorapetse (Willie) Kgositsile, he came to Moscow to participate in a poetry seminar organised by the Afro-Asian Writers' Association. He used the pen name under which his poems appeared, "A N C Kumalo".)

Among members of his small group was an African who was known in the ANC structures as September. (His real name was Glory Sedibe, but in Moscow, as was common with ANC cadres, he chose another name.) Two and half years later he disappeared in Swaziland and surfaced in South Africa as a collaborator of the regime (some ANC cadres were intercepted at the border immediately after his disappearance). Many believed that he had been planted by the South African security in the ANC earlier, others thought that in a cowardly act he saved his own skin by betraying his comrades. September was killed in South Africa, apparently by his Pretoria masters, who got rid of a number of turncoats who knew too much about their dirty tricks.

It would be interesting to know whether the invitation of the ANC military delegation to Mozambique and promises of greater support reflected the mood of the Mozambican leadership or whether it was just a bargaining chip in the Mozambicans' relations with South Africa. The fact that the ANC delegation was hosted not in a guest house but in an international hotel looked like a political statement, happening as it did on the eve of the talks which took place between Mozambican and South African officials in the border town of Komatipoort.

In 1983, both in domestic and in international affairs, Pretoria combined aggression and repression with political manoeuvres, trying to pose as a party looking for change. In the sphere of foreign affairs it promoted non-aggression treaties with neighbouring countries, and in the internal sphere constitutional reform, as well as the so-called Koornhof bills (after the Minister of Development and Co-operation). These bills, the "Black Persons Orderly Movement and Settlement Act" and the "Black Authorities Act", were meant to strengthen control over Africans living in urban areas, and to give some respectability to the puppet administrations in both the bantustans and the townships.

However, if in the international sphere Pretoria managed some success – the talks with Mozambique were making progress – the internal situation was far from encouraging. The tricameral proposals gave an unexpected boost from Pretoria to resistance, culminating in the formation of the United Democratic Front (UDF), initially in the regions and then, on 20 August 1983, as a national coalition of various non-governmental organisations.

To a large extent this was a response to the inadequacy of the reforms launched by Pretoria. The new constitutional dispensation made it clear that Africans would continue to be excluded from state power and that Coloureds and Indians would only be co-opted as junior partners of the White establishment.

It should be underlined that the initiative for the creation of the UDF came from inside the country. One of my ANC friends told me soon after: "If some of our people say that the UDF was made by us, don't believe them." But this same friend just a year later was enthusiastic about the way the UDF was developing.

Indeed, while it was not an "ANC front", from the very beginning many ANC veterans as well as members of the ANC underground took part in its formation and activities. Many more people found their way into the ANC through their participation in the UDF.

On 2 November 1983 a referendum was held among the whites in South Africa. The constitutional changes proposed by P W Botha, which envisaged the creation of the tricameral parliament – for whites, coloureds and Indians, with the complete exclusion of Africans – received 66% of the votes.

Africans outside the bantustans were entitled to elect only so-called "Black local authorities". Those elections were a complete failure. In Soweto only 10% of the voters came to the polling stations.

Parallel to the process of the formation of the United Democratic Front, other political forces, which included some leaders of the Black Consciousness Movement recently released from prison, convened a National Forum. At first this initiative was supported by some prominent figures, including Desmond Tutu and Alan Boesak; but at the very first session it became clear that, instead of being a forum, the meeting was convened to form a new organisation, as a rival to the ANC and the emerging UDF. Thereafter many lost interest in the Forum and it was a short-lived venture.

Meanwhile the South African authorities set themselves the goal of eliminating the ANC presence in the neighbouring states. They applied a carrot-and-stick policy to secure the neighbours' co-operation: on the one hand, promises of economic aid and the cessation of Pretoria's support for the anti-government forces, and, on the other, destabilisation, both military and economic.

These methods were intensively applied to Mozambique. At the meeting with the ANC representatives in March 1983, the Mozambicans for the first time reported on the contacts they had had with Pretoria. The Mozambican authorities insisted on the withdrawal of about 150 ANC activists from Maputo to an ANC camp in Nampula in the north of the country. At the same time they refused to allow the ANC to take arms for self-defence, even though Renamo was already active in the area. Neither would they allow their departure for Angola, protesting that the ANC was not being expelled from the country.

But at the same meeting it was decided to create a joint committee on military questions and security. The ANC, therefore, had reason to believe that the Mozambican talks with South Africa would not mean a rift between itself and Maputo.

After the Church Street explosion the South African Air Force carried out a revenge raid against ANC targets in Maputo on 23 May 1983. This was a complete fiasco. Of the six houses attacked, some had been vacated by the ANC up to a year earlier. The SADF claimed that 64 persons had been killed, including 41 "terrorists". In fact, the ANC suffered only one casualty, but several Mozambicans were killed. Pretoria's officials boasted that they had destroyed an ANC arms depot.

251

It turned out to be a jam factory.

However, as distinct from the Matola massacre in 1981, this attack had a negative effect on the Mozambican leadership. The issuing of visas to ANC cadres wishing to enter Mozambique was stopped. The registration of all ANC members was required, as was the confiscation of weapons. On 31 May the Mozambican Minister of Defence Chipande had a meeting with Piliso, Modise and Hani, and they discussed, in particular, the situation in the ANC camp in Nampula. The ANC wanted meetings such as this to be held regularly but that did not happen. A proposed meeting between Oliver Tambo and Samora Machel was postponed in May for the third time. It was later scheduled for 30 June, but was again postponed. The ANC was not informed of the content of the Mozambican negotiations with Pretoria.

By mid 1983 the Mozambican leadership, and Samora Machel in particular, became convinced of the necessity to improve relations with South Africa, almost at any cost. The pressure on the ANC increased. The Mozambicans regarded the 31 flats and houses where the ANC members lived in Maputo as a threat to their security. They wanted to cut down the number of ANC activists in Mozambique, and started detaining people coming from South Africa. The use of "corridors" on the Mozambican border with Swaziland was restricted, and ANC activists were evicted from some houses.

Press reports and other information about the talks between South Africa and Mozambique could not but worry the ANC leadership. In August 1983 in an interview with the Guardian, Oliver Tambo stated: "The Machels, Dos Santoses, Kaundas, Mugabes – they are all creations of liberation struggle. If they did what South Africa wanted them to do, to destroy the liberation struggle, they would be destroying their own independence ... There may be limitations as to what they can do in practice but they cannot be our enemies."[225]

The ANC President did not want to believe that Samora Machel would agree to Pretoria's demands. On another occasion Tambo recalled how in 1976 on the eve of the Soweto uprising the Mozambican leadership asked the ANC delegation "to help in the mobilisation of the people in support of the struggle for liberation of Zimbabwe". (Mozambique then introduced sanctions against Rhodesia.) However, in those areas, "the people wanted to mobilise for liberation of South Africa", and wanted to leave the task of liberating Zimbabwe to those in other regions of the country.[226]

Neighbouring Swaziland had by this time become a battleground for

the ANC. Many of its members and supporters were round
deported in 1982. After the death of King Sobhuza II, the a
the country's interregnum authorities towards the liberation m
deteriorated further. The carrot Pretoria used was a promise to
surrender to Swaziland the territory of the Kangwane bantustan as well
as a part of Natal, Ingwavuma, which would give Swaziland access to
the sea. That plan, however, met with strong resistance inside South
Africa. In particular, it threatened to sour Pretoria's relationship with
Buthelezi, and was abandoned.

The developments in Southern Africa and especially in Mozambique
were among the subjects raised by the ANC delegation, headed by
Alfred Nzo, which visited Moscow at the end of October 1983. The
delegation recounted how the creation of the tricameral parliament had
boomeranged and provoked the formation of the United Democratic
Front. During its first months the UDF brought together about 400
organisations with a combined membership of at least one million. The
ANC leadership, which still regarded the Freedom Charter as the
fundamental platform of the democratic forces, felt that the liberation
movement should embrace all democratic efforts in the struggle.[227]

Boris Ponomarev assured the delegation that Soviet support of the
ANC would continue and strengthen. Nzo and his colleagues were glad
to hear from Ponomarev that Mozambican hopes to secure an end to
Pretoria's assistance to Renamo in exchange for further restriction of
ANC activities were unfounded.

Usually ANC delegations visited the USSR for only a few days and
rarely travelled outside Moscow. But this time some of the delegates
flew to Volgograd (formerly Stalingrad) to see the historical sites of the
greatest battle of World War Two.

The gravity of the situation the ANC faced in Mozambique became
perfectly clear two months later when the Soviet Union informed the
Mozambican authorities that some goods of a purely civilian nature
requested by the ANC were to be sent to Maputo. Their response was
more than cool. They said that in the difficult situation they were in,
Pretoria could misconstrue even the supply of civilian goods and use
this against Mozambique. They explicitly told the Soviet diplomats
that the ANC should limit its military actions and concentrate on the
political struggle.

They admitted to an agreement already reached at a meeting in
Swaziland in December concerning the mutual cessation of military
assistance by Mozambique to the ANC, and by South Africa to

253

Renamo.

By the end of 1983 preparations for a meeting between Samora Machel and P W Botha were at an advanced stage. Originally several places were rumoured as the venue, from Cabo Verde to Swaziland. For the whole of that year Tambo had been unable to meet with Machel. Other Mozambican leaders in their discussions with the ANC asked them to understand the difficult situation Mozambique was in, and started hinting at a formal agreement with South Africa.

The ANC leadership tried to save the situation. It decided to send Oliver Tambo and Alfred Nzo to Mozambique on 9 January 1984, immediately after the celebration of the ANC anniversary. The Mozambican President received them in his country house on the island of Bilem. An emotional man, sincerely committed to the liberation of South Africa, he seemed unable to bring himself to tell the ANC leaders the exact truth. For about three hours he described the difficulties Mozambique was facing and the reasons for signing a treaty with Pretoria. He avoided discussing the position of the ANC in his country.

It was on the next day, 14 January, that the ANC leaders became aware of the facts of the situation. The Minister of Security Mariano Matsinha, on Machel's instruction, relayed to them Pretoria's demands, which Mozambique had virtually already acceded to. The ANC was to leave only a limited number of officials at the ANC office in Maputo. The ANC was to stop all military activity. The ANC was to recall several prominent ANC figures.

The ANC leadership had been ready for a "tactical retreat", as had already happened in Lesotho, for a withdrawal or replacement of part of its personnel in Mozambique. But now it had to face a strategic retreat without any prospect of return. What upset them most was the absence of consultation between Frelimo and the ANC.

The ANC National Executive Committee met for several days at the end of January and decided to try to talk to the Mozambican leadership again. A new delegation, headed by Tambo, was to convey to Machel and his ministers the view that the ANC regarded these developments as the most serious blow to the movement since its banning in 1960. The betrayal of the ANC would mean the betrayal of the revolutionary gains in Mozambique and in Southern Africa as a whole. The ANC had started its struggle long before the independence of Mozambique and would continue it.

Tambo and Nzo left for Maputo on 18 February, expecting an early meeting with Machel. At first he avoided this, but the meeting eventually took place on 26 February. Machel praised the ANC as a revolutionary vanguard; conceded its right to choose its methods of struggle, including armed struggle; but said that the treaty with South Africa was the only way out for Mozambique. Despite the depressing nature of the meeting, it took place in a cordial atmosphere. The ANC leaders were assured that no deportation list existed, and, in particular, that the departure of Joe Slovo from Mozambique was not a requirement.

The signing of the Nkomati Accord on the Mozambican-South African border on 16 March 1984 was hailed by the Mozambican government as a great diplomatic victory. But there was a hollow ring to it; even the practical arrangements of the ceremony were anything but triumphant. Machel could not secure the participation of any significant African leader; only the Prime Minister of Swaziland accepted his invitation. (Swaziland itself had signed a similar agreement with Pretoria in 1982.) On the eve of the ceremony Julius Nyerere paid a short visit to Maputo, apparently in a bid to dissuade Machel from going ahead, but without success.

In an interview given in New York on 18 March 1984 Johnny Makatini recalled that early in 1984 Tambo had been waiting in Maputo for "some occasion for discussion" with Machel.[228] Like other ANC leaders, Makatini correctly insisted that Umkhonto was not launching its attacks from Mozambique, and (less than entirely truthfully) that operations were not planned from there. He was worried that Maputo would make more concessions to Pretoria: "Mozambique has given a yard, and they will demand a mile. And they'll eventually get a lot of mileage."[229]

But only a week later the bitter truth of the agreement between Pretoria and Maputo became known. Mariano Matsinha invited Joe Slovo and the ANC representative in Mozambique to his office and informed them that, as they spoke, searches were already being conducted in the ANC houses and offices.

The number of ANC activists in Maputo had to be limited to ten, all supplies of arms to the ANC were banned, the ANC camp in Nampula had to be closed. All other ANC activists had to leave Mozambique, but were not to go to countries adjacent to South Africa. Only the ANC President and Secretary General had the right to visit the country at any time. A limited number of people on a special list would be exempted from entry visas. All others had to request visas in advance.

Matsinha's instructions were recorded (apparently to be played back to Pretoria's representatives), but the recorder was immediately switched off when Joe Slovo started asking questions.

The searches continued for two days. While Slovo was talking to the Minister of Security, officials of the same ministry broke into his apartment and seized a quantity of arms. A significant sum of foreign and local currency was seized in Moses Mabhida's apartment. More flats and houses were searched. All this was done in broad daylight, apparently to draw public attention to their zeal in carrying out the agreement with Pretoria. Some security officials wore gas masks. This was ostensibly in case of resistance, but ANC activists were convinced that the gas masks covered the faces of South Africans.[230]

Among the goods seized by the Mozambican authorities were over 700 Soviet-made wristwatches, allegedly to be used as fuses for explosives. But the real history of those watches is much more curious. In 1982 the ANC leadership submitted to Moscow its regular request for equipment. It was considered, approved, and, as part of the consignment, one thousand watches were sent to Mozambique.

When this information reached us in the International Department, we were amazed: the quantity was several times more than the total number of ANC activists in Mozambique. The explanation was simple. The watches were intended for the one hundred Umkhonto fighters in the camp in Nampula, and an ANC typist had made a mistake, putting three zeroes after the figure 1, instead of two. Having spotted the mistake, the secretary tippexed it out, but the third zero was apparently still noticeable. So, if the friends requested one thousand, let it be one thousand ...

When we investigated the case, the explanation was innocent enough. The officials of the Ministry of Foreign Trade (responsible for the supply of civilian goods, like watches) rightly maintained they had no knowledge of the strength of Umkhonto in Mozambique; that was not their field. And the Ministry of Defence officials had their explanation too: watches were civilian goods, and therefore not their responsibility.

Would that such things happened only with wristwatches.

Relations between the ANC and Mozambique continued to deteriorate. Of the ten people proposed by the ANC to run the office, only one person was approved by Maputo. The list submitted by the ANC of the ten to be allowed entry without visas was apparently compared with the list received from Pretoria, and four names were excluded from it. In April virtually all other activists left Mozambique: military cadres mostly for Angola, political figures for Zambia, others for Tanzania. But even in those conditions the ANC leadership was determined to maintain relations with Frelimo.

On 8 June Oliver Tambo visited Maputo again, to attend the funeral of Machel's father. A short meeting of the two leaders took place, but nothing substantial came of it. Machel spoke of the need for the ANC to talk to Pretoria, recalling his role in the Zimbabwe settlement (thus virtually proposing himself as mediator). He promised to assist the ANC after the elimination of Renamo. In practice, that meant that any radical improvement of relations with the ANC was excluded for the foreseeable future.

As was mentioned above, Frelimo had established direct relations with the SACP as well. The SACP was planning to set up a printing works in Maputo to distribute Umsebenzi and other materials inside South Africa. But, despite this positive relationship, the Mozambicans refused even to discuss the Nkomati Accord with the SACP leadership. On 5 May 1984 Moses Mabhida was required to leave Maputo for Lusaka, which for the rest of the decade became the SACP Headquarters. Before his departure, in spite of the difficulties, Mabhida managed to visit Lesotho to meet Party activists there.

The effect of the Nkomati Accord on the South African liberation struggle was equivocal. It obviously created many practical problems for the ANC. But on the eve of the Accord many Umkhonto fighters were evacuated from Maputo – not to the North, further from South Africa, but to the South, to Swaziland. Many of them were intercepted there and deported, but quite a number reached home.

Needless to say, the Nkomati Accord and the resulting actions of Mozambican officials caused indignation among ANC activists, especially among the radical youth who were determined to return to South Africa to intensify the armed struggle. If the Umkhonto Command had tried in the past to avoid operations close to the Mozambican border, after the Nkomati Accord those restrictions no longer applied.

In addition, Nkomati provided a powerful counter to the view that decisive assistance to the liberation struggle would come from beyond South Africa's borders. Alan Boesak said on the eve of the Accord: "Mozambique, Angola and Zimbabwe will not fight our struggle for us. If you want human rights you have to do it yourself."[231] Professors Jakes Gerwel and Pieter le Roux of the University of the Western Cape

257

predicted that "Nkomati and similar accords might force the ANC to develop a stronger internal base."[232]

Meanwhile step by step the situation began to change, mainly due to the failure of Pretoria to honour the Nkomati Accord, which promised an end to its support of Renamo. The lists of the staff of the ANC office and of those who had a right to visit the country were agreed upon. At the celebration of the 9th anniversary of Mozambican independence on 25 June, Samora Machel introduced Oliver Tambo as a guest of honour. Before the ANC delegation left Maputo, the Mozambican President was very friendly and co-operative.

Apart from the betrayal of faith by Pretoria, one more circumstance influenced Machel's position. The Nkomati Accord was not supported in Africa. The communiqué of the meeting of the Front Line States, which took place in Arusha on 29 April, contained a very cautious formulation on the Nkomati Accord. It identified the "abolition of apartheid by whatever means are necessary" as the objective of the Front Line States and liberation movements.[233]

Giving "strong preference" to peaceful means, the leaders of the Front Line States insisted that this was possible only "through a process agreed upon in free discussions between the present South African regime and genuine representatives of the people of South Africa, who are unrepresented in the present government structure of that country."[234]

The release of Nelson Mandela and all other political prisoners was named as a precondition for such talks. "Difficult as this step may be in the eyes of the present South African Government, there is no way to peace in Southern Africa except through discussions between the South African Government and the African people of South Africa."[235]

Julius Nyerere, the head of the group, played a very positive role. The ANC was again allowed to open a camp for Umkhonto on Tanzanian territory. Zambia, too, changed its attitude to the ANC. Oliver Tambo was provided with proper security and invited to live in the Presidential complex in Lusaka.

After the Nkomati Accord, Pretoria increased its pressure on the Lesotho government. But Lebua Jonathan and his colleagues used a skilful tactic to resist such pressure. They organised "pitsos", meetings all over the country to discuss their policy, and so in their contacts with Pretoria they could refer directly to the people's opinion.

The Lesotho government also developed its international contacts. After a trip to the Far East, Jonathan spent some days in Moscow.

When the delegation of the Soviet Afro-Asian Solidarity Committee visited Maseru in July 1984, Jonathan expressed his gratitude for the Soviet supply of arms. While he underlined Lesotho's determination not to capitulate, the ANC itself understood Lesotho's vulnerability and withdrew some of its cadres. (All in all, about 250 activists of the ANC lived in Lesotho, including about 80 who had some training.)

For me personally the flight from Maputo to Lesotho in a small plane over South African territory gave me my first sight of South African soil after fifteen years of involvement with South Africans. That is not strictly speaking accurate as earlier, in 1978, I had glimpsed South African territory through "the Pioneers' Gate", a checkpoint at the Botswana-South African border. A delegation of the Soviet Afro-Asian Solidarity Committee was hosted by the ruling Botswana Democratic Party. Our short stay there gave us a better understanding of the situation in South Africa. For example, observing the heavy traffic of African-driven cars and trucks across the Botswana-South African border, I became convinced that Pretoria could not stop the penetration of ANC cadres (and equipment) into South Africa.

The visit to Lesotho was even more exciting. In Maseru it was hard to believe that very near the residence of the Soviet Ambassador, just across the Caledon River, lay South Africa. In our discussions with Lesotho officials we tried to strengthen their resolve to resist the pressure from Pretoria. While some members of the cabinet were inclined to agree with Pretoria, a very important role in withstanding such pressure was played by Vincent Makhele, Secretary General of the ruling party, who later became the Minister of Foreign Affairs.

Mozambican control over the movement of ANC activists continued to be very strict, sometimes ridiculously so. For example, in August 1984 a Lesotho student on his way to Maseru was sent back from Maputo all the way to Moscow because the Mozambican immigration officials suspected him of being an ANC member.

From July 1984 the Mozambican media started to criticise South Africa, but a real breakthrough in ANC-Mozambican relations occurred only much later, during Moses Mabhida's funeral in March 1986.

Initially the SACP and ANC leadership intended to take Mabhida's body to Lusaka, but Samora Machel insisted that the funeral should take place in Maputo. The Mozambicans organised the funeral extremely well. Mabhida's widow, a blind Zulu woman, together with his daughter and other relatives, came from inside South Africa; ANC and SACP leaders and activists came from Lusaka and elsewhere. The UDF was represented by its co-president Archibald Gumede and by its National Chairman Curnick Ndlovu, a former Umkhonto commander, who had recently been released from Robben Island.

The funeral ceremony took place under the scorching sun in the cemetery where Ruth First's grave and those of the victims of the Matola massacre are located, and was followed by the traditional hand-washing ceremony. All this represented a symbolic reconciliation between Frelimo and the ANC: the participants carried both Oliver Tambo and Samora Machel on their shoulders. Talking to Soviet delegates, Machel even called the ANC Frelimo's "elder brother".

The liberation movement used this rare occasion to meet leaders and activists from inside the country for extensive consultations. Some arms, I heard, were brought to Maputo in the luggage of the ANC delegates from other African countries, later to be smuggled into South Africa. We also used the opportunity to discuss the situation in South Africa with those who had come directly from South Africa, in particular Curnick Ndlovu.

Different from that pertaining in Mozambique, the ANC position in Angola at that stage was politically very secure. This was confirmed earlier when a delegation of the SACP, which included Moses Mabhida, Joe Slovo and John Nkadimeng, had official talks with a delegation of the MPLA - Party of Labour in 1983. The Angolans gave the assurance that in their contacts with South Africa, which had commenced not long before, they would not discuss questions concerning the ANC, in particular the ANC camps in their country, without preliminary consultations with the ANC leadership.

However, in July of that year the situation deteriorated, particularly in the province of Melange. The UNITA offensive threatened both the line of supplies and the ANC camps themselves. In this situation the Angolan government requested the ANC to participate in the counter-offensive. A substantial contingent of SWAPO's People's Liberation Army of Namibia was also mobilised and airlifted from Southern Angola to the North.

A special delegation of the ANC was invited to Luanda to discuss specific issues concerning Umkhonto's involvement. Initially this was quite successful. In October, at a meeting with Oliver Tambo, the Angolan President Jose Eduardo Dos Santos expressed his gratitude and promised to continue support to the ANC, including the training of its cadres on Angolan territory. He was also interested in broadening the ANC military operations inside South Africa and was emphatic that every Front Line State should carry out the decisions of the 1982 Maputo summit in support of the ANC.

The talks which the Angolan government had with South Africa at that time and their results – the Lusaka Agreements of 16 February 1984 – were quite different from Nkomati. Johnny Makatini made the point after Tambo's meeting with Eduardo Dos Santos: "We are happy with their rejection of any idea of a non-aggression pact. We are confident they [Angola] will not dump SWAPO."[236]

The leadership of SWAPO was nonetheless worried about the forthcoming agreement between Angola and South Africa. It felt, rightly, that it would mean a serious limitation of SWAPO's freedom of action in Southern Angola.

This growing tension between SWAPO and the Angolan government was one reason for a working visit of the International Department's officials in January 1984 to meet with Sam Nujoma in Lubango, where SWAPO's main training base was situated.

Before leaving Luanda we, of course, saw both the ANC representatives and the Soviets who worked in the ANC camps. We learned from our chief adviser, "Comrade George", that there had been a serious "case of disobedience to the Umkhonto Command". Our position was clear: "This was an internal ANC matter, the Soviets should not interfere in any way."

Later, after our return to Moscow, we were informed of events, amounting to mutiny, which had occurred after we had left. These events are described in detail in the report of the "James Stuart Commission", released by the ANC recently, as well as in Ronnie Kasrils's book and in a number of interviews with Chris Hani and other ANC leaders.

Now that more information is available, it is possible to assess the events more clearly. At the time the ANC leadership identified a lower level of the regional leadership and of the security machinery in Angola as the main source of the disaffection. Among the reasons advanced for the mutiny were the long periods (up to six years) spent by activists in the camps, exacerbated by weak political and educational work, shortages in supplies of materials, and poor medical care.

The first human losses in the fighting against UNITA had a totally negative impact. The sight of the mutilated bodies of comrades, killed thousands of miles away from home, demoralised some of the ANC activists. The old accusation, repeated for many years by Pretoria propaganda, that the ANC leadership was sending young people to die in foreign countries, for foreign interests, was taken up by the dissidents, supported, of course, by Pretoria's agents. Chris Hani told us later that several Pretoria agents had been among the instigators. Some of them had been uncovered three years earlier and had undergone a nine-month course of re-education. Others had arrived from South Africa not long before.[(237)]

But there was one more reason for the lowering of the cadres' morale, which made them susceptible to provocation. This was the foreign policy manoeuvres of Pretoria at the end of 1983 and the beginning of 1984, which later resulted in the Nkomati Accord and in the Lusaka Agreements. The fact that the ANC was again, as in the early 1970s, in danger of losing support from its allies in Africa was also a source of disruption.

The mutiny naturally created problems in Angolan relations with the ANC, despite the leadership of that country confirming that it would continue its assistance to the ANC. (Officially, however, Angola admitted the presence of only South African refugees on its territory).

But some good came of it as well. The convening of the ANC National Conference was overdue: fifteen years had passed since Morogoro. The decision taken by the ANC Executive in 1977 to convene the conference two years later had been all but forgotten. There were several reasons for the delays and postponements. One of them was the flow of young people from inside the country and the need for their orientation into the ANC, since many of them knew the ANC only as a symbol and were not acquainted with its political programme. Apart from this, time was needed to weed out Pretoria's agents from among the newcomers, as well as some uncommitted and criminal elements.

But perhaps the subjective reasons were more important: some of the ANC Executive members were not secure in their popularity, and so were unsure if they would be re-elected to leadership positions. As Chris Hani commented, it was the mutiny that finally made it impossible to delay the convening of the conference any longer.[(238)]

One more question was a subject of our discussion in Luanda with "Comrade George". He reported that recent field exercises proved that the ANC units were quite skilful in infantry combat and certainly superior to the armies of the bantustans. The first battalion was scheduled to complete its training soon, and, according to the directive of the ANC High Command, a total of least five battalions were to be formed.

We met this news with a considerable degree of scepticism. There was no doubt that the battalions could be successfully trained and properly equipped with Soviet assistance, but what would be their immediate use? There was no chance of the ANC regular-type units becoming involved in any military activity in South Africa for the foreseeable future. Mozambique's talks with Pretoria made this perfectly clear. The pressing need was to emphasise guerrilla-type operations and, even more urgently, to train the organisers of the armed underground.

I still think that our position was correct. It is true that the ANC needed more cadres properly trained in regular warfare than it had when the process of the integration of the armed forces started. But to put most of Umkhonto's strength into regular units many years before they were required would not serve the struggle against the racist regime inside South Africa.

Howard Barrel in his book *MK: the ANC's Armed Struggle* (perhaps the best academic book on the subject) claimed that by December 1983 "MK had trained about 8 700 combatants since 1977."[239] That figure seems to be a gross overestimation. A simple aggregation of courses undertaken by cadres can be misleading. I recall a conversation I had with one of Oliver Tambo's bodyguards, while we were waiting for him at Samora Machel's suite. "Comrade," he said, "I completed four different courses but I have never used any of the specialities I acquired."

After the Nkomati Accord, government propaganda described the Umkhonto actions as "a few parting shots of the ANC."[240] But in reality the level of armed activity inside South Africa, having declined, increased again after March 1984.

In May-June 1984, P W Botha made a trip to Western Europe. While governments received him more or less cordially, the anti-apartheid movements strongly protested and Pretoria failed in its bid to project itself as the peacemaker. Against the background of growing resistance inside South Africa, the UN Security Council on 17 August 1984 adopted a resolution declaring the new South African Constitution "null and void". Therefore, from the UN point of view all structures created on the basis of this Constitution – the tricameral parliament, the President, the cabinet – were illegal from the outset.

TALKS ABOUT TALKS: THE BEGINNING

The period immediately preceding and following the Nkomati Accord coincided (not accidentally) with growing pressure on the ANC to start talks with the South African government on Pretoria's terms. The ANC leadership came to the conclusion that the West was no longer willing simply to eliminate the ANC. By that time the ANC had acquired considerable prestige and the task of the West was to try to persuade the ANC in a "proper" direction. This was to be done in such a way that, while preserving the outward appearance of a revolutionary organisation, the ANC would become an instrument in the hands of those who were working for a neo-colonial solution of Southern African problems. One of the methods of achieving this was to play up so-called differences between the moderates and those who allegedly leaned towards the socialist countries.

Sometimes those attempts were ridiculous. A correspondent of a London newspaper phoned the ANC Headquarters in Lusaka and could not believe that it was the Secretary General who himself picked up the phone: the report was spread in London that Alfred Nzo had been detained by the "moderates", headed by Oliver Tambo.[241]

Trying to prove that the "[South African Communist] Party imposed on the ANC a rigid pro-Soviet line in foreign affairs", Ellis claims that "the ANC never even had a representative in Washington until as late as 1989."[242] But it was the US Administration that prevented this for many years. When the ANC opened its Mission to the UN, its Head could go no further than ten miles from the UN Headquarters. The opening of an official mission to Washington was out of the question for many years, and to establish its presence the ANC had to send an activist married to an American citizen.[243]

Although Reagan's Administration, after coming to power in January 1981, consistently maintained its hostile attitude towards the ANC, the upsurge of the liberation struggle inside South Africa forced it to seek contacts with the ANC leadership. The first such meeting took place between Thabo Mbeki and Crocker's assistant Robert Cabelly in August 1983, but the US representative argued that this was "not a meeting".[244]

He insisted that the ANC should renounce its alliance with the SACP and friendly relations with the USSR, stop the armed struggle (which,

264

he alleged, was imposed on the ANC by white communists), and become a part of "the policy of reforms" in the region. If this was not done, he threatened, the ANC would be "driven" out of the region; and he maintained that P W Botha wanted to move the ANC as far as Egypt.

Later the tone of the US representatives changed. In February 1985 a preliminary meeting took place. Chester Crocker's deputy Frank Wisner tried to convince the ANC representatives that forces within the South African government were interested in talks with the ANC. A further meeting took place in June. This time the US stated its readiness to establish official relations with the ANC and to propose the agenda, venue and time of the meeting.

The ANC representatives agreed to the proposal but wanted to know what was meant by the "establishment of relations". In October Robert Cabelly came to Lusaka again and did some back-pedalling. Some of the ANC's positions made things difficult for the US, he said, and official relations could not be established until the ANC changed its stand. At the same time he confirmed that the US wanted "contacts" as distinct from official relations.[245] Such vacillations in the US position apparently reflected a struggle within the establishment over the approach to South Africa.

No doubt Washington and Pretoria kept each other informed. Chester Crocker precisely quotes in his book the Soviet message to Pretoria transmitted through the South African Mission in New York in November 1983. But he misinterprets the motives of the Soviet initiative, claiming that the Soviets were trying to open a channel with the USA on Africa "without having to ask" or trying "to bluff Pretoria out of Angola".[246]

In reality the message was a rather simple but stern warning: if South Africa continued its aggression, Soviet assistance to the Angolan government would increase. As a rule Pik Botha deliberately distorted Pretoria's contacts with Moscow. In this case, however, he had to admit that the Soviet message "boiled down" to a warning that the USSR viewed the issue of Namibia in a more serious light than ever, and that the occupation of Angolan territory by South African troops, coupled with Pretoria's support for UNITA, was "unacceptable".[247]

There have been South African and British press reports of the praises which the then Prime Minister John Major and his colleagues showered on the ANC and its leaders following the formation of a democratic government in South Africa. These should not blind one to the fact that the British Conservative government had insisted that it would have no official dealings with the ANC because it had been dedicated to the "violent overthrow" of a government with which Britain maintained diplomatic relations.[248] Only very preliminary contacts with ANC members were made unofficially by some British intelligence officers (posing as diplomats).

1984 was a very difficult and in a sense tragic year for the ANC, but it also saw the first signs of the possibility of a political solution in South Africa. Perhaps this needs to be stressed, to counter numerous statements by both academics and politicians that the process of political settlement started with the "collapse of the Berlin wall", or the "collapse of communism", or at least with the advent of Gorbachev.

In fact even earlier the development of the resistance movement and the evident growth of ANC prestige and influence caused some forces within the South African establishment to raise publicly the possibility, hedged by many reservations, of talking to the ANC. The first probe in this direction was the article by Tom Vosloo, published on 9 January 1981 in the Afrikaans newspaper Beeld. He called the ANC the "mother-body of organised black politics in South Africa" and admitted that among its sympathisers were "probably millions of blacks in the Republic". But the same journalist demanded from the ANC "a purification concerning its pattern of behaviour". He set a number of conditions, which included not only acceptance of "the confederation/federation model" and the renunciation of "its Marxist strivings", but also the recognition of the "independent bantustans".[249]

In spite of all these reservations and preconditions, the very thought expressed by Vosloo that "the day will yet arrive when a South African government will sit down at the negotiation table with the ANC" was a shock to many in the country. More so, because Beeld at that stage was regarded as "the Transvaal mouthpiece of the Prime Minister, Mr P W Botha".[250]

But the official statements at the time were far more conservative. While South African Foreign Minister Pik Botha was regarded as a liberal (compared, that is, to the "verkramptes"), in an interview with the BBC in 1981 he answered the question "Will there ever be one man, one vote in South Africa?" with a flat "No." He refused to answer a question as to whether "in the end" he would be forced "to talk with Nelson Mandela", saying that Pretoria was "continuously talking with black leaders in this country."[251]

But by 1984 the situation had changed. Pretoria engaged in an experiment. Andimba Toivo ya Toivo had been arrested over seventeen years before and was serving a sentence on Robben Island. The government transferred him to a Namibian prison, and then freed him. Apparently there were several reasons for this action: to show Pretoria's readiness to make some concessions on Namibia and at the same time to cause a split in SWAPO, to set Toivo, one of its founders, against its President Sam Nujoma. It is possible, too, that this action was a kind of rehearsal for freeing ANC leaders. Their continued stay in prison was becoming more and more embarrassing for Pretoria.

After the signing of the Nkomati Accord and the Lusaka Agreement, the regime apparently felt that the "weakened and isolated" ANC could be pressed into talks on the regime's terms. The first open hint of this was a statement in May 1984 by the South African Ambassador to Paris, Robert du Plooy, that because the political situation in Southern Africa was changing so quickly "anything is possible – even the rapprochement with the ANC."[252] But the preconditions for discussions were the cessation of armed struggle, the recognition of the "sovereignty of the South African government", and the renunciation by the ANC of "links with the Soviet Union".[253] The ANC leadership publicly rejected such preconditions.

Accountability to ANC members and supporters on such a "sensitive" issue as "talks about talks" with Pretoria (headlined as such in *Sechaba*, September 1984)[254] was a matter of great concern to Oliver Tambo himself. Speaking in May 1984 in Mazimbu he said: "We would like our people to know that there are attempts to bring the ANC into discussions with Pretoria racists ... That campaign is building up all over ... they are under pressure. We are under pressure to talk to them." Tambo promised the ANC youth that, before making any step in this direction, the membership and especially the youth would be consulted. One thing was already clear: "You cannot ignore the ANC."[255]

Two months later Tambo said in Gaborone: "We have not been approached. But we know the question [of talks between the ANC and Pretoria] is being discussed." He declared that the ANC would be ready to meet P W Botha only after making sure that there would be "serious dialogue aimed at bringing an end to apartheid."[256] The precondition for such a meeting was, not surprisingly, the release of Nelson Mandela and other leaders and their participation in the talks.

However, the ANC leadership believed that the South African government was not yet ready for serious talks. The possibility of strictly unofficial contacts was not excluded. According to Piliso, the first visit to Lusaka by Professor Hendrik van der Merwe of the University of Cape Town, who was close to some important figures in the National Party, took place in August 1984. The ANC agreed to meet him because he was an "individual of apparently good faith." Van der Merwe said that as a Quaker he was "concerned about the state of violence in South Africa."[257] This meeting did not constitute the beginning of negotiations; Piliso said, "the ANC is not saying there never will be any talks."[258] In December another meeting took place in Lusaka between van der Merwe and the ANC leaders – Nzo, Mbeki and Simon (Sipho) Makana – though initially they were rather sceptical about his efforts.

The visits of van der Merwe, aimed at the promotion of a political settlement in South Africa, took place over a number of years. One hopes that at some time he himself will write in detail about his personal role in the lengthy process of "talks about talks".

The Soviet Union reacted positively to such meetings. We heard that van der Merwe proposed a meeting between National Party members of parliament and the ANC in Lusaka. The alternative was an unofficial meeting in France, in Grenoble, which could take the form of a free exchange of views with the four South African MPs and probably some French MPs. But at the same time he confirmed that Pretoria insisted on its conditions for talks with the ANC, including the severing of relations with the USSR and other socialist countries.[259]

Van der Merwe inundated the ANC Headquarters with messages after his return to South Africa. The ANC leaders, however, were in no hurry to respond to his proposal. They wanted both to think about the forms of the contacts and, more importantly, to explain the necessity of such contacts to their membership. The proposed meeting had to be a matter of public knowledge to avoid attempts to discredit the ANC.[260]

The very first signs of "talks about talks" showed up certain differences in the South African establishment. Prominent journalists and businessmen (the first of them was Tony Bloom, an old schoolmate of Ronnie Kasrils) were openly calling for talks with the ANC, though as a rule accompanying those calls with certain conditions, such as an end to violence. When the press wrote about the possibility of the MPs' visit to Lusaka, P W Botha declared, "No parliamentarian of the National Party will be allowed to do so."[261] However, public opinion among whites was changing: a poll conducted in 1984 indicated that practically as many whites were in favour of

talks between the government and the ANC as were against them.

All this was happening against the background of an upsurge of mass protest activity in various forms: about 150 000 workers participated in a general stay-away in November 1984 in the Transvaal; a massive rent boycott was started; black townships were exploding one after the other. Attacks were made on the houses of puppet mayors and councillors; barricades were set up, made of barrels, stones and burning tyres. All of this became daily practice in the second half of that year.

That upsurge had a very positive effect on the South Africans in exile. The depression provoked by Nkomati had lifted. We experienced this when an ANC delegation came to Moscow in December 1984. It included Alfred Nzo, Thomas Nkobi, John Nkadimeng and Joe Slovo. Oliver Tambo had come to the USSR a little earlier. When we fetched him from the airport late at night, he was totally exhausted. After a month first in hospital and then at a sanatorium, his health improved and he joined the delegation during the discussions at the CPSU Headquarters. That visit followed an important summit of the Front Line States in Arusha. Julius Nyerere had invited Oliver Tambo to attend, but when I brought this message to him he was hesitant, and his doctors insisted him that he should not interrupt his treatment. So the ANC was represented in Arusha by Alfred Nzo.

At the meeting with Boris Ponomarev, Tambo described the latest developments in South Africa and in the region. According to the South African Police, from 1976 to June 1984, ANC armed actions had caused damage amounting to about 600 million Rands. In June 1984 Bill Sutton, a member of the Presidential Council, declared that the revolution had already begun in South Africa. The task was "to contain it". [262]

When Tambo spoke about the summit of the Front Line States in Arusha a strange expression of disbelief – or at least doubt – appeared on Ponomarev's face. "We have received different information," he said and instructed an official to translate, for the benefit of the delegation, a message received from a Soviet embassy. Now it was the turn of the ANC leaders to express doubt. "This is not the meetin~ I participated in," commented Nzo.

Kobus Meiring, then South African Deput~ Affairs, said in September 1988 that there had come to the realisation that the ANC h the nose with falsehoods about the situation i

But by the end of 1984 it became clear even to those Soviets who were somewhat reluctant to be involved in direct relations with the ANC that the prospect of a political settlement was a realistic one, and that therefore there was a need for diplomatic initiatives.

In that period the South African establishment could no longer silence the growing lobby for a political solution. But in trying to explain its growing influence, they did not go beyond conspiracy theories. Police Major General F M A Steenkamp, at the press briefing mentioned elsewhere, said that the "terror onslaught by the ANC/SACP revolutionary alliance" was "the direct result of an organised communist conspiracy, which since at least 1902 had aimed at the creation of a socialist people's republic in South Africa as one of the world-wide family of such states."[265] Notice the words "since at least 1902": that is even before the Bolshevik Party was founded in Russia!

He called the ANC "an extension of the Communist Party", "a puppet of the SACP", and claimed that "the SACP in its turn is a creature of the International Department of the Communist Party of the Soviet Union."[266]

But behind closed doors Pretoria's officials were much more realistic. As was mentioned above, Pretoria deliberately organised the leaking of information about every contact with the USSR, in whatever field. Apparently the only serious contact which it was discreet about was a Soviet-South African meeting in August 1984 in one of the European capitals.

Indisputably Pretoria was much more interested in contacts with the USSR than vice versa. While the Soviet delegation was headed by a Deputy Head of the Third African Department, their South African interlocutors were led by the Deputy Director General of the Department of Foreign Affairs, not to mention the inclusion of the Head of the National Intelligence Service, Neil Barnard.

Pretoria tried to use the meeting to procure recognition of South Africa as a "regional [read: dominating] power" before she embarked on the road of substantial changes in domestic policy. In exchange, a very doubtful promise was made to distance the country from the West. The South African delegates were unable to hide their disappointment when the Soviets declined to swallow this bait.

More important was a statement that Pretoria was ready to get rid of the "Namibian burden", to carry out Security Council Resolution 435, provided that, simultaneously, Cuban troops left Angola and the SADF left Namibia. The South African representatives also claimed that Pretoria had stopped supporting Renamo.

Whereas the South African government used the "communist bogey" as a threat inside the country and in their relations with the West, they now tried to scare the Soviets with stories of the growth of the ultra-conservative elements among the whites, the only viable alternative, they asserted, to P W Botha. It is also worth mentioning that at this meeting the South African side (and not the Soviets) tried to introduce the issue of possible joint control of the world market of several strategic raw materials.

Increasing international attention to the problems of South Africa was evident in September 1984 at the Arusha conference held at the initiative of the Socialist International. Its participants included many prominent West European leaders, the Prime Ministers of Sweden and Portugal among them. Applauding those social democratic parties which had proposed measures to isolate South Africa, Oliver Tambo added: "In honesty we should, however, also say that these actions have been small relative to the enormity of the problem we face in Southern Africa and in terms of the extensive backing that the apartheid regime receives from the countries of Western Europe."[267] The ANC President stressed that the ANC "had got over the shock" of Nkomati. "We have adjusted."[268]

A striking feature of the conference, which I attended as a *Pravda* correspondent, was that the African leaders did not mince their words when they criticised US collusion with Pretoria. The twisting of their arms by Chester Crocker and his assistants caused some bad feelings. More than once I heard the US diplomat referred to as "Crooker".

Robert Mugabe said that P W Botha started to speak very arrogantly "soon after his meeting with Dr Chester Crocker, US Assistant Secretary of State for African Affairs ... We cannot avoid the feeling that we have all along been cheated. But may I state, emphatically, that although cheated, yes, we have been, blackmailed we shall not be!"[269]

GORBACHEV, ACCELERATION AND PERESTROIKA

1985 was a special year both for South Africa and for the USSR. In South Africa the mass protests, which had begun after the introduction of the Constitution in the previous year, resulted, in July, in the government's declaring a State of Emergency in many areas, and in engaging in a new wave of mass repression.

In the USSR in March 1985 Mikhail Gorbachev was elected General Secretary of the CPSU Central Committee. Almost immediately he proclaimed a new policy, based on accelerating the social and economic development of the country, which had allegedly stagnated in the late 1970s and the early 1980s. Initially his approach was technocratic and focused on the development of the Soviet machine-building industry as a basis for new technologies.

However, before the economy had made any breakthrough, the slogan of "perestroika" was coined, which, roughly translated, meant "rebuilding" or "restructuring" both the economic and political life of the Soviet Union, while keeping intact or even strengthening its socialist foundation. The idea of marrying socialism and democracy became highly attractive to most Soviet citizens as well as to many people abroad. Both hoped for a new era of dynamic leadership that would turn aside from the blunders of the past, and institute a more consistent and active internal and external policy.

A song about a "fresh wind" became popular at this stage. Expectations were very high and Gorbachev initially seemed to meet them. In his first statements Gorbachev was clear in his stand. "People abroad who share our views may rest assured: in the struggle for peace and social justice the Party of Lenin will as always closely co-operate with fraternal Communist, workers' and revolutionary-democratic parties and will champion the unity and co-operation of all revolutionary forces," he declared in his acceptance speech on 11 March.[270]

The "perestroika" period in Soviet relations with the ANC and its allies deserves special study. In many articles and books by academics, published both in South Africa and in the West, it is described mostly as a period of the USSR's "alienation" from the ANC and its "rapprochement" with Pretoria. The truth is much more complicated and often remains obscure and even distorted.

In May 1985 the USSR celebrated the fortieth anniversary of the victory over Nazi Germany. Among foreign delegates who were invited to the occasion was Joe Slovo.

The old bureaucratic traditions which lingered on in the CPSU were often embarrassing. For example, officials of the International Department had to determine which of the foreign guests should be seated "in the presidium", that is on the stage, and which in the auditorium; who should be given the floor at the "main" plenary meeting, and who at the meetings of the regional or grassroots organisations. How were we to explain to Slovo, for example, why the leader of the Cyprus AKEL Party should sit "upstairs" and Slovo, also a World War Two veteran, "downstairs"?

Apart from the official ceremonies (the military parade and the "solemn meeting" in the Kremlin), the spirit of the celebrations captivated Slovo. On Victory Day we strolled in Gorky Park, listened to the spontaneous singing of songs and reading of poetry, watched a fireworks display in the evening at the Lenin Hills near the Moscow State University, and joined groups of singing students, including some Africans. "This is the Chairman of the South African Communist Party," I whispered to one of them. She looked at me with utter disbelief. Slovo was warmly received by the workers and engineers of the famous "Krasny Proletariy" (Red Proletarian) Machine Building Plant in Moscow, especially when the chairman mentioned his participation in World War Two.

Ellis and "Sechaba" wrote: "South African government propaganda alleged that Slovo was a colonel of the Soviet KGB, but that seems rather unlikely in view of Slovo's South African nationality."[271] The fact is that for several decades the South African authorities refused Slovo a South African passport and he was officially regarded as an "alien" even when he was already engaged in the vital talks on a political settlement.

After Slovo's death Dennis Herbstein in the *Cape Times* described how "the SAP department of dirty tricks" made Slovo a colonel in the early 1980s: "Make him a captain in the KGB, suggested one. Good idea, said Williamson, but why just a captain? The bigger the lie the more readily people will swallow it. The KGB colonel was born."[272]

However, even later there was some uncertainty about Slovo's supposed rank. The *Cape Argus* alleged in 1984 that he was "the KGB General" and had a dozen passports.[273] Pik Botha, being his usual contrary self, "demoted" him. "The power behind ANC is the Communist Party and the power behind the Communist Party is Joe Slovo, a major in the KGB," he declared at a pre-election meeting in 1987.[274] One wonders how Pik Botha, himself a "South African Air Force Honorary Colonel", later allowed himself, at the cabinet meetings of the Government of National Unity, to sit with someone of a "lower rank"? And what did Botha really feel when he participated in Slovo's state funeral in January 1995 at the Orlando Stadium in Soweto?

However, other accusations have been more serious. For anybody who had a chance to meet and talk with "Comrade J S", the insistence of Ellis and "Sechaba" that he is "a fundamental believer in classical Marxism-Leninism of the Soviet school"[275] is something of a joke. Slovo's sober approach to "real socialism", his understanding of mistakes committed in the course of social transformation, was evident long before "perestroika" even began. "In South Africa we are not going to nationalise every street vendor," he told me during one of our (very) informal discussions in a small bar in the famous Oktyabrskaya (October) Hotel, now known as the President Hotel.

Joe was always an independent thinker, able to adjust Marxist doctrine to realities, to enrich it with experience. His creative mind is well known. Moreover, his relationship with the Soviet establishment was not exactly a cosy one. For example, his criticism of the "socialist orientation" concept irritated some influential people in Moscow. One of the academics of the Moscow Africa Institute even prepared a 30-page document criticising Slovo's "theoretical mistakes" in the early 1980s, and it took quite an effort on the part of the CPSU officials to convince the Institute Director to refrain from publishing it. Besides, contrary to the claim of Ellis and "Sechaba" that the SACP supported Joseph Stalin's approach to the national question,[276] Slovo publicly criticised it.[277]

Later, when interviewed by the Western (and South African) press, Slovo explained that "because he had been an official visitor" in the USSR he "had not met the people"[278] and had not seen their living conditions. By and large this is true, but the fault lay mainly with his personal schedule. He was always an extremely busy man, and could rarely stay in the USSR for even an extra day. It happened more than once that while other members of the ANC or SACP leadership would go outside Moscow "to meet the people" and "to see the conditions", he would dash off to, say, Berlin or London. Until the late 1980s he had

275

never been in the USSR for a rest (traditionally after a stay at a sanatorium the guests would be invited to visit one or two republics or regions in the USSR). It seems that the meeting at "Krasny Proletariy" was the only time that Slovo visited a factory in the Soviet Union.

The paradox is, however, that those who knew Soviet life "better", who were "meeting the people" every day and so were in a position to assess the pros and cons (for example, South African political and military students), as a rule returned from the USSR with warm feelings and often as convinced socialists. Getting acquainted with the Soviet system in its various aspects, the majority compared the reality not with, say, Clifton or Sandton, but with Khayelitsha or Phola Park.

Slovo's criticism of "real socialism" did not develop into a rejection of the socialist idea. After the collapse of the Communist-ruled governments in Eastern Europe at the end of 1989 we were glad to read Slovo's booklet *Has socialism failed?*, and it was published in Russian in two issues of *Africa and Asia Today* magazine. Later, in April 1991, he said in an interview with a *Pravda* correspondent: "Some Eastern European countries after some time will inevitably feel a nostalgia for the indisputable advantages of the socialist idea and practice, first of all of such as social justice."[279] He was proved right: soon the mood of the people changed and the electoral victory of socialists in several countries in Eastern Europe as well as 40% of votes received by the Chair of the Communist Party in the Russian Presidential election in 1996 attest to that.

Slovo admired Gorbachev's initial actions on the democratisation of the CPSU and the Soviet Union as a whole, but he condemned his desertion and betrayal in 1991: "It is saddening that some of those in the Soviet Union who helped diagnose the disease have now allowed themselves to be pushed into a treatment which addresses the disease by killing the patient." Slovo criticised Gorbachev for issuing "a Stalinist decree" to dissolve the CPSU "as if it were his personal property."[280]

Two weeks after this statement by Slovo, Gorbachev finally capitulated to those who "dissolved" the Soviet Union without reference to the people. He agreed to resign as the USSR President without any resistance. Apparently, a "golden handshake" from Boris Yeltsin played a role, although it should rather be called a "brick-and-mortar" handshake: he received as a kind of "retrenchment allowance" the premises of the International Lenin School (Institute of Social Sciences) to house his newly established "Gorbachev Fund".

I have no doubt that Slovo would have been delighted to hear that the Russian people totally rejected Gorbachev's opportunism when they had a chance to do so: in the 1996 Presidential election the former leader received a pathetic 0,51% of the vote.

But in May 1985, when Slovo visited the Institute, nobody could have imagined such a deal between Gorbachev and Yeltsin, then two Secretaries of the Communist Party Central Committee.

Slovo met both groups of South African political students, those of the SACP and of the ANC. Although in fact practically all the SACP members were also members of the ANC and some members of the ANC group were communists, they lived and studied in two different places. The complex of buildings in Moscow, on Leningradsky Prospect 39 on the way to the international Sheremetyevo airport, was at that stage reserved for communists, while a small campus in a forest in Nagornoye, about 50 km north west of Moscow, was reserved for "revolutionary democrats". (Later the allocation was changed around.) However, the programme of training for both groups was quite similar.

In an informal atmosphere on that campus outside Moscow (shortly before Gorbachev's prohibition rule) Slovo said: "You took us seriously all these years, even when almost nothing remained."[281]

This phrase reminded me of another, which I heard from Oliver Tambo many years earlier, before the Soweto uprising: "The Soviet Union was helping the ANC permanently, as if the situation was always favourable."[282]

277

Among the issues discussed in Moscow at that time were the first signs of the "talks about talks". Apart from Professor van der Merwe's mission, a rather peculiar development was the permission given by Pretoria to British Conservative Lord Bethell to visit Nelson Mandela in prison (just two weeks earlier Edward Kennedy was refused such a meeting). According to Bethell, Mandela told him: "The armed struggle was forced on us by the government. And if they want us to give it up, the ball is in their court."[283]

Perhaps one more phrase from Mandela's interview should be remembered, especially nowadays: "Personally I am a socialist and I believe in a classless society. But I see no reason to belong to any political party at the moment."[284]

By and large the Bethell visit was regarded as Pretoria's attempt to sound out Mandela without entering into direct talks with him. But at the same time P W Botha added a further condition to his previous demand that Mandela reside in the Transkei in the event of his release: that he reject violence unconditionally.

A clear reply was given by Mandela to those demands in the message read by his daughter Zindzi at a rally in Soweto on 10 February: "I cannot and will not give any undertaking at a time when I and you, the people, are not free. Your freedom and mine cannot be separated. I will return."[285]

Nevertheless the government continued its overtures. The possibility of negotiations was mentioned on 15 February 1985 by Botha himself: "If the ANC and other organisations concerned also decide to reject and renounce violence, the government is willing to talk to them."[286]

The position of Oliver Tambo and his comrades was clear: "We see talks as a final stage in the whole struggle we have been involved in. They will take place when there is a general agreement that apartheid has to end."[287]

On 25 April the ANC National Executive Committee issued a statement, with an optimistic opening: "The future is within our grasp." It assessed the developments in the first months of 1985 and advanced the slogans: "Make apartheid unworkable. Make the country ungovernable."[288]

The spirit of growing resistance to the apartheid regime dominated the ANC's Second National Consultative Conference in Kabwe (in Zambia) in June 1985. The decision to convene it was taken a year earlier, soon after the mutiny in Angola. It was preceded by regional conferences, which discussed major problems confronting the ANC and elected delegates to the national conference.

For example, at the regional conference in Angola, which took place in March, the mutiny was resolutely denounced, though the delegates criticised the activities of the ANC Security Department. The delegates suggested that the inclusion of non-Africans in the National Executive Committee be discussed. The names of Joe Slovo and Ronnie Kasrils were mentioned. The conference in Tanzania also supported the opening of the ANC membership to all races, though it was suggested that the three highest positions should be occupied by Africans.

The venue of the National Conference remained secret, even for delegates, until the last moment. The delegates who came from abroad were initially accommodated at the ANC farm some miles from Lusaka. Earlier some had suggested that the conference be held in Mazimbu, but that idea was rejected in order to avoid giving too "humanitarian" a character to the conference. Luanda was discussed as well. However, the increasingly friendly attitude of Zambian President Kenneth Kaunda was decisive in the final choice of the Citizens' College, the school of the ruling UNIP party. A battalion of Zambian troops protected the venue from possible attack by Pretoria.

The conference took place during the new upsurge of the struggle in South Africa and it strengthened the feeling of unity. There were no serious conflicts or confrontations. Oliver Tambo, Alfred Nzo and Thomas Nkobi were returned unopposed to their positions. The NEC election had a specific procedure. The delegates received a list of 40 nominations recommended by Oliver Tambo. Delegates were asked to elect 30 members, and were free to choose from the full list of about 250 names. As it happened, all 30 NEC members were elected from the list of 40. The maximum number of votes was received by Chris Hani and John Nkadimeng.

(Nkadimeng's son Vernon, named after Vernon Berange, an advocate in the Treason Trial, was killed by a car bomb in Gaborone on 14 May. On the eve of the conference, on 14 June, another attack on the ANC, unprecedented in its scale, took place in Botswana.)

The US academic Michael Radu claimed in his article in the *Problems of Communism*, a magazine published by the US Information Agency, that delegates voted in Kabwe by blocs, including "groups that had been part of the Congress Alliance (SAIC, Sactu, CPC, SACP, COD)."[289] This was not merely wrong but unthinkable: how could communists vote by bloc when only two or three of them were officially known?

The Conference decided to open membership of the ANC to South Africans of any race. There was almost no opposition: two delegates voted against and three abstained.[290] Joe Modise made an emotional speech lauding this proposal. Brian Bunting cautioned delay, considering that the ANC inside South Africa had not been adequately consulted, but his view did not gain support from the delegates.

Almost all members of the old Executive Committee were re-elected. One who lost his position was John Motshabi, who at this stage was trying to organise some kind of opposition to the leadership. There was even talk of his introducing an alternative list of candidates, but he did not muster much support. Earlier, in 1983, he had been expelled from the SACP Central Committee[291] for factional activity and violation of discipline. This example shows again (as at Morogoro) that when differences arose in the ANC they were not between communists and non-communists but across the organisational spectrum.

Two Indians, Mac Maharaj and Aziz Pahad, two Coloureds, Reginald September and James Stuart (Hermanus Loots), and a white, Joe Slovo, became members of the highest organ of the ANC. The new Executive Committee had the right to co-opt five more members. Later this provision was used to co-opt Ronnie Kasrils.

Oliver Tambo himself delivered a special report on security problems. Its purpose was to draw attention to these problems, but it served also to soften the attitude towards the ANC security apparatus, members of which had been strongly criticised for abuse of power. The report conceded: "Some of the comrades manning these organs have made bad, sometimes terrible mistakes. They have over-reacted in some situations and employed unacceptable methods, thus distorting the image of the Department of Intelligence and Security."[292]

For the first time concern about Tambo's health was made public at the Conference, when he made a pledge: "Whatever little is left of my health will be consumed in struggle."[293]

One of the questions discussed at the Conference was so-called "soft targets". This issue has been grossly distorted by the South African and Western media. They linked it to Oliver Tambo's call to bring the struggle to the white areas. This led them to interpret the intention to attack "soft targets" as the ANC's decision "to shoot down white civilians, pregnant women and children, to indulge in an orgy of slaughter, bloodshed and general mayhem in order to achieve its objectives."[294] In reality, however, the idea was to attack and eliminate the personnel of the security forces: the SADF and police.

Nevertheless, there was a change in attitude to the possibility of civilian victims. Joe Slovo wrote in 1986: "One can say that up to a few years ago we were very anxious to avoid civilian casualties. We still are anxious. But there were moments in our military activity when we could have engaged the enemy effectively but opted out of that possibility because of the danger of civilian casualties. We are no longer completely guided by that consideration."[295]

In actual fact not much was done in this respect. For example, during several years the question of a mortar attack against military personnel was canvassed (some advice was requested by the ANC from the Soviet instructors in Angola) but it had never been realised. However, public debate and considerable media attention to the question of attacking "soft targets" helped the government propaganda to present a distorted image of the ANC to whites inside the country, and in the West.

At Kabwe the delegates decided to convene the ANC conferences and re-elect the NEC once every five years. It affirmed that the next conference would be held inside South Africa. (This idea was contained in Nelson Mandela's message from prison, read to delegates by Oliver Tambo.) So five years became the time frame for radical change in the country. This aim was very nearly achieved, though for practical reasons the next conference was delayed and took place in Durban six years later.

1. *Southern African Information Service*. International Defence and Aid Fund, London, vol. 4, part II, p.806.
2. *Sechaba*, N 5, 1975, p.16.
3. Ibid. p.7.
4. MCHP, ANCLonC, Matters arising from the Revolutionary Council meeting March 17-20, 1975, Morogoro, for the attention of the National Executive Committee, p.1.
5. Ibid. pp.2-3.
6. Ibid. p.2.
7. *Sechaba*, N 5, p.16.
8. *Declaration of the African National Congress* (1975, s.l.) p.4.
9. *Pravda*, 9 April 1975.
10. Discussion with A. Nzo, Moscow, 11 August 1975.
11. Quoted in: Janke P, Southern Africa: End of Empire, in *Conflict Studies*. London. N 52, December 1974, p.116.
12. Discussion with M.P. Naicker, Moscow, 5 July 1975.
13. *Sechaba*, N 8-9, 1975, p.23.
14. *Echo*, Op. cit.
15. MCHP, YDC.
16. Discussion with C. Hani, Moscow, 27 April 1992.
17. CSCD, Minutes of the Secretariat, N 177, item 54g, 16 July 1975.
18. Statement of the African National Congress, p.1.
19. Discussion with O. Tambo and A. Nzo, Moscow, 3 March 1976.
20. *African Communist*, N 64, 1976, p.11.
21. CSCD, Minutes of the Secretariat, N 191, item 15g, 30 October 1975.
22. Ibid. N 200, item 43g, 9 January 1976, N 203, item 11g, 30 January 1976.
23. Discussion with J. Makatini, Moscow, 9 February 1976.
24. Discussion with A. Nzo and T. Nkobi, Moscow, 3 February 1976.
25. Ibid.
26. Ibid.
27. Discussion with O. Tambo and A. Nzo, Moscow, 3 March 1976.
28. *Sechaba*, 1976, 3rd Quarter, p.31.
29. Brooks A. and Brickhill J. *Whirlwind before the Storm. The Origins and Development of the Uprising in Soweto and the Rest*

of South Africa from June to December 1976. International
Defence and Aid Fund, London, 1980.

30. Quoted in: *Rand Daily Mail*, 9 August1976.
31. *Echo*, Op. cit.
32. *African National Congress. National Consultative Conference June 1985. Report of the National Executive Committee presented by the Secretary General Comrade Alfred Nzo.* African National Congress, Lusaka, s.a., p.18.
33. Ibid.
34. Discussion with M.P. Naicker, Moscow, 5 July 1975.
35. Quoted in: *Spotlight on Soweto.* World Peace Council - African National Congress publication. Helsinki, 1976, pp. 8-9.
36. de Villiers C.F., Metrowich F.R. and du Plessis J.A. *The Communist Strategy.* The Department of Information, Pretoria, 1975, p.65.
37. *Rand Daily Mail*, Johannesburg, 20 August 1976.
38. *South African Digest*, Pretoria, week ending 29 July 1977, p.12.
39. *Morning Star*, London, 7 July 1976.
40. Lodge T. *Black Politics,* p. 296.
41. *Sechaba*, London, N 5, 1975, p.6.
42. Discussion with J. Makatini, Moscow, 9 February 1976.
43. Archive of the SAASC, SAC. Alfred Nzo to the Secretary, South African Students' Union (SASU), 12 June 1979.
44. CSCD, Minutes of the Secretariat, N 24, 3 January 1972, item 42g.
45. Archive of the SAASC, SAC, Summary of discussion with O. Tambo, Moscow, 6.12.1979.
46. *African National Congress. National Consultative Conference June 1985. Report of the National Executive Committee,* p.13.
47. MCHP, ANCLusC, *African National Congress. National Consultative Conference. June 1975. President's Statement to Conference,* p. 11.
48. *Sechaba*, First Quarter 1977, p.65.
49. Karis T. and Gerhart G. *Challenge and Violence.* p.785.
50. *African National Congress. National Consultative Conference. June 1975. Report of the National Executive Committee,* p.19.
51. *Dawn*, Souvenir Issue, p.49.
52. MCHP, YDC, (Unsigned Report), p.1.
53. *Rand Daily Mail*, Johannesburg, 26 January 1977.
54. *Citizen*, Johannesburg, 29 September 1977.

55. *Rand Daily Mail*, 2 February 1978.
56. *Sechaba*, First Quarter 1978, p.5.
57. Tambo O. *Preparing for Power*, Heinemann, London, 1987, p.126.
58. Discussion with A. Nzo, Moscow, 21 December 1976.
59. Ibid. 20 August 1976.
60. Ibid. 23 December 1976.
61. Discussion with J. Jele, Moscow, 4 October 1976.
62. Ibid. 2 October 1975.
63. Quoted in : Nel P. *Perceptions, Images and Stereotypes in Soviet - South African Relations - A Cognitive-Interpretive Perspective.* University of Stellenbosch Annale, 1992/4, Stellenbosch, 1992, p.33.
64. *Izvestiya*, Moscow, 6 November 1977.
65. *Rand Daily Mail*, 19 August 1976.
66. Palme O. *Social Democracy and the Liberation Struggle in South Africa. SI Congress, Geneva, November 26-28 1976,* p.3.
67. Bushin V. *Social Democracy and Southern Africa (1960s-1980s).* Moscow, Progress Publishers, pp. 97-98.
68. *Sechaba*, February 1979, p.27.
69. Ibid. Third Quarter 1978, p.42.
70. *Daily Telegraph*, 31 January 1978.
71. Discussion with O. Tambo, Moscow, 5 October 1978.
72. Discussion with O. Tambo and J. Slovo, Moscow, 8 June 1977.
73. Ibid.
74. *Sechaba*, First Quarter 1978, pp. 1-2.
75. Ellis S. and Sechaba T. *Comrades*, p.59.
76. *Sechaba*, First Quarter 1978, pp. 1-2.
77. MCHP, YDC, Report to members on recent NEC meeting held in Lusaka 25-28 February 1978, p.1
78. Ibid. p. 8
79. *Pravda*, Moscow, 7 October 1978.
80. Discussion with O. Tambo, Moscow, 5 October 1978.
81. MCHP, ANCLonC, Speech at the graduation ceremony of the Moncada Detachment of Umkhonto we Sizwe, Angola - December 1977.
82. Kasrils R. *"Armed and Dangerous". My Underground Struggle Against Apartheid.* Heinemann, Oxford, 1993, p.270.
83. MCHP, YDC, Nelson Mandela to Oliver Tambo.
84. Ibid. The words "prison" and "cautious" in square brackets were

added by the person who typed Mandela's message after it was smuggled out.

85. Ibid.

86. MCHP, YDC, (Letter from the Robben Island Prison), pp. 1-2.

87. Ibid. Yusuf Dadoo to the CC CPSU, 16 March 1977.

88. *African Communist,* London, N 70, 1977, p.31-34.

89. Ibid.

90. MCHP, YDC, Main Decisions of the Plenary Session of the Central Committee Held in Walter, 21 to 24 April 1977, pp.1-3.

91. *African Communist,* N 70, 1977, p.34.

92. Quoted in: *African Communist,* N 68, 1977, p.51.

93. *Problemy Mira i Socialisma* (Russian edition of the World Marxist Review), Prague, 1978, N 3, p.15.

94. MCHP, YDC, Guidelines. February 1978.

95. CSCD, Minutes of the Secretariat of the CPSU CC, N 97, item 1g, 15 March 1978.

96. *Report on the Labour Movement and Our Task.* (s.a. e.l.)

97. Ibid. p.1.

98. Ibid. p.3.

99. *African National Congress. National Consultative Conference, President's Statement to Conference,* p. 14.

100. *Imperialist offensive against the African National Congress of South Africa (1969-1978),* (s.a.e.l), p.9.

101. Ibid. p.16.

102. Discussions with J. Jele, Moscow, 20 August 1977, 10 February 1978.

103. MCHP, YDC, (Yusuf Dadoo's notes.)

104. *Sechaba,* October 1979, pp. 16-17.

105. Quoted in: *African Communist,* N 84, 1981, p.90.

106. Discussion with J. Nkadimeng, Cape Town, 25 November 1994.

107. *Resolutions and documents adopted by the Revolutionary Council meeting held in Luanda from the 3rd to the 5th January 1979.*

108. *African National Congress. National Consultative Conference. June 1985. Report of the National Executive Committee,* p.20.

109. *Archive of the SAASC, SAC.*

110. *Sunday Express,* Johannesburg, 23 August 1979.

111. *Sechaba,* April 1979, p.4.

112. Tambo O. *Preparing for Power,* p. 146.

113. Ibid. p.147.

114. Quoted in: *The Weekly Mail and Guardian,* Johannesburg,

8 to 14 October 1993.

115. Tambo O. *Preparing for Power,* p.180.

116. *Sechaba*, May 1979, pp. 13-14.

117. *Star*, Johannesburg, 15 May 1979.

118. *Internal Statement. The enemy is intended to eliminate us physically.* 26 March 1979. (Lusaka).

119. Kasrils R. *"Armed and Dangerous",* p. 186.

120. Discussion with O. Tambo, Moscow, 6 December 1979.

121. Ibid.

122. Discussion with T. Nkobi, Moscow, 6 December 1979.

123. MCHP, ANCLonC, Island: Regional Committee comments, p.1.

124. *African Communist*, N 84, 1981, p.21.

125. Tambo O. Op. cit. pp. 203-204.

126. *Kommunist*, Moscow, 1981, N 11, p.102.

127. *African National Congress. National Consultative Conference , President's Statement to Conference ,* pp. 19-20.

128. *Sechaba*, August 1980, p. 2.

129. Ibid. p.4.

130. ANC *Weekly News Briefing*, London, 1980, N 11, p.1.

131. Ibid. p.2.

132. *Morning Star*, London, 20 August 1980.

133. Discussion with A. Masondo, Moscow, 1 October 1980.

134. *African National Congress. National Consultative Conference, President's Statement to Conference,* p.20.

135. *Star*, Johannesburg, 4 December 1980.

136. *Rand Daily Mail*, 3 June 1980.

137. Ibid.

138. *Guardian*, London, 4 June 1980.

139. Discussion with J. Slovo, Moscow, 10 May 1985.

140. *Dawn*, Souvenir Issue, p.18.

141. *Sunday Times*, Johannesburg, 27 January 1980.

142. *Guardian*, 23 January 1980.

143. *Sechaba*, February 1979, p.29.

144. ANC *Weekly News Briefing*, 1980, N 4, p.3.

145. MCHP, An Operational Analysis of the Schoon Network, August 1980, (Pretoria).

146. *Servamus*, Pretoria, September 1981.

147. *Sunday Times*, Johannesburg, 27 January 1980.

148. Ludi G. *Operation Q-018,* p.101.

149. *Sunday Times*, Johannesburg, 27 January 1980.

150. Venter A. (edit.) *Challenge. Southern Africa within the African Revolutionary Context. An Overview.* Ashanti Publishing, Gibraltar, 1989, p.278.

151. MCHP, An Operational Analysis, p.1.

152. Ibid. p.5.

153. MCHP, An Operational Evaluation of the ANC/CP with emphasis on the Internal Reconstruction and Development Department (IRDD), Pretoria, 1980, p.1.

154. MCHP, Draft. Strategy and Tactics of the ANC/CP. Compiled by K.Z. Edwards. May 1980. N.I.S. Head Office, pp. 2-3.

155. Ibid. p.6.

156. MCHP, Draft. ANC/CP Methods of Spotting and Recruiting of Agents within the RSA. Compiled by K.Z. Edwards. May 1980. General Remarks and Conclusions Concerning the ANC/CP, (Pretoria), p.1.

157. *Star*, 3 November 1983.

158. Quoted in: *Washington Post,* 1 January 1984.

159. Sole D. *This Is Above All. Reminiscences of the South African Diplomat.* (D.S. Sole, s.a.e.l.), p.48.

160. *Sechaba*, May 1982, p.7.

161. *Star*, 1 April 1982.

162. *The Role of the Soviet Union, Cuba and East Germany in Fomenting Terrorism in Southern Africa. Addendum.* US Government Printing Office, Washington, 1982, Vol. 2, pp. 350-387.

163. Ibid. p.8.

164. Ibid. p.7.

165. Quoted in: *African Communist*, N 91, 1982, p.90.

166. *Soviet, East German and Cuban Involvement in Fomenting Terrorism in Southern Africa. Report of the Chairman of the Subcommittee on Security and Terrorism to the Committee of the Judiciary. United States Senate.* US Government Printing Office, Washington, 1982.

167. Ibid. p.22.

168. Ibid. p.23.

169. Quoted in: ANC *Weekly News Briefing*, N 19, 1982, pp. 5-6.

170. Tambo O. Op. cit. pp. 92-93.

171. Maharaj S. in: Nelson Mandela. *The Struggle is My Life.* London, International Defence and Aid Fund for Southern Africa, London, 1978, p.220.

172. *Africa Confidential*, N 3, 1981, p.1.

173. *Evening Post,* 10 June 1981.

174. *Izvestiya*, 30 December 1988.

175. *Sowetan*, Johannesburg, 10 August 1981.

176. *Times*, London, 18 December 1981.

177. *Evening Post,* Johannesburg, 21 April 1981.

178. *Cape Times*, 2 September 1981.

179. *The Role of the Soviet Union,* Addendum. Vol. 2, pp. 800-801.

180. *Pravda*, Moscow, 2 September 1981.

181. Discussion with T. Mbeki, Moscow, 6 January 1982.

182. Ibid. 9 January 1982.

183. *Sechaba*, April 1982, p.8.

184. Ibid. June 1982.

185. Discussions with T. Mbeki, Moscow, 6, 9, 10 January 1982.

186. MCHP, Draft. The Internal Reconstruction and Development Department (IRDD) and S.R. "Mac" Maharaj. (Pretoria, 1980). pp. 5-6.

187. *Sechaba*, October 1982, pp. 25-26.

188. Discussion with T. Nkobi, Moscow, 29 September 1982.

189. MCHP, YDC, Minutes of P.B. Meeting 17 February 1983 in Maputo, p.2.

190. *Sechaba*, December 1982, p.20.

191. Quoted in: Crocker C. *High Noon in Southern Africa. Making Peace in a Rough Neighbourhood.* Jonathan Ball Publishers, Johannesburg, 1993, p.81.

192. *Rand Daily Mail*, 20 December 1982.

193. Ibid. 10 December 1982.

194. MCHP, ANCLonC, Traitors.

195. *Sechaba*, January 1983, p.3.

196. *African Communist,* N 93, 1983, p.71.

197. Ibid. N 92, 1983, pp. 81-82.

198. Discussion with C. Hani, Moscow, 20 May 1983.

199. MCHP, YDC.

200. *Southscan*, London, 11 June 1993.

201. MCHP, YDC, Secretariat activities since formation.

202. MCHP, YDC, Minutes of the P.B. Meeting, 17 February 1983 in Maputo, p.3.

203. *Star*, 3 November 1983.

204. *Sunday Times*, Johannesburg, 29 May 1983.

205. Ibid.

206. Ibid.
207. *Weekend Argus*, Cape Town, 7/8 January 1995.
208. Tambo O., *Preparing for Power*, p.163.
209. MCHP, ANCLonC, Mandela to Mota [Yusuf Dadoo], 1 November 1975.
210. *African Communist,* N 96, 1984, pp. 6-7.
211. MCHP, YDC, (Yusuf Dadoo's letter to his friends in South Africa).
212. Ibid.
213. MCHP, Profile of Mac Maharaj, with emphasis on his friends and family. Pretoria. 1980.
214. Dadoo Y. *South Africa's Freedom Struggle.* Kliptown Books, London, 1990, p.288.
215. *Cape Times*, 13 December 1982.
216. *Golden City Press*, 12 December 1982.
217. MCHP, YDC, Minutes of P.B. Meeting 17 February 1983 in Maputo, p.6.
218. Kasrils R. *"Armed and Dangerous"*, p. 274.
219. Discussion with M. Mabhida, Moscow, 26 November 1984.
220. *London Review of Books*, London, 5 August 1993.
221. Ibid.
222. Ellis S. and Sechaba T., Comrades against Apartheid, p.145.
223. MCHP, YDC, Structure March 1983, p.1
224. Ibid.
225. *Guardian*, 6 August 1983.
226. *African National Congress. National Consultative Conference, Presidential Statement to Conference*, p. 21.
227. Discussion with A. Nzo, 28 October 1983.
228. Makatini J. New York. 18 March, 1984. *Interview by Jim Casson and Richard Knight of the American Committee on Africa,* p.1. (I am indebted to Prof Gail Gerhart for the text of this interview).
229. Ibid.
230. Discussion with Joe Slovo, 25 November 1985.
231. *Sowetan*, 16 March 1984.
232. *Rand Daily Mail*, 18 April 1984.
233. *Sechaba*, June, 1984, p.4.
234. Ibid.
235. Ibid.
236. Makatini J, New York, p.4.
237. Discussion with Chris Hani, Moscow, 25 November 1984.

238. Ibid. 27 November 1992.

239. Barrel H. *MK: the ANC's Armed Struggle.* Penguin Books, London, 1990, p. 52.

240. Quoted in: *Sechaba*, November 1984, p.87.

241. Discussion with A. Nzo, Moscow, 20 June 1984.

242. Ellis S. *The South African Communist party and the ANC in exile.* (Amsterdam), 1992, p.6

243. Discussion with J. Jele, Johannesburg, 25 November 1993.

244. Discussion with T. Mbeki, Moscow, 21 October 1985.

245. Ibid.

246. Crocker C., *High Noon in Southern Africa*, p. 180.

247. *Times*, 6 January 1984.

248. *Guardian*, 26 June 1984.

249. Quoted in: *Cape Times,* Cape Town, 15 January 1981.

250. *Cape Times*, 10 January 1981.

251. *Rand Daily Mail*, 16 June 1981.

252. *Citizen*, 12 May 1984.

253. Ibid.

254. *Sechaba*, September 1984, p.1.

255. Ibid. October 1984, p.14.

256. *Zimbabwe Herald*, Harare, 7 July 1984.

257. Quoted in: ANC *Weekly News Briefing*, 1985, N 2, p.3.

258. Ibid.

259. Discussion with A. Nzo, Moscow, 14 February 1985.

260. Ibid.

261. *Rand Daily Mail*, 22 December 1984.

262. *Star*, 19 June 1984.

263. *Argus*, Cape Town, 13 September 1988.

264. Discussion with J. Slovo, 14 December 1984.

265. *Press briefing for accredited foreign correspondents*, p.6

266. Ibid. p.17.

267. *The Arusha Conference,* London, Socialist International 1985, p.132.

268. *Guardian*, 6 September 1984.

269. *The Arusha Conference,* pp. 86-87.

270. Quoted in: *African Communist,* N 102, 1985, p.79.

271. Ellis S. and Sechaba T., *Comrades*, p.58.

272. *Cape Times*, 9 January 1995.

273. *Argus*, 30 April 1984.

274. *Daily Dispatch*, Port Elizabeth, 29 September 1987.

275. Ellis S. and Sechaba T., *Comrades,* p.58.

276. Ibid. p.88.

277. Slovo J. *The Working Class and Nation-Building. In: van Diepen M. (edit.) The National Question in South Africa.* London, Zed Books, 1988, pp. 142-143.

278. *Cape Times,* 5 December 1994.

279. *Pravda,* 27 April 1991.

280. *Cape Times,* 6 December 1991.

281. Discussion with Joe Slovo, Nagornoye, 10 May 1995.

282. Discussion with Oliver Tambo, Moscow, 3 March 1976.

283. Quoted in: ANC *Weekly News Briefing*s, 1985, N 4, p.2.

284. Ibid.

285. Quoted in: ANC *Weekly News Briefing*s, 1985, N 7, pp. 2-3.

286. *Argus,* 15 February 1985.

287. *Guardian,* 8 February 1985.

288. *Statement of the ANC National Executive Committee,* 25April 1985, Lusaka, Zambia.

289. *Problems of Communism,* Washington, July-August 1987, p.10.

290. MCHP, ANCLusC, The Second National Consultative Conference of the African National Congress held in Zambia, 16-23 June 1985, p.10.

291. MCHP, YDC, Minutes of the P.B. Meeting, 17 February 1983 in Maputo, p.3.

292. MCHP, ANCLusC, Report on Security and Intelligence, p.4.

293. Quoted in: Van Wyk, C., Callinicos, L. *Oliver Tambo,* Maskew Miller Longman, Cape Times, 1994, p.57.

294. *African Communist,* N 103, 1985, p.13.

295. *Dawn,* Souvenir Issue, p.49.

PART THREE
THE ROAD TO POWER (1985-1991)

TALKS ABOUT TALKS: CONTINUATION

The first years of Gorbachev's rule witnessed a much more active USSR foreign policy on many different levels. Overdue moves, for example, were made to initiate contacts with legal opposition organisations in South Africa, within the framework of the 1981 Central Committee decision. Two special workshops took place in the International Department of the CPSU in June 1985 with representatives of the Soviet NGOs, publishing houses and research bodies.

Two months later several South African writers were invited to attend the International Book Fair in Moscow on the recommendation of the ANC. One person managed to come. He was Chris van Wyk, then the editor of *Staffrider* magazine and also representing Ravan Press. Other black writers recommended by the ANC were unable to attend.

Attempts to bring to the USSR representatives of the legal opposition in South Africa were initially unsuccessful. The UDF leadership wanted a delegation of young people from inside South Africa to go to Moscow to the Festival of Youth and Students in July 1985, but just one young woman managed to attend, only to be detained as soon as she returned to South Africa.

After discussion with the ANC the Youth Festival International Preparatory Committee also invited Bishop Desmond Tutu and Rev. Alan Boesak. Although the number of Boesak's flight from Paris had already been communicated and people were at the airport to meet him, he did not arrive, apparently because of the imposition of the State of Emergency in South Africa. It is interesting to note that some of the ANC representatives had doubts about the wisdom of this invitation, which they felt could have negative consequences for Boesak.[1] Both Tutu and Boesak did, however, visit Moscow later. The next ANC-recommended visitor from South Africa was Jennifer Mohamed, a daughter of Professor Ismail Mohamed, a prominent figure in the UDF. Officially she came to see her brother, who was studying at the University, but we involved her in many discussions.

The Soviet side requested and received from the ANC a list of organisations and personalities to invite to the USSR. Among them were the UDF, AZASO, NUSAS and the End Conscription Campaign (ECC). However, the ANC proposed that initially "moderates", such as students from the University of Stellenbosch, be invited.

The CPSU Central Committee also took a special decision in 1985 to speed up anti-racist propaganda. The introduction of specialised studies on South Africa, including a course of Afrikaans in the Moscow State University, were part of this plan. An important role in its elaboration and implementation was played by the late Boris Asoyan, at that stage heading a section in the CPSU Department of External Propaganda (publicly known as the Department of International Information). Asoyan was strongly supportive of the struggles of the ANC and Umkhonto, and encouraged journalists to write about them. He wrote that actions such as the bomb attack on the South African Air Force Headquarters in Pretoria in May 1983 caused foreign investors to reconsider investing in South Africa and therefore helped deepen the crisis of the racist regime. "The observers were unanimous in their opinion: the operation in Pretoria promoted a further rise of ANC authority, an increase of the flow of the people to it."[2] In October 1985 Asoyan participated in talks with a special delegation of the ANC, headed by Thabo Mbeki, then the Head of its Information and Publicity Department, who came to the USSR to discuss co-operation in information and other fields.

By that time it had become evident to both friends and foes that a solution in South Africa could not be found without the involvement of the ANC, which was the acknowledged spearhead of the militancy sweeping the country. Steve Tshwete, then an underground leader of the UDF, reflected this militancy when he said to 70 000 people at the funeral of eighteen victims of the regime that the whole country could be burned to the ground so that a new society would emerge from the ashes of apartheid.[3]

The first serious sign of concern among the South African establishment was seen when a delegation of businessmen met with the ANC leadership in the Mufume Lodge in Zambia on 13 September 1985. The meeting was hosted by President Kaunda. The business leaders were responding to the upsurge of popular struggle and the apparent inability of the Pretoria regime to find a viable way out of the crisis.

Emissaries had twice before been to Lusaka, but the ANC had initially delayed the meeting with the businessmen. After P W Botha's "crossing the Rubicon" speech of 15 August 1985, which dashed hopes that the National Party would agree to substantial reform and disappointed those who had hoped for a change of heart by Pretoria, the time was ripe to go ahead. The ANC agreed to the meeting but, contrary to the businessmen's proposals, insisted that the meeting should not be secret. This was done to avoid speculation about possible ANC contacts with the regime.

One more factor played a role: business was finding itself in the direct line of fire. Umkhonto we Sizwe was targeting monopoly companies involved in disputes with their workers. On 30 April 1985 bomb explosions occurred at the headquarters of the country's two largest corporations: Anglo-American (whose Chairman Gavin Relly headed the delegation to Zambia) and Anglovaal. The explosion, "believed to have been caused by powerful Russian limpet mines", occurred after Anglo-American sacked 14 000 workers, followed by the dismissal of 3 000 Anglovaal workers. [4]

Not surprisingly, the business delegation posed questions about the relationship between the ANC and the USSR. The categorical ANC response was that in all its dealings with the Soviet Union and other socialist countries there had never been attempts to influence its views or to instruct it on what to do.

The businessmen agreed in principle with the need to abolish apartheid and create a united democratic South Africa. Thabo Mbeki's assessment during his visit to Moscow in October 1985 was that South African big business had drifted away from the National Party rulers, but that it was worried at the prospect of nationalisation envisaged in the Freedom Charter. Business desired to transform the ANC into a "moderate force", and to draw in other groups to achieve a "moderate" solution. That would mean that political power would be transferred from the ruling party to "moderate" politicians, and not to the ANC, at least initially.

Practical steps in the above direction were taken just a week after the return of these business people from Zambia. On 21 September the Alliance for a National Convention held its inaugural conference. It was hoped the Alliance would unite all those who were "against apartheid and against revolution". A delegation of the Progressive Federal Party, headed by Frederick van Zyl Slabbert, visited Lusaka to try to sell the idea of the Alliance to the ANC. But the ANC refused to support it for at least two reasons: firstly, one of the Alliance participants was to be Buthelezi, and, secondly, the alliance would be in direct competition with the UDF, which was already successfully uniting democratic forces.

After the imposition of the State of Emergency in July 1985, thousands of activists belonging to the UDF and other legal opposition organisations were detained. This hampered the anti-apartheid movement, but a positive result was the recognition of the need for tighter underground organisations, bringing the UDF and the ANC even closer to each other.

All this was happening against the background of attempts by certain Western countries to win the UDF away from the ANC. Because of the broad nature of the UDF, they hoped to find among its ranks those who would be acceptably moderate and at the same time part of the legitimate opposition. The government of West Germany offered a large sum of money to the UDF for it to open an office in the FRG.

Thabo Mbeki noted during his Moscow visit that the ANC leadership was taking the USSR's support too much "for granted" and was concentrating its diplomatic and information work in countries whose governments had been hostile to the ANC. This had resulted, for example, in his visit being delayed for three years.[5] Unfortunately this recognition that it was necessary to be more proactive in relations with the USSR was never properly acted upon in practice, even though this necessity grew in the following few years.

The South African situation was extensively discussed at the Commonwealth summit held in the Bahamas in October 1985. Both here and within the European Economic Community, Margaret Thatcher held out against the imposition of sanctions against Pretoria. A compromise of sorts was found in the creation of a special Eminent Persons Group (EPG), which would try to mediate between the government and the liberation movement.

The attitude of the ANC leadership to this decision was very restrained, not to say negative. They feared that Britain was trying to shift part of the responsibility for the lack of progress in finding a political settlement in South Africa on to the developing countries. They were worried that the EPG could become a permanent body, like the Western "contact group" on Namibia, which would sideline the UN and OAU when it came to South African issues.[6] The ANC decided it would not agree to the continuation of the EPG's activity beyond the six months decided upon at the Commonwealth summit.

There were valid reasons for this concern. A report was received in Moscow from Lagos that even a person as eminent as the EPG co-chairman, former Nigerian Head of State General Olusegun Obasanjo, was showing some susceptibility to Pretoria's approaches. After his visit to South Africa where he met with Nelson Mandela, Obasanjo stressed that there was a lack of unity in the opposition ranks and felt that the regime could withstand economic sanctions. To him Mandela resembled a man who was standing on a station platform after the train had left. He felt that Mandela's release would exacerbate the perceived leadership problems. Obasanjo felt that the government was ready for the talks but with the "non-communist" part of the ANC. These impressions, which revealed a spectacular misreading of the situation, were in no small measure influenced by misinformation provided by the regime.

Even while the EPG was speaking to Pretoria, the regime continued to attack the ANC in the neighbouring states. A group of ANC activists were killed on 21 December 1985 in Maseru. The USSR offered to provide some assistance to the Lesotho government, but in practice it was a difficult assignment. Although Maseru managed to negotiate with Pretoria the transit of Soviet-made arms to Lesotho, efforts were made to stop this transfer.

When Vincent Makhele, Lesotho's Foreign Minister, arrived in Moscow as a guest of the Soviet Afro-Asian Solidarity Committee at the end of 1985, he was received by newly appointed Foreign Minister Eduard Shevardnadze, even though this was not an official visit. Makhele informed us that the Lesotho authorities were expecting further problems from Pretoria. Before he left Moscow, it was agreed that Lesotho would buy a YAK-40 plane to help combat South African pressure. On 1 January 1986 Pretoria introduced an effective blockade of Lesotho by applying strict vehicle search measures at the South African border. Ten days later a coup followed, and the new military government insisted on the deportation of all ANC cadres from Lesotho. Vincent Makhele and a fellow minister, Desmond Sixishe, who was also close to the ANC, together with their wives, were murdered by the military.

Other governments in the region were also feeling Pretoria's grip at this time. Although Botswana resisted pressure to sign a treaty with South Africa, it officially demanded that the ANC representative and his deputy leave the country.

On the other hand, disillusionment with the Nkomati Accord was moving the Mozambican leadership closer to the ANC again. Mozambican officials began directly criticising the South African government for violations of the Nkomati Accord, and referring to the aggressive nature of the apartheid regime. Samora Machel put forward a confidential proposal for the release of Nelson Mandela. One of the conditions was that he would be given political asylum in Mozambique. (A similar proposal was made by the French government.) Machel hoped to organise a meeting between representatives of the ANC and the apartheid government.

The ANC leadership insisted that such talks could take place only after the release of the political prisoners (who should have the right to remain in South Africa) and the unbanning of the ANC. And the ANC was in no hurry to react to Mozambique's overtures; when Machel invited Tambo to Maputo in October 1985, the ANC President delayed for several months before going. Meanwhile, Joe Slovo was using a Mozambican passport (with a false name) to travel abroad. When it expired in 1986, the Mozambicans agreed to issue a new one, and dated it 1983, the year before the Nkomati Accord was signed.

By that time it was widely recognised in the West that apartheid could not survive. The question was: What would replace it? And by what kind of arrangement? Pretoria and the Western governments were still hoping to find some "moderate" elements in the liberation movement that could be counterposed to the "radical Lusaka leadership".

Recently the impression was given that Nelson Mandela conducted the preliminary discussions with various South African officials without the ANC leaders in exile having any knowledge of the situation. However, even the limited information that reached Moscow during that period proves that the opposite was true.

On 14 November 1985 I received the following telex message sent from Lusaka through the Soviet Afro-Asian Solidarity Committee:

"From DIP [Department of Information and Publicity] Thabo 14.11.85

Comrade Vladimir Shubin must phone Thabo Mbeki presently in Nairobi Kenya on number (2542) 725189. It is a matter of urgency."[7]

Within days, Thabo Mbeki was in Moscow to pass on to Oliver Tambo (who was back in Barvikha) an urgent personal message from Nelson Mandela which needed a reply before 1 December. Tambo persuaded his doctors to complete his treatment, and, against their advice, left Moscow much earlier than planned. Back in Zambia, Tambo was visited by Mandela's lawyer, George Bizos, who briefed him fully and assured him, on Mandela's behalf, that Tambo and his colleagues "should not worry, that he wouldn't do anything without their concurrence." [8]

The situation at which the struggle was poised in 1984-5 made the

...negotiations a reality for the first time. For the Soviets ... were a matter of expediency. In an academic paper, ... end of 1984 and presented in June 1985 (when the term ... was still unheard of), I wrote: "South African freedom fighters did not reject the possibility of negotiations but they are not going to conduct 'negotiations for the sake of negotiations'. They believe that the negotiations will be justified when a real possibility arises for the liberation movement to force its adversary to make cardinal concessions, and this, in its turn, depends on the current balance of forces both in South Africa and in Southern Africa as a whole."

I continued, "The history of the national liberation movement in Africa and on other continents has already brought to light a regular pattern: even before winning a military victory over the colonisers the liberation forces compel them to start negotiations and the struggle, victorious in its essence, often ends with a peace agreement of one kind or another, containing a large degree of compromise." [9]

In February 1986, at the 26th Congress of the CPSU (the ANC was represented by Alfred Nzo and Joe Modise, and the SACP by Joe Slovo and Eric Mtshali), Gorbachev emphasised the need for regional conflicts to be settled politically. Later that step was presented by many academics and politicians as something entirely new in Soviet policy. However, the Soviet Union had been involved in a search for political solutions in many military conflicts during the previous decades, *inter alia* in Korea, Vietnam, South Asia and the Middle East. The difference now was that Gorbachev's statement was forcefully articulated and followed by dynamic diplomatic activity.

The atmosphere of that CPSU Congress and the mood of delegates were quite different from previous party congresses. Joe Slovo arrived in Moscow from Lusaka after midnight, just hours before the congress opened. Gorbachev's report impressed him greatly. With his usual sense of humour Slovo said: "The proof is that I did not fall asleep."

The Soviet leadership was unequivocal that the ending of apartheid was part of the agenda for settling the conflicts in Southern Africa. At a dinner in honour of the Angolan President Jose Eduardo Dos Santos in May 1986 Gorbachev declared: "There exists a reasonable and realistic alternative to bloodshed, tension and confrontation in Southern Africa. It presupposes an end to aggression against Angola and other liberated states, the speedy granting to Namibia of independence – but of genuine independence, not fictitious

300

independence, as the USA and the RSA would like – and finally, the liquidation of the inhuman apartheid system." [10]

These remained the three pillars of Soviet policy towards Southern Africa throughout the 1980s and, indeed, this was the way the conflict was finally resolved.

The first concrete proposals for political settlement in South Africa were put forward by the Commonwealth's Eminent Persons Group, mentioned above. Their brand of shuttle diplomacy failed, however, when the South African government attacked targets in Lusaka, Harare and Gaborone on 19 May 1986. The targets were described as ANC bases, but not for the first time poor intelligence let Pretoria down.

Soviet protests against Pretoria's aggressive acts intensified when the South African special force damaged Soviet vessels and sank a Cuban vessel in an Angolan port on 5 June 1986: "The RSA is responsible for an act of terrorism in the Port of Namibe in Angola. Actions of this kind cannot go unpunished." [11]

The growing attention being paid to the ANC by Western countries became clear to me during a trip to the US in May 1986 to participate in the Soviet-American Conference on Sub-Saharan Africa at Berkeley. I was impressed by the seriousness of some researchers in South African studies in the US, especially Professor Thomas Karis. But at the same time some of our counterparts could hardly hide their desire to see the ANC weakened and split. One of them even talked about "four ANCs: non-communist, communist, internal and military." I spoke in Berkeley about the necessity for an "orderly transfer of power" to the ANC, bringing home the point that apartheid was doomed and that the only alternative to a negotiated settlement was a further escalation of revolt, chaos and economic disintegration. I also jokingly reminded the Americans that Moscow had not sent either red flags or people to hoist and carry them to South Africa but, nonetheless, from mid 1985 the red flag had become a regular feature of many South African political rallies and funerals.

At the State Department in Washington we encountered confusion among the Africanists. While voicing their criticism of the "acts of terror" committed by the ANC, they insisted that the State Department did not include the ANC in its list of "terrorist organisations". We had an odd conversation with Jeffrey Davidow, later the US Ambassador to Lusaka. He was concerned about the influence of the SACP inside the ANC, but at the same time suggested that "all the Party members could be accommodated in an elevator." I had no interest in debating the numerical strength of the SACP with him (or the fact that elevators are quite spacious in the State Department), but reminded him that tens of thousands of Africans had participated in the rallies in memory of Moses Mabhida two months earlier.

The rapid developments in Southern Africa necessitated increased discussions and closer co-ordination of efforts between the liberation movements and their supporters. In March 1986 Oliver Tambo paid a visit to Cuba, followed later by Joe Modise and Ronnie Kasrils, opening the way for more intensive co-operation, particularly with regard to the training of the ANC military cadres. Far from pushing the ANC towards intransigent positions, the Cuban side suggested that the clause of the ANC programme on nationalisation frightened many whites and hampered the creation of a broad coalition with white opposition forces in South Africa.

When the Umkhonto leaders described the difficulties of transporting personnel and arms into South Africa, the Cubans reminded them that they had "the longest friendly border" possible: a sea coast. The Cubans obviously had considerable experience in this field, but the ANC, seldom involved with the sea and with ships, did not seriously consider this avenue.

Regular consultations were also being conducted by Angola, Cuba and the USSR on a rotating basis in the respective capitals. The idea arose to have similar consultations on a broader basis, to include the participation of the ANC and SWAPO. Plans were made for high-level meetings to be attended by the leaders of the liberation movements, ministers, and Central Committee Secretaries, and a date was fixed for the end of June 1986. But during a short meeting in Paris with the newly appointed Soviet Deputy Foreign Minister Anatoly Adamishin at the UN International Conference on sanctions against South Africa, Oliver Tambo suddenly announced that the date did not suit him and suggested postponing the meeting. This showed a lack of co-ordination within the ANC as the names of the ANC delegates had already been sent from Lusaka to Moscow.

On the surface it seemed a purely technical matter. However, the reasons for Tambo's postponement were more deep-seated. To clear up the issue I was asked to go to the GDR in August 1986 to meet with the ANC President. He was spending time there for heart treatment. We had a good and frank discussion in his medical suite in the hospital. Tambo explained that he was worried about being involved in a broad meeting of such a nature. He was not sure that the leaking of information could be avoided. In a situation where hostile propaganda presented the ANC as a "Soviet proxy", such a meeting could be used against the ANC. In addition, apparently, before and during the Conference in Paris the ANC President had expected Western resolutions on sanctions against South Africa, and he wished to avoid any complications in this respect. For these reasons Tambo preferred bilateral or multilateral talks of a more specific character. Joe Slovo and Chris Hani, whom I also met in Berlin – where they were both on holiday – agreed with Tambo's opinion.

Informally Chris and I discussed a variety of issues over drinks at a café on the Spree river. "Who will replace Mabhida as the next SACP General Secretary? Why not you?" I asked. "Speak to J S," came the answer. And to my enquiry after Tony Yengeni and his wife and whether their studies in the Lenin School had been useful, the reply was "Yes, we're planning to send them inside."

Oliver Tambo also discussed with me the prospects of a political settlement in South Africa. He said that, while the State of Emergency hampered the development of the struggle, it also had the effect that even the moderate elements were now not prepared to co-operate with the regime. He even said that – depending on developments – the possibility existed that the ANC could in the future suspend the armed struggle.

THE USSR STRENGTHENS RELATIONSHIP WITH THE ANC

Soon after my return from Berlin, Joe Slovo asked on behalf of Tambo if a meeting could be arranged with Gorbachev in Moscow. It was felt that the high prestige enjoyed by the Soviet leader could work to the advantage of the ANC. International perceptions of the ANC were changing rapidly. In May 1986, for example, the US for the first time officially described the ANC as a "liberation organisation". Slovo also said that Western attempts to influence Oliver Tambo had failed, as he was "100% on anti-imperialist positions."

The growing influence of the ANC made a meeting with Gorbachev quite feasible. The personal conditions were favourable too. Gorbachev was, at least initially, much more dynamic with regard to Africa than his predecessors: during 1986 he received six heads of independent African countries in Moscow.

The first (and last) discussion between the ANC President and the Soviet leader took place in the Kremlin on 4 November 1986. Oliver Tambo arrived in Moscow at the head of a strong ANC delegation, but at the meeting itself he was accompanied only by Thabo Mbeki. Tambo had flown to Moscow from Maputo, where he had attended the funeral of Samora Machel, who was killed when his Tupolev-134 plane crashed inside South Africa.

The circumstances of this tragedy are still to be fully investigated, as the report by the Margo Commission, appointed by Pretoria, was far from convincing. The Soviet investigators were firmly of the opinion that some outside interference with the navigation of the plane had occurred. In the International Department, we tried to find out the truth at source, as it were, and Deputy Minister of Civil Aviation Vasin described to us how the plane had been lured off course by a false beacon.

The Soviets were especially offended by the allegations made by Pik Botha concerning the supposed "drunkenness" of the Soviet crew. [12] He claimed that in some cases there were traces of alcohol in their blood. Later he tried to explain away these assertions in the context of defending his country.[13]

What is interesting is that Botha and the South African authorities were ready to use every opportunity, even when inappropriate, to engage with the USSR. After the crash, a middle-rank official of the USSR Embassy in Maputo had to visit South Africa to visit a Soviet flight engineer who had been admitted to hospital there. Botha immediately tried to make political capital out of this. He received the official personally and tried to use him to send a political message to Moscow. Pretoria was ready to maintain a position of "political neutrality" in international relations and wished to establish relations and develop co-operation with the USSR in every field, including the marketing of gold, diamonds and other minerals. Pretoria also sent a senior official from the Department of Foreign Affairs to accompany the technical specialists who went to Moscow to investigate the black boxes containing information about the fatal flight. (The Soviet Embassy in Mozambique mistakenly issued him with a visa without prior approval from Moscow.) However, the official met only a low-ranking Soviet diplomat, an attaché or a third secretary, and then only informally, during the meeting of air safety specialists. Later the South Africans tried in vain to find out what the Soviet response was to the matters raised by their so-called emissary.

There were also other attempts at opening contacts, such as when the good offices of an Italian businessman Giovanni Mario Ricci were used to approach the Soviet Embassy in the Seychelles. It was hardly coincidental that Craig Williamson, by that time a director of the Longreach Company (funded by South Africa's Department of Military Intelligence) should become a member of the board of Ricci's GMR Company. [14]

At the Tambo-Gorbachev meeting, the latter gave evidence of sound knowledge of the situation in South Africa and the region. Even though he had no notes in front of him, he had studied all the material we had prepared for him. The discussion, intended to last 45 minutes, continued for an hour beyond that time, in an atmosphere of friendship and mutual understanding. There were no points of disagreement, or perhaps just one: the ANC leader was insistent that Gorbachev visit Southern Africa (he had already been invited by several countries, including Zimbabwe and Tanzania), but Gorbachev, while agreeing in principle, pleaded for "revolutionary patience". In their communiqué the two leaders appealed "to all who are interested in the peaceful and free future of the peoples of Southern Africa to collectively search for ways to solve the problems." [15]

Gorbachev informed Tambo confidentially that P W Botha was "knocking on our door through a third, even a fourth, party. But," he added, "we are not in a hurry." He assured the ANC President that any step in this direction in future would be taken only after consulting Tambo and his colleagues.

At the press-conference which followed, Oliver Tambo reported: "We emerged from that meeting strengthened by the knowledge that the Soviet Union stands firmly with us in the struggle for a united, democratic and non-racial South Africa, an independent Namibia and a peaceful region of Southern Africa. We draw immense satisfaction and inspiration from the fact that the Soviet Union is resolved to contribute everything within its possibilities and, within the context of our own requests, to assist the ANC, SWAPO and the peoples of our region to achieve these objectives. The Soviet Union is acting neither out of consideration of selfish interest nor with a desire to establish a so-called sphere of influence."[16]

Oliver Tambo's words did not accord with the fantasies of Stephen Ellis and his co-author "Sechaba", who used anonymous and highly dubious sources to describe Soviet intentions and policies after the famous Gorbachev-Reagan summit in Reykjavik in October 1986. The meeting was not the first between the two leaders, as Ellis claims, neither did it "set a groundwork for a comprehensive deal."[17] On the contrary, Gorbachev was greatly disappointed both by the failure to reach an agreement on the reduction of nuclear missiles and by the American interpretation of the talks. I witnessed how he criticised Reagan's behaviour in the strongest terms at his meeting with Tambo.

There was no "redefining zones of influence" in Reykjavik and, contrary to Ellis's claims, the Soviet government did not "commit itself to withdraw its forces or to refrain from seeking the overthrow of the existing order [in South Africa], leaving the field to the USA and its allies on the ground." One can only shake one's head at reading that South Africa was allegedly included in Reykjavik "in the category of countries where the USSR would henceforth refrain from aggression" and that the Soviet Union agreed it would no longer "throw its weight behind the effort by the ANC and the SACP to ferment a revolution in South Africa."[18]

The reality *at that stage* (the emphasis is to be noted, as the situation did change later) was exactly the opposite. The Gorbachev-Tambo meeting in 1986 not only symbolised a new, higher level of contact, but also resulted in a number of important practical steps. The day after meeting with Gorbachev, Oliver Tambo led his delegation to a meeting in the Soviet Ministry of Defence, where it was received by Army

General Valentin Varennikov, then the First Deputy Head of the General Staff.

(I met the General for the first time in Angola in January 1984, when he was inspecting the Soviet military mission and discussing the counter-offensive against UNITA with the Angolans and Cubans. Later he became famous as one of the accused in the Moscow "Treason Trial" of the leaders of a so-called coup in August 1991. As distinct from all the other accused, he refused an amnesty granted by the Russian parliament in January 1994, and was later acquitted by a Military Collegium of the Supreme Court. He is now an MP.)

Varennikov started the meeting with a half-hour lecture about the Soviets' desire for peace and readiness to reduce weapons. I got the impression that the General had neither read *Pravda* that morning nor been briefed by his assistants about Tambo's meeting with Gorbachev. So he was not aware that general questions of peace and disarmament had already been discussed with Tambo. "Our military are the most peaceful people," I scribbled in a note to Joe Slovo. He nodded with a chuckle.

A comprehensive discussion took place between the delegation and the officials of the International Department, which was headed at that stage by the CPSU International Secretary Anatoly Dobrynin. His appointment to this post in March 1986 to replace the 81-year-old Ponomarev rejuvenated the Department. Dobrynin combined his internationalist and patriotic feelings with an efficiency no doubt acquired during his 25 years in Washington. The two and a half years that he was in office, through to November 1988, were the best for the Department.

Oliver Tambo and his colleagues wanted the USSR to strengthen its position and maintain a higher profile in Southern Africa, and not leave the field to the Western powers. The visible presence of the USSR was needed, especially against the background of an increasing number of visits by representatives from other countries. They emphasised that a trip by Gorbachev to Southern Africa would "transform the situation", especially after Reagan had snubbed the leaders of the Front Line States by rejecting their invitation. In Joe Slovo's words, it would "electrify the region. People are looking for the support of a friend." Dobrynin promised to speak to Gorbachev again about this idea. He assured the delegation of the USSR's "100% support" for the ANC – and, "if you want it, 120% support."

At the same time Gorbachev and Dobrynin fully supported the ANC proposal to explore the possibility of joint Soviet-American actions against apartheid. The USA had been forced to change its attitude to the ANC and it was now hurriedly trying to establish official contacts. On 20 September 1986 Oliver Tambo had a meeting with Chester Crocker that was a prelude to his meeting with the Secretary of State George Shultz in January 1987. The US Ambassador in Lusaka was even interested in the shape of the table for future talks. The traditional hostility to the ANC had begun to melt, but the numbers game concerning SACP members in the ANC NEC ("Were there 15? 13? 19?") continued, and the ANC's relations with the USSR were a permanent issue in discussions.

One of the questions raised by Dobrynin was whether Pretoria had atomic weapons. The delegation assured him that South Africa was in a position to produce them. The question of atomic weapons, naturally, worried those in the USSR who dealt with South Africa. It was Moscow who warned the USA and other Western powers about the preparations for nuclear testing in the Kalahari in 1977. I am not aware if the top Soviet leadership had hard information about the actual production of bombs by South Africa, but certainly that possibility was always considered.

However, after the outgoing apartheid regime admitted producing six atomic bombs, some academics claimed that this nuclear capacity had played a major role in shaping developments in the region. Professor Renfrew Christie in his paper on South Africa's nuclear history advances this as "an attractive hypothesis": "By threatening to test or to use its atomic bomb, South Africa had relieved itself of the Soviet-backed military threat which it had so long feared, and had saved itself the need to build a very expensive fighter aircraft." He admits that there is not enough information to judge whether an atomic test threat was made by South Africa in 1987, "nor what effect it had on the war [in Angola] or on negotiations." Nonetheless, he insists: "The most likely understanding is that President P W Botha successfully used the threat of a nuclear explosion, in the process of getting Cubans to leave Angola. If this is true, Apartheid's atom bomb strategy paid off."[19] To the best of my knowledge, this was not so. The Soviet executive and other papers concerning the talks on Angolan-Namibian settlement never referred to this as an issue of leverage.

The mood of Tambo's delegation was upbeat, in spite of the regime's visible success in suppressing legal opposition. On 20 May the ANC issued its latest "call to the people": "From ungovernability to people's power".[20] In particular, the ANC statement called for a general strike on 16 June 1986. To counter it, Pretoria re-introduced the State of Emergency (lifted the previous March) throughout the country. As Chris Hani explained, the regime managed to beat off the visible part of the flame of resistance, to weaken the emotional effect of the events in South Africa on the international public, especially in the West. Prevented from mobilising resistance through mass rallies, the democratic forces had to concentrate on organisational activity in virtually underground conditions, mostly at the grassroots level. And that created new problems for the regime: while the national leaders were well known and could easily be detained, the security forces, who had lost virtually all their informants in the black community, were unable to cope with the lower echelons of resistance. The flame, extinguished on the surface, was in fact spreading more widely beneath it.[21]

It is worth recalling how Chris Hani in 1986 envisaged the future of South Africa. My notes reveal that he thought the next government would be an ANC government, or, rather, a government formed by the ANC, with some places in it allotted to organisations and individuals not connected with the ANC, including representatives of the white population. In his opinion, the main subject of the future talks with the government would be the convening of a Constitutional Assembly. But at that time the ANC had not accumulated enough strength to force the government to start genuine talks. A meeting between the ANC and a group of National Party MPs was expected, despite its having been banned by P W Botha. The ANC would then explain in more detail its social economic policy.[22]

After the meeting in the Kremlin between Tambo and Gorbachev, the official press release, agreed by both sides, declared that a political settlement in Southern Africa could be achieved. It would need to be based on three major conditions: an end to Pretoria's acts of aggression against independent African states; the granting of independence to Namibia in accordance with UN resolutions; and the removal of the apartheid regime in South Africa as "the primary cause of the conflict situation in the region."[23]

In January 1987 an ANC delegation led by Johnny Makatini, the Head of the International Department, visited Moscow to participate in the commemoration of the ANC's 75th anniversary. In his discussions in Moscow Makatini indicated that while the USA and the UK had become "resigned to the reality" with regards to the ANC, he was convinced they had a "hidden agenda". This was to promote the "Natal option" - Buthelezi - and to support the so-called Genscher initiative to convene a conference on South Africa of the Lancaster House type. [24]

During Makatini's visit the forthcoming opening of the ANC Mission to the USSR was officially announced. This matter had been extensively discussed during Oliver Tambo's visit in November 1986. Philip Nel writes in his book on Soviet-South African relations that "The clearest indication of the traditional Soviet uncertainty about the true potential of the ANC is to be found in the fact that the USSR only allowed the ANC to open an office in Moscow in 1986 ... Why did the USSR wait for so long? The obvious explanation is that the USSR was definitely sceptical about ANC claims that were not always a reflection of the real state of affairs."[25] What was "obvious" to a South African "Sovietologist" was not obvious to the Soviets themselves.

The ANC leadership and Oliver Tambo in particular were cautious about a Moscow office, even after an informal ANC office was opened in Washington and the logical move would be to have one in Moscow to balance the equation. Though Tambo always publicly acknowledged the role of the Soviet Union in support of the South African liberation struggle, at the same time he was concerned about the accusation that the ANC was a Soviet proxy. That was particularly the case because he imagined that the office would be financed by the Soviet Government.[26] In the event, when the ANC Mission was finally opened, it was financed through the Soviet Afro-Asian Solidarity Committee by the non-governmental Soviet Peace Fund.

Years earlier the ANC representatives had informally raised the question of Anthony Mongalo, the ANC representative in the GDR, being given representative status in Moscow as well. But this idea seemed strange to the Soviets. Neither were they happy when Alfred Nzo requested in January 1985 that Moscow accept an ANC representative with the limited function of maintaining contacts with South African students and relevant Soviet organisations. It was acknowledged that the handling of the ANC students' affairs was not an easy task: in 1986 they were scattered in fourteen cities in different parts of the vast country. However, it was felt that so limited an office would not be only detrimental to the ANC's prestige, but could also cause confusion about Soviet attitudes to the ANC. If the office was to be established, it would have to be a fully-fledged operation. Probably encouraged by the positive processes in the USSR in 1985-6 and by the more assertive stance of the ANC in the international arena, Tambo finally made an official request for an ANC Mission to be opened in Moscow.

From the very beginning the Mission enjoyed all diplomatic privileges, even though it was accredited to an NGO, the Soviet Afro-Asian Solidarity Committee. They included, for example, diplomatic immunity and the right to hoist the ANC flag on the premises and use it on the official car.[27]

Unfortunately the ANC delayed the opening of the Mission and in fact never used it to its fullest extent. Steve Tshwete, who was a guest of the Soviet Afro-Asian Solidarity Committee in May 1987, wrote in his report: "The whole trip – from the beginning to the end – was one grand experience with the Soviet people whose depth of commitment to our struggle is immeasurable." At the same time he shared the Soviets' concern about an ANC office: "The Soviet Solidarity Committee and other comrades I have met harped on the urgency of an ANC office in the Soviet Union."[28] After his arrival in Moscow in mid November, the Head of the Mission Simon (Sipho) Makana wrote to Alfred Nzo: "Yesterday I was at the office of the Soviet Afro-Asian Solidarity Committee ... This [opening of the Mission] seems to be a more serious affair than we have thought."[29] Though originally two people with diplomatic status were to staff the Mission (in addition to several Soviet employees), the Head of Mission was helped by a Deputy for only a small part of the three years of his stay in the Soviet Union.

Relations in the military field were also being strengthened at this time. From 1986 there was an increased number of ANC members coming for all kinds of training, including Military Combat Work – a highly specialised course for organisers of the armed underground. The letters MCW became very popular in Umkhonto and the ANC. A decision was taken in 1986 that an annual intake of 60 people should come for training in the MCW and related subjects over a five-year period, to 1990. In fact, the intake was greater than was planned for.

In 1986, even before the Gorbachev-Tambo meeting, the first group of ANC members arrived for a full course for motorised infantry officers in Simferopol. Starting from 1987, full-course training (four to five years) was organised for the ANC in several fields in various Soviet cities: helicopter and later jet pilots, as well as aircraft engineers, in Frunze; naval officers in Baku; armour officers in Kiev; communications officers in Ulyanovsk; political officers in Minsk. (By way of comparison: an officer's training course in the South

African Defence Force was from six to twelve months long.) Joe Modise had raised this issue earlier, but the usual rule in the Soviet Army was to train foreign personnel for the type of arms and equipment to be supplied. However, after Tambo's meeting with Gorbachev, an exemption was made for the ANC: the need to train an officers' corps for the future armed forces of a democratic South Africa became obvious and we managed to persuade the Ministry of Defence to agree to this.

One more problem was discussed in Moscow during Oliver Tambo's visit: the need for the re-organisation of the ANC's security apparatus. By that time the top ANC leadership and especially Tambo himself were worried that the security department could spin out of control (or had already done so). As has been seen, the situation in this field was critically assessed at the Kabwe conference.

In recent years much has been said about the incidence of malpractice committed by ANC security personnel, especially in Camp 32 or Quadro camp in Angola. As an organisation the ANC accepted collective responsibility for this. The conditions of underground struggle and the need to counter the enemy's penetration into ANC ranks created, if not a spy mania, at least a culture of suspicion. One of the ANC papers on security declared: "Our guiding principle must be that 'every new individual is "suspect" until proved innocent'."[30] In another document the use of force during interrogation was rejected, but for practical and not for ethical reasons: "Force - poor technique as it may evict [sic] false information."[31] In fact, that paper was simply a summary of a US manual on the subject.

The ANC was often lenient in the punishment of offenders in its ranks. For example, I heard that Ellis's "co-author", who camouflaged himself as "Sechaba", twice could not account for his disposal of large sums of money amounting to 30 000 Zimbabwean dollars. He was investigated and disciplined by being sent to a farm in Angola. Not only was he allowed to appeal but also to go to Zimbabwe to collect his belongings. Instead, he sought refuge in the Canadian Embassy in Harare, later finding his way to the USA,[32] following in the steps of Lennox Sebe's niece, Kave (mentioned earlier).

Some "experts" are fond of making the SACP a "scapegoat" in these cases. Ellis and "Sechaba" are in the forefront of making such allegations. They admit that "the rank and file of Umkhonto we Sizwe, including the mutineers [of 1984], generally commended the Party," but claim they did not know that the ANC security department "was a

Party fiefdom".[33]

It is not for me to judge when this or that action of ANC security was justified: the whole truth may come out only if and when the archives of Pretoria's security services are opened for inspection (that is, provided the secrets have not been shredded). But those documents which are already available show that the SACP (and the USSR for that matter) were actively concerned to prevent abuses.

On 29 November 1982 immediately following Moses Mabhida's return from Moscow at its meeting in Maputo the SACP Central Committee Secretariat discussed "the question of the method of interrogation in the MK".[34] Information (or at least rumour) of unacceptable methods of interrogation in the ANC had reached Moscow, and we raised the matter with him. Both then and later we reminded the SACP and ANC leaders and activists of the tragedy of the Soviet Union when some of its best people were lost during Stalin's days because of a spy mania.

At the next meeting of the SACP Secretariat it was decided: "The question of interrogation in our camps to be further looked into."[35] The matter was referred to the SACP Politbureau, which took a decision: "Luanda delegation to discuss this question further with selected comrades." [36]

During his visit to Moscow in November 1986 Oliver Tambo, in the presence of Joe Modise and Chris Hani, repeated a request forwarded earlier for a Soviet security expert to be sent to the ANC in Angola. For one reason or another the Soviet side declined to respond. I still believe that was a mistake because such an expert could have exerted a positive influence on the practices of the ANC.

Ronnie Kasrils writes in his book: "Whatever might be thought about interrogation methods in communist countries, I found that Soviet and East German training emphasised the need to depend on brain work and not beating to arrive at the truth."[37] For a number of years ANC security personnel were trained mostly in the GDR. If any blame is to be laid at the feet of their instructors, it is perhaps that they were not sufficiently insistent that ANC cadres should never use methods of physical intimidation and torture.

It is not by accident that Oliver Tambo requested new personnel to be trained in the security field at the precise time when changes in the NAT (the ANC's Department of Intelligence and Security) became imperative and he was keen to rid the organisation of the blunders and abuses of the past.

Soon after Tambo's visit to Moscow, in February 1987, the National Executive Committee finally decided to reorganise the ANC Security Service: "The present Directorate of NAT will be dissolved, effective as from the date the Presidential Committee formally announce it."[38] That announcement was to be made on 20 February.[39] The top officials of the Department were informed that they would all (except Sizakele Sigxashe) be transferred to other missions. In particular, Piliso became the Head of the Department of Manpower Development.

Almost simultaneously, in January Oliver Tambo announced an amnesty for "those who were expelled and have now recognised their errors and wish to return to the field."[40] A reduction in the term of sentence or, in some cases, a reprieve was recommended "for prisoners and other detainees". [41]

The most amusing of the claims made by Ellis and "Sechaba" is that in September 1987 the Angolan government offensive against the SADF-backed UNITA was "supervised in part by a Soviet General Konstantin Shaganovitch".[42] In the first place, the term "supervised" does not correctly express the role of the Soviet military advisers and specialists in Angola, but, leaving that aside, the fact is that in the early 1980s there was a Soviet General in Angola whose name was Vassily Shakhnovich, who was a Chief Military Adviser. Also, the Soviet documents captured by South Africans during their invasion into Angola and published as an addendum to the Denton Report in Washington contain a reference to "Chief Military Adviser in the People's Republic of Angola Lieutenant-General V. Shakhnovich", dated April 1980. [43]

The General left Angola for the USSR around 1982 and before long died in Moscow. The obituary was duly published in the Soviet official military newspaper *Krasnaya Zvezda* (Red Star), but apparently neither SADF personnel nor their friends read it. One of Shakhnovich's successors was Colonel-General Konstantin Kurochkin. So it seems that Ellis managed to merge someone dead with someone alive. Kurochkin himself left Luanda in 1985, though according to him he "visited Angola later on an invitation of the President." [44]

So, if *Comrades Against Apartheid* is fact, what is fiction? Ellis's and "Sechaba's" book is full of "Konstantin Shaganovitches" of one kind or another.

But Ellis was not alone. Fred Bridgland, a leading British journalist, used "General Shaganovitch's offensive" as the title for a section of his book describing military actions in Angola. The non-existent

"Konstantin Shaganovitch", according to Bridgland, was "a known chemical warfare expert", and this is used to substantiate the claim that the Angolan Brigade that faced the SADF had "chemical weapons in its armoury." [45]

The same author invented one more Soviet, namely "Shaganovitch"'s subordinate "Mikhail Petrov, first deputy on the Soviet Politbureau in charge of counter-insurgency policy."[46] There was no such post, and in any case nobody in the Politbureau would be specifically in charge "of counter-insurgency policy". Perhaps Bridgland meant Marshal Vassily Petrov, Commander-in-Chief of the Soviet Ground Forces and later the First Deputy Defence Minister? If so, Petrov was first and foremost "in charge of" regular warfare, and could by no stretch of the imagination be described as junior to "Shaganovitch".

Chris Louw, prefacing his interview with Ellis, wrote: "African National Congress leaders in exile more than once found that next day after a secret meeting the editors at *Africa Confidential* were fully informed of what had been discussed behind closed doors."[47] Louw does not indicate a source for this intimate knowledge of the mood of the ANC leaders, but in any case the reality was quite different.

Ellis had become the editor of *Africa Confidential* in August 1986. The level of the journal's "knowledge" from then on is reflected in an article on the ANC, published on 10 December of the same year. It contained distorted information on virtually every member of the ANC Executive Committee. Alfred Nzo was wrongly described as "a recipient of the Lenin Peace Prize"; Pallo Jordan became an "SACP member"; Joe Nhlanhla was "currently Chairman of the ANC Youth League" (which had been defunct for over 25 years) and "one of the 1976 generation" (despite having left South Africa in the mid 1960s). Josiah Jele's first name was "unknown" to *Africa Confidential*, despite his involvement for over fifteen years in the international activities of the ANC. *Africa Confidential* also referred to him as "apparently SACP Secretary General",[48] although Joe Slovo had just been elected General Secretary at a meeting of the SACP Central Committee in Bulgaria in November-December 1986. His post of National Chairman was allocated to Party veteran Dan Tloome. At the written request of the SACP Slovo was relieved of his duties as Chief of Staff of Umkhonto in February 1987 by the ANC National Executive Committee, so that he could "devote more time to his responsibilities as General Secretary of the SACP."

The "confidential" nonsense about the ANC spread by *Africa*

315

Confidential was part of a broader campaign orchestrated against the ANC. The *Problems of Communism* magazine, put out in Washington by the US Information Agency, published an article by another "expert", M Radu, already mentioned above. Apparently Radu was highly regarded by the US establishment, because the Agency reprinted and widely distributed his article. In it he described Chris Hani as "a veteran of the Soweto riots", and Nelson Mandela as the "*de jure* President" of the ANC from the 1960s.[49]

In spite of the propaganda onslaught and Pretoria's pressure, the position of the ANC in Africa was improving. In discussions with the Soviets, leaders of the Front Line States were demonstrating their increased sympathy for the ANC and showing a greater commitment to help it. When Robert Mugabe was in Moscow in June 1987 he confidentially informed Gorbachev that Zimbabwe had started facilitating Umkhonto crossings into South Africa. The Tanzanians, too, again opened some military facilities for the ANC. They also helped transport ANC cadres to some forward areas via flights from Dar es Salaam which avoided Mozambican territory.

The ANC was slowly and cautiously increasing its presence in Mozambique. While the quota of ten was officially maintained, by mid 1986 about a hundred activists were based in Mozambique. Before his death Samora Machel suggested that, in the event of problems, the ANC representative should make direct contact with the Central Committee of Frelimo, effectively side-stepping the Ministry of Security.[50]

However, the Mozambican position remained unstable and unpredictable. In December 1986 the new Mozambican President Joachim Chissano met Oliver Tambo. Although the discussions with Chissano were friendly, the Mozambicans suddenly informed the ANC that Pretoria had demanded the deportation of most of the ANC office staff in Maputo, including Jacob Zuma, Indres Naidoo, Sue Rabkin, and Bobby Pillay (Sonny Singh).

A dramatic improvement in Beijing's attitude to the ANC and the SACP was apparent in the mid 1980s. A Chinese delegation visited Zambia in November 1985 and agreed to supply the ANC with uniforms and small arms, and offered to train its cadres in China. The Chinese met Joe Slovo in his capacity then as the SACP Chairman and invited him to China, having expressed regret that for twenty years there had been no contacts between Beijing and the SACP.

In September 1986 Slovo headed an SACP delegation to China and relations were restored. At Slovo's request on the eve of the visit a specialist on China from the CPSU International Department came to Lusaka to brief the SACP group.

Meanwhile, the relationship between the USSR and the ANC was continuing to develop in a number of ways. Apart from general political delegations, several specialist delegations were received; for example, one on education. In March 1987 an important seminar of social scientists took place in Moscow. Among its participants were the ANC Executive members Dr Pallo Jordan and Simon Makana, and several prominent South African researchers, including Dr Ivy Matsepe, now Premier of the Free State.

The ANC received assistance in improving communications between its units in different areas, a need long recognised by the Soviet specialists. On one occasion, when an ANC delegation was in Moscow, the Soviet military organised a communications demonstration in one of the "special flats" to illustrate the need for the ANC to request more sophisticated equipment. "This is the first time," Slovo whispered to me, "that I've heard of people begging others to request goods from them for free." The formal request duly followed and the ANC was supplied with a multitude of radio installations, from truck-mounted equipment for reliable long-distance communication between, say, Luanda and Lusaka, to sophisticated portables for use in the underground. Special equipment to ensure the safety of communications was also provided. Jackie Molefe, the ANC Head of Communications (Jackie Sedibe, now Major General in the SANDF) and her Deputy spent several weeks in Moscow for consultations relating to this project.

Various other visitors continued to come to Moscow, such as an ANC activist, whose passport name was Peterson, who arrived on 24 June 1986 for medical treatment. This was none other than Gordon Webster. He had been arrested and wounded while carrying out an ANC operation, and was in police custody in hospital. In a daring escapade he was "kidnapped" by his fellow fighter Robert McBride. Webster had two bullets in his body and, though his condition improved in the Moscow Hospital, doctors remained hesitant about removing the two bullets from his chest. Webster was determined to return to South Africa, which he did, and was arrested again.

While these contacts were occurring in 1986 and 1987 and relations between the USSR and the ANC were being conducted on ever higher levels, reports by foreign academics and journalists began to appear

317

which suggested a rift between them. The first of these was largely the consequence of a paper presented by Professor Gleb Starushenko, the then Deputy Director of the Africa Institute, at the Second Soviet-African Conference in June 1986. Speaking strictly in his personal capacity, Starushenko called for "comprehensive guarantees for the white population" in South Africa.[51] This private initiative by Starushenko was quite acceptable within the process of democratisation of both political and academic life then taking place in the USSR. Some of his proposals were realistic, even though they contradicted the existing public positions of the ANC. Others were whimsical and uninformed, such as a proposal for a chamber in a future South African parliament "possessing the right of veto, on the basis of the equal representation of four communities."[52]

Starushenko's paper and an interview subsequently given by another former Deputy Director of the Africa Institute, Victor Goncharov, provided a feeding frenzy for foreign "Sovietologists". Speculating on whether or not Kremlin leaders approved Starushenko's remarks on white minority rights became the fashionable thing to do. The *Soviet Review*, published by the Institute of Soviet Studies at the University of Stellenbosch, commented in 1987: "Since taking power, Gorbachev has been using academics more and more for foreign policy purposes, often as vehicles to introduce new ideas (see for instance Starushenko's and Goncharov's ideas about South Africa)."[53] In reality, however, neither Gorbachev, nor any other significant political figure, "in the Kremlin" or beyond its walls, either knew about or was interested in "Starushenko's and Goncharov's ideas".

The Soviet Union's open support of the ANC, including the armed struggle, was again underlined at a very high level in November 1987 when Andrei Gromyko, the Soviet Head of State, presented the Order of People's Friendship award to Oliver Tambo in a ceremony in the Kremlin. We felt that it would be a proper occasion to re-state the Soviet position on the ANC, and the armed struggle in particular, and drafted Gromyko's speech accordingly.

Following the third Gorbachev-Reagan summit in Washington in December 1987, the CPSU Central Committee sent a confidential letter to the ANC and other friendly organisations which assured them: "While discussing the problems of regional conflicts and other issues with Americans we have stressed the point that our aspiration for a dialogue with the US by no means should be construed in such a way that we give up the solidarity with the liberation struggle of peoples or ignore the interests of the developing countries. Never and under no circumstances shall we deviate from the course of supporting the right of nations for independent development, never shall we go for any accord with Americans at the expense of or to prejudice the peoples of developing countries. For us a solidarity with those who struggle for national liberation, against imperialism and neo-colonialism remains a permanent factor which is not influenced by the temporary changes."[54]

The Soviet position with regard to a political settlement in South Africa was elaborated by Gorbachev in a speech at a dinner in honour of Joachim Chissano in August 1987. Gorbachev's words led to some speculation that he was announcing a departure in policy, but this was not the case. He said *inter alia* that "we don't believe in the thesis 'the worse the better'. There is no doubt that the elimination of racist rule by means of a political settlement is in the interests of all the people in South Africa, black and white. We should seek and find the ways which lead to such a settlement. It is time for Pretoria to understand that too. We are in need of new ideas, a new approach and collective efforts."[55]

Some South African and Soviet academics latched on to this supposed departure from the previous policy, which they alleged followed the principle "the worse the better".[56] Vladimir Tikhomirov, then from the Africa Institute (now resident in Australia), commented that the officials of the International Department had not been consulted and that "the new shift in Soviet policy towards Southern Africa came quite unexpectedly for both the CPSU bureaucrats and the ANC-SACP leaders."[57]

There was no need for "CPSU bureaucrats" to be consulted because the International Department was in fact a co-author of Gorbachev's text. When the first draft came from the Ministry of Foreign Affairs various changes, modifications, deletions and additions were made in the usual way. Nevertheless Gorbachev's key phrase – "We don't believe in the thesis 'the worse the better'"[58] – did indeed come from the Foreign Ministry. Its origin, however, lay further afield, in the Soviet Academy of Sciences. Its author was Professor Apollon Davidson, mentioned above.

As for its being a surprise to "the ANC-SACP leaders", the truth was quite the opposite. The "closed door" multilateral consultations involving the ANC, Cuba and the Soviet Union which had been mooted earlier finally took place in Moscow in September 1987 and proved again that there was a commonality of vision on all major issues, including the approach to the political settlement.

Oliver Tambo had expressed the need for these tripartite talks soon after his meeting with George Shultz in January 1987. The ANC President had come away from that meeting satisfied by the US administration's formal recognition of the ANC. But he was worried that the USA wished to be the only mediator in future talks.

The ANC delegation to the Moscow meeting included all the senior office bearers of the organisation. The approach to the political settlement was one of the major subjects discussed. Oliver Tambo and his colleagues described in particular the offers of various parties to be mediators or intermediaries between the ANC and Pretoria.

The "talks about talks" process was far from smooth. When the question of the exchange of prisoners was discussed at the ANC Working Committee in March 1987, for example, Johnny Makatini and Pallo Jordan suggested that Hendrik W van der Merwe be used to sound out Pretoria's position, but proposed that this be followed up by a neutral government. "Botha repudiated van der Merwe last time. He could do likewise on this occasion," Jordan commented.[59]

PROSPECTS IMPROVE FOR A POLITICAL SETTLEMENT

As the impetus towards political settlement in Southern Africa built up in 1987, the ANC leaders began to receive questions from the membership. What is the ANC's policy with regard to negotiations? Is the leadership prepared to enter into negotiations? What has the ANC achieved in the talks with Shultz? What are our aims and objectives in these and other such talks in the future?[60]

Shortly after the September 1987 tripartite consultations in Moscow, therefore, the ANC NEC decided to publish a statement on the issue of negotiations and to organise briefings for the membership, the Mass Democratic Movement, Front Line and other African states, and socialist countries.[61] The ANC reaffirmed that the movement "and masses of our people as a whole are ready and willing to enter into genuine negotiations provided they are aimed at the transformation of our country into a united and non-racial democracy. *This and only this should be the objective of any negotiating process.*"[62]

The bottom line easily agreed on by the ANC leadership was that "Our organisation had built a following in South Africa, this must be always remember[ed] ... We need to keep our mass base firm and strong, our people must always be taken along with us."[63]

The Executive underlined the fact that the international mood was to find political settlements for regional conflicts, and that the process had been started in Angola. At this early stage the ANC leadership was already anticipating that a Namibian settlement could include a stipulation that Angola should not allow ANC bases on its territory. The ANC NEC was convinced that the South African regime was not yet ready for negotiations, and pointed out that "this must be explained as we go on the offensive ... We may negotiate at some stage in the interests of the struggle. But the burden is on Botha." The Executive concluded that, as long as the regime "has not yet been weakened sufficiently", the ANC would resist the pressure "to negotiate on the least favourable terms ... with all the might at our disposal."

Leaders like Thabo Mbeki who were involved in international contacts emphasised the necessity for early preparations for the talks. The ANC Executive members felt that a number of questions had to be considered: who would participate in talks, who would preside, would there be a Constitutional Assembly?[64]

An important step in bridge-building with the white and, especially, Afrikaner community was the meeting with academics and intellectuals from South Africa in Dakar in May 1987. It was thoroughly prepared by the ANC. Initially Paris was suggested as a venue but preference was given to Dakar. Aziz Pahad was given the role of the liaison person.[65]

When both Thabo Mbeki and Chris Hani came to Moscow for a short holiday in 1988 there was a chance to discuss the prospects of political settlement. "When will you win?" was a question I put, very informally, to each of them. "Ten years more," was Chris's reply. "We shall be at home in 1990," said Mbeki. As different as these replies were, essentially both of them were right: the ANC leaders did return home in 1990, but after the general election of April 1994 the Interim Constitution made it mandatory for the ANC to be in government together with the National Party for at least five years. So, while there was a victory, the ANC can be victorious (in the full sense of the word) only after the 1999 elections, that is, even later than Hani forecast.

It was a pleasure to see Hani and Mbeki together in Moscow after reading speculations in *Africa Confidential* and other similar publications about splits in the ANC leadership. Some forces undoubtedly tried to drive a wedge between the two most popular figures of the younger generation of the ANC leaders. Usually they tried to juxtapose the two, counterpointing their different work styles and life stories.

But were their lives so unalike? A closer look helps one to see many similarities. Both Chris Hani and Thabo Mbeki were born in the same area (the Eastern Cape) in the same month, June 1942. They studied at the same school (one a year earlier than the other), both were initially attracted by the radical ideas of the "non-collaborationist" Unity Movement. Both soon gravitated towards the ranks of the ANC. Both had to leave the country, and spent many years in exile.

Their ways parted in exile: Mbeki began his studies at a British university and Hani at a Soviet military training centre. However, afterwards their life stories converged again: Chris was admitted for additional training in the early 1970s in the USSR just a year or two after Thabo, and even at the same camp in the environs of Moscow.

Two or three years later, when Chris was heading the ANC machinery in Lesotho, Thabo began operating in Swaziland. Both of them were detained for some period by the local authorities.

322

Much later, in July 1991, at the ANC Conference in Durban, Hani gained the most votes in the elections for the NEC and Mbeki was second by a small margin.

Some people believe that an unspoken competition between the two of them in the ANC leadership ended only when Chris Hani was assassinated as a result of a right wing conspiracy. This was not so: Chris himself opted out of it when he acceded to the pressure of rank and file SACP members in December 1991 and accepted the position of General Secretary.

By 1987 the need for a more active diplomatic role by the USSR in South Africa was becoming obvious. The Soviet Union was not initially involved in the talks on the Angolan-Namibian settlement. As a result, the Luanda government had to confront, not only its adversary Pretoria, but also the Americans who were supposed to be neutral mediators. We felt therefore that in South Africa, with the prospects for a political settlement growing (due primarily to the upsurge of the anti-racist struggle), it was essential to establish a line of communication between the USSR and the South African government. This could obviously be done only after consultation with the ANC.

We first put forward such a proposal in May 1987. After some hesitation, it was endorsed, and during the tripartite consultations in Moscow in September Anatoly Dobrynin confidentially raised the issue with Oliver Tambo. The ANC President's attitude was positive, though he suggested waiting a short while until the ANC had again been in contact with Pretoria's informal go-between. Then there would be more clarity on the regime's intentions.

Speaking at the Africa Institute in Moscow in September 1987, Joe Slovo elaborated on the possibility of a compromise (he compared it to the peace treaty between Soviet Russia and Germany signed in Brest-Litovsk in 1918), provided such a compromise was in the interest of the revolutionary advance: "We don't say there will be no moment for us to make a compromise but we cannot support now the scheme which would mean perpetuation of their minority rule, like the veto for minorities."[66]

In the final analysis both the political and military leadership of the ANC were united in their assessment of the situation. Addressing the meeting of the Soviet Solidarity Committee on 18 September 1987, Joe Modise, for example, described the situation as substantively new. He spoke of the possibility of talks, perhaps forced on the ANC, and underlined that in this "new kind of struggle" the ANC should not be

323

alone.[67]

The SACP, too, was responding to the new conditions. In a paper prepared by Joe Slovo for the International Meeting of delegations from many countries, which took place after the celebration of the 70th anniversary of the October Revolution in Moscow in November 1987, he wrote: "There are certain regional conflicts (and our own struggle is one of them) when the prospect of political settlements or real negotiation does not yet depend on diplomatic manoeuvre but rather on the building up of the strength of the liberation forces and escalating blows against the Apartheid regime ... This does not mean that those who run the apartheid state will never be forced to seat themselves around a *genuine* negotiation table."[68]

That the ANC and Soviet positions coincided was confirmed by Oliver Tambo's speech at the celebration: "The concern of the imperialist powers is that any change in South Africa must preclude any alteration of the capitalist system in our country and leave South Africa within the orbit, and as an integral and dependent part of the world imperialist economy and under its political domination. The imperialists are concerned that any transformation in South Africa which actually brought about the changes they fear would affect not only our country but would also have a decisive and strategic impact on the greater part of our continent."[69]

However, speculation about Soviet policy intensified. Christopher Coker, a US academic, wrote in 1988: "The [all-white] election was a blow to those in the Kremlin who were committed to the Leninist proposition that a split in the ruling class was a necessary if not a sufficient precondition for a revolution."[70] But "in the Kremlin" (interestingly, apart from the weekly Politburo meetings, the real centre of power was outside the Kremlin walls in those days) hardly anybody noticed the results of that election – although in fact they did indicate significant splits within the white community.

Coker alleged that a "radical reassessment of Russian support for the ANC" was happening in 1987 and quoted an unnamed member of the Soviet Central Committee as saying during a visit to the West in 1988 that "We cannot carry the ANC into the Union Buildings and we don't wish to do so."[71] Again, I doubt whether any CC member even knew what the Union Buildings were.

On the contrary, in 1987-8, relations between the USSR and the South African liberation movement reached their highest peak, strengthening the position of the ANC, and thus helping to create a climate conducive to a political settlement. At the same time an overall relaxation of international tension was overturning the "total onslaught" bogey.

We in the International Department who were dealing with South Africa continued to encourage exchanges between different social forces in the USSR and South Africa in consultation with the ANC. A decision of the Central Committee Secretariat was adopted in 1988, which stressed the need for closer relations with forces in South Africa that were "critical of apartheid".

The first South African journalist invited to Moscow was to have been Allister Sparks, but he postponed his visit. Meanwhile Tim du Plessis of *Die Beeld* and Johan Vosloo of *Rapport* had met some Soviets at the ANC-organised international conference in Arusha in 1987 and indicated that they wished to visit Moscow. After consulting the ANC and the SACP, the CPSU Secretariat gave its approval.

There began a kind of "pilgrimage" to Moscow by prominent anti-racist figures from South Africa. Bishop Tutu came in June 1988 for the celebration of the Millennium of the Russian Orthodox Church, followed by Alex and Jenny Boraine from the Institute for a Democratic Alternative for South Africa (IDASA). At IDASA's initiative a conference was convened in Leverkusen in West Germany in October 1988 where Soviet academics, prominent members of the ANC (including Joe Slovo) and South African liberal (in the broad sense of the word) academics met for the first time. It was a significant step in clearing up misconceptions about Soviet policy.

This process was paralleled by the growth of contacts between the ANC and the broad spectrum of forces within South Africa. After the meeting in Dakar the idea was raised of a meeting between Umkhonto and the South African military establishment. Although it finally happened only in 1990, in Lusaka, it should be noted that from about 1987 the ANC started receiving messages from influential people in the South African military establishment that either an agreement would have to be reached by 1990 or the country would be destroyed.

The South African government played a rather risky "Soviet card" in March 1988 when Minister of Defence Magnus Malan, referring to the planned Soviet withdrawal from Afghanistan, directly suggested that the USSR make a bilateral deal with South Africa over Angola. The Head of the Press Department of the USSR Foreign Ministry Gennady Gerasimov responded by saying that the only similarity between Angola and Afghanistan was that they both started with the letter A.

Boris Pilyatskin of *Izvestiya* in 1988 became the first Soviet journalist to visit South Africa. The leadership of both the ANC and the SACP informed the CPSU International Department that they had no objection to visits to South Africa by Soviet journalists who would, in particular, contact legal oppositional organisations there. The content of the *Izvestiya* reports was by and large reasonable but the leadership of the United Democratic Front was somewhat concerned about the circumstances of this visit. The programme was prepared by the government's Department of Foreign Affairs and its officials accompanied the *Izvestiya* correspondent everywhere.

As early as 1983 Boris Asoyan had commented: "They don't like foreign journalists in the RSA. If they are let into the country, they are surrounded by so many full-time propagandists that to an unprepared newspaperman it might seem: the apartheid is not so dreadful and Africans in the RSA live quite decently. Such a correspondent or rather a tourist returns home and publishes in his paper an advertising article about the racist regime. The authorities in Pretoria do not spare money for bribing and propaganda treatment of journalists."[72] The same methods were subsequently quite successfully applied to several other Soviet journalists.

The beginning of talks about talks disturbed not only the rank and file but also some ANC leaders. The main concern was to ensure that all of the ANC top leadership guided the process. Joe Nhlanhla, who not long before became the Head of the Intelligence and Security, put it this way at the meeting of the ANC Working Committee in February 1988: "There are lots of people who are meeting people from home without any consultation, let alone co-ordination. There are more and more workshops being organised which involve people from home. There is a loss of control." Chris Hani supported him: "One consequence of this uncontrolled contact is that people from home complain that we are saying different things to them."[73]

Chris Hani was particularly worried about a meeting in London between an ANC group, headed by Thabo Mbeki, and Afrikaner intellectuals. "On whose authority [did] Cde Thabo enter into discussions with these Afrikaner intellectuals?" Hani asked at the Working Committee meeting. "Does the NEC/NWC know anything about this? It is very disturbing."[74] A fiery discussion followed and was continued at the next meeting: "There was unclarity as to the actual decision, we must assume Cde Thabo acted in good faith ... The issue was not Cde Thabo *per se* but the principle of prior consultation and a mandate from the NWC ... Cde President had raised the objection in principle to the idea of our interlocutors specifying whom they would like to meet in the NEC."[75]

That discussion, however, did not mean the end of the contacts. In fact, Thabo Mbeki was absent from that meeting, as Alfred Nzo explained, because: "He was in London to attend the Commonwealth Conference on the Media and was delegated by the Presidential Committee to meet representatives/intermediators acting on behalf of the regime to discuss the issue of political prisoners."[76]

The state of Soviet contacts with anti-racist forces and the prospects of political settlement were important subjects for discussion with the delegation of the SACP in April 1988. It was headed by Joe Slovo and included Chris Hani. In Moscow the SACP delegation met with Yegor Ligachev (who was *de facto* second in the Party hierarchy) and Anatoly Dobrynin. The South African Communist leaders were pleased to hear from Ligachev that "The South African revolutionaries are better placed to assess the situation and to work out a combination of all the necessary forms of the struggle – organisational, political and armed. We support such a course; though the communists would prefer the peaceful solution, the time has not come yet." Whether Ligachev was sincere or whether he merely wished to placate the visitors, he insisted that there were no differences in the Soviet leadership on matters of policy, simply debates about how to implement it. In fact, by that time Yeltsin had already been removed from the Politbureau and the struggle between Ligachev and Alexander Yakovlev was becoming very bitter.

Ligachev clearly said that the USSR supported the ANC and the SACP in combining various forms of struggle, including the military one. However, when a draft press release was shown to him, even he, regarded as a hard-liner in the Kremlin, demanded that the word "armed" be crossed out in the phrase "armed struggle".[77] This word was becoming unfashionable in Moscow, though support for the ANC's armed struggle persisted and was in fact intensified.

The SACP leadership wrote in the Party Internal Bulletin that this was the first visit by a special SACP delegation to Moscow in five years. In fact, it was probably closer to ten years. Contacts in the intervening years had tended to be made when SACP leaders came for Party meetings, or as ANC representatives, or in transit. This official visit was described as a most useful and inspiring experience. Very importantly for Joe Slovo and his colleagues, the CPSU agreed that its annual financial assistance to the SACP, though modest, be increased.

Joe Slovo was pleased by the changes in the USSR in the first years of *perestroika*. Speaking at the Institute of Social Sciences during that visit in April 1988, he said that socialism still had to prove its superiority. The distortions it suffered created a negative impression but the successes would have a greater effect. "We may be coming into the world when the struggle between the classes, between the oppressed and oppressors, would be carried out at the negotiation table, without using traditional forms."[78]

My notes of the time show that he was more realistic about the prospects for national and social liberation in South Africa and the role of the SACP: "The regime is strong, it is not on the verge of collapse. Most probably the struggle will be protracted. But we must be ready for rapid changes as well. There is a drive towards socialism among the workers but in a simplified form. The Communist Party has not yet won the soul of the workers. The SACP is for political settlement. The experience of the national liberation movements in other countries proves its feasibility. Besides, the regional confrontation threatens world peace. The question is not 'to talk or not to talk?' but 'with whom to talk and about what?'"[79]

Slovo commented that at that stage Botha could not agree to negotiations, except on his stated conditions; and if the ANC initiated negotiations it would lose its prestige and would be sidelined as a leader of the liberation movement. But the situation would change when the pressure on the regime from inside and outside increased.

Apart from regular groups of students who came for a year or two, there were activists who came from time to time for semi-clandestine studies in the Institute of Social Sciences. One of these was Janet Love, now Chairperson of the Portfolio Committee on Agriculture and Forestry. Her short stay in Moscow in 1986 was part of her preparation for illegal work at home. I knew what she was about to go into, and our farewell in the lobby of the Institute among the crowds of students and lecturers was an emotional moment.

Another person who was expected in December 1986 was Jennifer Schreiner, a leading member of the SACP committee in Cape Town (now an MP), but she was unable to make the trip. Many years later I jokingly admonished her that, if she had come, a short course in underground activity might have saved her from arrest in Cape Town shortly afterwards.

In 1987 and 1988 the ANC's armed struggle intensified. Joe Modise

328

and Ronnie Kasrils visited Moscow in March 1988 and informed us that in 1987 Umkhonto had carried out more operations than in previous years (over 250); Pretoria tried to suppress reports of those activities. It was not alone in attempting to downplay the importance of the armed actions. Chester Crocker wrote: "The armed struggle never amounted to much more than a costly inconvenience to the security forces – an inconvenience that was gradually eliminated during the course of the 1980s."[80] In fact, however, "during the course of the 1980s" the actions of Umkhonto and its supporters, far from being "eliminated", became such an "inconvenience" that the security forces lost their control over many townships physically and, more importantly, psychologically. The people had been freed from fear, and, as the regime suppressed legal opposition by the democratic movement, it succeeded only in creating a mass militant response.

Combat groups inside South Africa started emerging. They were a new phenomenon, acting without permanent contact with the ANC Headquarters, following instead a general direction and general types of targets. These groups had simple weapons: hand grenades, mines, and some small arms. But their actions were often more effective than those of groups sent from outside: they were legally in the country and it was difficult to detect them.

The spirit of defiance spurred individual fighters on, to fight and even die alone, sometimes taking on hundreds of soldiers, and with thousands of township residents as onlookers. However, Modise and Kasrils described numerous problems as well: lack of discipline, the leaking of information by captured fighters, and, especially, the appearance of askaris, turn-coats who created great difficulties for Umkhonto members returning to South Africa. That also increased the need to train recruits inside the country.[81]

The ANC military leaders requested Moscow to train more cadres in MCW, including the transition from legal activities to underground. They expressed delight at the military coup in the Transkei, where there was an indirect ANC involvement through some officers who had ANC connections. But the coup in Bophuthatswana, which was suppressed by the SADF, came as a surprise to the ANC leadership.

A growing participation of fighters, trained in South Africa in armed actions, had another, negative aspect: the number of attacks against civilian targets increased, something which was contrary to ANC policy. The problem was discussed at a meeting of the ANC NEC in August 1988 in Lusaka. When one of its members expressed his concern, Oliver Tambo supported him. The Committee issued a statement, which read: "Some of these attacks have been carried out by cadres of the people's army, Umkhonto we Sizwe. Inspired by anger at the regime's campaign of terror against the oppressed and democratic forces, both within and outside South Africa in certain instances operational circumstances resulted in unintended casualties."[82]

At the same time the ANC emphasised that "the agents of the Pretoria regime have been detailed to carry out a number of bomb attacks deliberately to sow confusion among the people of South Africa and the international community, and to discredit the African National Congress."[83]

After the NEC issued the above statement the number of such attacks decreased sharply. This convinced many people in South Africa and abroad that the ANC leadership exercised overall authority over combat groups inside South Africa.

An important step in preparing for a political settlement was made by the ANC in 1988 when it published "Constitutional Guidelines for a Democratic South Africa".[84] By that time different organisations from South Africa were trying to contact ANC Headquarters, looking for guidance, "as if the ANC had answers to all the questions."[85] Meanwhile, a massive national and international campaign for the release of Nelson Mandela and other political prisoners was making itself felt. The Release Mandela Campaign was one of the most successful single-issue campaigns undertaken in the South African struggle. It had been well planned by the ANC and the SACP, together with their internal and international allies. The momentum built up to such an extent that Nelson Mandela's release by Pretoria became a distinct possibility. In October 1988 the National Working Committee held an emergency meeting after receiving information from Beyers Naude that the regime was seriously considering freeing Mandela. A plan of action to organise his reception was immediately prepared.[86]

It was at this time that a new problem arose, involving the so-called Mandela Football Club, Winnie Mandela's group of self-styled (and spy-infected) bodyguards. At the National Working Committee meeting Oliver Tambo proposed an approach which would "protect the movement and Nelson Mandela at the expense of Winnie Mandela without being part of the forces aiming to destroy her."[87]

It is interesting to note that as early as the 1960s serious consideration has been given to organising Mandela's escape from prison. Among the papers in the Mayibuye Centre Historical Papers

Archive is an unnamed two-three page document, apparently drafted in the 1960s or 1970s, which calls for "an exhaustive study" of all the information pertinent to such a project. It noted: "It is possible that even the objective itself may be determined by such a study, i.e. Rescue of all political prisoners on Robben Island, or Rivonia group or one or two of the latter."[88] A great number of related questions needed to be answered, ranging from shipping routes in the area to marital status and numbers of children of prison personnel. The sources of information were also to be diverse: from the British Museum to "Employment of special agents" (this last line was a hand-written addition to the typed text).[89] But despite various reported plans no escape attempt was actually made.

The degree of mutual trust that existed between the ANC and its allies and the USSR was illustrated when the ANC top leadership sought Soviet assistance in preparing the operation which later received much publicity as Operation Vula. The issue was initially raised with me in strict confidence by Oliver Tambo, and Joe Slovo, at the time of the September 1987 tripartite consultations.

The question of exiled leaders going back inside South Africa or of the internal leaders going underground was one that had been on the agenda for decades. It was not at all easy to put into practice. For example, when two prominent figures in the democratic opposition left South Africa legally at the end of 1988, in preliminary discussions the ANC proposed to them that they "assume leadership underground". They "appeared to be taken aback and expressed the view that they considered themselves inadequate for the assignment."[90] Oliver Tambo was considerate, as always: "We should avoid giving them tasks that would get them into trouble even before they are ready."[91]

Now history seemed to be repeating itself. As was the case once in 1961, two leaders were entrusted with the duty of selecting people for the difficult task of creating an armed underground, and one of them was again Joe Slovo.

When Oliver Tambo broached the subject with me, the ANC delegation was staying at Stalin's former dacha, the same place where the 1970 SACP meeting had taken place. One evening I was invited to Tambo's suite. He explained that he and Slovo envisaged a limited Soviet role. It entailed mainly covering-up what was expected to be a long-term absence of Mac Maharaj and Siphiwe Nyanda ("Gebuza" in MK, now Head of the South African National Defence Force). The idea was that the former would be "admitted to a Soviet hospital" and the latter was "to start a long course of military training". Tambo also mentioned a third name to me, that of Chris Hani, but his departure was later postponed.

The cover story (the term "legend" was commonly used) required that the Vula operatives come to Moscow and then secretly travel home to South Africa from there. In a book *Operation Vula*, published by the Dutch anti-apartheid activist Conny Braam,[92] she describes how she and other supporters in the Netherlands provided the ANC underground with various disguises. But it would seem that, when the most crucial part of the operation started, professionals needed to replace the amateurs. Assistance of a more technical nature was requested by the ANC leadership, which we provided in July 1988. It helped ensure a safe journey for Mac and Gebuza to Southern Africa. The USSR was not involved in any way with their activity inside the country.

Allister Sparks writes in his book, apparently after discussions with Mac Maharaj: "the Soviets, always helpful to the ANC, fitted him out with false passports...."[93] Maharaj and Nyanda were neither the first nor the last members of the liberation movement who used Soviet-made documents. After the August 1991 events in Moscow, the press was full of stories about the "sudden discovery" of a kind of workshop on the fifth floor of the International Department building in Moscow where false documents for clandestine operations had been found. In the pictures accompanying the press disclosures one could see South African passports and identity documents, alongside Chilean and Portuguese documents.

It is still too early to recount the full story of the CPSU's assistance to the South African liberation movement in this regard, but some archive documents speak for themselves. In July 1977 Yusuf Dadoo made this request to the CPSU:

"... Dear Comrades, we request you to forward the following items to LUANDA as per arrangement for delivery made by Comrade Joe Slovo with Comrade Alexei Makarov:-

(i) 150 Reference Books

(ii) Swazi and Lesotho Passports [The USSR did not have diplomatic relations with these two countries]

(iii) Tax Exemption Forms

(iv) Embossing Stamp (Congrave) as appears on the back page of the Reference Book enclosed herewith ...

N.B. The enclosed Reference Book must be sent back to us as it will be required for the use for the owner.

(v) If it's possible we would appreciate investigations on how to replace photographs in documents both congrave and ordinary types. All that is required is the principle to guide us."[94]

The next letter was even more detailed:

1. "We require an additional 150 reference Books.

2. We have run out of Swazi and Lesotho Passports and we would appreciate a supply of a further 75 of each ...

333

3. We did not receive any Tax Exemption Forms and we hope you can forward these ...

5. We would also appreciate early delivery of the rubber stamps which comrade Slovo requested when he was on a visit in May."[95]

Similar requests continued to arrive over the years and as time went on the numbers increased dramatically. Maximum secrecy was maintained in this kind of assistance. The unit mentioned above was for many years headed by the late "Comrade Ivan", an experienced specialist in his field. Once, when some South Africans were waiting for the lift in the building of the International Department, "Comrade Ivan" emerged from the lift and bumped into Moses Mabhida. They embraced and greeted one another. "Who is this comrade?" asked another SACP Politbureau member. "This man does not exist," Mabhida replied.

Other forms of technical assistance for underground activity were also given. In response to a request from the SACP top leadership, the CPSU Central Committee Secretariat took a decision "to organise in March-April 1981 a course of special training [in the USSR] for a SACP representative on the party technique for the period up to six weeks." (As in other sensitive documents the words "party technique" were hand-written into a blank space: even trusted typists were not to know the nature of the training.)[96]

The importance of such training can be seen in the report of an unnamed South African activist: "After an initial survey of the problems I encountered in the work and also in my techniques and methods, the instructor decided that I needed a training course from scratch." Describing the methods of secret writing he/she adds: "All these methods even if heavily scrutinised and checked with those special security techniques should not be detectable. These methods were all developed by USSR experts and are not generally known of by Western intelligence agency – except of course in the instances which we are aware of."

The recommendations of the activist included the following reference:

"(1) That Ronnie [Kasrils?] is given sufficient time for me to teach him in the way that I was taught and with equal thoroughness so that our standards correspond. (I am assuming that apart from Ronnie there isn't anyone else who train(s) people regularly.)"[97]

It was amazing, and amusing, to observe all the preparations for Mac and "Joe" (Nyanda's name in Vula). Changes were made to their appearance and some practical "consultations" were given in which Mac, especially, showed considerable survival skills.

Slovo came to Moscow specifically to brief them before their trip. On the hot and rainy evening we sat in a modest apartment on the tenth or eleventh floor in one of Moscow's apartment blocks. There were four of us: Maharaj, Slovo, I – and a comrade who was directly responsible for taking care of Mac. (Gebuza has already left a day earlier.) Two bottles, whisky and cognac, were on the table but were hardly touched. The atmosphere was emotional. Mac said, "Don't say I am brave, I am also scared. I want to live but I know I must go home. If I die, don't say 'He was a hero', say 'He started the process of opening the way, of coming back'."

I could not sleep properly that night. We had had a serious problem: the ANC comrade who had planned Mac's trip had not been thorough enough and we suddenly had to find a flight for Mac from Moscow to Amsterdam that would connect with the flight that would take him to the meeting point with Nyanda in Africa. I joked with the lady who made the travel arrangements for us in the Party hotel, assuring her that the people of South Africa would not forget her, as I begged her to sort out the muddle. She did, finding a small, little-known German airline which was flying to Amsterdam from a suitable place, Brussels. Mac would have just an hour or two to make the connection.

Dawn is very early in Moscow in summer and I awoke to find that a heavy fog had descended on the city. What would the weather be like at the airport? What would happen with Mac's connection? With his meeting with Gebuza? Fortunately for us, as we were driving Mac to the airport, the fog lifted and the Sabena plane took off almost on time. We drove back to Moscow and happily informed Joe Slovo, who was staying "legally" at the hotel, that Mac had left.

It is not for me to describe all the problems that Mac and, especially, Gebuza encountered on their way to Swaziland and then to South Africa. One day, I hope, they will tell the story themselves. The cover story (or "legend") for Mac, that he was sick, was a reasonable one. His health was far from perfect, and in 1985 he had spent several weeks in a Soviet hospital. But to expect that he could stay in a Moscow hospital for several months without any South African visitors was absurd. So, instead of his (alleged) kidney problems and besides his (real) knee problems, we looked for something else, and came up with the story that he had a serious lung condition. The sanatorium for tuberculosis patients was situated in the Eastern Crimea, a remote area, usually closed to foreigners. Mac left us a batch of letters that we had to post to his family on specific dates. However, it was still a bit difficult to explain to some of his close friends why they could not even contact him by phone.

Nyanda's story was simpler. There were many military training institutions in the USSR and most of them were some distance from Moscow. Apart from the top leadership, nobody would ever ask for permission to visit them or telephone. It worked, and we were happy to read in Ellis's magazine the "confidential" information that "Leading Umkhonto commander Siphiwe Nyende [Nyanda] has left the beleaguered military to study in the Soviet Union, disenchanted with the ANC leadership."[98]

But at the end of 1988 a new problem arose: Mac's wife had a bad car accident. Treatment was organised in Zimbabwe but later it seemed as if she was in danger of losing her sight. Oliver Tambo, knowing that Moscow (and those few who knew where Mac really was) would support his request, personally persuaded the USSR Embassy in Lusaka to issue her with a visa and ticket. Zarina was successfully operated on in Moscow. We then suggested – almost insisted, since she was eager to return to her children – that she spend a week in Yalta in the Crimea. From there a trip was organised to the sanatorium where Mac supposedly was, so that she was better equipped later to describe where her husband had stayed.

Later we received a message indicating that some people in Lusaka were beginning to doubt whether Mac was really in the sanatorium. At the request of Tambo and Slovo, we sent an official message to the Soviet Embassy in Zambia asking them to inform the ANC leadership that Maharaj's health was deteriorating and that doctors were recommending an operation. That deception apparently worked: even the Ambassador Oleg Miroshkin found out the real purpose of that message only much later, when we told him the whole story after Mac was already back.

I was pleasantly surprised to get a message from Mac through the ANC channels, addressed to "comrade-it-is-possible" and dated 4 March 1989. Mac wrote: "Looking forward to the day when, in spite of Gorbachev – or is it Ligachev in this case? – we shall sit around a bottle of well-chilled vodka! Keep well and keep telling effective lies about me ... (Oh, how one lie will lead to a lifetime of lies ...)" With his sardonic sense of humour he added: "[We] are keeping well and busy (we hope productively but more likely making a bigger mess)."[99]

Another message came, sent from Lusaka on 17 June 1989:

"Dear Comrade

Re: Tony [Maharaj]

We are arranging for Comrade Tony to consult with us and at the same time to strengthen his legend. Your assistance is critical for the success of this mission.

At the moment, neither the timing nor the route have been finalised. We expect that due to so many variables we will only know the details at a late stage.

We can only outline the ideas and give you confirmation later using the code name "TONY"

1. Tony will arrive via ... (As far as we know, ... does not stamp SA passports).

2. From there he travels to Moscow on another SA passport, supplied by us together with a ticket corresponding to the new name.

3. Once in Moscow, he will need your assistance to normalise his appearance. He will thereafter make a "public appearance": i.e. see Simon [Makana] etc. He will apply for a visa to Britain, where he joins his wife who is receiving medical treatment.

4. Thereafter the whole family goes to Moscow for a holiday for approx. one month.

5. At same time our team (of three) will meet him for consultations.

Our requests are:

1. Ticket for Tony from ... to Moscow. Tony to pick up ticket and our passport (which we will forward to you) from ...

2. Assistance for normalising his appearance.

3. Ticket from Moscow to London. He will travel on his old Indian passport.

4. Ticket for Tony and family to Moscow. A month holiday.

5. The return by Tony and family for various destinations will be discussed later.

6. Tickets for our team of three (OR [Tambo], JS [Slovo] and Ivan [Pillay]) from Lusaka to Moscow and back.

7. Facilities for consultation.

Tony will exit his present area sometime in July.

Best regards

J.S."

Everything went according to the plan, the only exception being that "Tony" and his family could not find time for a holiday in the USSR.

When we met again the following month the vodka was rather warm, because I had put a bottle in my briefcase when I went to the airport. However, in spite of what he had written in his message, Mac always preferred cognac and had brought along a bottle of fine Martell, bought somewhere on the long journey back from South Africa to the Soviet Union.

We spent the following days and nights being regaled by stories about Mac's and Gebuza's travels, border crossings, and work at home. We never asked Mac where they had stayed, what their mission had been, who else had been involved; our only business was to assist with the continuation of the operation. To show how mindful of security both sides were, we heard the name "Vulindela" ("Open the way" in Zulu) or simply "Vula" ("Open") for the first time only after the operation had been uncovered and revealed by the South African security forces in July 1990. Mac told some fascinating stories, such as how one prominent South African writer gave him refuge during a difficult time; how Nelson Mandela initially could not believe that Mac was inside the country; and how a young woman sent inside from Lusaka told Mac (whom she had not recognised because of his disguise) that according to persistent rumours Mac was mentally ill in the Soviet Union. He also told us about the police knocking at their door one morning after they had received arms and had been too tired to conceal them. Fortunately for them, the police were investigating a car theft and did not enter the house.

A couple of days after Mac's return, a number of important guests turned up: Oliver Tambo, Joe Slovo, and Ivan Pillay. As for the claim that by that time the USSR had "dropped" the ANC, suffice it to say that in July 1989 Moscow was still the safest place for the ANC leaders in exile to meet the head of their underground machinery.

Maharaj was accommodated in one of the special flats, and a dacha in Serebryany Bor was prepared for Tambo and the others. It soon became clear that for practical reasons they needed to stay together. It therefore became necessary for one more person to be informed about the whole project: the Head of the ANC Mission, Simon Makana. (Makana had, I am sure, guessed that Mac was not in the Crimea, but as a man with a strong feeling of discipline and responsibility he had not asked any questions.)

Mac spent enough time in Moscow for his appearance once again to match the picture on his legal passport and to get a visa for Britain, where his family stayed. Even in mid 1989, the British Embassy was in no hurry to issue a visa to this ANC Executive member. Fortunately

Mac's trademark, his goatee beard, soon grew enough for him to go to the British Embassy himself and to squeeze a visa out of them. Of course, Maharaj did not waste any of his time in Moscow. For example, when he heard that Frank Chikane, Secretary General of the South African Council of Churches, was in Moscow as a guest of the Russian Orthodox Church, he decided to meet with him. Chikane was stunned to see him: they had met in South Africa just a week or two earlier. "I knew you were going to Moscow and decided to follow you," Maharaj joked.

Another secret mission from South Africa to Moscow involved Billy Nair, who after spending 20 years on Robben Island became a prominent leader in the UDF. In February 1988, when Oliver Tambo was again in the Barvikha sanatorium, we received a message that Nair was in the GDR and would be able to visit Tambo. A few days later I accompanied a relatively young-looking (disguised) man with a black beard to Barvikha. It was moving to watch them meet again after almost thirty years, and amusing to notice the expression on the face of Tambo's bodyguard, who could not fathom who this clearly important South African was.

We were watching the news in Nair's hideout, one of the special flats in Moscow, when the regime announced the ban on the UDF and other organisations. But it was clear that the government was not in a position to carry this banning out in practice. Nair was sure that the banning would lead to something like a "People's Front Against Apartheid", and that is, in fact, what happened with the creation of the Mass Democratic Movement. It was interesting for us to hear from someone at the heart of the internal struggle. He described how big business in South Africa was eager to maintain contacts with the UDF. In his opinion, the imperialists were worried that, if talks were further delayed, it would all be too late. They feared the generation of young people who were coming to play an active role in the mass movement, many of whom had been brutalised by detention and repression when they were 15 or 16. But the regime was still trying to preserve the status quo, until a more serious threat of revolution developed.

From the previous chapters it is clear that in the first three or four years of the *perestroika* the ties between the Soviets and the ANC were becoming more regular and wide-ranging; assistance in all fields grew. A common approach towards a possible political settlement in Southern Africa was worked out and followed. The democratisation of the political system in the USSR and the working methods of the ruling CPSU also affected the South African liberation movement. The ANC (and the SACP) adopted more critical attitudes towards outworn dogmas, and undertook more comprehensive and realistic analyses of the situation in South Africa.

The Soviet Union supported an intensification of FAPLA operations against UNITA, and assisted in the build up of Cuban forces in Southern Angola in 1987-8. That helped ensure strong resistance from the Angolans and Cubans at Cuito Cuanavale and later their advance to the Namibian border. The Soviets were, in fact, with the Angolans at Cuito Cuanavale even before Cuban reinforcements arrived, and suffered some fatalities there.

On the eve of the Angolan-Namibian settlement, Gorbachev was still following a no-nonsense approach *vis-à-vis* Pretoria. In his discussion with Jose Eduardo Dos Santos in Moscow at the end of October 1988 he told the Angolan President that the Soviet response to the South African government's request for contact had been made subject to the resolution of the Namibian problem. And, moreover, when this happened Moscow would first consult the ANC on the matter.

But the situation started to change rapidly, commensurate with changes in Gorbachev's general policies. Gorbachev's rule can be divided into two periods with the watershed occurring some time in 1989, when "perfection of socialism" and "democratisation" started turning into the restoration of capitalism and authoritarian decision making, and when "new political thinking" became his search for applause from the West at whatever cost. A description of this process is beyond the scope of this book, but it is obvious that there was no clear-cut moment of rupture; the process was initially very slow, indeed hardly discernible, and therefore much more difficult to resist.

This division is relevant to the Soviet attitude to the ANC and its allies as well. The first disjuncture between Soviet policy and that of the liberation movement happened in the months December 1988 to January 1989. During the talks on the settlement in South Western Africa the Soviet diplomats agreed with the American proposal to cut down the number of UN troops to be deployed in Namibia in the pre-election period. The reason was not political, but financial: even with the reduced number, the USSR was making a large contribution to the budget of the United Nations Transition Assistance Group (UNTAG). Subsequently events showed that this reduction did not affect UNTAG's functioning, especially since the number of UN police officers was increased. But what was disturbing was the way the agreement was reached, without the knowledge of either Cuba or SWAPO. Cuban delegates, for example, were informed of the arrangements by the Americans.

The decision, which caused political complications for the USSR, was taken by the Foreign Minister Eduard Shevardnadze, acting almost single-handedly. Only later, to be on the safe side, did he seek and receive the approval of the CPSU leadership. Subsequently this practice of replacing the collective leadership by the decisions of one person or at best by agreement between Shevardnadze and Gorbachev became commonplace. Valentin Falin, the last International Secretary of the CPSU, wrote about Shevardnadze's actions: "It is difficult for me to judge the motives and the real reasons of Eduard Amvrosievich [Shevardnadze] ... What induced him even to violate the directives of the President? Apparently something highly serious ..." Falin said Gorbachev expressed his dissatisfaction and suggested that Shevardnadze should act independently only in very extreme circumstances. More often than not Shevardnadze got away with "the violation of the state discipline."[100]

The negotiations on an Angolan-Namibian settlement served as a kind of early warning signal to the ANC: it might find itself in a position where talks in South Africa would be inevitable, even if they were considered to be premature. The ANC also understood that the political settlement in South Western Africa would affect its right to have training camps in Angola.

While the talks were progressing, the ANC leadership was worried that their organisation "was being surrounded in an offensive to cut it from the decision making process."[101] The ANC was alarmed about contacts between the independent African countries and Pretoria, and about media speculation around a Southern African summit including P W Botha. Speaking about the position of the African states, Joe

Slovo said: "Some of our friends eager to avoid conflicts were tempted to encourage the process [of "moving towards a détente"] and leaving impressions that even in the Soviet Union there was a bias towards pushing for a negotiated settlement."[102]

Even as late as 1988, when it was clear that the ANC would be a leading force in the future South Africa, the ANC experienced considerable difficulties with some independent African countries. Botswana, for example, rejected an appeal for amnesty for ANC members imprisoned in that country. Chris Hani, who himself spent time in a Botswana prison, suggested raising with Botswana the implications of their actions. "We are quiet now but will not be always quiet." He proposed sending a delegation there "to let them know that it could embarrass them if we told the world about what happens to us in some of these African states for fighting for freedom in South Africa. The main task of the delegation must be to secure the release of our comrades."[103]

In Angola the situation of the ANC again deteriorated. UNITA launched orchestrated attacks on ANC convoys, and at the National Working Committee meeting on 7 June 1988 Tambo drew attention to "the high rate of casualties in the west [Angola]".[104] It was decided to approach "at the highest level" the ANC's friends for immediate assistance. The committee resolved that "The Soviet delegation led by Shubin will be approached when they are in town and JS [Joe Slovo] will follow when he passes through SU [Soviet Union] on July 4th."[105]

We had a comprehensive discussion with the ANC leaders in Lusaka on our way to Harare that resulted, in particular, in providing urgent medical assistance for a group of MK wounded. It was not the first time when discussions had to be made on the spot. Once, while in Luanda in transit, I met Modise who came to the airport for discussions with me. He was growing increasingly disturbed about the condition of wounded ANC fighters, especially Timothy Makoena, who was in danger of losing his leg. We took a decision on the spot and sent all of the wounded fighters to Moscow on the next flight for medical treatment. Timothy had to spend many months in Moscow, initially in the Central Clinical Hospital, and then in the Burdenko Military Hospital, which proved more successful in treating his wounds. Though he had to return to Moscow for further treatment, Makoena's health was finally restored and as a result he later joined the new South African National Defence Force as Major General Godfrey Ngwenya, his real name.

As far as Slovo's "passing through SU" is concerned, he was actually going to Moscow specifically to meet Maharaj and "Gebuza" before their departure for South Africa, as has been mentioned above. But initially only a few of the ANC leadership (and three or four persons in Moscow) knew about it and that ensured the safety of the whole operation. As somebody jokingly remarked at the time, at least these people were definitely not traitors.

In the short term, developments in South Western Africa created serious problems for the ANC. Fortunately the leadership had anticipated them. The lesson had been learnt from the pre-Nkomati period, when there were many rumours which the ANC failed to heed.[106] The issue of evacuation from Angola, and even the possibility of withdrawal from Zambia, was discussed several times at meetings of the ANC ruling bodies. At the meeting of the National Working Committee on 1 November 1988 Oliver Tambo said: "Our problems are moving Eastward ... we need to be near [the ANC cadres, who were to be transported to Tanzania and Zambia]."[107] The ANC President realistically assessed the difficulties facing the ANC as a result of the regional settlement: "We are moving from the West [Angola], virtually demolishing our Army and retreating from strategic positions. When the whole Army is moving from the West, who will say No to an order to move? Things have changed, comrades, our people must understand that ... We must move before the Maputo kind of situation [post-Nkomati] overtakes us."[108]

But the full independence of Namibia was worth the high price paid for it. After Pretoria's withdrawal from its so-called fifth province, it would have to take steps towards a political settlement inside South Africa itself. The developments in Namibia caused a radical change in the psychological climate in South Africa, more so because of Pretoria's acknowledgement of the strong possibility that SWAPO would come to power in Namibia. If its "enemy" – that is, SWAPO – could come to power in neighbouring Namibia, why not the ANC in South Africa.

Contrary to the misinformation given out by South African and Western "Sovietologists" and the media, no pressure whatsoever was applied by the Soviet leadership for the ANC to withdraw from Luanda. Among the points made during discussions at the meeting of the National Working Committee on 4 October 1988 was the following: "We need to revive contacts with the Soviet leadership in order to ensure we are on the same wave-length."[109] That was done during Alfred Nzo's visit to Moscow in November. He raised the question of assistance in transferring ANC personnel and equipment from Angola. Nzo reported: "Soviet comrades were concerned lest their (unilateral) participation in transfer operations should spark off anti-Soviet campaigns. They would prefer countries of the region to be seen to be involved. They wanted to know what would happen to materials requested and already in the pipeline. They wanted to know if we intended to vacate Angola altogether. Response was that we could not hope to remain in Angola in significant numbers. The Soviets had said that though they had air transport means, it was in hands of Angolans ... We need to answer the question immediately as to what we do with material in the pipeline."[110]

Oliver Tambo appreciated the Soviets' concern and suggested that the ANC "should go to the Front Line States with specific requests when they meet."[111] Some assistance had already been solicited, particularly from Zambia. Tambo said that at that stage "general supplies" from the USSR should still be sent to Angola, because the ANC was not in a hurry to move personnel from there, except from Camp 32.[112] Regarding "the tricky aspect" of military supplies being delayed by the Soviets "until there is clarity on delivery point", Tambo proposed that the ANC "get back to them when the issue is clear."[113] Later Dar es Salaam was designated as the port of delivery instead of Luanda.

An NEC delegation, headed by Joe Modise, was in Angola in December 1988. It briefed the Angolan authorities and ANC cadres at ten different venues in the country. "The thrust of the briefing was that racists want to use our presence in Angola as an excuse. Comrades understood.... The Soviet instructors were also briefed and they expressed willingness to continue serving the ANC."[114] These extracts from the ANC Working Committee minutes clearly show that the USSR continued actively supporting the ANC after the agreement on Angolan-Namibian settlement. In fact, a small group of Soviets remained for two more years with the Umkhonto cadres who stayed on in Angola, ostensibly to take care of the remaining materials.

The transfer of the Umkhonto camps and other facilities from Angola was a very difficult task. The main headache involved those people who were sentenced or detained by the ANC. Dakawa in Tanzania was initially proposed as a venue for them, but later the Ugandans agreed to "clear one (or section thereof) prison to accommodate Camp 32."[115] While the Soviet Union was ready to assist the ANC in moving personnel and goods to Tanzania and Uganda (where the Head of State, Yoweri Museveni, had expressed a willingness to accommodate most of MK), they made it very clear that they would not wish to get involved in dealing with the detainees. A special task force of the ANC, which was created to deal with the transfer from Angola, "decided that Camp 32 should be lifted at ANC expense."[116]

The ANC NAT suggested that the inmates should be divided into three categories: those who ought to be released unconditionally, those who did not qualify for release but should not be held in that camp, and so-called serious cases. These last, it was recommended, should be considered by a Tribunal, convened by the ANC Officer of Justice Zola Skweyiya, after which "cases involving capital punishment" would be referred to a Review Commission.[117]

Joe Slovo and Dan Tloome visited Moscow in January 1989, soon after a meeting of the SACP Central Committee in Hungary. That meeting discussed the preparations for the Seventh SACP Congress to be convened in Havana. The draft SACP programme, prepared on the basis of several years' work, provoked a heated discussion, especially the last chapter, which was written mostly by Slovo himself: "people's way out … people's power … insurrection." The revolutionary strategy, including an insurrectionary perspective, in some cases armed, remained in place.

The Seventh Congress of the SACP, held in Havana in April 1989 (for security reasons only made public on 15 June 1989), adopted a new party programme and elected a new Central Committee, which included younger people. Of some 50 participants, seven came from inside South Africa. The growth of the Party inside South Africa in the previous six-to-nine months had been higher than in the previous twenty years. By that time about a quarter of the party membership was inside the country, of whom 60% were workers.

One SACP activist was not in Havana: the young woman mentioned earlier, who had sung a Russian song at the closing of the previous SACP Congress. Later she came to Moscow for training again, this time for a crash course in MCW. We heard that she was to be working underground either in a forward area or inside South Africa.

But we soon learned that she was in trouble. While in London she was asked to go to Lusaka. There she was detained under suspicion of being an agent. Not everybody in the ANC (and SACP) leadership believed that. Both Joe Slovo and Chris Hani expressed their doubts, arguing, for example, that, if she was working for the regime, why did she not stay in London instead of agreeing to fly to Africa? Others, who said they "suspected her long ago", had a different view.

Some time later I spent over an hour sitting on a bench in Gorky Park in Moscow, expressing my concern to a member of the ANC Executive who was involved in investigating this case. He stressed that she was not being ill-treated, that she could even be released to continue her studies, say, in Britain, provided she was frank in reporting the damage she had caused. He was absolutely convinced that Rose was an agent. I was not. Perhaps I just did not want to believe it.

I later heard more of the story from Chris Hani, when he was in Moscow in April 1992. In his answers to my questions, I could sense his persisting doubts. He told me that, after being released from detention in Uganda, she came to the SACP Headquarters. He immediately asked if she had been an informer, and she emphatically denied it. For Chris the matter was not yet closed and needed further investigation. However, one has to take into account the fact that Chris was a bit of a "softie" when questions of detention and interrogation came up.

While in Moscow Joe Slovo and Dan Tloome assessed the impact of the Angola-Namibian settlement: "The right-wing in South Africa called it betrayal; the people [on the other hand] were inspired." But many problems remained for the ANC and the SACP. The situation in Mozambique again deteriorated. Once every six months Pretoria presented a list of ANC members it deemed undesirable, and the Mozambican authorities would insist on their departure. "There is not even a show of dignity," Slovo commented bitterly.[118]

The second Soviet South African seminar of social scientists took place in February 1989, after several postponements. Only two of the five members of the ANC team, Pallo Jordan and Rob Davies, managed to attend. The ANC representative in Moscow and some students joined them. Even though discussions revealed some differences between the Soviet and South African academics, mostly in the approach to ethnic problems, Pallo Jordan emphasised that "In the last instance we are on the same side of the barricades, comrades in arms in a common struggle ... History may some day judge *perestroika* and *glasnost* as a third Russian revolution."[119]

Oliver Tambo visited Moscow with a senior delegation in March 1989 at the invitation of the Central Committee of the CPSU and the Presidium of the USSR Supreme Soviet. In the Kremlin he and his

346

colleagues met Anatoly Lukyanov, the first Deputy to Gorbachev in the state structures, and Valentin Falin, recently appointed Head of the CPSU International Department. The fact that Tambo was received not by Gorbachev but by his First Deputy was interpreted by some journalists as a snub to the ANC President. By this time it was becoming more and more difficult to involve Gorbachev in anything which concerned liberation movements and developing countries. He concentrated his energies on contacts with the West in the vain hope of receiving credit and the transfer of technology. Gorbachev was, in effect, avoiding meetings with African leaders. For example, when the Politbureau entrusted him with meeting Sam Nujoma in April 1988 (which he had earlier agreed to do), he shuffled the task over to Andrei Gromyko. When Gorbachev's previous assistant for African affairs, Vladimir Sharapov, left to take up an ambassadorship, his job was given to a newcomer. Although he was a well-intentioned person, Africa became ancillary to his main task of catering to the international activities of Raissa Gorbacheva.

We felt that in the new situation created by the Angolan-Namibian settlement it was not worth waiting for an opportunity for Tambo to meet Gorbachev. The ANC President himself had not insisted on such a meeting. It was much more pressing for the ANC to have discussions in Moscow on the rapidly changing situation in Southern Africa.

Another person conspicuous by his absence was Alexander Yakovlev, the CPSU Politbureau member and International Secretary, who consented to the ANC delegation visiting Moscow on the precise days when he was due to be on a short vacation.

Yakovlev was a great disappointment to me and to most of the officials of the International Department. Having replaced Dobrynin in late 1988, Yakovlev, a close confidant of Gorbachev and often regarded as "an architect of *perestroika*", behaved in a way that was strange to us. He met his own staff only once in the two years he occupied the post, and that just two months before his resignation. Behind the "democratic" image and the screen of "socialist pluralism", he rejected anything contrary to his own views. When a delegation of the "conservative" Indian Communist (Marxist) Party disagreed with him, he warned the official who accompanied them: "If you bring to me such people again, write a resignation letter."

As to Africa, he was at best completely indifferent. In his two years in office he received precisely one African – a Mozambican minister with a message from President Chissano – and that was on the direct instruction of Gorbachev. Yakovlev sabotaged the work of the special commission on Ethiopia, which was supposed to help stabilise the situation and the peace process in that country. After being appointed as its chairman by the Politbureau, he simply failed to convene the commission.

(Yakovlev's political career ended miserably. Having moved to vicious anti-Communist positions and having agreed to become the Head of the State TV and Radio under Yeltsin, he twice, in 1993 and 1995, tried to get into parliament – as a candidate of two different election alliances – and twice failed.)

During his meeting in the Kremlin Oliver Tambo described the developments in South Africa and noted that, after its departure from Angola (and the forthcoming departure from Namibia), Pretoria would have to look to a new survival strategy. It was seeking contacts with the ANC, but its own propaganda had made the ANC "untouchable" and so it was afraid to deal publicly with the ANC. Tambo said that, although Pretoria had used anti-communism as a weapon from 1950, the West now recognised that "communists or non-communists, terrorists or non-terrorists, the problems of South Africa could not be solved without the ANC. They want to win us over to their ideas. Ambassadors, special representatives are trying to cultivate us." Tambo called on the USSR to play a greater role in the region. "We want the Soviet Union to be a part of the solution of the problem; the South African situation should not remain only the concern of the US, UK and other Western states."

For his part Anatoly Lukyanov confirmed that the USSR was firmly in favour of preserving the international isolation of the racist regime and the broadening of the economic and other sanctions, both within the UN framework and on a bilateral level. Lukyanov reiterated that the "unblocking" of the regional conflicts did not mean "sacrificing" the struggle for national and social liberation. The political solutions of the regional conflicts had to include the right of the people to determine their destiny. With regard to South Africa, freedom of choice meant the eradication of apartheid.

Lukyanov emphasised that the Soviet Union became an observer of the Joint Commission on South Western Africa (in which South Africa was a member) at the request of its friends, that is Cuba and Angola. "All our discussions with South Africans in the framework of that commission are limited by the questions concerning the implementation of the agreements on South Western Africa ... The attempts by South Africans to move the discussion to the questions of the bilateral relations were resolutely rebuffed by us. We want full clarity. If there will be any moves, you would be the first we consult, to seek advice from."

This clarification was needed, because Pretoria was trying to profit from contacts with the Soviets. For example, in December 1988 Deputy Foreign Minister Anatoly Adamishin, who came to Brazzaville for the final discussions on the Angolan-Namibian settlement, met Pik Botha and Magnus Malan. Though the content of the discussion was supposed to be confidential, Pik Botha immediately gave his version of it to the South African media.

Lukyanov also confirmed that, in broadening contacts with democratic and liberal circles in South Africa, the Soviet Union was acting on the advice of the ANC. "We cannot see everything: whom to support and whom to hold back for some time."

Discussions with Anatoly Adamishin on 10 March proceeded along much the same lines, though he did speak about "modifying, changing, reforming" as a way to get rid of apartheid. He also told the ANC delegation that *perestroika* was the last chance to save socialism.

As was the usual practice, the Central Committee left it to the state departments, particularly the Ministry of Defence and the Ministry of Foreign Economic Affairs, to consider the requests submitted by the ANC. In earlier years these departments would present joint proposals, covering both military and civilian supplies. But this time the military prepared their part much more quickly, with the civilians lagging behind. In fact, the Ministry of Foreign Economic Affairs delayed their proposals on civilian goods to such an extent that the ANC ended up receiving nothing from them.

Meanwhile changes in the USSR political system were gathering momentum, especially after the Congress of People's Deputies was convened in May 1989, and the Supreme Soviet headed by Gorbachev was transformed into a permanent parliament. As a result, in August 1989 the final decision on supplies to the ANC was made not by the Central Committee, but directly by the USSR Council of Ministers. This meant the role of the Ministry of Foreign Affairs was becoming more important, and here the military unexpectedly ran into problems.

The idea of the political settlement of conflicts became so enshrined that the Ministry officials tried to limit the military supplies made available to the ANC. A lack of experience and competence became evident in the way decisions were taken. For example, the ANC requested armoured personnel carriers to be delivered to protect its fighters against ambush. This idea did not receive support because APCs were considered too heavy a class of weapons, as if they would be able to travel into South Africa! Land mines were rejected as too dangerous, but SPM and MPM were allowed, simply because the officials did not know that those abbreviations meant "Small limpet mines" and "Medium limpet mines".

Despite these new dynamics, Soviet supplies to the ANC continued well into 1990. Arms badly needed by the ANC such as a large number of Stechkin automatic pistols were sent to the ANC via Tanzania. The Stechkin, a weapon invaluable for self-defence in underground conditions, lay somewhere between the famous Kalashnikov assault rifle and the smaller Makarov pistol. The supplies complemented a significant arsenal of arms held by the ANC. According to specialist assessment in Moscow, Umkhonto already possessed arms and ammunition sufficient to sustain training and armed actions for at least a year.

The training of ANC members in Soviet military academies and centres, both for the future regular army and in MCW and other sensitive fields, continued as well. In fact, the number who received training in 1989-90 was the highest in the long history of the Soviet co-operation with the ANC, except perhaps 1964.

In 1989 the USSR helped with the major task of relocating Umkhonto from Angola. The Soviet Air Force transport planes took MK fighters to Tanzania and Uganda. We also helped transport hardware and other equipment from Luanda to Dar es Salaam (by sea) and to Entebbe (by air). A very dangerous incident took place during the transportation of Umkhonto personnel. As attempts at sabotage were expected, security was intensified while the planes were being boarded. Despite this increased vigilance, one of the passengers, a white man, tried to hijack the plane to South Africa while it was in Tanzanian air space. Fortunately he was overpowered. A Soviet crew member was slightly wounded. The subsequent investigation showed that the oversight was probably the fault of the Soviets in Angola. They had understandably insisted on participating in the security check at the airport, and in fact virtually took it over. It may well be that one of them was lenient towards the culprit because he happened to be white.

Oliver Tambo described his visit to Moscow in March 1989 as "the most successful" yet. At a final press conference in Moscow he spoke about "no change at all" in the Soviet attitude to the ANC. But even before the delegation left Moscow, there was disturbing news from London. The BBC reported a secret meeting between Soviet, British and South African academics in Britain. The ANC had not been invited, and the press had a field day. Anatoly Gromyko, Director of the Africa Institute, claimed that the British and South African press had distorted the gist of what was said at the meeting; and he expressed regret that the British organisers had failed to comply with the Soviet request that representatives of the ANC be invited to the meeting.[120] But he and his colleagues had themselves not done much in this respect; they could (and should) have informed the ANC Mission in Moscow or its Headquarters in Lusaka in advance. This oversight (deliberate or not) permitted the Western and South African propagandists to present a slanted picture of the seminar and to overshadow the successful talks conducted with Oliver Tambo in Moscow. One participant in that seminar wrote that no Soviet academic of any repute wanted to see the ANC in power in South Africa; it was clearly not on their agenda.

Having failed to break ANC-Soviet ties, the South African government intensified its attempts to win over individual academics, journalists and even officials. But a visit to the USSR by an IDASA delegation headed by Frederick van Zyl Slabbert in April 1989 helped to clear up misconceptions about Soviet policy towards South Africa. The IDASA delegation said in a statement that: "It would be a dangerous distortion of reality to seize upon the *personal* view of any single academic or official to determine what the *official* policy of the USSR is or how it has possibly changed with regard to South and Southern Africa ...We found no evidence at all that the USSR is putting pressure on the ANC to abandon the armed struggle before the conditions for a negotiated settlement had been created by those in power in South Africa, or that the USSR is considering abandoning support for the ANC in favour of closer contact and relations with those who are in power in South Africa at present ... and we believe it would be a dangerous delusion for interest groups in South Africa to proceed on distorted or wrong assumptions in this regard."[121]

During the discussion in the CPSU International Department, van Zyl Slabbert emphasised that contacts between the USSR and South

351

Africa should not give an impression of co-operation with the regime. He welcomed the statement that, if Pretoria were to reject a political settlement, the Soviet Union would support the ANC armed struggle.

Other honest South African and international observers also commented that changes in Soviet policy towards South Africa would be consonant with changes taking place in South Africa itself. After a visit to Moscow in August 1988, Allister Sparks wrote: "Nor is it only the Soviet Union that is making this reassessment. Eighteen months before, in the course of a long interview in Lusaka, the leader of the South African Communist Party Joe Slovo told me of his belief that the transition in South Africa would come about through negotiations rather than military victory or revolutionary overthrow. There isn't a single struggle in the post-war [post-World War Two] period in the colonies which hasn't ended at the negotiations table ... If there were any prospects of settling this thing peacefully tomorrow, we would be the first to say let's do it."[122]

Nevertheless the psychological campaign surrounding the Soviet Union's supposed abandonment of the ANC, pursued by Pretoria and part of the Western media, was starting to bear fruit. If the discussion in the Kremlin removed any doubts Oliver Tambo and his comrades had about Soviet policy, they were soon to be worried again. On 2 May 1989 a special meeting of the National Working Committee discussed the problems of negotiations. The main report was prepared by Chris Hani, then the Chief of Staff of Umkhonto we Sizwe. He spoke about the pressure being applied by the major Western powers on the ANC and added: "Even in the USSR some academics and individuals in the Foreign Affairs Ministry have declared in favour of a negotiated settlement in South Africa. The regime came out on top in South Africa (they argued) and the MDM is exhausted and burned out. These views have had an effect on the membership, some of whom believe we are preparing for negotiations."[123]

Hani's argument did not mean he was against negotiations, but he and apparently the majority of the ANC leaders thought that the time to negotiate had not yet come. They argued that the ANC would need to be stronger before negotiating. The underground, therefore, had to be strengthened, training inside South Africa had to be intensified, and the penetration of cadres from outside had to be increased. An overriding concern expressed in the meeting was: "We need to assure people that we are not selling out." One of the members asked: "Can we be certain that the present Soviet position in our favour will hold?"[(124)]

Oliver Tambo insisted that negotiations and the armed struggle were not mutually exclusive. In his opinion there was both the capacity and the resources to intensify the armed struggle, "and our friends (including the Soviet Union) must accept this. It must be real armed struggle".[125] Tambo thought that the regime was not yet ready for talks and so talks had to be postponed. He warned against self-appointed brokers, and reminded his comrades about the "incredible pressure" the Front Line States put on the Patriotic Front of Zimbabwe in 1979.[126]

However, the ANC itself was now rapidly moving towards a negotiating position. At the National Working Committee meeting on 14 May 1989 the possibility of the suspension of armed actions was touched upon. The ANC NWC confirmed that the cessation of violence was an issue, and not a precondition, for talks. But there was also a proposal that the ANC should call for a moratorium on armed actions for three or four months, from, say, September 1989, if the regime agreed to unban the organisation, lift the State of Emergency, and meet some other conditions. "The effect would be to put the ball in the enemy's court." The ANC leadership discussed the possibilities for a broad package of preliminary arrangements as an approach to talks, including a control mechanism and the involvement of outside parties.

Pointing to the Namibian experience, Oliver Tambo underlined that the talks there coincided with a certain level of the armed struggle for independence.

Towards the end of 1989 an interesting initiative was brought to our attention by the South African Foundation through the newly established office of the Social Democratic Friedrich Ebert Foundation in Moscow. Anticipating that difficulties would arise in the coming talks, the Foundation suggested forming a small group of international figures, well known to both the ANC and the South African government. My name was proposed by the Soviet side. However, until the very end of the negotiations in March-April 1994 Pretoria refused to agree to any international assistance or mediation, and the ANC conceded this. The initiative was therefore stillborn, though it could perhaps have served a useful purpose.

It would be wrong to imagine that the process of Soviet policy making towards South Africa was engineered by a small group, isolated in the Kremlin, or in the CPSU Headquarters on the Staraya Ploshchad ("Old Square"). The International Department, which was primarily responsible for South African policy until the end of the 1980s, sought to involve a broad range of specialists. A regular "situation analysis" was held, involving both academics and experts from governmental and non-governmental organisations.

At such a meeting at the end of June 1989 there was a wide spectrum of opinions, not only among researchers, but among state officials as well. One diplomat who became popular among South African "Sovietologists" even tried to convince the meeting that the apartheid system should not be abolished, because the white minority power guaranteed the preservation of the highly developed South African economy and the Afrikaner nation. "Why do we need black majority rule? What progress of humanity? There are dangerous tendencies in the ANC, an age-long envy of the rich ... Why do we reject a variant, proposed by the National Party? The ANC is longing for power, but it does not have a programme. The assurances that they do not want to push whites into the sea are not substantiated." Chris Hani had good reason to worry about some individuals in the Soviet Foreign Ministry.

Even though the diplomat was speaking in his private capacity, most of the participants, including his direct superiors, were astonished. But he was not entirely alone in his views. An apparent expert from another government department characterised the ANC as a narrow exile organisation. In his opinion, none of the "Lusaka leadership" of the ANC would join a future South African government; in fact, he proclaimed, "they don't want to return."

What was behind such total ignorance? Unfortunately, the number of Soviets who dealt directly with the ANC was limited, both in Moscow and in the African capitals. Officials increasingly relied on the Western and South African media. And those who worked abroad were sometimes influenced by discussions with Western diplomats and casual meetings with whites from South Africa.

However, the general conclusions of the meeting were sound. It was expected that during future talks the ANC would have to make considerable concessions, but it would try to do this without sacrificing its major principles. Compromise solutions could be found, and the ANC demand for majority rule could be accepted but realised step by step. That is almost exactly what happened when the

355

Government of National Unity was installed in South Africa. It was also stated that the principle of a united South Africa did not exclude, especially during the transition period, elements of federalism. Again, the forecast was realistic. The opinion of most of the participants was that "It is difficult to imagine better tactics than the ANC now follows." The meeting concluded that the initiatives by Pretoria to establish relations with the USSR were primarily driven by its need to end political isolation and economic sanctions, and to use Moscow as an instrument for pressurising the ANC and the Mass Democratic Movement. Similarly, some forces in the West wished to exploit the "Soviet card". "We should not agree to play such a role, allotted to us by the West and by the RSA, we must have our own policy. By 'dropping' the ANC our country would not gain anything either in the economic or political field." Unfortunately this warning was soon disregarded by the outgoing leaders of the USSR and the incoming leaders of Russia.

Nevertheless, when Alfred Nzo came to Moscow at the end of June 1989 for a short visit, followed, as has been mentioned, by Oliver Tambo and Joe Slovo in July, their exchanges with Soviet representatives confirmed the congruence of views. When the ANC National Executive Committee met in June the prevailing view was to consider talks as a part of the struggle and not as a substitute for it. The ANC published a discussion paper on the issue of negotiations and suggested that its members debate the issue.

A draft paper spelling out the ANC position on possible talks was also prepared, to be kept confidential for the time being. The ANC's main idea was that the Front Line States should work on the basis of a paper drafted by the ANC and not on "Thatcher's one", as had happened during the Lancaster House Conference on Zimbabwe.

At the National Working Committee meeting on 29 July 1989 Oliver Tambo reported that, following authorisation from the NEC for him "to obtain comment on the [confidential] statement and to give it to (selected) people on a confidential basis and to seek their impact," the text was sent in particular to Nelson Mandela, Govan Mbeki, the leadership of the Mass Democratic Movement, Nyerere, Kaunda, Mugabe, and Masire. "Since then," Tambo continued, "we have received comment from the Soviet comrades but still not received [anything] from Havana."[127]

When Alfred Nzo and Simon Makana visited the International Department on 22 June, they asked us for our written opinion on the

ANC proposal, following a very lively and friendly discussion.[128] There was no time to report to the top leadership and to give an official response. As Nzo was leaving Moscow the next day, we drew up a report that night and called it "Informal notes by a friend", to reinforce its strictly preliminary and private nature.

While supporting the general thrust of the ANC draft and most of its concrete proposals, we nevertheless thought that some of them were too demanding. We were not sure, for example, whether it was realistic to install an Interim Government before general elections. (During the actual negotiations a middle position was found: the old government continued to function, but in several fields its activity was controlled by a Transitional Executive Council.)

The ANC document became the basis for the Harare Declaration of the OAU Ad Hoc Committee on Southern Africa, adopted on 21 August 1989 and later approved by the Conference of the Non-Aligned Movement and the UN.

The question remains: what happened in May and June 1989 to convince the ANC (and SACP) leaders that serious talks with Pretoria had become possible? Was it De Klerk's first moves as the leader of the National Party in February 1989 after P W Botha's resignation? Or was it information reaching them from Polsmoor Prison about Mandela's contacts with cabinet ministers?

The story of these contacts is graphically described in Nelson Mandela's autobiography *Long Walk to Freedom*, as well as in Allister Sparks's book *Tomorrow Is Another Country*.[129] There was an element of happenstance in the way contact between Minister of Justice Kobie Coetzee and Winnie Mandela was established: they chanced to speak while travelling on the same plane from Johannesburg to Cape Town. But contacts between Pretoria and Mandela (as well as between Pretoria and the ANC Headquarters in Lusaka) would have been established in any event. What really mattered was not the goodwill of one or other political figure, however important, but the development of the struggle, which led to growing pressure on the regime from inside and outside South Africa.

The regime quite obviously had its own agenda. They apparently hoped to soften Mandela by improving the conditions of his imprisonment. The information about that process worried at least some members of the ANC top leadership. Would Mandela, for so many years isolated from his comrades, be strong enough to resist the psychological pressure of people who were simultaneously his jailers

357

and his interlocutors? ANC friends sometimes shared these worries with us.

Neil Barnard admitted later that when Mandela was transferred in December 1988 to a kind of house arrest in Victor Verster Prison, the authorities "wanted him to be in a decent place where he could receive people and start playing the political role that we had in mind for him."[130]

Allister Sparks writes: "For four years before the rest of the world knew anything of it, the future of South Africa was being explored in secret conversations."[131] In Moscow we followed those developments step by step from late 1985 until July 1989, by which time the picture was clear. We kept the secrets of our friends and did not share them with the rest of the world.

Information about other meetings between members of the ANC leadership and Pretoria emissaries were reaching Moscow as well, although it was not always easy for us to distinguish between the discussions with liberal Afrikaner intellectuals and those with Neil Barnard's emissaries: sometimes the same people were involved. When information of such meetings first reached us I thought the reports were an exaggeration, but I was wrong. On the other hand, when members of the ANC leadership, Chris Hani in particular, expressed concern about meetings with Afrikaner intellectuals, they perhaps felt (or knew for sure) that the talks were moving beyond dialogue with the liberal opposition.

When Oliver Tambo and Joe Slovo came to Moscow to meet Mac Maharaj we had discussions with them on 11-12 July 1989. The meeting between P W Botha and Mandela had already taken place, on 5 July. But it was not yet clear to the ANC leaders what was behind it: was it an attempt by Botha to use Mandela in his power struggle against De Klerk, or a step towards Mandela's release? Tambo expected a statement from Mandela, but supposed that he was not in a position to make one. "Maybe he is not allowed to disclose anything? Maybe he himself was surprised by what they had told him?" the ANC President surmised.

The ANC leadership was aware that numerous meetings had taken place between Mandela and government representatives. Tambo mentioned about thirty or more. (According to Allister Sparks there were forty-seven.)[132] In his message to Tambo from prison, sent before his meeting with P W Botha and before Tambo's departure for Moscow, Mandela had promised his comrades to send more information, but there was clearly some delay.[133] The ANC President divulged to us the document stating Mandela's position, which Tambo had received the previous week from South Africa. He regarded this as Part One of Mandela's report. Mandela stressed that "no prisoner, irrespective of his status or influence, can conduct negotiations of this nature from prison ... The step I am taking should, therefore, not be seen as the beginning of actual negotiations between the government and the ANC. My task is a very limited one and that is to bring the country's two major political bodies to the negotiating table."[134]

Mandela clearly stated his position on the three issues which Pretoria tried to impose as preconditions for talks. Firstly, with regard to the armed struggle, he said, "We consider the armed struggle a legitimate form of self-defence against a morally repugnant system of government, which would not allow even peaceful forms of protest. It is more than ironical that it should be the government which demands that we should renounce violence. The government knows only too well that there is not a single political organisation in this country, inside or outside parliament, which can ever compare with the ANC in its total commitment to peaceful change ... It is perfectly clear on the facts that the refusal of the ANC to renounce violence is not the real problem facing the government. The truth is that the government is not yet ready for negotiations."[135]

Secondly, referring to the ANC's alliance with the SACP, Mandela declared that "No dedicated ANC member will ever heed the call to break with the SACP. We regard such a demand as a purely divisive government strategy. It is in fact a call on us to commit suicide. Which man of honour will ever desert a life-long friend among his people? Which opponent will ever trust such a treacherous freedom fighter? Yet this is what the government is in effect asking us to do: to desert our faithful allies. We will not fall into that trap."[136]

Finally Mandela said: "The government also accuses us of being agents of the Soviet Union. The truth is that the ANC is non-aligned, and welcomes support from both the east and west, from the Socialist and capitalist countries. The only difference, as we have explained on countless occasions before, is that the Socialist countries supply us with weapons, which the west refuses to give us."[137]

Apart from these political discussions, Tambo, Slovo and Maharaj requested further practical assistance, particularly in training ANC underground leaders and operatives, including those who would come illegally from inside South Africa. Assistance was also needed for the

359

return of Mac Maharaj and Ronnie Kasrils to South Africa. Tambo and Slovo requested us to help the ANC work on documentation, which involved producing reliable false documents and devices to camouflage messages. Nelson Mandela, a man of high integrity, was reluctant to deceive even prison officers. Still, some rather sophisticated hiding places in rather innocent goods were requested for better communications with him. This assistance and support for Operation Vula were given with the approval of the CPSU Secretariat during the period when the South African and Western media were feasting on rumours about the USSR abandoning the ANC.

Various ANC people came to us for advanced training. Most of the documents in the Moscow archives relating to assistance to the ANC have not yet been declassified. But there are declassified papers relating to this kind of work which are useful to quote from, for example, those relating to support for the Chilean Communist Party during General Pinochet's dictatorship (the words underlined were hand-written in the original document):

"1. To satisfy the request of the leadership of the Communist Party of Chile (CPC) and to receive in 1988 for a term up to three months 14 representatives of the CPC for training in methods of secret work (party technique, special photography, surveillance), who go from Chile or to Chile as messengers.

2. To entrust the International Department and the Administration of the CPSU CC with the reception and servicing of Chilean comrades and the USSR Committee of State Security [KGB] with their training, assistance in equipping and documenting.

3. The expenditure on travel of the Chilean comrades from the country of their residence to Moscow and from Moscow to Chile, their stay and equipping (including the expenditure in foreign currency), as well as other expenditures, connected with complying with the request of the leadership of the Communist Party of Chile is to be covered by the reserve in the Party budget."[138]

The archive contains a similar decision of the CC Secretariat on assistance to the Sudanese Communist Party, which was involved in resistance against a dictatorial regime. In that case, their reception, maintenance, and training were entrusted to the USSR Ministry of Defence, which covered all the expenses of their travel and stay in Moscow.[139] All such decisions were kept in a so-called "Special File", which contained the most sensitive documents. I will leave it to the reader to decide whether the relevant documents on South Africa differ much from this format.

Makana and I saw Tambo off at the Moscow international airport after his July 1989 visit. He was flying to London, then to Paris to participate in the celebration of the 200th anniversary of the French Revolution. Thereafter he planned to visit several African countries before flying to the Commonwealth Summit in Kuala Lumpur. Meanwhile, Soviet doctors were expecting him for a further check-up and treatment. At the end of 1988 he had a full cycle of treatment for the first time. This consisted of a couple of weeks in the Central Clinical Hospital (under a false name as he was anxious to avoid rumours around the deterioration of his health) and thirty days in Barvikha. His health improved greatly, but the doctors insisted that he should come back again after six months.

"There will be many Kuala Lumpurs," I said as I tried to convince him that he should follow the medical advice and return, while we were driving to the Sheremetyevo airport. He promised to do so in September, but in August, after travelling all over the Front Line States, in a small plane, soliciting support for the ANC draft of what would soon became the Harare Declaration, he had a serious stroke. Tambo was first taken to London and then transferred to a hospital in Sweden.

I am convinced that Oliver Tambo was a Christian socialist. During the last decades of his life he fully trusted his Communist colleagues in the ANC leadership, Joe Slovo in particular. Slovo described to me how, while in Barvikha after his election to SACP chairman in 1984, he and Tambo discussed the future prospects of the South African political organisations. Tambo welcomed Slovo's words that perhaps in the future the ANC and the SACP would merge in one organisation of a socialist character.

However, to the best of my knowledge, Tambo only once came out openly in favour of socialism. According to the Russian translation of his address to the Soviet Party Congress in 1971, he spoke about international socialist solidarity and said that the ANC was leading the masses towards the revolution for the overthrow of the fascist regime, the seizure of power and the building of a "socialist society".[140]

On several other occasions he made his Moscow interlocutors understand that his intentions went beyond the eradication of apartheid. During his last visit to the Kremlin in March 1989 Tambo spoke about the struggle for a national democratic revolution, the goal of which was political power, non-racialism, and an end to exploitation. "There are long-term goals as well," he acknowledged

361

and added, "we are not pushing them."[141]

I find the assertion by Breyten Breytenbach that Oliver Tambo "was completely protected by his Praetorian guard" ridiculous.[142] On the contrary, Tambo was too accessible. This was partly because of the tradition developed in exile while the ANC was still a relatively small body, but was mainly due to his warm-hearted nature.

As a result of the practical actions of the Soviet Union, especially in the first years of *perestroika*, Tambo was confident in his belief that he could rely on the USSR without sacrificing his convictions and his integrity in any way. Tambo always cherished his independence. It was not in his nature to serve as anybody's proxy or puppet.

The Harare Declaration was a major success for the ANC. It provided a sound basis for talks between the liberation movement and the regime on the ANC's terms, although some further concessions had later to be made by the ANC. This was no surprise, because the Declaration essentially reflected the positions of the ANC and the Front Line States.

Unfortunately at the very moment that the success of the ANC and its allies was becoming evident to the whole world, the first open disagreement occurred between the ANC and a Soviet official. The trigger was a *Pravda* article written by Boris Asoyan, who at that stage was a consultant in the African Department of the Ministry of Foreign Affairs.

Asoyan wrote about what he considered to be "the disunity and amorphousness of the anti-apartheid structures," and further claimed that over the previous eleven years "the colour of one's skin is losing significance as a determinant of economic life."[143] Joe Slovo criticised Asoyan, in the same newspaper, reminding him that 98% of the South African gross domestic output was the result of means of production owned and controlled by capitalists drawn exclusively from a white minority, which constituted less than 17% of the population. He also protested against the depiction of the ANC as merely one among many anti-apartheid forces, "just as the regime and Margaret Thatcher are endeavouring to do."[144] Asoyan had also described as "unexpected" the "decision by Pretoria to sit at the negotiating table with Angola and Cuba."[145] Slovo regarded this as "a tendency to obscure actual struggle." He emphasised that Cuito-Cuanavale marked a major shift in the balance of forces in the region and that that shift "delivered Pretoria to the negotiating table."[146]

Slovo questioned the reasoning behind Asoyan's "damaging detour", and asked: "Could it derive from an endeavour to force the South African reality into an abstract and universal strategic conception? We in the South African revolutionary movement greatly welcome the clearing in the world, to use Asoyan's words, of 'the mist of confrontation'. But the mist of universal conciliation can be equally damaging to correct analysis."[147]

Asoyan's article probably reflected Shevardnadze's line in the Ministry. By now Shevardnadze was a very different person from the enthusiastic young member of the Afro-Asian Solidarity Committee he once was, or from the CPSU leader who had headed a delegation to the Afro-Asian Solidarity Conference in Algeria in 1984, or even from the dynamic newly appointed minister.

Due to the changes in the Soviet political system many matters in the international field, previously dealt with by the CPSU, now became the domain of the Ministry of Foreign Affairs and other Ministers. Unfortunately these innovations, while well intentioned, were not accompanied by a redistribution of responsibilities within the state machinery, or the creation of relevant structures within Gorbachev's office. The result was a serious lack of co-ordination in the making and carrying out of Soviet foreign policy.

Persistent attempts to influence the Foreign Ministry line on South Africa were undertaken by Ambassador Vassily Solodovnikov, then back at the Russian Academy of Sciences. He sent several letters to Shevardnadze. In the first of them in September 1989 he wrote that Africans could hardly understand why, on the one hand, *perestroika* was characterised as a revolutionary process yet, on the other hand, South Africans, who stood against the apartheid system, were advised to strive not for revolution but for evolution and the reform of apartheid. He warned that while the USSR's contradictory attitude *vis-à-vis* the ANC had not yet led to an open and unavoidable clash, there was a danger that this could happen.

Another problem at this time was the nature of the ANC's relationship with its cadres being trained and educated in the USSR. The ANC leaders were so preoccupied with both the intensification of the struggle and the talks about talks in the late 1980s that they did not have the time to make regular visits to the ANC members scattered throughout the USSR. True, Ronnie Kasrils went to Ulyanovsk, and Chris Hani visited Minsk, but some of the ANC groups would go for three or four years without seeing any of their leaders from Headquarters. Meanwhile general demoralisation and deterioration of conditions of life in the Soviet Union affected them as well, though the situation differed from place to place. For example, while the Umkhonto members were praised in the Naval Academy in Baku, Makana found "a very sad and disturbing catalogue of repeated acts of indiscipline and general disorder" in Frunze.[148] He was specifically worried about the South Africans engaging in speculation: "The authorities explained that it is becoming a general disease affecting all sorts of people, local and foreign. Finally solution lies in political explanations to and careful selection of candidates. Discipline is generally declining among foreigners there. It is not only ANC cadres involved ... Once more the question of the visits of all these areas by the leaders was emphasised. Whatever they do cannot replace the role of the ANC/MK leadership."[149]

The release of prominent political prisoners in October 1989, including Walter Sisulu and all the Rivonia trialists except Mandela, was a clear confirmation that the government was being pushed to negotiate on conditions previously set by the ANC. There was a striking difference from the earlier experience of Govan Mbeki when, as the eldest of the Rivonia group, he was released in 1987 and Pretoria severely restricted his activities. The new batch of ex-prisoners immediately involved themselves in the mass actions of the MDM. Mandela's contacts with Pretoria were continuing, but he was now in a position to communicate with the rest of the ANC leadership through political channels and not only through his family, lawyers and other occasional visitors. In December 1989 Alfred Nzo and Thabo Mbeki were guests at the ZANU-PF congress, which completed the process of the merger of this party with ZAPU. I witnessed their excitement on receiving a message that Cyril Ramaphosa and Sidney Mafumadi, who had just visited Mandela at Victor Verster, were coming to meet the ANC leadership as Mandela's special representatives.

Pretoria proposed three options to Mandela: that he be allowed to visit Lusaka to confer with his comrades (an idea he liked), or that ANC Executive members whose security would be guaranteed be brought to South Africa for discussions with him, or that a meeting be organised in a "neutral place". However, Mandela proposed that his comrades in exile should not hurry to make a decision until Walter Sisulu and other released leaders had come to Lusaka to discuss the whole matter. Mandela was under the impression that there could be a dramatic development that included his own release.[150]

Thabo Mbeki and Aziz Pahad, who were heavily involved in talks about talks with informal emissaries of the South African government, flew to Moscow from Paris in December 1989 to discuss matters. Travelling in the other direction, two professors from Moscow – Apollon Davidson and Irina Filatova – became the first Soviet academics to visit South Africa at the invitation of IDASA. They participated in the Conference for a Democratic Future in South Africa in December 1989. The Soviet visitors were well received in anti-government circles as the trip had been discussed in advance with the ANC in Lusaka and, through it, with the internal Mass Democratic Movement.

Mac Maharaj returned to Moscow on his way back home on 9 January 1990. A week later Ronnie Kasrils followed him. This time they stayed in the special flat where the Chilean Communist leader Luis Corvalan had also stayed earlier before going home, also in disguise and with false documents.

Others who visited Moscow in January 1990 were Ivan Pillay and, towards the end of the month, Alfred Nzo and Joe Slovo. These two left on 2 February for Stockholm to meet with Oliver Tambo, Walter Sisulu, and the other released prisoners, who had gone to confer with the ANC President. In the VIP hall of the Sheremetyevo airport they were told of the unbanning of their organisations by Jonathan Steel, correspondent of the *Guardian* and an old friend of Joe Slovo and his assassinated wife Ruth First. Steel had rushed in for an interview with the ANC leaders.

Ellis and "Sechaba" commented: "The unbanning of the SACP and the ANC came as a surprise to the exiled leaders of both organisations ... The fact that the Communist Party was caught unawares threw it off balance."[151] Even such a thoughtful and experienced writer as Allister Sparks followed suit and wrote about De Klerk's speech: "This time the surprise was an announcement that went beyond anybody's expectations."[152]

Yet for us in Moscow, more than ten thousand kilometres from Cape Town, 2 February 1990 was not a surprise. On the evening of 1 February, the eve of the opening of the session of parliament, we had a long discussion with Joe Slovo. I had some doubts that the SACP would be unbanned along with the ANC, but its General Secretary was confident that it would be.

The situation in South Africa changed dramatically on 2 February 1990. "Should we cancel the booking?" I asked Mac jokingly, when the news of De Klerk's speech came. The ANC and the SACP were unbanned, the release of Mandela was secured, but the political process was far from irreversible. So Mac left "to go back to the sanatorium in the Crimea". His legend was maintained even while he spent some time with his family in Britain: we would remind all ANC and SACP members coming to Moscow that the doctors were insisting on his speedy return to the sanatorium.

Ronnie Kasrils also left for London and then flew to Moscow again "on his way to Vietnam". His legend was also of a "medical nature": a car crash in Vietnam was supposed to have incapacitated him for many months. In fact, he was expected to spend some time in Moscow for additional preparation. But the situation at home demanded his presence and he "left for Hanoi" earlier than expected.

The expanding (though still preliminary) contacts between the ANC and Pretoria in this period are vividly described in Allister Sparks's book. And again it proves that the regime's knowledge of the ANC was rather limited. Sparks describes how during the first (clandestine) meeting of the heads of the National Intelligence Service with the ANC representatives in Switzerland "with whispers and sideways glances Louw [then Deputy Head of the National Intelligence Service] pointed out to Barnard who was who at the ANC table. Only Nhlanhla had them stymied: the NIS men had no idea who he was."[153] Sparks himself describes Nhlanhla as "one of the guerrilla commanders". Perhaps it is expecting too much of the NIS bosses that they should know the face of a guerrilla commander, but Joe Nhlanhla had in fact been at the helm of the ANC Department of Intelligence and Security for two years by then. The saying "it takes one to know one" clearly did not apply here. Mike Louw had a good chance to improve his knowledge later; as the Head of a new South African Secret Service he was directly subordinate to Nhlanhla, Deputy Minister for Intelligence Services.

On the eve of Ronnie's departure, on 20 March, two prominent members of the ANC Executive came to Moscow on their way to

Havana. They described to us the rapidly changing situation: Jacob Zuma was leaving for South Africa the next day at a head of the ANC forward group to prepare for the arrival of the top leadership. Joe Nhlanhla was supposed to join the group the following week. Our discussion took longer than I expected. I needed to phone Ronnie. I spoke to him in Russian, as if I was calling my family. Compounding my problems was the fact that both comrades were Soviet graduates and understood Russian perfectly. Both of them were heavily involved in sensitive ANC matters and they probably knew about Kasrils's mission, but nonetheless we strictly followed the secrecy rules established earlier by Tambo and Slovo.

When I finally left them to join Kasrils at his special flat, even the bar at the hotel had closed and, contrary to Russian tradition, Ronnie and I had only a cup of tea to serve as "one for the road".

Because Kasrils was well known in the movement for his adventures, there was a feeling that his legend would be suspect. To strengthen it Ronnie suggested that his wife Eleanor also be "sent to Vietnam". This time Makana was involved from the very beginning. He dispatched a message to his London counterpart, Mendi Msimang, that Ronnie's condition was so serious that it required his wife's presence and that the Soviets were ready to organise her trip. Later in Moscow, Eleanor described to me how she nearly fainted when Msimang informed her of the accident, even though she already knew that it was not true. To match the timetable of flights to Hanoi, Eleanor spent some time in Moscow and even visited Leningrad. We invited a comrade from the International Department, who had worked in Hanoi, to brief her on all the details: the name of the Vietnamese Party hotel, the venue of the hospital, etc. Fortunately, some Vietnamese handicraft could also be bought in Moscow.

However, all the efforts to make the legend believable became superfluous when the first meeting of the ANC and government delegations took place at Groote Schuur in Cape Town in May 1990.

A new message came from Lusaka:

"(1) Ben [Mac's code name during the second phase of his underground activity]:

1.1. Ben is exiting again. Will you please arrange visa and ticket for Mr [Mac Maharaj] to be collected at ...

(2) Daniel [Ronnie Kasrils]

2.1. I am awaiting Daniel's parcels and photos ..."[154]

"Daniel" was soon withdrawn, however, but the rest of the

367

underground machinery remained intact.

Mac had a habit of giving one heart failure. After getting a message that he was due to visit Moscow again I found his (false) name on the airline computer, but he had changed his flight, arriving a day earlier than expected. Fortunately he knew the way to the ANC office and I had to rush there after his call. Ronnie's trip back, by a different route, also involved some difficulty. After arriving in Moscow his beard was soon dispensed with and he was no longer the successful businessman, but his old self again. However, he often forgot to limp. Besides, an excuse for his speedy recovery was needed and the only passable explanation was an Oriental miracle cure.

Wynand Malan, a former leader of the Democratic Party, also unwittingly became part of the legend and I am afraid we still owe him something of an apology. He was in Moscow during Ronnie's departure for London, and their respective flights practically coincided. So, supporting himself with a stick, Ronnie had to walk with great difficulty into the VIP hall at the airport. It was not so expensive to support revolution in those days: I bought that stick for just 1 Rouble and 25 Kopecks.

Wynand Malan, incidentally, was very realistic in his assessment of developments in South Africa. He expected (in June 1990) that the process of political settlement in South Africa would take four years. Malan felt that it would be wrong for the Soviet Union to establish bilateral relations with Pretoria. South Africa, he believed, should not be regarded as a state, because that would mean the recognition of the legality of the regime. The situation was one of "a number of parties trying to create a state," Malan said.[155]

The attempts to drive a wedge between the Soviet Union and the ANC intensified at the time of the ANC's unbanning. *The Star* newspaper in Johannesburg wrote on 19 January 1990: "In private discussions Soviet leaders have increased pressure on the ANC."[156] That was wrong: there were no "private discussions" whatsoever between the Soviet leaders and the ANC. And as far as official meetings were concerned, I was present at all of those held in Moscow for almost a decade, and I can testify that "pressure" was never put on the ANC.

This also applied to meetings between Shevardnadze and top ANC leaders. Shevardnadze met Mandela in Windhoek during the Namibian independence celebrations and confirmed an invitation for Mandela to visit the Soviet Union. That meeting was preceded by a lengthy discussion on 20 March 1990 in Lusaka between Shevardnadze and a group of ANC leaders, including Alfred Nzo, Joe Slovo, and Thabo Mbeki. In response to the Soviet Foreign Minister's suggestion that we "consult, talk and co-ordinate our actions,"[157] Thabo Mbeki made the ANC's position clear, warning against negative changes in Soviet policy: "We want the USSR to be a leader of anti-apartheid forces. That position should not be compromised ... The USSR should continue to be seen as not beginning to establish links with a system on its way out ... We wouldn't want a negative perception of the USSR among our people."[158]

Shevardnadze assured the ANC leaders of the continuation of Soviet assistance and agreed with them about the necessity of close co-operation during the negotiation process: "We would be ready to work with you on all of this. I think there must be a special person in our Foreign Ministry who would be in charge of contacts with our friends, in this matter. A person with whom you will be able to consult at any time ... We are ready to work with you in your revolutionary work." Referring to material aid, he confirmed that "the obligations we have pledged we will fulfil."[159]

When the Soviet Foreign Minister requested their opinion, the ANC representatives did not object to Shevardnadze's meeting with De Klerk: "President de Klerk will probably want to see me. Should I see him? Should I refrain? I would like to have some mandate."[160] The meeting with De Klerk took place in Windhoek and De Klerk did his best to convince Shevardnadze that he was ready for serious talks on a political settlement and the eradication of apartheid.

In conversation with the ANC leaders, Shevardnadze also hinted at the possibility of a permanent presence of Soviet diplomats in South Africa, which, however, he directly connected with the impending transference of the ANC Headquarters there: "Given you are transferring your offices we will have to think of new channels ... After your transfer we will have to think again. Some formal link without establishing formal relations."[161] There were no objections from the ANC side.

But, in spite of Shevardnadze's assurances, at the very time when several decades of anti-apartheid struggle were bearing fruit, Soviet relations with the ANC and its allies started to cool and even to deteriorate. First of all, serious administrative problems arose. For many years relations with the ANC had been conducted mainly through the CPSU and the Soviet Afro-Asian Solidarity Committee.

369

Now the Foreign Ministry officials had that responsibility. With the exception of some who had worked in the Front Line States, the Foreign Ministry people had limited experience in dealing with the ANC. Their specialisation in inter-governmental relations did not help them understand the complexity of the struggle in South Africa. As Joe Slovo put it once, "Soviet diplomats may have their heart in the right place, but they look at South Africa as at a chess board where some politicians were playing; they don't understand the role of the mass struggle."[162]

Besides these practical administrative factors, there were also more serious political reasons. The ongoing general change in the stance of Gorbachev and his collaborators led to talk of "de-ideologisation" of almost everything, from the economy through to international relations. Talk about the supremacy of "universal human values" became a camouflage for the process of "re-ideologisation" and the uncritical acceptance of Western values both in internal and external policies.

Economics was another factor in the changing relationship. Since the economic situation in the USSR was rapidly deteriorating, "the interests of national economy" started to become key words when choosing international partners. However, more often than not, these words tended to be used to conceal cover-ups for the narrow interests of groups of officials and emerging businessmen. In the case of South Africa, this approach was detrimental. "The interests of national economy" were used as a pretext for the violation or at least the relaxation of sanctions, when a better approach would have been to prepare for multifaceted co-operation in the future, once sanctions were removed.

The transfer of the ANC Headquarters to Johannesburg by mid 1990 created serious problems in communications. Contrary to Shevardnadze's promises and though some officials of the Foreign Ministry worked hard at trying to keep contact with the ANC, no "special person" was appointed to maintain channels of communication. Instead of consultations with the ANC, at best the ANC was informed about the diplomatic initiatives and actions, and that rather briefly. During this period American diplomats often gave the ANC a more detailed (though biased) version of their discussions with Moscow concerning South Africa than that provided by the Soviet Ministry of Foreign Affairs.

At the same time the South African government and local pro-government groups were working energetically (and often successfully) at exerting an influence on some Soviet individuals. Thus, after visiting the country at the invitation of the South African Institute of Race Relations, Vladimir Tikhomirov insisted in his report to the Africa Institute that "the ANC-UDF-MDM bloc" was much weaker organisationally than Inkatha, the BCM and even the PAC, and that in many places "charterists" were in the minority. "It is especially clearly seen in the second half of 1989 and in 1990 ... In the near future the ANC can lose its leading role among blacks," he declared.

In discussions with Soviet academics, journalists and even government officials, we had to warn them, sometimes repeatedly, against adopting a paternalistic attitude towards the ANC. We told them that the ANC knew its interests better than Soviets could. Unfortunately some of the Soviet scholars, who made reports to international conferences or met with foreign counterparts in bilateral discussions, had little competence in these matters. The picture some of them gave of Soviet policy sometimes bordered on the ridiculous. We used to joke: "It's the job of the academics to deceive the enemy about our real intentions."

However, as unprofessional and as biased as such researchers and journalists were, their ideas were reaching the ears of the Soviet "establishment", especially those who were sceptical about the ANC, and reflected increasingly the mood in Moscow: ANC methods of struggle, particularly armed actions, contradicted the new fashionable theories of a "non-violent world" advanced by Gorbachev and his coterie of assistants, especially Shevardnadze and Yakovlev.

In a speech to the UN General Assembly in September 1989 Shevardnadze pledged "to oppose ... resolutely all kinds of violence, no matter what had caused or motivated it."[163] The old South African hands in Moscow tried hard to counteract such statements.

During the last years of Gorbachev's rule an illusion was spread in Moscow academic and political circles that all major world problems could be solved by an agreement between Moscow and Washington. Proposals to guarantee jointly a political settlement in South Africa, including the rights of whites, were advanced. Trying to show the fallacy of this approach, I published an article, which I began with a quotation from Pallo Jordan's paper on Soviet-South African relations: "If today it appears that a negotiated settlement is likely, this owes more to the struggles waged by the South African people than to the strategies devised by policy-makers in either Moscow or Washington."

371

I criticised Shevardnadze's statement, as well as Alexander Yakovlev's absolutisation of "non-violence": "I believe it is equally dangerous for revolutionaries to make an absolute of violence (but at any rate neither the ANC nor the SACP can be accused of this) and to rule out even now any possibility of its use in response to violence from the authorities ... It would be an error to view new political thinking as the rejection of all the old forms and methods, as well as the policies pursued in the past, say prior to April 1985."[164]

Shevardnadze's lack of respect for the ANC's opinion was glaringly demonstrated when in August 1990 he gave his approval for a visit to the USSR by a delegation headed by Kent Durr, South African Minister of Trade, Industry and Commerce. Though such a visit constituted a very serious breach of the boycott policy, the issue was not discussed with either the CPSU leadership or the USSR parliament; it was, in fact, virtually hidden from both of them. Instead of the consultations (promised earlier by Shevardnadze) with the ANC, a message, purely for-your-information, was sent to them at the last moment, when it was in any event too late.

This delegation was invited to the USSR by the Ekoprom, a consortium of state-owned enterprises, dealing with environmental problems. The government press-agency, TASS, reported that South African firms had offered "to provide technology and equipment for emergency measures to clean up after the [Chernobyl nuclear] disaster."[165]

TASS reported that the delegation toured Kiev, the Chernobyl nuclear power station, and "surrounding areas". Yet in reality the South Africans also visited the Kirovsky machine-building factory in Leningrad (to investigate the potential for co-operation in the automobile industry) and even famous resorts on the faraway Black Sea coast (where the Soviet hosts tried to induce them to become involved in a major construction project for a tourist hotel).

The South African press reports about the visit only footnoted the discussions with the Ekoprom people, who had extended the invitation.[166] The emphasis was put on Durr's discussions "with ministers" in Moscow. Durr did meet a couple of ministers, though not of the Soviet government, but of the government of the Russian Federation, formed by Boris Yeltsin in the summer of 1990 after his election to the post of Chairman of the Russian Supreme Soviet. Thus a "Russian card" began to be played by Pretoria in dealing with the Soviet Union. While in Moscow, Durr invited some twenty people, including Yeltsin's Minister of Foreign Economic Affairs (and then close confidant) Victor Yaroshenko, to make a reciprocal visit to South Africa.

Another attractive aspect of Durr's visit was a promise to assist in building three townships, one in each republic, affected by the Chernobyl disaster: the Ukraine, Russia and Belarus, on very favourable terms (at least $ 300 million soft credit for 20 years). It became clear, however, that Chernobyl was little more than an excuse for Durr and some of his Soviet counterparts to touch on wider issues. Durr himself described his visit as "opening the gates to Eastern Europe", vital because South Africa "had no other way" of doing it.[167]

Simon Makana had good reason to state at a meeting at the CPSU International Department in October 1990: "Something is cooking behind our backs." The visit of the Director General of the Department of Foreign Affairs, Neil van Heerden, in July 1990 was one such case. Officially he was supposed to be in Moscow only in transit to Tokyo, but the South African press immediately blew it up. The ANC was only informed at the last moment. "What happened to geography?" asked Makana. "Why is the way to Japan via Moscow?"[168]

A delegation from Ekoprom visited South Africa on a reciprocal visit in November-December 1990. This time at least some damage-control measures were taken. The delegation met the ANC leadership in Johannesburg to explain the purpose of its visit and to secure the ANC's support for the proposed involvement of South African companies in the Chernobyl zone projects. But some forces within the Russian government tried to use this visit to make a "breakthrough" in dealings with South Africa. Yaroshenko planned to lead the delegation, but at the last moment the Russian government decided to cancel his trip on the insistence of the USSR Foreign Ministry. Meanwhile the South African press had already been informed that the Russian Minister had arrived at Jan Smuts airport, "heading an official Soviet trade delegation." The Zimbabwean *Sunday Mail* newspaper pointed to the violation of the UN boycott.[169] The actual head of the delegation, Andrei Chernukhin, was promoted by the press to the "Soviet Ministers' Council".[170] At the end of the day, all Durr's promises remained paper proposals, but Pretoria had scored a propaganda victory.

In February 1991 a group of "Russian businessmen", headed by the so-called "Director General of the Moscow-based International Projects Centre", visited South Africa for talks with Pik Botha and some other high officials. The "Director General" said in an interview that the Russian Federation was not under the same constraints as the Soviet government when it came to sanctions against South Africa: "The Russian government has never voted for sanctions."[171] This statement was, of course, welcomed by the South African establishment. The visitors even discussed with the Mayor of Pretoria the question of Moscow becoming a twin city with the South African capital. The delegation had no mandate from the Moscow City authorities to discuss any such issue, and the USSR Foreign Ministry officials were not able to trace an "International Projects Centre" in Moscow.

An important (and controversial) development in Soviet-South African relations during this period was the signing of a five-year deal on the sale of Soviet diamonds to De Beers. A direct agreement was concluded with De Beers (or, to be technically precise, with the Swiss-registered subsidiary De Beers Centenary) for the first time in almost thirty years. The agreement was criticised on various fronts. The Russian government protested that a billion-dollar deal was closed without its participation. Besides, many experts believed that this arrangement was not profitable for the USSR and that all it did was strengthen the Oppenheimers' monopoly. The agreement caused concern in the South African liberation movement as well. We could sense this when the COSATU delegation, which included Jay Naidoo and Alec Erwin, who are both now ministers, came to Moscow in September 1990.[172]

Valery Rudakov, who for many years was the head of "Glavalmazzoloto" (Main Department of Diamonds and Gold, a kind of mini-Ministry, directly subordinate to the USSR Government), virtually admitted in October 1990 that, even after the introduction of sanctions in 1963, Soviet diamonds still went to the same old destination. The diamonds were no longer sold through the London branch of De Beers, as in previous years; now they went to the "City West East Limited" company, registered in London. Rudakov said: "I quite assume that a part of our diamonds could get to the Central Trading Organisation through that firm."[173] He was equivocating: he and his associates had known all along about the involvement of De Beers in the London-registered company.

When the public controversy over "the deal of the century" broke, I phoned Rudakov and insisted on a briefing from his organisation. He sent to my office two of the "culprits", Igor Gorbunov, the head of the Almazyuvelirexport, a selling branch of the Glavalmazzoloto, and his Deputy. They did their best to convince me that the agreement with De Beers was the greatest thing that had ever happened. However, when we then met other officials, who were trying to develop the diamond-finishing process in the USSR, a different picture emerged. They explained in detail how De Beers manipulated prices. They claimed *inter alia* that the so-called independent dealers who came to Moscow every year to buy five percent of the Soviet stockpile of diamonds (so that the Soviets could check whether De Beers prices were fair or not) were very often De Beers proxies.

The diamond business has always been a highly secretive matter in the USSR. It was only recently made public that several attempts had been made to break the grip De Beers had on the Soviet diamond industry, but that all had failed. Nikolay Ryzhkov, the former Prime Minister, revealed that once, in early 1989, the government gave authority "to sell a small lot of diamonds, sidelining De Beers ... To tell the truth, we wanted to check to what extent De Beers 'swindled' us. But the company quickly caught us. As soon as we sold diamonds ... the company representative protested to our Ambassador. We had to settle this affair."[174]

Steps taken by researchers to organise a better cutting and finishing process for the Soviet diamonds were stopped, too. Strangely, a laboratory set up for this purpose was based in room N 626 of the editorial office of *Pravda* newspaper, under the patronage of its Editor-in-Chief Victor Afanasyev, and not in the responsible state organisation. Perhaps it was precisely that circumstance that allowed the laboratory to function unhindered for several years. Afanasyev explained later that specialists on the systemic analyses and theories of operations were trying to stop this "refined and prodigious ... form of robbery" of the USSR's natural resources by De Beers.[175] The *Pravda* group made hundreds of "electronic models" for diamond-cutting. After a successful experiment Afanasyev reported to the Politbureau, and Gorbachev ordered that the matter be followed up. But, as Afanasyev put it, "the Oppenheimer brothers sniffed out about our work. One of them came to Moscow. He was honoured to be received by the President. The incident, so to say, was settled." When Afanasyev resigned as Editor of *Pravda* in late 1989, "the laboratory was immediately disbanded."[176]

The De Beers protests undoubtedly carried additional weight because the company was (and remains) highly sophisticated in public relations. Only months earlier Nicholas Oppenheimer donated a large sum of money to the Soviet Culture Fund, of which Raissa Gorbacheva was a Board member. A sum of 300 000 dollars was mentioned in the Moscow press.[177] This money was used for hosting and entertaining

Fund officials on their visits to London.

As for the 1990 agreement, the official in the African Department of the Soviet Foreign Ministry who initialled the deal turned out to be the same person who had been worried about the prospects of the elimination of apartheid at the workshop referred to earlier. He later had his wife appointed to a highly paid post in the De Beers office in Moscow.

The true story of the Soviet relationship with De Beers is still to be told in full. It was revealed, for example, that in April 1984 a group of mid-level USSR government officials prepared an analysis of the Soviet export of diamonds and precious metals for the then Prime Minister Nikolay Tikhonov. They made "a systematic study of the operations of Israel, NATO and the RSA on bleeding the USSR economy and rendering it financially lifeless through the annual mass buying up of Soviet gold, diamonds and platina by the Oppenheimers' transnational De Beers Company." The 1984 report severely criticised "the export of gold, diamonds and platina into the same hands – to "Oppenheimer's TNC" for 25 years. The conclusion was shocking: "In the present regime of the interaction of the monetary financial systems of the USSR and of the other side, the USSR will be able to exist normally economically, independently from the West for not more that 20 years."[178]

This sensational report was studied and resolutely rejected by top government officials, including the Minister of Finance, the Chairman of the State Bank, and the President of the Academy of Sciences. The main reason for this was not the financial implications of the paper but the political conclusions: the authors connected De Beers not so much with South Africa as with "World Zionism" and Israel. Unfortunately the CPSU officials who dealt with South Africa and the Middle East were never informed of this report. Had they known of it, perhaps the grain in it could have been separated from the chaff, and proper decisions could have been taken.

END DAYS: MANDELA-VISIT MUDDLES, MILITARY MATTERS AND THE DISINTEGRATION OF THE SOVIET UNION

By mid 1990 another disturbing issue surfaced in the relations between the USSR and the ANC: the question of Nelson Mandela's visit to Moscow. Mandela's release on 11 February 1990 was, of course, greeted in the Soviet Union with deep satisfaction. A draft message to this effect, prepared in advance, was immediately sent by the International Department to Gorbachev's office. But apparently it was not of the highest priority to his staff, and the message was approved and made public only two days later.

An invitation "on behalf of the USSR leadership" for Mandela to visit the USSR and a message of congratulations from Gorbachev were sent to him via the Soviet Ambassador in Lusaka and the ANC Headquarters there. When we received the final version of the message from Gorbachev's office we noticed that a paragraph of the original draft prepared by us had been omitted. It was a reasonably significant one: "I hope to meet you in Moscow soon." It appears that that line was crossed out not by Gorbachev himself but by one of his assistants.

A delegation of the Soviet Afro-Asian Solidarity Committee, headed by Vassily Solodovnikov, a well-known figure in Southern Africa, went to Lusaka to greet Mandela. Mandela warmly acknowledged the Soviet Union's support of the ANC's armed struggle, though, he was quick to add, both the ANC and the USSR would always have preferred a political solution. "We in the ANC believe," he said, "that the Soviet Union will support us at the present crucial stage of the struggle."[(179)]

In April 1990 Mandela was awarded the Lenin Peace Prize, but unfortunately he has never had the opportunity to receive it. We regarded his visit to the Soviet Union as a matter of the highest priority. Simon Makana, the ANC representative in Moscow, reported as follows to the ANC on 11 April 1990: "A few days ago I met the local cdes. Their main interest was to find out if cde Mandela's programme will allow some space for him to come in this direction. But their appeal is that HQ should indicate in good time for them to prepare."[(180)]

But confusion followed: first, ANC Headquarters suggested dates at

378

the beginning of June that virtually coincided with Gorbachev's visit to the USA. Then, the Soviet side proposed mid September, but all of Mandela's foreign visits for that month had been cancelled. Then the ANC suggested October, but at the last moment it was found that the time was not suitable. In his message Gorbachev had proposed that a final date be jointly determined before the end of 1990, but this did not happen. After further planning the ANC announced that the visit would take place at the end of May 1991. Unfortunately in each case the ANC officials were over-hasty in announcing the dates of the visits before confirmation from Moscow had been received. When this visit too was postponed, an emotional dimension was added to the problem.

Elements in both South Africa and the Soviet Union tried to use the postponements of Mandela's visit to aggravate relations between the USSR and the ANC. Tikhomirov (distorting the facts) wrote: "The visit of Nelson Mandela, contemplated for last June-July [1990] was postponed because he decided to prolong his tour to the United States."[181]

Although valid reasons were given by Moscow for Gorbachev's failure to meet Mandela, the main reason for the delay of over eighteen months was simply that Gorbachev and his close advisers were concentrating their foreign activity on a limited number of (mostly Western) wealthy countries in the hope they would get meaningful support for their "reforms".

Anatoly Chernyaev, Gorbachev's assistant for international affairs, later wrote: "Gorbachev had a kind of good nose for the persons who had no prospects and were 'useless for us' ... He 'froze' his meeting with Mandela, though both academics and Foreign Ministry officials (true, with some resistance from my side) more than once argued wordily that it must be done: that one [Mandela] travelled all over the world, everywhere – at the highest level – and yet could not come to Moscow! Gorbachev did not believe that by feeding up the ANC and supplying it with arms we were assisting the correct process in the RSA. He did not stop it 'automatically', he had no time to do it. And he realised that it was one thing to receive Mandela even in Washington and another thing in 'red' Moscow, suspected of the expansion of communism."[182]

Gorbachev's nose was apparently not so good after all: Mandela soon became a President of world stature and Gorbachev an ex-President. Chernyaev's story is a typical attempt to improve on history. In reality, as we have seen, Gorbachev supported virtually all the ANC's requests in the first years of his rule, whether they were political or military. Far from curtailing assistance, he warmly received Oliver Tambo in "red" Moscow in 1986, when Reagan's anti-Soviet delirium was still high. And in 1990-1, when the issue of Mandela's visit arose, nobody could possibly have suspected Gorbachev of promoting the "expansion of communism".

The traditional anti-Communist card was once again played by Pretoria, and particularly by Pik Botha, when the security police, to its utter surprise, uncovered the existence of Vula in July 1990. Arrests of underground operatives, including Siphiwe Nyanda, followed. Two of them, Charles Ndaba and Mbuso Tshabalala, who had unaccountably disappeared in Durban, were shot after refusing to cooperate with the police. Their bodies were wrapped in wire mesh, weighted down and tossed into the shark-infested river mouth.

The arrest of Mac Maharaj was an entirely vengeful act, the payback for Pretoria's inability to uncover his presence in South Africa any earlier. Ronnie Kasrils, Janet Love and some others were put on the "wanted" list by the South African Police. They were described as "armed and dangerous", a provocation to the public to use whatever means necessary to arrest them.

Some ANC activists were not happy with what they regarded as the tepid reaction on the part of the top ANC leadership to the Vula arrests. They attributed this to a kind of euphoria prevailing after the beginning of talks; they felt that some of the leading members were trying to distance themselves not only from Vula but also from the underground struggle in general.

Among those arrested by the police were people who had nothing whatever to do with the operation. The security forces overreacted when they managed to read information found on captured computer disks. Despite the arrests, contact between ANC Headquarters and the Vula underground machinery was re-established a week later. This machinery remained largely intact at a time when the Umkhonto structures inside the country were in a state of some disarray after the ANC top leadership reached an agreement with Pretoria in August 1990 which included the unilateral suspension of "armed actions and related activities". The formulation of the Pretoria Minute differed from the relevant clause of the Harare Declaration (which referred to "mutual cessation of hostilities"). The ANC's flexibility was regarded by Pretoria as a weakness. By December 1990 only a hundred of the three thousand political prisoners had been released; and the return of exiles had also been delayed.

Our co-operation with the ANC underground continued. A short message with greetings came to me from Ronnie Kasrils who was still underground. Ever an enthusiast of Military Combat Work, he added, "The three little words have been our safeguard."[183]

Ivan Pillay came to Moscow at the beginning of 1991 for medical treatment as well as discussions. Though Ronnie Kasrils had to remain underground, he managed to see Siphiwe Nyanda after his release on bail, to assess the damage. Joe Slovo tried to visit Mac Maharaj in hospital, dressed as a doctor, but was recognised and refused access to him.[184] In Moscow we were asked to help those who remained underground, especially with new disguises and identity documents. A bad mistake was only just avoided in one case: the Vula people requested a passport for a young woman and provided the accompanying data, but according to the digit code given to us she was born in the 1990s.

The ANC and SACP leadership having left for home, it was now getting more and more difficult to follow developments in South Africa. But visitors did keep coming from South Africa. One delegation from the University of the Western Cape, including the rector Professor Jakes Gerwel and Professors Jaap Durand and Colin Bundy, visited the USSR in October 1990. They enlightened us about the complexity of the situation at home: "The ANC still needs to explain, especially to the youth, the suspension of the armed struggle."[185]

We were glad to hear that the launching of the legal SACP on its 69th anniversary at the end of July 1990 had been extremely successful. The list of the SACP Interim Leadership Core was impressive and included many members of the ANC NEC.

When later, in December 1991, a new leadership of the SACP was elected at the Eighth Congress, missing from the list of names were several people who were prominent when the Party was illegal. They had either left the Party or simply allowed their membership to lapse. There were various reasons: some thought that they could better serve their people (and continue working for socialism) from the ranks of the ANC, others were disillusioned after the collapse of the socialist states in Eastern Europe. But not one of them, to my knowledge, publicly denounced the Party.

Sad news was the death of Francis Meli (real name Alan Madolwana) in a Johannesburg hotel. Meli's story was tragic. A very able man, he destroyed himself through alcohol, as had some others in exile. He tried to fight his illness, abstaining for long periods, but then succumbing again. By 1989 it had become clear that he was unable to control his problem. As a result, Meli became a source of information about ANC and SACP activities for all kinds of shadowy characters. His behaviour became so erratic that he was banned from attending the SACP Congress in Havana, something which the Party leadership had to explain to Oliver Tambo.

Soviet government relations with the ANC deteriorated slowly but steadily. Simon Makana was worried about the attitude of some Soviet diplomats, hinting that any information he gave them was possibly relayed to Pretoria. He said the questions were: "If to brief, whom do I brief? Whom do I trust? What are they up to? Why should we inform Neil van Heerden through the Soviet diplomats?"[186]

In this situation, we took steps to maintain Soviet contacts with the ANC at the highest possible level. In November 1990 Walter and Albertina Sisulu were invited to visit the USSR for a rest. Apart from their holiday, they took part in various political discussions. While in the Crimea, they also visited the Umkhonto group in the training centre in Perevalnoye, which had by then been officially reorganised into a Ground Forces College. Commanders, instructors and the cadets gave them a warm reception. Sisulu was accompanied by his bodyguard, Edward Mbundu, for whom that trip was especially moving. He had studied there ten years earlier, before being imprisoned on Robben Island. "I want to continue my military studies," he said to us back in Moscow. "But I can't go to Simferopol: everything – classes, dining room, firing range – reminded me of classmates who fell in battle or were assassinated."[187]

The routine official delegation of the ANC followed Sisulu in December 1990. Henry Makgothi, ANC Deputy Secretary General, and Rashid Patel (now Major General Aboobaker Ismail), a member of the Umkhonto High Command, had discussions with Gennady Yanaev, Member of the Politbureau and International Secretary of the Communist Party. Yanaev made it clear that, while "clumsy statements by some Soviet representatives could create a wrong impression about the position of the Party and the Soviet state, the USSR reiterates its solidarity and support to the ANC." He added: "The [South African] problem is not finally solved and the process is not yet irreversible." Yanaev's assurances gained extra weight when he was elected two weeks later to the newly created post of USSR Vice-President.

The ANC delegation also had meetings with the Ministries of Foreign Affairs and Defence, as well as with other Soviet organisations. It emphasised the need for supplies of arms, and the training of large groups of Umkhonto fighters for the future regular army.

The Umkhonto Command had ambitious plans for the training of its cadres, requesting USSR assistance for both basic training of the recently recruited cadres as junior officers, and refresher courses for veterans. In discussion with the Soviet Defence Ministry, the delegation asked for at least one Soviet expert in regular army training and a specialist in radio maintenance and repair to be sent to Lusaka.

At that time about 600-700 fighters were inside South Africa and over two thousand outside the country. As many as 95% of all the members of the ANC in exile were trained. In addition 200 to 300 young people were leaving South Africa every week to join Umkhonto.[188] These figures from authentic sources differ radically from the information contained in Howard Barrel's book on Umkhonto we Sizwe. He wrote that from 1976 to the end of 1987 more than 6 000 guerrillas had been deployed inside South Africa. Subtracting from that figure the 694 captured or killed (according to police figures), he concluded that "there was no evidence to suggest that 5 000 or more MK cadres were active inside the country." Barrel observed that a small percentage crossed over to the security forces, some others had involved themselves in political organisations, but "perhaps as many as 30 per cent had, in effect, abandoned their missions."[189] Such cases definitely occurred, but Barrel's calculations are not correct. The figure of 6 000 that he mentions is in my opinion an overestimation. Barrel also forgets that many fighters returned to the forward areas; in fact, in the late 1970s and early 1980s most MK cadres were sent inside the country only on short-term missions.

Our reaction to the ANC delegation's requests was, as usual, sympathetic, particularly with regard to the request for training, but a formal reply was frozen, pending the visit of Mandela. Meanwhile the ANC had not used all the facilities offered by the Soviets. Since 1988 there had been talks about students coming directly from South Africa for academic studies in the USSR. The Soviet Afro-Asian Solidarity Committee was prepared to allocate at least 30 scholarships annually. It was clear by then that a political settlement was on its way and that future graduates would not be stranded abroad for years. But in spite of promises by ANC Headquarters to act on this, nothing was done.

Meanwhile hundreds of South Africans were leaving for the USA and other Western countries.

Openly hostile attitudes to the South African liberation movement (and not just clumsy statements) were now beginning to appear regularly in the Soviet media. Some born-again "democrats" were ready to reject or ridicule any policy previously conducted by the USSR. Others had already been co-opted and were anxious to get on the gravy train circuit of visits, conferences and honoraria.

One of the strongest advocates of ties with Pretoria was Pilyatskin, an *Izvestiya* correspondent, mentioned above. Writing in September 1990, he said: "There is every reason to believe that as an increasing number of Soviet enterprises and companies enter the foreign market and as the Union republics become increasingly independent economically, the process of establishing ties of mutually beneficial co-operation with South Africa will gain momentum despite opposition from the conservative [anti-racist] forces reluctant 'to forgo their principles'."[190]

The part of the Soviet press calling itself "democratic" was simply repeating stories from Western and South African media. For example, President de Klerk was portrayed as playing the role of wise mediator between the predominantly Xhosa ANC and the exclusively Zulu Inkatha, locked in battle for the soul of the black population. South Africa was increasingly portrayed as a land of milk and honey. So-called experts from a newly established Centre for Social Strategic Studies claimed that South Africa could absorb 1,5 million emigrants from the USSR in ten years, perhaps even 4,5 million if "the extreme right forces come to power."

While analyses of this kind, wishful thinking rather than informed assessments, were becoming more common, there was no radical change in official Soviet policy. Cases of sanctions-busting, be it spontaneous or authorised by the USSR Foreign Ministry or the Presidential officials, were still exceptions to the general rule. In fact, a special meeting was held in the Foreign Ministry on 1 March 1991, chaired by the Ambassador Vladimir Kazimirov (who replaced Yukalov as the Head of the African Department), to caution against euphoria concerning the prospects of Soviet relations with Pretoria. Representatives from various government departments as well as non-governmental and business organisations and the missions of the Union Republics to Moscow were warned that sanctions against South Africa remained in force. A formal circular letter from the Ministry to this effect followed. Though officially Boris Yeltsin's Russian government also abided by sanctions, the representative of the Russian Foreign Ministry complained at the meeting that the terms of the boycott were too stringent.

Kazimirov emphasised that an agreement on 26 February 1991 to exchange liaison missions between the USSR and South Africa (attached to the Austrian Embassies in Pretoria and Moscow) did not mean the establishment of diplomatic relations. The whole matter had been discussed with the leadership of the ANC and the SACP, who raised no objections. In fact, since they had left Lusaka for Johannesburg, the maintenance of bilateral contacts without a permanent Soviet presence in South Africa had become complicated.

To emphasise the limited nature of the new missions, the Soviet Foreign Ministry stressed in a press statement that: "The creation of the Sections of interests does not mean the establishment of diplomatic or consular relations ... and [they] are deprived of the right to use the national flag, emblem and other state symbols."[191] The positive attitude by the leaders of the liberation movement to this development was greatly reinforced by the appointment of Dr Alexei Makarov to head the new Soviet Mission. He was personally known to most of the ANC and SACP leaders, having been involved with them since the early days in Odessa, and especially after 1970.

The briefing in the USSR Foreign Ministry, mentioned above, was followed by a new "Situation Analysis" in the CPSU International Department in April 1991. There was broad participation, and, as before, a variety of views was expressed. Apart for one or two participants who were rushing to establish trade links with South Africa, the overwhelming consensus confirmed the importance of strengthening relations with the ANC and giving it active assistance. The participants noted that: "A curtailment of ties with the ANC will inevitably bring the Western countries to fill the vacuum, and that is already partially taking place." While the experts anticipated that the talks in South Africa to be derailed, perhaps even several times, they expected that the tendency towards a settlement would prevail. This is exactly what happened.

The last top-level contact between the CPSU and the SACP was in April 1991, when Joe Slovo came to Moscow for a short working visit. Slovo met the late Vladimir Ivashko, Deputy to Gorbachev in the CPSU, on 23 April 1991. They discussed, not only the present situation in both countries and inter-party relations, but also "the prospects of relations between the USSR and a future democratic South Africa."[192] Meanwhile, they decided, co-operation between the two parties would continue. A new intake of party cadres, for example, was expected at the Moscow Institute of Social Sciences. "A nice guy," commented Slovo after the meetings. Ivashko was an honest, modest person. But during the August 1991 crisis in the USSR he proved not to be strong enough to replace Gorbachev when the latter deserted the Party.

During his last visit to Moscow Joe Slovo expressed concern about the state of the dialogue between the ANC and the South African government. Pretoria was conducting the talks and at the same time trying to weaken the ANC, particularly by using Inkatha. It was trying to split the ANC, putting the blame on "communist radicals", while acting against the organisation as a whole. The trust that ANC supporters had put in the negotiation process was starting to falter. Slovo informed us that the SACP had about ten thousand members, but that that figure was expected to rise to thirty thousand before the forthcoming congress, scheduled initially for July 1991 but later postponed to December.[193]

The ANC National Conference, convened at the beginning of July 1991, gave me my first opportunity to visit South Africa. Technically I had been there once before, in November 1989, when I spent a night quarantined in a hotel at Jan Smuts airport while in transit from Windhoek to Maputo.

On that occasion I was part of a delegation to Windhoek to monitor the Namibian general election. Even though visas for all of us had been negotiated in advance and guaranteed by the South African Missions in New York and in Windhoek, the immigration authorities refused us entry and our luggage was taken back to the Zambian Airways plane that had brought us from Lusaka. A low-ranking coloured policemen and a black Zambian airline representative tried to force us to board the plane again but we flatly refused. Only after the vigorous efforts of Pavel Pavlov, the Head of the Soviet Liaison Mission in Windhoek, were we allowed in. Then a top-ranking white officer appeared on the scene.

When I arrived in South Africa in 1991 I was expecting more of the medicine I had been given then. But this time the situation was completely different: there was no problem at the airport or anywhere else.

The ANC Congress was unforgettable. Over two and half thousand delegates rose and started applauding as soon as Walter Sisulu, who was chairing the session, mentioned "our natural ally", even before he said the words "the Soviet Union". He invited me to the stage to read the message of the Central Committee of the CPSU, but I felt that the words in it, smooth and correct as they were, were not enough. More needed to be said, especially about our respect for those who had perished in the struggle or had not lived to see that day. Their names were in my memory, their faces before my eyes. There was a renewed wave of applause when I spoke about future co-operation between a democratic South Africa and a renovated Soviet Union.

We had a very interesting discussion with General Bantu Holomisa, who thanked us for training some Umkhonto cadres who by that time had been incorporated in the Transkeian Defence Force and participated in defeating a coup attempt instigated by Pretoria in November 1990. Holomisa expressed the wish to send more cadres to the USSR for more sophisticated training, a realistic proposition at that stage, provided his soldiers were sent through the ANC channels. He said there was a lack of information about Soviet policy on South Africa, and this made Africans believe that the ANC had stronger links with the West than with the USSR, and consequently that the destiny of South Africa depended on the USA and Britain.[194]

After the conference we discussed its results with Slovo. He was delighted with the composition of the new NEC. "We, as the SACP, haven't done any caucusing. However, the Executive could not be better."[195]

Nelson Mandela received the Soviet delegates in Durban on 3 July 1991. He put it very simply: "Without your support we would not be where we are now." He was worried about the delay in his visit to the USSR. I told him that there were no political reasons for this delay. Also, it was desirable that the visit should happen in the near future, as I had been given assurances on this score from Gorbachev's entourage before my departure from Moscow.[196]

As soon as we returned to Moscow, the urgent need for Mandela to be received in Moscow was brought to Gorbachev's attention. Having read my short (and strongly worded) report about the meeting, Gorbachev again made promises that the meeting would take place soon. To defuse the situation, Deputy Foreign Minister Valery Nikolaenko (the fourth Deputy Minister in six years to deal with Africa) was urgently sent to South Africa in August 1991 to meet with Mandela and discuss the matter yet again. Nikolaenko conveyed to Mandela Gorbachev's "[verbal] message, in which the invitation to the

ANC leader was confirmed."[197]

We tried to apply some public pressure as well. Vice President of the Soviet Afro-Asian Solidarity Committee Seitniyaz Ataev, a World War Two veteran from Turkmenistan, in his capacity as a USSR People's Deputy officially asked Gorbachev why Mandela had not yet been received in the USSR. The reply was in the form of a telephone call from Anatoly Chernyaev, who assured Ataev that Gorbachev was eager to see Mandela, and that it could perhaps be arranged during Gorbachev's holiday in the Crimea in August.

But by now Gorbachev was clearly playing a double game. When I was leaving Moscow for Namibia in March 1991 I saw some familiar faces in the VIP hall at the Sheremetyevo airport. We were on the same flight, but our ways parted in Harare, with me going to Windhoek at the invitation of SWAPO to celebrate the first anniversary of Namibian independence, while they were going to Johannesburg. It became clear that, contrary to his earlier promises to Tambo, Gorbachev was establishing direct contacts with Pretoria without the knowledge of either the ANC or the CPSU that he was (at least on paper) still heading.

Further trouble arose in August 1991 when the USSR government, headed then by Valentin Pavlov, took a decision to stop the free military training of foreigners in the Soviet Union. This step was not directed specifically against the ANC – the aim was to get badly needed hard currency – but the decision was a blanket one, taken without an analysis of the situation in each case, and it affected the ANC negatively. Its leadership was deeply concerned by these developments. Urgent steps were taken to clarify the situation. On Friday 16 August the CPSU International Department urged the continuation of Umkhonto training on the previous free basis, this contained in a report sent to the Crimea, where Gorbachev was on holiday at his luxurious dacha in Foros.

However, over the weekend the situation in the USSR changed dramatically. On Monday 19 August, a group of top government leaders, including the Vice-President and Prime Minister, took actions which were later described as "a very strange coup".[198] A kind of counter-coup followed, technically bringing Gorbachev back to office but in effect giving all control in Moscow to Boris Yeltsin. Gorbachev resigned as General Secretary of the CPSU, clinging to the Presidential post. The Party was banned in Russia by Yeltsin's decree.

After these dramatic events the traditionally sober approach of the

USSR government towards South Africa was maintained at an official level, but not for long. In an article published in the November 1991 issue of *International Affairs* (and written a month or two earlier) Nikolaenko named the "incompleteness" of the process of eliminating apartheid as an obstacle to the establishment of full-scale diplomatic relations and the development of ties between the USSR and South Africa. Even then Nikolaenko was speaking of "maintaining and consolidating our tradition of friendly relations" with the ANC.[199] But this "line of defence" crumbled within weeks, when Pik Botha paid a "private and unofficial" visit to Moscow. Botha wanted to meet with both Gorbachev and Yeltsin.[200] Although he was unable to meet them, the South African Foreign Minister signed a protocol with the new USSR Foreign Minister Boris Pankin on 9 November 1991, formally restoring consular relations between the two countries. Pankin promised that it would not be long before full diplomatic relations were established, and he added that the USSR would "certainly not be the last" to abandon the sanctions imposed by the United Nations.[201] No preliminary consultations with the ANC took place. ANC spokesperson Carl Niehaus called the decision "premature".[202]

But the tide had turned and it was announced soon afterwards that F W de Klerk would undertake an "unofficial and transit" visit in December 1991. Trying to keep some balance or at least save face, Gorbachev at very short notice proposed dates for Mandela's visit to Moscow. It did not work. The ANC Mission in the USSR issued an unusually strong statement on 26 November 1991, after receiving an instruction from Johannesburg. The ANC Headquarters asked their mission to convey to Moscow not only regrets but "our deep surprise as to the timing of the visit, without prior consultations with us, and the manner in which the invitation has been extended to us." The proposed dates were 3 to 6 December, when, as it had already been announced, Mandela was planning to be in New York. The message emphasised the fact that "this sudden invitation" was extended "on the eve of a scheduled visit by the President F W de Klerk to Moscow. This is highly irregular, to say the least."[203]

So, the Mission went public: "Since his release from prison on 11 February 1990 Cde N. Mandela has been invited thrice to the USSR and thrice the visit did not materialise as it was cancelled at the request of the Soviet side." The Mission expressed regrets over "unfortunate and slanderous rumours that have accompanied the indefinite postponements of the visit," such as claims in some Soviet media that "the ANC is no longer interested in the USSR and is searching for new allies in the West ... The ANC permanent Mission would like to make it known to the people of the USSR that the President of the ANC, Cde Nelson Mandela, is looking forward to visiting the Soviet Union for the specific purpose of thanking them and their government for the immeasurable support and assistance rendered to the ANC and the cause of our people during the last three decades, and to renew the bonds of friendship between our peoples."[204]

De Klerk's visit was postponed after the "Belovezhskaya troika" – the leaders of Russia, Ukraine and Belarus: Yeltsin, Kravchuk and Shushkevich – decided to dissolve the USSR on 8 December at their meeting in the Belovezhskaya Pushcha forest near the Soviet-Polish border. The dissolution of the Soviet Union, which former Prime Minister Nikolay Ryzhkov called "the greatest tragedy of this century",[205] heralded the end of an epoch in world history, and an end to the close relationship between the ANC and one of the two great powers of the post World War Two era.

1. Discussion with F. Meli, Moscow, 15 June 1985.
2. *Novoye Vremya* (Russian edition of *New Times*), Moscow, no 16, 1985, p.25.
3. *Newsweek*, New York, 16 September 1985.
4. *Star*, 30 April 1985.
5. Discussion with T. Mbeki, Moscow, 15 October 1985.
6. Archive of the SAASC, SAC, Summary of discussion with J. Nhlanhla, Moscow, 19 May 1986.
7. Archive of the SAASC, SAC, ANC DIP/Thabo to V. Shubin, 15 November 1985.
8. Sparks A., *Tomorrow is Another Country: The Inside Story of South Africa's Negotiated Revolution.* Struik, Sandton, 1994, p. 30.
9. Shubin V., "From the History of the Liberation Movement in South Africa." Paper, presented at the seminar on African nationalism at the Institute of General History, Moscow, June 1985, pp. 1-2.
10. *Pravda*, Moscow, 9 May 1986.
11. *Izvestiya*, Moscow, 9 June 1986.
12. Discussion with O. Tambo, 6 November 1986.
13. Ibid.
14. *Weekend Argus*, Cape Town, 28/29 January 1995.
15. *Pravda*, 5 November 1986.
16. Tambo O., *Preparing for Power*, p.233.
17. Ellis S. and Sechaba T. *Comrades*, p.182.
18. Ibid.
19. Christie R. "South Africa's Nuclear History". Fourth International Conference. Sofia-Antipolis, Nice, France, 23-27 June 1993. pp. 55-57.
20. *From Ungovernability to People's Power. ANC Call to the People.* (Lusaka, 1985)
21. Discussion with C. Hani, Moscow, 10 November 1986.
22. Ibid.
23. *Pravda*, 5 November 1986.
24. Discussion with J. Makatini, Moscow, 9 January 1987.
25. Nel P. *A Soviet Embassy*, p.57.
26. Discussion with J. Jele, Moscow, 16 May 1982.

27. MCHP, ANCLusC, Rules, governing the privileges and immunities granted to the Mission of the African National Congress (ANC) of South Africa.

28. Ibid. Report on "Week of solidarity with the peoples of Southern Africa" compiled and prepared by Steve Tshwete.

29. Ibid., S. Makana to A. Nzo, 15 November 1987.

30. MCHP, ANCLonC, Draft document on security. p.2.

31. Ibid. Principles of interrogation, p.2.

32. Discussion with J. Jele, Johannesburg, 23 November 1993.

33. Ellis S. and Sechaba T. *Comrades*, p.202.

34. MCHP, YDC, Secretariat activities since its formation, p.3.

35. Ibid. p.4.

36. Ibid. Minutes of P.B. Meeting 17 February 1983 in Maputo, p.3.

37. Kasrils R. *"Armed and Dangerous"*, p.257.

38. MCHP, ANCLusC, Final Version. Decision and Recommendations of the N.E.C. Meeting, 11 to 15 February 1987, p.8.

39. Ibid. p.14.

40. Ibid. p.15.

41. Ibid.

42. Ellis S. and Sechaba T. *Comrades*, p.183.

43. *The role of the Soviet Union*, vol.2, Addendum, p.801.

44. Nezavisimaya Gazeta, Moscow, 8 August 1992.

45. Bridgland F. *The War for Africa. Twelve Months that Transformed a Continent,* Ashanti Publishing House, Gibraltar, 1990, p.62.

46. Ibid. p.17.

47. *Die Suid-Afrikaan*, Cape Town, April-May 1992, p.66.

48. *Africa Confidential*, 10 December 1986, pp. 1-2

49. *Problems of Communism*, Washington, July-August 1987, pp. 11, 17.

50. Archive of the SAASC, SAC, Summary of discussion with J. Zuma, Addis Ababa, 30 July 1986.

51. Starushenko G. *Problems of Struggle against Racism, Apartheid and Colonialism in South Africa*, Africa Institute, Moscow, 1986, p.12.

52. Ibid.

53. *Soviet Review*. Stellenbosch, N 4, 1987, p.30.

54. MCHP, ANCLusC, Our assessment of the outcome of the Washington summit between General Secretary of the CPSU

Central Committee Comrade M.S. Gorbachev and the US President R. Reagan.

55. *Izvestiya*, 4 August 1987.
56. Nel P. *A Soviet Embassy,* p.8
57. Tikhomirov V. *The States in Transition: Russia and South Africa,* International Freedom Foundation, Bryanston, 1992, p. 49.
58. *Izvestiya*, 4 August 1987.
59. MCHP, ANCLusC, Minutes of N.W.C. Meeting 25 March 1987 p.3.
60. Ibid. Memorandum to the NWC on membership questions that need our attention, p.1.
61. Ibid. Decisions of the National Executive Committee Meeting 5-9 October 1987, pp. 1-2.
62. *Unite for Freedom. Statements by the African National Congress on the Question of Unity and Anti-Apartheid Coalition. 1985-1990* (ANC DIP, Lusaka) 1990, p.10
63. Consensus, (Lusaka, 1987) p.1.
64. Ibid.
65. MCHP, ANCLusC, Decisions of NWC Meetings 27 February - 12 July 1987, p.2.
66. Presentation by J. Slovo at the Africa Institute, Moscow, 19 September 1987.
67. Presentation by J. Modise at the Soviet Afro-Asian Solidarity Committee, Moscow, 18 September 1987.
68. Statement of the delegation of the South African Communist Party to the meeting of delegations, 5 November 1987, p.4.
69. Statement of President of the ANC Comrade Oliver Tambo at the International Meeting Held on the Occasion of the 70th Anniversary of the Great October Socialist Revolution, November 2-3, 1987, p.4.
70. Coker C. "South Africa and the Soviet Union". In: A. Venter (edit.), *Challenge*, p.310.
71. Ibid. pp. 311-312.
72. *Zhurnalist*, Moscow, no 8, 1983, p.74.
73. MCHP, ANCLusC, Minutes of NWC 22 February 1988, pp. 1-2.
74. Ibid. p.1.
75. Ibid. Minutes of the NWC Meeting 9 March 1988, p.1.
76. Ibid.
77. *Pravda*, 28 April 1988.
78. Presentation by J. Slovo at the Institute of Social Sciences,

Moscow, 29 April 1988.

79. Ibid.

80. Crocker C. *High Noon in Southern Africa. Making Peace in a Rough Neighbourhood.* Johannesburg, Jonathan Ball Publishers, 1993, p.311.

81. Discussion with J. Modise and R. Kasrils, Moscow, 20 March 1988.

82. *Statement of the NEC of the ANC 17th August 1988,* Lusaka, Zambia, p.1.

83. Ibid.

84. *ANC Perspectives. Policy Documents and ANC Statements,* (ANC, Lusaka), 1990, pp. 18-19.

85. Discussion with S. Makana, Moscow, 15 November 1988.

86. MCHP, ANCLusC, Emergency Meeting of the NWC 28 October 1988, pp. 2-7.

87. Ibid. Minutes of meeting of N.W.C. 14 February 1989.

88. MCHP, ANCLonC. (No title).

89. Ibid.

90. MCHP, ANCLusC, Minutes of Meeting of NWC 11 January 1989, p.3.

91. Ibid.

92. Braam C. *Operatie Vula.* Muelenhoff Nederland bv. Amsterdam, 1992.

93. Sparks A. *Tomorrow Is Another Country: The Inside Story of South Africa's Negotiated Revolution*, Struik, Sandton, 1994, p.62.

94. MCHP, YDC, The SACP Chairman to the CPSU, 18 July 1977.

95. Ibid. The SACP Chairman to the Central Committee, Communist party of the Soviet Union, 19 August 1977.

96. CSCD, Collection of declassified documents, Decision of the CPSU CC Secretariat St 240/46 gs of 5 December 1980.

97. MCHP, ANCLonC, (No title).

98. *Africa Confidential*, 8 September 1989, p.4.

99. S. Maharaj to the author, 4 March 1989.

100. *Komsomolskaya Pravda*, Moscow, 26 January 1994.

101. MCHP, ANCLusC, Meeting of NWC 4 October 1988, p.3.

102. Ibid.

103. MCHP, ANCLusC, Minutes of the NWC Meeting 7 June 1988, p.9.

104. Ibid. p.1.

105. Ibid. p.3.

106. Discussion with J. Modise and R. Kasrils, Moscow, 16 March

1988.

107. MCHP, ANCLusC, Meeting of NWC at SACTU 1 November 88, p.3.

108. Ibid.

109. MCHP, ANCLusC, Meeting of NWC 4 October 1988, p.4.

110. Ibid. Meeting of NWC 2 December 1988, p.2.

111. Ibid.

112. Ibid.

113. Ibid.

114. MCHP, ANCLusC, Minutes of the Special Meeting of NWC 21 December 1988, p.3.

115. Ibid. Meeting of NWC 12 December 1988, p.2.

116. Ibid. p.4.

117. MCHP, ANCLusC, Minutes of the Special Meeting of NWC 21 December 1988, p.3.

118. Discussion with J. Slovo and D. Tloome, Moscow, 10 January 1989.

119. *Social Scientists' Seminar*. (ANC, Lusaka), 1989, part 2, p.2.

120. *Press-Release, Novosti Press Agency*. Lusaka, 23 April 1988.

121. Statement by IDASA delegation on their visit to the USSR. (s.a.e.l.)

122. Sparks A. *The Mind of South Africa*, Alfred A. Knopf, New York, 1990, p. 366.

123. MCHP, ANCLusC, Minutes of the NWC Meeting 2 May 1989, p.1.

124. Ibid.

125. Ibid.

126. Ibid.

127. MCHP, ANCLusC, Emergency meeting of the NWC 29 July 1989, p.1.

128. Discussion with A. Nzo and S. Makana, Moscow, 22 June 1989.

129. Mandela N. Long Walk to Freedom, pp. 609-668; Sparks A. *Tomorrow is Another Country*, pp. 21-67.

130. Sparks A. *Tomorrow is Another Country*, p.39.

131. Ibid. p.36.

132. Ibid.

133. Discussion with O. Tambo and J. Slovo, Moscow, 11 July 1989.

134. The document, (s.a.e.l.) p. 1

135. Ibid. pp. 2-3.

136. Ibid. p.4

137. Ibid.

138. CSCD, Collection of Declassified Documents, Decision of the Secretariat of the CPSU CC, N St 36/132g, 18 January 1988.

139. Ibid. N St 86/256 gs, 24 June 1988.

140. 24 s'ezd KPPS. Bulleten N 10. (24th CPSU Congress, Bulletin N10) Izdatestvo *"Pravda,"* 1971, p. 54

141. Discussion with O. Tambo, 7 March 1989.

142. *Weekend Argus*, Cape Town, 4/5 December 1993

143. *Pravda*, 20 August 1989.

144. Ibid. 1 October 1989.

145. Ibid. 20 August 1989.

146. Ibid. 1 October 1989.

147. Ibid.

148. MCHP, ANCLusC, On MK Cadres - Expulsion. 24th November 1989. Sipho Makana, Head of the ANC Permanent Mission to the USSR, p. 1.

149. Ibid. p.2

150. Discussion with A. Nzo and T. Mbeki, Lusaka, 25 December 1989.

151. Ellis S. and Sechaba T. *Comrades*, p.198.

152. Sparks A, *Tomorrow is Another Country*, p.6.

153. Ibid. pp. 117-118.

154. I. Pillay to the author, 13 May 1990.

155. Discussion with W. Malan, Moscow, 12 June 1990.

156. *Star*, 19 January 1990.

157. MCHP, ANCLusC, Report on the ANC Meeting with the Soviet Foreign Minister. 20 March 1990. p.1

158. Ibid. p.4.

159. Ibid. p.6.

160. Ibid. p.4.

161. Ibid. p.6.

162. Discussion with J. Slovo, 10 January 1989.

163. *Izvestiya*, 27 September 1989.

164. *Asia and Africa Today*, Moscow, no 2, 1991, pp. 8-15.

165. Quoted in: *Soviet Revue*, N 3, 1990, p. 53.

166. *Citizen*, Pretoria, 14 August 1990.

167. Discussion with A. Chernukhin, Moscow, 22 November 1990.

168. Discussion with S. Makana, Moscow, 12 October 1990.

169. *Sunday Mail*, Harare, 28 April 1991.

170. *Executive*, Johannesburg, August 1991, p.52.

171. *Business Day*, Johannesburg, 14 February 1991.

172. Discussion with the COSATU delegation, Moscow, 25 September 1990.

173. *Izvestiya*, 12 October 1990.

174. *Moskovsky Komsomolets*, Moscow, 19 October 1991.

175. *Pravda*, 28 October 1991.

176. Ibid.

177. *Argumenty i Fakty*, Moscow, no 35, 1992.

178. *Pravda*, 2 December 1992.

179. Archive of the SAASC, SAC, Summary of discussion with N. Mandela, Lusaka, 28 February 1990.

180. MCHP, ANCLusC, S. Makana to A. Nzo, 11 April 1990.

181. *Nezavisimaya Gazeta*, Moscow, 25 May 1991.

182. Chernyaev A. *Shest Let s Gorbachevym* (Six Years with Gorbachev), Progress - Kultura, Moscow, 1993, p. 195.

183. I. Pillay to the author, 10 March 1991.

184. Discussion with I. Pillay, Moscow, 30 January 1991.

185. Discussion with the UWC delegation, Moscow, 25 October 1990.

186. Discussion with S. Makana, Moscow, 12 October 1990.

187. Discussion with E. Mbundu, Moscow, 2 December 1990.

188. Discussion with H. Makgothi and R. Patel, Moscow, 5 December 1990.

189. Barrel H, *MK*, p. 64.

190. *Moscow News*, Moscow, 9 September 1990.

191. *Pravda*, 28 February 1991.

192. Ibid. 24 April 1991.

193. Discussion with J. Slovo, Moscow, 24 April 1991.

194. Discussion with B. Holomisa, Durban, 2 July 1991.

195. Discussion with J.Slovo, Johannesburg, 7 July 1991.

196. Discussion with N. Mandela, Durban, 3 July 1991.

197. *Izvestiya*, 12 August 1991.

198. Mkhulu. Moscow Tragedy. In: *African Communist*, First Quarter 1992, pp. 63-68.

199. *International Affairs*, Moscow, no 11, 1991, p.25.

200. *Pretoria News*, Pretoria, 5 November 1991.

201. Quoted in: Anderton N. *From Gorbachev to Yeltsin. Moscow-Pretoria Relations at a Time of Change*. Unpublished paper. University of Stellenbosch, 1994, p.11.

202. *Pravda*, 11 November 1991.

203. Archive of the SAASC, SAC, To: Themba Thabethe Chief Rep from Stanley Mabizela Deputy Director DIA.

204. ANC (S.A.) *Permanent Mission to the USSR. 26 November 1991.*
  Press Statement on the visit of the President General of the
  ANC Cde Nelson Mandela to the USSR.
205. *Pravda*, 30 October 1992.

POSTSCRIPT

THE END OR THE BEGINNING?

The relationship between the USSR and South Africa, especially with the ANC and its allies, had a profound though contradictory influence on developments in South Africa. Much has been said and written about the negative effects of the links with the Soviet Union on the South African liberation movement. One has to admit that certain aspects of Soviet society such as leader-worship, dogmatism, lack of broad discussions before taking crucial decisions, limitations in inner-party democracy were not the best features to emulate. But even if some borrowing of these characteristics did take place, the influence was negligible and was undoubtedly outweighed by the positive effects of co-operation with Moscow.

The Russian press has calculated that, from 1963 to 1991, 1 501 ANC activists were trained in Soviet military institutions.[1] This figure is not all-inclusive as far as Umkhonto training is concerned. About two hundred ANC members completed training in Soviet tertiary institutions, mostly with Masters and some with PhD degrees (the official government figure is smaller, but it does not include those South Africans who were registered as citizens of Lesotho, Zambia and other Southern African countries). About two hundred ANC and SACP members studied at the Institute of Social Sciences, and dozens in trade union and youth schools. Several hundreds visited the USSR for rest and medical treatment.

To judge purely by the figures, about three thousand South Africans stayed in the USSR for relatively long periods. Often, the same people would, for example, complete a university degree and then also undergo military training. So, a realistic figure for South Africans who lived in the USSR under the auspices of the ANC and its allies is appreciably smaller. There were, of course, many hundreds of South Africans who visited the Soviet Union as members of delegations or in transit.

More than two hundred Soviet specialists and interpreters were stationed with the ANC in Angola in the period 1979-91.[2] According to the Chief Department of Military Technical Co-operation of the Ministry of Foreign Economic Relations, the total value of assistance to the ANC (from 1963 to 1990) was about 61 mln roubles, including 52 mln supplies (36 mln - "special equipment" and 16 mln - civilian goods). The rest is "technical assistance", mostly training of ANC cadres in the USSR and sending Soviet specialists to Angola.[3] These figures are also not all-embracing, because they do not include the material assistance provided by the Soviet non-governmental organisations, such as the Soviet Afro-Asian Solidarity Committee. Even the accurate figures would not reflect the true picture. These sums are counted in roubles and their simple conversion into dollars at any given rate of exchange can only further distort the picture: many goods, especially military supplies, were exceptionally cheap in the USSR.

A more detailed description of the equipment might give a clearer picture: several thousand AK-47s of various modifications, over three thousand SKS carbines, over six thousand pistols, 275 grenade-launchers, 90 Grad-P missile launchers, over 40 Strela 2M anti-aircraft missile launchers, 20 Malyutkas, over 60 mortars, etc.[4]

However, I am convinced that the Soviet Union's greatest contribution to the elimination of apartheid was not material assistance, or the provision of training facilities, but the encouragement of non-racialism in the ANC.

It is sometimes amusing to see how supposedly sober and experienced diplomats and politicians become victims of their own wishful thinking. Chester Crocker writes in the preface to his book: "This book tells the story of peacemaking in Africa the 1980s. It is a record of an American diplomatic strategy which helped us to win the Cold War in the Third World."[5] We in the Soviet Union have never looked at our assistance to the liberation movements and Front Line States as waging "the Cold War". But even if one uses Crocker's terminology, who is ruling in Namibia now: SWAPO or the so-called Democratic Turnhalle Alliance? Who is President of South Africa: Mandela or Buthelezi? Of Angola: Dos Santos or Savimbi?

What should be emphasised, however, is that the changes in Southern Africa and in South Africa in particular, the emerging political settlements, were the result, first and foremost, of internal dynamics and not of "Gorbachev's *perestroika*" or the "collapse of communism". Perhaps the previous rulers in Pretoria, and especially the military and security hierarchy, found in these theories a kind of consolation for themselves: unable to admit their failure (not to say "defeat"), they were trying to explain their retreat in terms of "global changes". It is more surprising when academics sometimes follow suit. I was astonished, for example, to find in one of the supposedly serious magazines a calendar of negotiations on South Africa, which starts with: "November 1989. The Berlin Wall collapses, signalling the end of Marxist-Leninist ideology."[6] Have those politicians, academics and journalists forgotten that the Pretoria regime (or at least some people

401

in contact with it) started to seek (very preliminary and very informal) contacts with the ANC as early as 1984, when the name "Gorbachev" was familiar to almost no one outside the USSR? That Gavin Relly and other prominent businessmen met the ANC leadership in 1985? That the Commonwealth EPG had real hopes for starting the settlement process in 1986? That the ANC National Executive Committee had an in-depth discussion on the matter in 1987?

I am not suggesting that the break-up of the Soviet Union did not influence the political process in South Africa. While the end of the Cold War, or, should I say, a cease-fire in 1988-9, undoubtedly facilitated the move towards the eradication of apartheid by political means, the collapse of the Soviet Union and Moscow's cessation of both political and practical assistance to the ANC in 1991 undoubtedly had a negative effect on the talks. It is hardly accidental that the government of the day adopted an intransigent position in 1992 after the establishment of diplomatic relations with Moscow and the assurances given to De Klerk in the Russian capital. Besides, the collapse of the "Second World" harmed prospects of deep social and economic transformation in the interests of the majority in South Africa.

"The SACP, believing in the depth of its being that the Soviet Union was the true home of international socialism," Ellis and "Sechaba" write, "considered that betrayal from this source was unthinkable."[7] So what? Was the SACP (and the ANC for that matter) wrong? No. If we are to apply the word "betrayal" (strong as it is), it has been committed not by the Soviet Union, but by those who destroyed it.

***

In a paper "From Gorbachev to Yeltsin: Moscow-Pretoria Relations at a Time of Change", Nicholas Anderton, then of the University of Stellenbosch, claimed that after the accession of President Boris Yeltsin to undisputed power in the Kremlin in December 1991, "a clearly defined policy towards South Africa, based exclusively on Russia's national interest, emerged."[8] Exactly the converse was true. After that date foreign policy in Moscow was initially largely determined by personalities or clans, acting either in their own narrow interests or blinkered by "re-ideologisation", and certainly not in Russia's national interests.

Two striking examples which reinforce this point occurred in relation to South Africa. When the Russian government took the decision to establish full diplomatic relations with Pretoria in February 1992 (thereby violating the UN General Assembly resolutions) the ANC was not consulted. The then Russian Foreign Minister Andrei Kozyrev did inform Nelson Mandela about the Russian government's intentions during his visit to South Africa, but that was done at the last moment, when the matter had already been settled. Fortunately for Kozyrev, the ANC President did not directly protest against this step, even though he was no doubt offended by it.

When the SACP criticised the move as "premature and counter-productive", Kozyrev responded: "Seventy years of history has made us aware of communist movements and dogmatic communist movements. One has to listen to them and do the opposite."[9] The irony is that Kozyrev for many years claimed to be a committed communist; but, setting aside his cynicism, his statement showed both a lack of professionalism for a diplomat, as well as a complete ideological somersault: a true diplomat would rather listen to various people, be they communists or not, and then act according to the interests of his country.

The second example was even more deplorable. In June 1992 F W de Klerk made an official state visit to Russia. Yeltsin assured De Klerk that "Mandela would not be received as the ANC President in Moscow but would be visiting the Russian capital as an international figure, a fighter for human rights."[10] Knowing the high level of professionalism among diplomats in the African Department of the Russian Foreign Ministry (as distinct from their former "boss"), I am convinced that they would not have written such a phrase into Yeltsin's notes. It was most probably prompted by someone within his close circle with an undisguised animosity to the ANC. So one should not be surprised if Mandela appears to be in no hurry to visit Moscow and if, in 1997-1998, his visit has been twice postponed by the South African side.

On many major issues of foreign policy the Russian Government until recently followed in the footsteps of the West. But, as far as South Africa is concerned, it went beyond the pale even by the standards of the Western countries. While major Western powers were doing their best to build or strengthen bridges with the ANC, which they had often ignored or opposed in the past, the Russian government was busy developing ties with the white-minority government still in the Union Buildings in Pretoria at the expense of contacts with the ANC Headquarters in Shell House in Johannesburg.

At the same time that consular and diplomatic relations were established with South Africa, financial support for the ANC office in

Moscow was stopped. While Pik Botha was welcomed in Moscow, Joe Modise and Chris Hani, who wished to negotiate the continuation of military training in the USSR, were not. It is true that Mandela was invited to Moscow, first by Gorbachev in November 1991 and then by Yeltsin in May 1992, but in both cases the invitations were issued after the visit by De Klerk had been agreed upon, and was the sugar-coating on what must have been for the ANC a bitter pill.

After August 1991 the anti-ANC propaganda in the Russian press intensified. The degree of pro-Pretoria bias in pro-government papers was illustrated by the claim of the *New Times* correspondent Yakov Borovoy that Umkhonto we Sizwe "had turned a long time ago into a gang of criminals."[11]

The right wing so-called International Freedom Foundation made special efforts to discredit the ANC. In 1992 it paid for the publication in the Moscow *Nezavisimaya Gazeta* of an open letter addressed by an MK defector Mwezi Twala to the Academician Evgeny Primakov, then Head of the Russian External Intelligence Service (now Russian Prime Minister). Twala requested him to "make public all information that is available in Russia about the nature and workings of the ANC security apparatus ... in order to assist the true ANC democrats."[12]

According to Chris Hani, Twala was first withdrawn from Swaziland to Maputo, "because he did not carry out instructions of MK in terms of preparing routes for infiltrating cadres into South Africa. He also failed instructions on recruiting." In Maputo "he was caught stealing and selling ANC blankets and was therefore taken back to Angola."[13] Twala was later charged by the ANC tribunal for his role in the 1984 mutiny, but later granted amnesty.

The IFF claimed that Twala, who found a political home in Inkatha after deserting from the ANC, had been "trained as a political commissar by the KGB in Rasdori in Moscow."[14] The truth is that he was never trained by the KGB either in "Rasdori" or anywhere else. And, in any event, the training of political commissars for the liberation movement was very far removed from the functions of the USSR State Security Committee.

Recent disclosures in the South African press have confirmed what had been suspected for a long time: the "international" body – the IFF – was created and financed by Pretoria's Military Intelligence. Craig Williamson commented : "Because of its anti-ANC campaigning, the IFF's clandestine funding ought not to surprise many people." The ex-spy admitted: "The only chance [for the Pretoria regime] of manipulating things to survive just a little bit longer was to paint the ANC as a project of the international department of the Soviet Communist Party."[15]

In May 1993, when negotiations were successfully resumed in South Africa, Pilyatskin wrote: "Intransigent opposition in the upper echelons of the ANC and the Communist Party is actively preparing for the X Day, when a signal will be given to start widescale violent actions, called "the revolutionary struggle of the masses.""[16]

Similarly, writing in a tone that would have made former head of the notorious BOSS General Hendrik van den Bergh proud, Vladimir Abarinov alleged that the ANC had hidden five "Russian tanks" in Angola. He tried to convince readers that those tanks could roll into South Africa to prevent national reconciliation. He wrote: "The Soviet tanks in Southern Africa will crush not apartheid but an attempt at national reconciliation."[17] One recalls the statement of Magnus Malan, mentioned earlier, but for Abarinov, who had close links with right-wing forces in South Africa, not hundreds, but just five tanks were enough.

Another "prophet of doom" was Yury Skubko, who wrote: "The Government of Frederick de Klerk ... is inexplicably in a hurry today to capitulate to pro-communist totalitarianism ... Formally democratic general elections in the RSA in the present situation will almost for sure bring in a bloody dictatorship, right or left, 'black' or 'white', and possibly dismember the country."[18]

These reports fed directly into South African right-wing debates. Several South African papers were ready to print material which could discredit the ANC by distorting the nature of its past connections with the Soviet Union. The *Citizen* newspaper, for example, published a letter from "Siza", who claimed to have been the bodyguard of Ronnie Kasrils. He wrote: "I was also present when Ronnie Kasrils and a Russian instructor, Vladimir Boris, tortured people in Zambia."[19] Kasrils immediately refuted those allegations as "sheer fabrications".[20] But since "a Russian instructor" was mentioned, it is worth making the point that the USSR did not send instructors to the ANC in Lusaka, except for one or two visits by our specialist in radio maintenance who went there from Luanda. If the editors of the *Citizen* knew anything about Russia, they would also have known that a Russian could be either Vladimir or Boris, but never "Vladimir Boris".

The crowning piece of bad-taste commentary came from the selfsame Pilyatskin, who wrote in *Izvestiya* in December 1993 that:

"One could understand if the [Nobel] Peace Prize were awarded to De Klerk three years ago when he single-handedly changed the course of the state ship away from apartheid. But what did Nelson Mandela have to do with it? It was De Klerk who released him from prison and provided the opportunity to legalise the ANC."[21]

What were the reasons for the drastic changes in the attitude of both governmental and other structures in Russia towards South Africa? The Russian Communist Workers Party, a hard-line left grouping noted that: "The sources of the mutual sympathy of the ruling circles of Russia and South Africa are obvious: both of them are trying to ensure the prosperity of a small section of population (10-15%) at the expense of continued impoverishment of the overwhelming majority of people of Russia and South Africa. We are clearly dealing with the practical manifestation of class solidarity between the bourgeois governments of the two countries."[22] But the reality is much more complex. It seems that originally the main reasons for changing policies were attempts by Gorbachev and later Yeltsin to find short cuts to get quick credit, loans and investments, almost irrespective of the source.

A second factor was the personal benefits which people who started dealing with the South African regime and the white establishment in general received, either directly or indirectly. Unscrupulous journalists, academics, and even some officials climbed on the bandwagon.

Philip Nel divided Soviet specialists into two groups, "strategists" and "diplomats", on the basis of their different approach to South African problems.[23] A more relevant, though less academic, division would be those with integrity on the one hand (and in this group I would include a broad spectrum of people from the "moderate" Gleb Starushenko to the "hard-liner" Vyacheslav Tetyokin), and, on the other hand, those whose actions were dictated by their personal interests. One of these wanted to be an Ambassador in Pretoria, and therefore called for the early establishment of diplomatic relations. Another, as a correspondent operating from an impoverished Front Line State wanted to move to "prospering" Johannesburg, and tried to please South African authorities with articles which emphasised his political acceptability. A third, eager to get a Chair at a South African University, called for the immediate end of the academic boycott. Such people were "co-optable" by the same methods that had been tested by Pretoria in the West earlier: free trips, high honoraria, etc.

A third reason for the turnabout in policy was an obsession to break with old allies and policies of the Soviet Union as part of a "re-ideologisation" process. If the ANC (not to mention the SACP) maintained friendly relations with the CPSU, it could not be a benign organisation. And those who opposed the liberation movements and were hostile to the Soviet Union could not be but right.

The final and perhaps most disgraceful reason for changing attitudes was the rise of xenophobia and outright racism, which came to the fore as living standards deteriorated in Russia in the course of "reforms". The flipside of this coin was a show of sympathy for the whites in South Africa, who were portrayed in the media as potential victims of "black majority rule".

In the final analysis, however, the successful completion of negotiations, the triumph of the ANC in the general elections, the election of Nelson Mandela as President, and the formation of the Government of National Unity emphatically refuted the predictions of all these "experts". It should be emphasised that the result of the negotiations, though clearly a compromise, was more than somewhat removed from what De Klerk had wanted to achieve after his 2 February 1990 speech.

I was in the public gallery at the opening ceremony of South Africa's first representative parliament in Cape Town on 9 May 1994, and I was happy to see among the members many familiar and friendly faces. The next day I was at the Union Buildings in Pretoria for President Mandela's inauguration, and many warm meetings took place on the official podium and on the lawns on that historic day. But I could not help observing that many who should have been there were missing – such as Chris Hani, the beloved son of South Africa, who died at the hands of the hired murderer, Janusz Walus, on 10 April 1993, and Oliver Tambo, who succumbed to his long illness two weeks later, no doubt affected by Chris's death.

***

Mark Phillips, who visited Moscow in November 1989 as a member of the Johannesburg Democratic Action Committee, commented on Soviet policy towards South Africa: "Much pressure on the Western countries to 'do something about apartheid' comes from broad-based and popular anti-apartheid movements. Policy making in the Soviet Union has historically been much more elite-oriented, and in consequence, apartheid is not a mass issue in the Soviet Union itself."[24]

Unfortunately this statement was by and large correct. It would be wrong, however, to think that the Soviet people were ignorant about developments in South Africa. In 1988 I happened to visit the village of Vyvenki in the Koryak National District in the Far East, North of Kamchatka and South of Chukotka, where the people are mostly deer breeders and fisherfolk. A local young activist, watching a TV programme, pointed out Winnie Mandela to me and described her as "the wife of Nelson Mandela" (she did not know that I was in any way involved with South Africa). I was happy to report this episode to Joe Modise, who happened to be in Moscow at the time.

However, the fact that Soviet citizens were involved in South African affairs only as members of the CPSU or party-controlled trade unions and other NGOs made it difficult to counter the negative changes in the policy after the CPSU was banned.

But this did not mean that the deviation in USSR/Russian policy towards South Africa went unchallenged. Criticism of the new course was voiced by the left and broad patriotic forces within the Russian parliament – the Supreme Soviet and later the State Duma – as well as by newly formed left organisations.

Three of these groups published a joint statement on 11 December 1991, calling F W de Klerk's visit to Russia "premature" and expressing "deep concern over plans to establish diplomatic relations with the present South African government ... The diplomatic relations with the minority regime will obviously complicate our relations with the future democratic South Africa."[25]

These and other organisations warned again on 21 February 1992, on the eve of Kozyrev's visit to South Africa, that "the establishment of diplomatic relations with the government of white minority that is leaving the political scene constitute a violation of the international obligations of Russia and in political terms serves as a means of supporting one side in the South African conflict."[26]

On 28 May 1992 a group of opposition leaders issued a statement expressing "concern over the invitation" to De Klerk and insisting on the postponement of the visit: "The trip of Mr F W de Klerk may probably be regarded as an effort by the South African President to solve his domestic problems at the expense of Russia's relations with the democratic forces of South Africa."[27]

At the same time that Yeltsin welcomed De Klerk in the Kremlin, Themba Thabethe, then Head of the ANC Mission (now the High Commissioner to Zambia), was invited to the premises of the Russian Supreme Soviet. There he discussed with the Co-ordination Council of the Opposition "the present stage, and the prospects, of political, economic and cultural relations between Russia and South Africa." A message of support to Nelson Mandela, signed by a group of opposition leaders, was presented to the ANC envoy.[28]

Traditional contacts between the ANC, the SACP and left-wing groups in Moscow have been maintained and developed. When the SACP delegation headed by Chris Hani visited Moscow in transit to Pyongyang and Beijing in April 1992, it met with representatives of both the left-wing political organisations and the leaders of the opposition in the Russian parliament to discuss the state of, and prospects for, bilateral relations.

John Nkadimeng, then ANC MP and a member of the SACP Central Committee, was warmly welcomed by the delegates of the Congress of the Communist Party of the Russian Federation in Moscow in January 1995.[29]

However, because of the absence of a broad-based anti-apartheid movement in Russia, the actions of the opposition, while irritating the government and forcing it to think twice before reaching out towards Pretoria, were unable decisively to influence policy. It was mostly the developments in South Africa and the growing recognition by the whole world that the ANC was going to lead a future South African government that finally caused some positive changes in Russia. In May 1993 Thabo Mbeki and Joe Modise visited Moscow en route from India. They had meetings with the then First Deputy Foreign Minister Anatoly Adamishin, in the Ministry of Foreign Economic Affairs, as well as in the Ministry of Defence. According to Thabo Mbeki, it was "very important that after a lengthy interval, caused by the changes in our countries, that the relations of the ANC with Russia are maintained at the state level."[30] Meetings with representatives of Russian NGOs and Opposition parliamentarians also took place.

The then Head of the African Directorate of the Foreign Ministry Grigory Karasin explained the official position of the Russian government on South Africa in May 1993: "As far as the RSA is concerned, in the relations with that country we are maintaining a balanced "equal distance" approach to the development of our ties with all constructive forces, including the government and the African National Congress."[31] While the need for a balanced approach could hardly be questioned, "equal distance" to the government and to the ANC was not justified, either from the point of view of history, or of prospects for the future. Such a stand was, however, more sober than the previous one-sided statements of the top leadership in Russia.

The initial euphoria in Russia about economic relations with South Africa was soon replaced by a more realistic assessment. It became clear that political gestures could not substitute for a thorough study of the markets and conditions of trade. Thus the 100 million Rand revolving credit to Russia announced after De Klerk's meeting with Yeltsin remained entirely a paper agreement.

New problems also arose between the Russian state bodies and De Beers. The former Head of the Komdragmetal (the State Committee dealing with precious metals and stones) Yevgeny Bychkov, who was involved in the unsuccessful attempts to break the stranglehold of De Beers on the diamond trade, publicly stated that the co-operation with De Beers was costing Russia a 30% loss of profits on raw diamonds and up to 50% on the final product. Bychkov revealed that the plans to develop a diamond-cutting industry in Russia had met with resistance from De Beers, and suggested that some articles in the Russian press, criticising the policy of his Committee, were sponsored by that company. For its part De Beers accused Russia of breaching the 1990 agreement.[32] Talks between the two sides continued in a somewhat strained atmosphere. A new deal was signed only in 1998.

The 1994 general election and the inauguration of President Mandela gave the Russian leadership a good opportunity to put right earlier lapses in their approach. Unfortunately this opportunity was not used to good advantage. The official Soviet observer at the election was Nikolay Ryabov, former Vice-Speaker of the Supreme Soviet, who crossed over to Boris Yeltsin's side during the tragic events in Moscow in September-October 1993. Having been rewarded with the post of the Chairperson of the Central Electoral Commission, he did not exactly distinguish himself in his new position and had to leave that post with a consolation prize – an Ambassadorship in the Czech Republic.

The official to represent Russia at Mandela's inauguration was also somewhat controversial. He was Vladimir Shumeiko, then Chairman of the Upper House of the Russian parliament, earlier suspended from the government while under investigation for corruption. After he had returned to the office as Minister of Information, he banned several opposition publications in a flagrant violation of the law during the political crisis in Russia in October 1993. Shumeiko lost his parliamentary post in January 1996.

However, a group of Russian MPs actively observed the election procedure and met several leading South African political figures during this time. It included deputies from various factions. One of them, communist Gennady Seleznev was elected Speaker of the State Duma after the December 1995 election, and another, Arthur Chilingarov, is Vice-Speaker.

There have also been changes in the foreign policy of the Russian leadership, which has departed from an openly pro-Western position towards a more independent one. These changes were initially slow but gained momentum in 1994-5. The visit by the South African Foreign Minister Alfred Nzo to Russia in September 1994 was the beginning of healthier relations between Moscow and the new South Africa. It was followed by the visit of Minister of Defence Joe Modise to Moscow in July 1995. Simon Makana again came to Moscow, this time as South African Ambassador, having resigned as an ANC Senator.

The visits of the South African Foreign and Defence ministers were not reciprocated by the Russian side. This is not to say that South Africa didn't attract prominent visitors from Moscow. The catalogue is lengthy and includes, apart from the two former ministers mentioned above, ex-First Deputy Prime Minister Soskovets, ex-Chief of General Staff Kolesnikov, ex-Commander-in-Chief of the Air Force Deinekin, ex-Minister of Atomic Energy Mikhailov and ex-Minister of Home Affairs Kulikov.

This list of "exes" reflected a serious problem within the Russian establishment or, as they say in Moscow, "the party of power": while until September 1998 there were no radical political changes after the "dissolution" of the Soviet Union, there was an ongoing process of reshuffling in the Russian government; this lack of continuity hampered the foreign relations of the country.

However, this is not the only obstacle to the development of Russian-South African relations. True, several members of the South African government, dozens of members of Parliament, and a majority of the new SANDF generals and officers have firsthand experience of Russia or other former republics of the USSR and are well aware of their potential. But for the average South African information about our part of the world, supplied mostly by Western mass-media, is limited to horror stories about "Russian Mafia" and presents Moscow as "a backyard of Europe". In the same way some Russian papers often relying on the same Western information and financial sources write about "white terror" having being replaced by "black fear" in South Africa. These misconceptions or deliberate lies have to be resisted and overcome. [33]

The recent developments in Russia, especially the success of left and patriotic forces in national and local elections and the formation of a new government, headed by Yevgeny Primakov show that more changes in Russia are inevitable, and they will lead to a further improvement in relations with the new South Africa.

There is the potential for Russia and South Africa to interact in several important spheres. Both countries are among the major producers of minerals in the world, and this could mean either mutual understanding or fierce competition. Technology and tertiary education are also possible areas of co-operation.

Russia and South Africa have a long history of interaction. The peoples, if not the rulers, of the two countries managed to co-operate under the most difficult conditions. Now, when the situation is improving on both sides, reflected in Thabo Mbeki's successful visit to Moscow in November 1998, such co-operation is imperative.

Moscow - Cape Town - Moscow

1991-8

1. *Segodnya*, no 3, 1993.
2. Ibid.
3. *Nezavisimaya Gazeta*, 8 August 1992.
4. Ibid.
5. Crocker, C. *High Noon*, p.17.
6. *Towards Democracy*, Durban, First Quarter 1993, p.8
7. Ellis, S. and Sechaba, T. *Comrades*, p.124.
8. Anderton N. *From Gorbachev to Yeltsin*, p.11.
9. *Star*, Johannesburg, 28 February 1992.
10. *Rossiyskaya Gazeta*, Moscow, 2 June 1992.
11. *New Times*, Moscow, no 29, 1992, p.23.
12. *International Freedom Foundation,* no 11, vol. 5, 1991, p.4.
13. *New Nation,* Johannesburg, June 22-28 1990.
14. *International Freedom Foundation,* no 11, p.4.
15. *Sunday Independent,* Johannesburg, 16 July 1995.
16. *Izvestiya*, 28 May 1993.
17. *Nezavisimaya Gazeta,* Moscow, 8 August 1992.
18. Ibid. 11 February 1993.
19. *Citizen,* Johannesburg, 15 March 1993.
20. Ibid. 21 March 1993.
21. *Izvestiya*, 10 December 1993.
22. *Support democracy in South Africa. Statement of the Russian Communist Workers Party,* 25 June 1992.
23. Nel, P. *A Soviet Embassy,* p.75.
24. Phillips, M. *Beyond Raspberry Diplomacy? Current Soviet Policy Toward South Africa* (University of Witwatersrand, Johannesburg), 1990, p.16.
25. *Statement by a group of left-wing parties of the USSR,* 11 December 1991.
26. *The establishment of diplomatic relations with South Africa is premature. Statement by a group of political parties and organisations of Russia,* 21 February 1992.
27. *To the visit to Russia of South African President F.W. de Klerk. Statement by group of People's Deputies of the Russian Federation,* 26 May 1992.
28. *Press Release. The meeting between a leading member of the*

    Supreme Soviet of the Russian Federation and the ANC Chief Representative in Moscow, 4 June 1992.
29. Discussion with I. Nkadimeng, Cape Town, 4 February 1995.
30. *Izvestiya,* 5 June 1993.
31. *Rossiyskaya Gazeta,* 25 May 1993.
32. *Ibid.* 11 March 1994
33. *Komsomolskaya Pravda,* 23 May 1998.

Abarinov, Vladimir 82, 405

Abdel Nasser, Gamal 31

Adamishin, Anatoly 302, 349, 409

Afanasyev, Victor 376

Africa and Asia Today 276

Africa Confidential 32, 82, 224, 315, 316, 322, 315

Africa Institute, Moscow 32, 275, 318, 319, 323, 351, 371

Africa Report 234

African-American Labour Centre 193

African Communist 14, 17, 20, 29, 39, 76, 85, 96, 122, 126, 138, 190, 239

African Liberation Centre 158, 208

African National Congress (ANC)
Angola and 160, 164, 165, 166, 168, 178, 179, 186, 187, 196, 197, 205, 206, 209, 211, 243, 251, 257, 260-262, 279, 281, 321, 341-345, 350, 400; banning of, 10; armed actions, see under; Umkhonto we Sizwe; Botswana and 29, 50, 66, 77, 79, 80, 84, 85, 88, 97, 101, 105, 109, 112, 131, 132, 137, 138, 177, 179, 207, 208, 212, 226, 231, 259, 279, 342; Britain and 65, 69, 181, 266, 309, 338, 339; Bulgaria and 37, 131, 196;

China and 31, 68, 97, 209, 210, 316; Cuba and 186, 196, 197, 209, 302, 319, 356; Denmark and 181; Department of Information and Publicity (DIP) of 185, 249, 299; Department of Intelligence and Security (NAT) of 86, 87, 205, 206, 219, 248, 249, 279, 280, 312-314, 345, 366; Department of Manpower Development of 314; Department of Ordnance of 196, 211-212; Department of Personnel and Training of 175, 205; Durban conference of 49, 39, 281, 323, 386, 387; Egypt and 31, 107; Ethiopia and 30, 31, 103, 130; External Co-ordinating Council of 249; External Mission of 47, 50, 26, 175; Finland and 181; GDR and 37, 68, 125, 131, 165, 188, 302, 310, 313, 339; Ghana and 34, 50, 131; Holland and 210; Hungary and 37, 131; Italy and 123, 210; Internal Political and Reconstruction Department of 185, 201, 219, 232; International Department of 131, 185, 207; Iran and 209; Iraq and 209; Ireland and 210; Kabwe Conference of 93, 128, 168,

Nikolaenko, Valery 387, 389

Nkadimeng, John 175, 188,
195, 234, 237, 249, 260,
269, 279, 409

Nkadimeng, Vernon 279

Nkobi, Thomas 78, 91, 92,
136, 163, 211, 212, 217,
230, 249, 269, 278

Nkomati Accord 246, 255,
257, 258, 261, 262-264, 267,
269, 270, 272, 298, 343

Nkomo, Joshua 82, 179, 193

Nkondo, Zenjive (Matlou,
Victor) 214

Nkruma, Kwame 34, 49

Nokwe, Duma 33, 70, 75, 83,
91-94, 102

Non-Alligned Movement 357

Novo Catengue, ANC camp at
196

Nujoma, Sam 183, 261, 267,
347

Nyanda, Siphiwe (Gebuza)
332-336, 338, 343, 380, 381

Nyerere, Julius 99, 130, 160,
208, 255, 258, 269, 356

Nzo, Alfred 88, 91, 92, 109,
114, 131, 159, 163, 164,
168, 173, 178, 195, 204,
230, 231, 249, 253, 254,
264, 268, 269, 279, 300,
310, 315, 327, 344, 356,
364, 365, 369, 411

Nzula, Albert (Jackson, Tom)
121

Obasanjo, Olusegun 297

Odendaal, Andre 8

Odessa, military training at
63, 64, 81, 385

Okhela 110

Olshannikov, Nikolay 233

Operation J 101, 103-107

Operation Mayibuye 45, 55-
58, 196

Operation Protea 229

Operation Vulindela (Vula)
237, 332-338, 360, 380, 381

Oppenheimer, Harry 39, 377

Oppenheimer, Nicolas 376,
377

Organisation of African Unity
(OAU) 31, 68, 79, 97, 98,
135, 159, 160, 212, 297, 357

Orlando, attack against a
police station at 211, 275

PAFMECSA (Pan African
Freedom Movement for
East, Central and South
Africa) 67

Pahad, Aziz 182, 280, 322, 364

Pahad, Essop 190

PAIGC (African Party of
Independence of Guinea
and Cape Verde) 123

Palestine Liberation
Organisation (PLO) 209

Palme, Olaf 180

Pan-Africanist Congress
(PAC) 10, 15, 16, 49, 50, 61,
65, 68, 81, 97, 172, 180,
193, 205, 207, 209, 217,
232, 233, 371

Pankin, Boris 389

Paton, Alan 56

Pavlov, Pavel 386

Pavlov, Valentin 388

PEBCO (Port Elizabeth
Black Civic Organisation)